RUSSIA IN THE AGE OF
TOLSTOY AND DOSTOEVSKY

Walter G Moss

Titles by the same author:

Russia In The Age of Alexander II, Tolstoy and Dostoevsky

Walter G Moss

Anthem Press
London

Anthem Press is an imprint of
Wimbledon Publishing Company
PO Box 9779, London SW19 7QA

This edition first published by Wimbledon Publishing
Company 2002

British Library Cataloguing in Publication Data
Data available

Library of Congress in Publication Data
A catalogue record has been applied for

ISBN: 978 1 89885 559 0
1 3 5 7 9 10 8 6 4 2

Printed and bound in Great Britain by
Marston Book Services Limited, Oxford

INTRODUCTION
ABOUT THE AGE OF ALEXANDER II

The Russian word "*istoriya*" can mean either history or story; *The Age of Alexander II* attempts to be both and is written for anyone who enjoys readable history. While emphasizing the "story" in history, I have taken no liberties with the facts, and even minor details such as descriptions of the weather on a particular day are based on solid historical sources. This book's subject is the reign of Alexander II of Russia (1855–81) and some of the fascinating writers, thinkers and revolutionaries who made this the Golden Age of Russian literature and thought. It interweaves the personal and public lives of such individuals as Dostoevsky, Tolstoy and Turgenev, but it also has a central thread woven throughout: Alexander II, his policies and the reactions they called forth from the book's other central characters, most of whom could be considered intellectuals.

This drama occurs in a psychological atmosphere as real but elusive as a St Petersburg fog. It is one of raised but then dashed hopes, of confusion, conflict and alienation, but also one of yearning for love and a sense of community. It is one of a lonely Dostoevsky in Siberian exile discovering the necessity of becoming one with the common people; of the radical Sophia Perovskaya rejecting the world of her influential father and going among the workers and peasants to both teach and radicalize them; of a Leo Tolstoy so miserable that he contemplates suicide until he also discovers new hope among the peasants. It is one of the poet and philosopher Vladimir Soloviev seeking a vision of Sophia, the oneness of the universe, in an Egyptian desert. And finally, it is one in which even Tsar Alexander II seeks refuge from the complexities and conflicts of the time in the arms of a woman younger than his oldest children.

Although numerous books have been written on various aspects of this period, most are of a specialized nature. I know of no other historical work which incorporates the lives and ideas of the period's great writers into the story of Alexander's turbulent reign and at the same time offers some reflections on why its outcome was so tragic. Thus, it should be of interest to students and scholars of the period, as well as to more general readers.

The collective biographical approach used here, as opposed to an exclusive concentration on the politics or ideas of the era, not only provides history that is more readable, but more existential, more grounded in everyday reality, and, therefore, more understandable. As the German historian Wilhelm Dilthey wrote: "How can one deny that biography is of outstanding significance for the understanding of the great context of the historical world?"[1] This method also has something in common with the "polyphonic" method that the Russian critic M.M. Bakhtin attributed to Dostoevsky's novels. Such novels, Bakhtin thought, are marked by a "plurality of independent and unmerged voices and consciousness, a genuine polyphony of fully valid voices."[2]

This book strives for both objectivity and compassion in presenting the contrasting lives and ideas of many of the era's leading personalities. They found themselves in a difficult period of history with no easy answers available for solving their country's problems. If these individuals were sometimes foolish, dogmatic and impractical, at other times they were courageous and noble in their behavior. Although this work is mainly a narrative history, some analysis is interspersed throughout the chapters. Finally, the Epilogue summarizes what the preceding pages have revealed about Russia and its intellectuals under Alexander II and offers some thoughts about the relevance of these findings for post-Soviet Russia.

The first draft of this work was completed in 1987 and grew out of a course team-taught with Russ Larson on "Russia in the Age of Tolstoy and Dostoevsky." I wished to provide our students with a lively, readable but accurate portrait of the reign of Alexander II and the leading thinkers, writers and revolutionaries of that period. Many of the pictures that appear here were first taken by me in the 1980s and early 1990s as I visited Russian and Western European cities, estates and houses important in the lives of the manuscript's main characters and then later showed them as slides to our students. After beginning work on my two-volume *A History of Russia* (McGraw-Hill, 1997), I put the manuscript aside, except for course purposes, for about a decade. In 2000, I placed an updated version of the work on the Internet (*http://www.emich.edu/public/ history/moss*) under the title *Alexander II and His Times: A Narrative History of Russia in the Age of Alexander II, Tolstoy and Dostoevsky* (with links to hundreds of images and other materials), where it can still be found. Soon after placing the work there, Kamaljit Sood of Anthem Press (Wimbledon Publishing Company) inquired about the possibility of printing a revised book version of this work, and it is this version that is now before the reader.

Two difficulties that face every Western historian dealing with Tsarist Russia are those of dates and spellings. Since the Russian calendar in the nineteenth century was twelve days behind the Western calendar, I have used the Russian dates for events occurring within Russia and the Western calendar for those that occurred outside its borders. In regard to the transliteration of Russian spellings, I have slightly modified for use here the Library of Congress system. The most noteworthy modifications of it are the use of "yu" and "ya" instead of "iu" and "ia." Thus Milyutin not Miliutin, and Perovskaya not Perovskaia. I have, however, maintained the more common English spellings of names such as Maria and Natalia rather than Marya or Natalya. Other minor variations will be noted by the specialist, but need not concern the general reader.

In the many years I have sporadically worked on this manuscript I have accumulated many debts of gratitude. At Eastern Michigan University (EMU), I have been indebted to Ira Wheatley, Russ Larson, James Waltz, Dick Goff, David Geherin, Margot Duley, Gersham Nelson and the now-deceased Bill Hauer, as well as to many helpful people at EMU's library. I also wish to thank the libraries of Harvard University and the University of Michigan, especially the latter, which furnished most of the books I have consulted for this project. During and after putting my online version of this book on the Internet, I have received encouragement from Nathaniel Knight, Marshall Poe, John Randolph and Benjamin Sher, though none of them bear any responsibility for whatever failings this work may have. I am also very grateful to Kamaljit Sood at Anthem Press for his many efforts in encouraging and overseeing the publication of *The Age of Alexander II*. As always, my greatest debt is to my wife, Nancy.

CONTENTS

PART ONE

PART TWO

PART THREE AND EPILOGUE

PART ONE

A new era will begin for Russia. The emperor is dead ... A desolate page in the history of the Russian empire has been completed. A new page is being turned in by the hand of time. What events will the new ruling hand write in it; what hopes will it fulfil?

A. V. NIKITENKO

> Everyone tried to discover still new questions,
> everyone tried to resolve them;
> people wrote, read and spoke about projects;
> everyone wished to correct, destroy and change things,
> and all Russians, as if a single person,
> found themselves in an indescribable state of enthusiasm.

L. TOLSTOY

1

AN EMPEROR'S FUNERAL

It was finally time to move the body. The funeral bells were tolling in the churches of St Petersburg. For nine days the corpse of the dead Emperor, Nicholas I of Russia, had remained within the red walls of the Winter Palace. On some of these days the odor of his decomposing body had been almost unbearable. But it was now Sunday, February 27th 1855, and the winter sun was shining brilliantly.

As the procession began to move, the new Tsar and "Emperor and Autocrat of all the Russias," Alexander II, walked behind the coffin of his father. In his Cossack overcoat he was tall and regal, and his blue-gray eyes stared straight ahead. He was thirty-six years old, and the heavy responsibility of ruling a country at war was now his.

His father had also come to power under difficult circumstances: a group of conspirators opposed to autocracy and serfdom – they were later called Decembrists – had tried to prevent him from coming to the throne. And so his reign had begun with bloodshed and the arrest of these revolutionaries, among whom were a number of aristocratic young army officers.

But the difficulties now facing Alexander II were, if not as dramatic, more complex. Despite inferior equipment, shortages of supplies and diplomatic isolation, he somehow had to successfully conclude the present war in the Crimea. That, however, was just the first of his problems. For Nicholas I had bequeathed to him what one critic called, no doubt with some exaggeration, "a thirty-year tyranny of madness, brutality and misfortunes of all sorts, the likes of which history has never seen."[1]

The ruling ideology of the deceased Emperor was contained in three words: Orthodoxy, Autocracy and Nationality. But Russian Orthodoxy, whatever its inherent value, was tainted by state control and itself in need of reform. Furthermore, it was the religion, if one subtracts the schismatic Old Believers as well as those of other faiths, of only about two-thirds of the empire's peoples. As for autocracy, it seemed more and more outdated in an increasingly complex age which demanded the co-operation of an educated citizenry. The principle of nationality was even more unrealistic. For how in an age of nationalism could an emphasis on the Russian nationality unite an empire where only about half of its people were Russian?

Besides a spent ideology, Alexander inherited a backward country. At least it seemed so to believers in one of the West's most cherished concepts: Progress. Compared to one of her chief enemies, Great Britain, the most industrialized nation in Europe, this backwardness was especially evident. Despite Russia's much greater size – easily over sixty times the size of the British Isles – it only had about one-tenth the railway track and produced an even smaller ratio of pig iron. While half of the English people were already living in urban areas and more than half the population could read and write, nine-tenths of Russia's population still lived in the countryside and four-fifths of the country's subjects were illiterate peasants, almost half of them enserfed to noble masters. Living in poverty in their small huts, their babies were almost twice as likely to die in infancy as an English child. And the backward nature of Russian agriculture, as well as its poor climate and growing conditions, necessitated the work of about three Russian peasants to produce as much as one Englishman could.

Dispirited by the thirty-year reign of the man whose body was now moving slowly towards its final destination, Russia's small educated class was conscious of the beginning of a new era. And they were anxious and unsure about what it would bring. Many yearned for an enlightened leader, for a Tsar whose ideas they could support. But was Alexander II such a man? And did he possess any such ideas, any banner, which they could rally around?

Although some in the streets of St Petersburg on this sunny February day hoped that Alexander II could soon end the war, even if it meant compromise or defeat, others were encouraged by his assurances that Russia would not retreat before its enemies. The day Alexander came to the throne a large bell from the Ivan the Great Bell Tower in Moscow's white-walled Kremlin came crashing down and killed several people. An evil omen, some thought. But others recalled that a bell had fallen from the same tower on the day when the French had left Moscow in 1812 and begun their retreat. Was the present event then not a sign that Russia's foes in the Crimean War would also soon be on the defensive?

The funeral procession continued for two hours. Soldiers lined the route as the crowds looked on. The clanging of carriage wheels, the pealing of church bells and the funeral music of the military bands filled the air. The procession wound its way toward the Nicholas Bridge, over the frozen Neva River to Vasily Island and then finally over the Tuchkov Bridge to the Sts Peter and Paul Fortress, where many of Nicholas's enemies had been imprisoned. There a needle-like golden spire, extending high in the air from the island fortress cathedral and glittering in the sun, acted like an enticing magnet slowly pulling the mourners to itself from miles away.

After entering the fortress cathedral the coffin was placed on top of a catafalque covered in red velvet and sitting under a large silver brocade and ermine canopy. The rays of the sun and the lights of thousands of candles combined to illuminate the cathedral.

For another week the body lay in state as dignitaries and commoners filed past; lay there with a crown on its head, painted up and perfumed, but still smelling of decay. Finally, on another beautiful winter day there was one last service. During it the dead Emperor's widow stood by his coffin. Then she kissed him one last time and her children followed, making their last farewells. After the imperial mantle was taken from the coffin and carried to the altar, the new Emperor and his brothers carried the coffin on their shoulders to the tomb. As salvos of guns thundered, it was lowered into the ground. Handfuls of dirt were thrown upon the coffin and the tomb was closed. The body of Nicholas I joined those of other Russian Emperors and Empresses in the fortress cathedral.

2

LIEUTENANT TOLSTOY
IN THE CRIMEA

During the week that the dead Emperor's body lay in state in the cathedral, Sub-lieutenant Leo Tolstoy was stationed more than a thousand miles to the south. He was in the Crimea, near the besieged city of Sevastopol. Here nature was already beginning to display its crocuses, snowdrops and hyacinths; and larks, linnets and brilliant goldfinches were twittering and singing their songs. On March 1st, the lieutenant wrote in his diary: "The Emperor died on February 18th, and now we are to take the oath to the new Emperor. Great changes await Russia. It is necessary to work and be manly to take part in these important moments of Russia's life."[1]

No doubt he was exhorting himself as he often did. His mother had died when he was almost two and his father, Count Nicholas Tolstoy, when he was almost nine. Kindly relatives completed the upbringing of the five Tolstoy children, but from an early age Leo exhorted and chastised himself as if he were his own parent. He was always setting goals for himself. When he was nineteen, for example, and about to leave Kazan University before obtaining a degree, he set out a two-year educational plan for himself. He would study the following: "the entire course of judicial science needed for the final exam at the university ... practical medicine and part of its theory ... French, Russian, German, English, Italian and Latin ... agriculture ... history, geography and statistics ... mathematics ... music and painting ... the natural sciences."[2] In addition, he intended to write a dissertation, as well as compositions on all the subjects which he studied. Whenever he failed to live up to his self-imposed high standards, he berated himself in his diary, especially for his frequent lapses into lust and gambling. He had been in the south four years now, most of it in the Caucasus as part of a Russian military force trying to subjugate Islamic mountain tribes. In these years he also became a writer. His short novels *Childhood* and *Boyhood* appeared in the journal *The Contemporary*. In these works the orphaned Tolstoy displayed for the first time his nostalgia for a mother he had hardly known and for the world of which she had been a part. The feeling of having been orphaned and the often accompanying feeling of not being loved enough were ones that often visited the young man. He did not make friends easily, and despite his noble birth, he generally felt uncomfortable in high society. Yet he longed for love and oneness with others.

Despite his promising start as a writer, he still was unsure about his future plans. In early March he wrote that he felt capable of devoting his life to a new religion, based on Christ, but purged of mysticism and dogmas, one that would not promise heavenly bliss, but happiness on earth. By the following month, however, he had more pressing thoughts on his mind.

He and his artillery battery had been moved back to Sevastopol. This time they were sent to the most forward bastion of the defense, only about a hundred yards from the French lines, and under constant and heavy bombardment. For the next month and a half, he alternated days at the bastion with off days back in the center of the city. In both places he found time to continue working on a sketch about Sevastopol at the end of the previous year. At the front he wrote in a bomb-proof dugout with the sounds of cannons booming in his ears. By the end of April, he sent the sketch off to *The Contemporary*.

Within a few months the educated public, including the new Emperor and his wife, were applauding this work of L.N., even though many did not yet know whose initials these were. In it they read of a cart with creaking wheels and heavy with corpses approaching a cemetery and of a government building converted to a hospital, where blood-splashed surgeons pitched amputated limbs into a corner. They also read about the earth shelter where the cannoneers lived and from which they shelled the enemy while incoming cannon and mortar shells whizzed and hissed near them and over dead and wounded bodies covered with mud and blood.

More than this unprecedented realistic description of the war, the Emperor probably appreciated Tolstoy's praise of the patriotism and courage of the soldiers and sailors who defended these fortifications. Even though Tolstoy privately believed that the common soldiers were treated like slaves, that many officers were involved in graft, and that supply and hygienic conditions were far from desirable, he did not mention these dissatisfactions in his sketch. Earlier that year he had planned to address some of these problems by writing a *Plan for the Reform of the Army*, but like many of his grandiose projects he soon forgot it.

By early summer he completed another sketch about Sevastopol. By this time he was commanding a mountain battery, fourteen miles from the fighting in Sevastopol. The new sketch reflected some of his doubts about the war, and when the censors in the capital received it from the editors of *The Contemporary* there was trouble. Toward the end of it he had described a scene in which the Russians and French declared a short truce in order to gather their dead. While collecting the bodies, soldiers from both sides chatted with each other. Spontaneously, a Frenchman and a Russian exchanged cigarette holders, and a French officer asked a young Russian cavalry lieutenant to say hello to a Russian officer whom he knew. Tolstoy then wrote:

> Yes, on the bastion and entrenchments white flags have been placed, the lowering valley is full of dead bodies, and the beautiful sun descends from the transparent sky to the undulating blue sea, which sparkles under the golden rays of the sun. Thousands of people crowd together, look at, speak to, and smile at each other. And these people, who are Christians, confessing one great law of love and self-sacrifice, looking at what they have done, do not suddenly fall with repentance on their knees before Him who has given them life, who has placed in the soul of each, together with the fear of death, the love of the good and beautiful. They do not embrace like brothers with tears of joy and happiness. No! The white flags are lowered, and again whistle the instruments of death and suffering, again flows innocent blood, and groans and curses are heard.[3]

When the piece appeared in the September issue of *The Contemporary* this passage and others had been changed by the censors. Some deletions had been made and words inserted justifying the war for the Russians on the grounds of defense of their native land.

No doubt in his desire to build a society based upon secularized Christian principles and to live in one where men would not kill each other but live in harmony, Tolstoy manifested utopian aspirations. But such hopes were common for intellectuals who grew up in the stifling atmosphere of Nicholas I's reign. Many of them, blocked by a reactionary government from participating in any practical, meaningful service, retreated into a mental world where anything seemed possible.

This utopian tendency was further encouraged by the intellectuals' isolation from their less fortunate and less educated contemporaries. The great majority of intellectuals were still from the gentry class, which made up less than two per cent of the population. And even within their own class, they stood out by virtue of their education and intellectual interests. Only about half of the men of gentry status had received more than a primary education. In all of the empire's six universities, there were not quite four thousand students, all male of course. Except for some institutes that educated young ladies to be "empty-headed dolls,"[4] the government largely ignored female education.

Higher and even some secondary education usually implied an increased exposure to Western ideas. This only increased the gulf between those who were educated and the vast masses who were illiterate or who had had little education. Between the rural, illiterate, Orthodox peasant and the city-educated noble, who had often become hostile or indifferent to Orthodoxy, there could be little in common. At times they even spoke a different language. Although Pushkin, the greatest of the Russian poets, picked up Russian from family serfs, he was formally taught as a young child to speak only French. The father of the radical Alexander Herzen hated to read a Russian book; and as with Pushkin's father, his personal library was filled with French works. In the fashionable salons of the capital, even during the reign of the nationalistic Nicholas I, one heard French more commonly than Russian. For nobles serving at court it was more important to know the court language of French than it was to be fluent in Russian.[5] At the Smolny Institute, a sort of "finishing school" for young noble women, they spoke French except in Russian classes. In no other major European country were the educated so isolated from so many of their countrymen. At times an educated, westernized noble seemed as "foreign" in his own country as an Englishman in India or a Frenchman in Algeria.

During the quarter century of Alexander II's reign, the intellectual's isolation from the Russian masses and a passionate Russian desire to overcome it, to be part of some larger community, would appear and reappear. This phenomenon would take many forms. It would vary in intensity. It would sometimes be conscious and sometimes not. But it would always be there.

For the new Tsar this longing for community, as well as the utopianism of the intellectuals, presented both an opportunity and a major challenge. In the days ahead he would need the support of idealistic, but basically patriotic, men such as Tolstoy. He would need to temper their utopianism with doses of political realism and yet convince them that he shared some of their strongest-felt sentiments. It was yet unclear, however, whether Alexander had the will or skill to do so.

In early August, Tolstoy and his battery were at the battle of the Chernaya River, on the outskirts of Sevastopol. As the Russians crossed the river and started up the hillside in the morning sunlight, their lives ended in clusters as French and Sardinian shells exploded around them. Before the morning was over the Russians were forced to retreat, leaving thousands of their dead comrades behind. Tolstoy was depressed and angered by the slaughter and believed much of it was due to incompetent generals and staff. He vented his anger by composing, along with a few others, some satiric stanzas, which soon gained widespread popularity among Russian soldiers.

By late August, the year-long defense of Sevastopol was nearing its end. The Russian forces were short of powder, projectiles and reinforcements; and the English and French bombardment increased. Tolstoy had volunteered for duty in the city and arrived at a fort on the north side of the bay just in time to see the French taking the Malakhov Hill Bastion on the other side. Once this key to the defense of the south and main part of the city fell, the Russians began to hasten down to the bay and to cross a floating bridge to the northern side. Before leaving the southern side they blew up their abandoned forts and ammunition and set the town afire. Lieutenant Tolstoy would later describe the scene in still another Sevastopol sketch. But he would not mention there that on the day after his arrival, seeing the French tricolor flying over the former Russian bastions and the town below in flames, he wept. It was August 28th, his twenty-seventh birthday.

3
THE TSAR VISITS MOSCOW

Several days after the fall of Sevastopol Alexander II, his mother, wife and four sons were on a train to Moscow. From there he would go south to encourage his troops. Soldiers and soldiering had always been important to him. Since childhood, he had loved military activities such as parades and war games, and he had become a full general while still in his mid-twenties. In addition, it appeared that Alexander had decided to demonstrate that his rule reflected not just power but also the mutual love of tsar and people for each other. The Tsar's family had left the baby, Maria, back in Tsarskoe Selo, one of the Tsar's summer residences near St Petersburg. It was early morning when they had departed, and now as they approached Moscow, a little over four hundred miles away, it was late evening. Although it was a long day's journey, it must have still seemed a great improvement over the carriage trip necessary before this line, Russia's first major one, had been completed just four years earlier.

The spring and summer had been difficult for the new Tsar. Although conscientious and provided with considerable experience by his father, Alexander II lacked a creative and agile mind. His thinking seemed almost as traditional as that of his reactionary father, and as uninspired. He also lacked vigor and real enthusiasm for his work. When he was young his tutors had discerned that he was easily discouraged by difficulties. As the dispatches from the Crimea got worse, his spirits fell. After the collapse of Sevastopol, he and his wife cried.

Still, there had been some happy times, especially during the spring and summer months spent at Tsarskoe Selo and Peterhof, another summer residence close to the capital but located on the Gulf of Finland. Among large, luxurious palaces, magnificent grounds, trees, flowers, lakes and fountains the family had spent some idyllic and peaceful moments. The marriage of Alexander and Maria of Hesse-Darmstadt had been based on love, not any special needs of state. In fact, at first there had been some parental opposition to it. But after fourteen years of marriage, the reserved young German princess had proved herself to be a serious, conscientious wife and Empress. And if some of

Alexander's youthful ardor toward her had cooled and there had been some talk at court about him and a flirtatious lady-in-waiting to the Empress, still he often relied on Maria for advice and support.

While the Emperor's train approached Moscow, large crowds waited for him in the rain along the route from the station to his eventual destination at the Kremlin Grand Palace. The people of the city had followed the defense of Sevastopol closely and contributed bandages, money and other needed supplies to the war effort. They had seen prices rise steeply during the war and, more importantly, sons, brothers, fathers and friends sent to the front. The censored press told the people of the righteousness of their Orthodox cause in the war against the infidel Turk and his European allies. It spoke confidently of the ability of Sevastopol to withstand the siege. When it fell, the news came as a shock to many. Some of the common people groaned and crossed themselves as if to ward off any future unknown dangers. Others crowded for solace into the city's taverns. Yet the news was not unexpected in all homes. Years of government propaganda had created a certain skepticism, even among the uneducated, and some of the more intelligent and insightful had foreseen Russia's eventual collapse at Sevastopol. Although it was said that Moscow was more patriotic, more Russian, than the more cosmopolitan St Petersburg, there were also those in this ancient capital who thought that the war was folly.

Toward Alexander, however, many Muscovites felt kindly. He had been born in their city, and this seemed to mean something to them. Those who blamed the government for failing to wage war more successfully could recall that Alexander had inherited the war and most of his ministers and generals from his father. Few were yet ready to judge him too harshly.

As the train pulled into Moscow, the rain let up and fireworks illuminated the sky. The sounds of bells and shouts of "hurrah" rang through the air. At the station imperial carriages appeared, and the monarchs' monograms, "A" and "M," were visible everywhere. Along the crowded route to the Kremlin, the Emperor and Empress stopped at one of the entrances to Red Square in order to enter the little Chapel of the Iberian Mother of God. There they knelt for a moment before the chapel's famous icon, believed by the faithful to work miracles.

For the next week the Tsar took part in prayer services, reviewed troops, met with his generals and received delegations from the city. As Alexander looked about, he saw once again a very different city than the St Petersburg from which he had just arrived. It was less symmetrical, less full of uniformed officials, and here one saw more Asiatic faces and attire. Despite its large size, it seemed more rural than St Petersburg. Gardens and greenery were scattered in abundance around white walls and low-lying houses. One might also see a cow or two wandering along a broad street or on a narrow, twisting, dirt road. Green and red rooftops, blue and golden domes, multi-colored cupolas and golden crosses sparkled everywhere in the sunshine as one looked down on them across from one of the hills of the city. And in the midst of it all, the ancient Kremlin! In Alexander's time not only were the brick crenellated Kremlin walls painted white, but so were many of the churches and other structures within, including the large new Great Kremlin Palace. From afar, along with the golden cupolas and crosses of the Kremlin's Ivan the Great Bell Tower and Assumption and Annunciation cathedrals, the white walls and exteriors helped to give the whole ensemble a magical appearance.

On the day after his arrival, Alexander went to several of the Kremlin churches to ask for God's help in Russia's hour of need. At the Cathedral of the Assumption (or Dormition), which Napoleon had once desecrated by using as a stable, the gray-bearded Metropolitan Filaret assured the Tsar of the justness of Russia's war effort and of the prayers of millions of Russians for its just cause. On that same day Alexander sent a letter to his Crimean commander, Prince Gorchakov, telling him not to despair, to trust in God and to remember that two years after Napoleon had captured Moscow in 1812, Russian troops had been in Paris. Later in the week Metropolitan Filaret presented the Tsar with a banner depicting the Blessed Virgin appearing before St Sergius. It had earlier accompanied Peter the Great and Alexander I on important campaigns, and the Tsar could now pass it on to Gorchakov.

For centuries, whether in war or in peace, the Tsars had relied upon the Orthodox clergy for support. They preached to the Russian people patriotism and submission, and Filaret, the most important clergyman of his time, was more than willing to continue the practice. In the words of Alexander Herzen, a man we shall soon meet, he "combined the mitre of a bishop with the shoul-dertabs of a *gendarme*."[1] In addition, although he supported reform in some areas, he defended the flogging of peasants for offenses against their masters, and opposed emancipating Russia's serfs on the grounds that such "theoretical progress" would only stir the peasants' "false hopes and baser appetites."[2] Although there can be little doubt that the support of such clergymen was helpful in keeping the country's illiterate masses faithful to the Tsar and state authority, supporters like him also inadvertently helped to discredit both state and church in the minds of Russia's progressive thinkers.

A week after the Tsar's arrival in Moscow and on the twelfth birthday of his oldest son, Nicholas, Alexander left his family and headed south. First, how-ever, there was one more service at the Cathedral of the Assumption, where Alexander's mother blessed him. The Tsar, Maria and his mother were all misty eyed as he prepared to depart. Amidst the clamorous shouts of the crowds, he left by carriage for Nikolaev, a town Alexander now considered the key to Russia's southern defenses. It was over seven hundred miles away, and the lack of a railway to the south not only inconvenienced Alexander, but had created serious supply problems for the troops.

In Nikolaev the Tsar approvingly overlooked the improvement of the Nikolaev defenses by General Totleben, the engineer whose fortifications had made it possible for Sevastopol to hold out for almost a year. He also visited a military hospital, and a correspondent for a semi-official newspaper wrote of the deep mutual affection of the Tsar and the wounded soldiers.

Before returning in early November back to Moscow, and then by train to the capital, the Tsar also visited both the headquarters of his army in the south at Bakhchisari and the northern side of Sevastopol. Like Tolstoy, he looked down across the bay on the ruins of the now-captured southern side of Sevastopol. He also visited the sick and wounded and thanked the defenders of the besieged city. Despite hearing tales of corruption and inefficiency, Alexander was in general encouraged by his trip to the south. He returned to the capital still hopeful that Russia could escape defeat.

4

A PROFESSOR AND A BANQUET

Late in February 1856, the city of Moscow gave a hero's welcome to some of the naval defenders of Sevastopol. By this time Russian diplomats were already in Paris working on the peace treaty that would end the war. Alexander had finally heeded the advice of his Foreign Minister and others and accepted the terms of his enemies. But not without bitterness, especially at the future prohibition of Russian naval forces in the Black Sea. His advisors, however, told him that Austria and perhaps even Prussia and Sweden might join the war against Russia. They emphasized the strength of the British navy and its ability to strike at Russia's coasts almost at will. They mentioned the difficulties of keeping so many troops (almost two and a half million, counting irregulars, militia and the navy) under arms in preparation for attacks from various directions, and they pointed out the tremendous financial strain of the war. They did not apparently stress the large number of Russian lives already lost in the war. In fact, an accurate count was not kept. But by the time peace finally arrived, about half a million had died, many from disease.

Welcoming the Sevastopol defenders was one way for Muscovites to assuage their wounded national pride. For more than a week they hosted and toasted these men: they greeted them with bread and salt, a traditional Russian welcome, and with hats thrown in the air and military marches; they invited them into their homes and cheered them as they rode through the snow-covered streets in troikas; and they held church services honoring the defenders' dead comrades.

On one occasion, the Merchants' Club hosted the officers for a dinner. The halls were decorated and flowers were strewn along the staircase. Wealthy merchants, nobles, scholars, artists and even some students were present, as toasts were drunk to the Emperor's health, and "God Save the Tsar" was sung. Among the speakers who addressed the heroes were three of Moscow's most prominent intellectuals. The most sober and moderate of them was Professor Sergei Soloviev of Moscow University, whose father was an Orthodox priest who had been teaching religion at the Moscow Commerce School for almost forty years.

Although only thirty-five, the son had been teaching at the university for a decade, and in each of the last five years he had published a volume of his *History of Russia from Ancient Times.*

As speakers before him mentioned the heroic deeds of the men of Sevastopol, he perhaps remembered those of his own father-in-law, Vladimir Romanov. Naval Captain Romanov had been decorated for bravery under enemy fire during the final evacuation across the Sevastopol Bay.[1] In 1848, Soloviev had married Romanov's attractive dark-haired daughter, Poliksena, and since then she had given birth to six children, although two died in infancy.

With several of the speakers who spoke before him, Soloviev had considerable differences. First, there was the bearish and broad-lipped publicist and panslavist M.P. Pogodin. He was one of the few intellectuals who had been born into a serf family. In addition to his humble origins, he was known for his ardent Russian nationalism, tactlessness and avariciousness. He was a former professor of Soloviev's and his predecessor in the chair of Russian history at the university. But he had resigned in anger in a dispute with administrators and colleagues and, contrary to his own expectations, was never asked to return. Bitter at being replaced by his former student, he had often found reasons to criticize Soloviev's work.

One of the major differences between the two men was also one of the most significant that divided Russian intellectuals in general. Soloviev shared the viewpoint of most thinkers that Russia was an integral part of European civilization, but Pogodin thought of Russia as a unique and superior civilization. As he characteristically overstated it: the Russian differed from the European in "temperament, character, blood, physiognomy, moral outlook, cast of thought, faith, ideals, dress, desires, pleasures, relationships, history – everything!"[2] Pogodin's relationship with Nicholas I and Alexander II was also noteworthy. Despite being a strong defender of Orthodoxy, autocracy and nationality, Pogodin was more than a humble servant of state and church. On occasion he sent unsolicited advice to his ruler, and he could be quite critical, especially privately, of Tsarist activities of which he did not approve. Like almost all intellectuals, he believed the police-state measures taken by Nicholas I, especially after the European revolutions of 1848, were excessive. He also believed that the government had been guilty of serious foreign policy errors. He had long dreamed of a panslavic union stretching from the Pacific to the Adriatic. It would also include Constantinople and, most importantly, recognize Russian hegemony. But to achieve this goal he thought that Russia would have to realign its traditional diplomacy away from friendship with Prussia and Austria, the latter especially resentful of any Russian intentions regarding the Slavic peoples of the Balkans. The month before the banquet, Pogodin wrote to the Tsar and advised him to rally the Russian people for a struggle against its enemies. In the following words, he even dared to advise Alexander regarding his own behavior:

> The Tsar lives in twenty rooms, let him occupy no more than five and have only five heated in the winter. He is served six dishes at table; let them give him three or four. The Tsaritsa will wear only a black dress ... she will seem lovelier and sweeter to us. Three lumps of sugar are put into their children's tea; let them sip it through a single lump [as was the Russian custom] ... and when they complain of its not being sweet, tell them it is because the French are in the Crimea and the English at Kronstadt."[3]

Another speaker who preceded Soloviev was the Slavophile Constantine Aksakov. He was a passionate man with a "leonine physiognomy,"[4] known for his Moscowphilism, his dislike of the more westernized St Petersburg, his glorification of the Russian peasant and his ardent desire to see Russia's alienated intellectuals return to the native Russian traditions. He was such an enthusiast of older ways that in the 1840s he had walked around Moscow wearing "old Russian" attire and an old-fashioned beard. One of his ideological opponents joked that this only led to his being mistaken for a Persian. In 1849, however, part of his old-fashioned look had to go. Because in the West beards were sometimes a symbol of revolutionary inclinations, the government of Nicholas I banned the "Russian beard," at least for members of the gentry class like Aksakov.

Despite being almost forty, his idealistic convictions and his devotion to his father, the novelist Sergei Aksakov, made him seem younger. Like Soloviev, Aksakov had also once been a pupil of Pogodin, and the latter was a longtime friend of the Aksakov family. Soloviev and Aksakov had also once been close enough for the latter to become the godfather of Soloviev's first daughter, but more recently Aksakov had become quite critical of Soloviev's historical views and in the next few years would increasingly attack them in reviews of Soloviev's multi-volume history.

The personal relations of Soloviev with Pogodin and Aksakov and the advice which Pogodin showered upon the Tsars both point to an important characteristic of the times. The prominent people in Russian society – the Tsar and his family, members of the court, leading government ministers and the significant intellectuals – were relatively few, and a great many of them were related, personally acquainted, or at least had access to each other.

Concerning Aksakov's ideas, Soloviev thought that due to his nostalgia, anti-Westernism and anti-progressivism, he was guilty of falsifying history. The professor also believed that Aksakov was more of a dilettante than a serious scholar and that he overemphasized the historical role of the Russian people. Both Soloviev and Pogodin stressed more the importance of Russia's rulers and government.

Like Pogodin, Aksakov also had sent a letter to the new Tsar. It deplored evils such as government corruption, romanticized the era prior to Peter the Great, and blamed Peter for being a despot and beginning the westernization of Russia's nobility. It also tried to convince Alexander II of the necessity of ending despotism, although not autocracy. For although Aksakov considered Russia fortunate to have a government that enabled its people to concentrate on their spiritual life and not be involved in any inherently corrupting political body such as a parliament, he nevertheless believed that a Tsar should allow and seriously consider freely expressed opinions. He even suggested that as the need arose the government might wish to convene representatives of different classes for advice.

Whatever the merits of this memorandum of Aksakov's, it is questionable whether the Tsar ever read it. And if he did, it had little effect. Despite wishing to encourage a limited amount of "openness" (*glasnost*), especially within government circles, Alexander was opposed to unshackling public opinion to the extent suggested by Aksakov.[5]

Despite Soloviev's differences with Pogodin and Aksakov, he probably did not disagree with much the two men said at the Merchants' Club. Although their extravagant nationalistic excesses might bother him, he shared their praise of the heroes of Sevastopol.

When his turn finally came to say a few words the solidly built, already balding Soloviev greeted the officers with words that he said were dear to their ancestors. He welcomed them as "sufferers for the Russian land, who had gloriously stood on guard for the native land."[6] Those who were familiar with his work knew that he believed that Russia was continuing in the tradition of Greece, Rome and the Christian medieval world in its fights against barbarian Asia. They were aware that he justified Russia's past wars against the non-Christian Mongols, Turks and other Asiatic powers because he believed that Russia was furthering the cause of European Christian civilization.

When the Crimean War broke out one of the causes had been Russia's insistence on her rights to intercede in behalf of Orthodox Christians within the Muslim Turkish Empire. Nicholas I had written at the time: "Waging war *neither for worldly advantages nor for conquests*, but for a solely Christian purpose, must I be left alone to fight under the banner of the Holy Cross and to see the others, *who call themselves Christians*, all unite *around the Crescent to combat Christendom*?"[7] Soloviev's feelings about the justness of the war were not essentially different.

Years later, however, Soloviev made it clear that Nicholas I was not one of his favorite Emperors, and he placed much of the blame for Russia's failures in the war on Nicholas. Despite Soloviev's patriotic feelings, he had even been a bit reluctant to see Russia win the war. For a victory might strengthen Nicholas's despotism, while a defeat might bring the progressive kind of changes that Soloviev believed Russia needed. With the accession of Alexander to the throne, Soloviev had thought there was still hope for victory. As he later explained it, a forceful, bold, knowledgeable ruler could have tapped the patriotism of the Russian people, while diplomatically splitting her enemies. Long after Alexander had given up the belief, Soloviev still thought that the fall of Sevastopol, like that of Moscow in 1812, could have been followed by a new beginning, one that would have eventually forced the allies to sign a peace treaty more to Russia's liking. But in the eyes of Soloviev, Alexander was too weak to accomplish the task.

The views of Pogodin, Aksakov and Soloviev, all three critical of the despotism of Nicholas I, but also all strong patriots and defenders of Russian autocracy and Orthodoxy, were illustrative of a serious problem facing Alexander II. All three of these men were confident that they knew better than the Tsar how the government should be run. The reign of Alexander's father had especially encouraged, inadvertently of course, this type of feeling. Although radical leftist criticism, emanating especially from St Petersburg intellectuals, would eventually attract more attention, the faultfinding of Muscovite supporters of autocratic government should not be overlooked.

Even at court in St Petersburg there were a few who agreed with some of the criticisms and reservations about the government's actions which were expressed or harbored by these three Moscow thinkers. One such person was Anna Tyutcheva, a lady-in-waiting to the Empress. She was the daughter of the poet and panslavist Fedor Tyutchev, and ten years after the Moscow banquet for the heroes of Sevastopol she would marry Constantine Aksakov's younger brother Ivan.

When she first heard rumors of the possibility of Russia's accepting unfavorable peace terms put forth by Austria, she became alarmed. On January 6th, the feast of the Epiphany and a day on which the Tsar took part in the ceremony of the Blessing of the Waters along the Neva, she wrote in her diary that if the Tsar offended the honor of Russia by agreeing to an unfavorable peace, she would not be able any longer to love him. Two days later she told the Empress that the Ministers of War and Finance were ignoramuses and should be replaced. And three days after that she recorded her belief that unfortunately Alexander was not the strong and energetic man that Russia needed in such trying times.

On January 16th, a young adjutant of the Tsar read to her and others a new letter written by Constantine Aksakov which expressed many of her sympathies about the undesirability of accepting unfavorable peace terms. She borrowed the letter and read it to the Empress, but it failed to have the desired effect.

Following Soloviev's words of welcome to the Sevastopol defenders, the millionaire merchant Vasily Kokorev, who had planned many of the activities of these February festivities, also made a speech. Not to be outdone by the historians, he also compared the Sevastopol heroes with those of earlier times.

Before the honored guests departed the Merchants' Club for a costume ball at the governor's house that February evening, they moved to a neighboring room. There hung a full-length picture, decorated with flowers, of the Emperor. With drinking glasses in hand and in loud voices they sang "God Save the Tsar." Pogodin then toasted the Tsar, and the guests in good Russian style threw their glasses to the ground, shattering them into thousands of pieces. The bearish Pogodin, as usual given to excesses, expressed the hope that all the Tsar's enemies might be dealt with in a similar fashion. Then once again the guests sang "God Save the Tsar" and departed.

5
TOLSTOY IN THE CAPITAL

Three months earlier, on November 19th, 1855, Lieutenant Tolstoy had arrived in St Petersburg by train. He remained there for most of the next six months. While Moscow's thinkers focused primarily on the war, St Petersburg's intellectuals seemed more concerned with political reform.

Although the Neva remained frozen throughout most of Tolstoy's stay, the spirit of the capital and Russia itself seemed to be experiencing a thaw after the frozen immobility of Nicholas's final years. Signs of renewed life were sprouting up everywhere. New journals were begun. Previously forbidden works were now printed. As Tolstoy later wrote: "Everyone tried to discover still new questions, everyone tried to resolve them; people wrote, read and spoke about projects; everyone wished to correct, destroy and change things, and all Russians, as if a single person, found themselves in an indescribable state of enthusiasm."[1]

Tolstoy came to the capital to meet the leading literary men of his day. One of the most prominent was Ivan Turgenev, the author of *A Sportsman's Sketches*, a work applauded for its humane depiction of the Russian peasants. Turgenev had just recently completed a draft of a novel, based in part on the life of a friend, Michael Bakunin, a radical currently in prison. Almost immediately after arriving at the train station, Tolstoy headed for the large first floor apartment of Turgenev. It was just off the Nevsky Prospect near the Anichkov Palace, where the widow of Nicholas I now resided. Turgenev had earlier written to Tolstoy and praised his work; he now invited him to stay with him.

For over a month Tolstoy remained as Turgenev's guest. Although still in the military, Tolstoy's duties were minimal. He soon shocked the more sedate, fastidious Turgenev by his carousing in this city of canals, columned palaces and pastel-colored buildings of green, yellow, blue and red. Turgenev was only ten years older than Tolstoy, but his hair, mutton-chop whiskers and mustache were already noticeably graying. At first he tried to restrain the younger writer from his excessive gambling, drinking and cavorting with gypsy women. But he soon gave up and resigned himself to preventing Tolstoy from being disturbed as he slept in the drawing room until the late morning or early afternoon.

Tolstoy was not alone in this custom, for St Petersburg during the winter season was not a place where the nobility rose early unless obliged to by their work. Evenings often kept them out late. There were theaters and concerts, operas and ballets, parties, banquets and balls. At the dances the bejeweled women, bare-shouldered in their full-length gowns, waltzed with officers and officials resplendent in uniforms with sashes and medals indicating their accomplishments.

St Petersburg was not only the home of many officers and government officials, it was also the most modern, fashionable and Western of Russian cities. Its architecture, like many of its nobles, reflected European influence. Baroque and neoclassical facades struck the eye on both sides of the Neva and along many of the city's canals. Even some of its main churches, such as the Kazan Cathedral, on the Nevsky Prospect, and St Isaac's Cathedral, which still was not quite completed after three and a half decades, looked more like they belonged in Rome than in Russia. While Italian Opera flourished, thanks to generous government support and its own popular appeal, native Russian opera languished. The prima donnas who captured the imagination of young men sang in Italian, not Russian. One such woman, Pauline Viardot, so mesmerized Ivan Turgenev that now, twelve years after first meeting her, he still idolized her as he did no other woman.

Despite its modern Western appeal, the city Tolstoy now found himself in was still nevertheless a mid-nineteenth-century Russian city. There were still vacant lots scattered about. Smoking was not permitted on the street. Almost all the city traffic was on foot or in horse-drawn sleighs or carriages. Omnibuses, also pulled by horses, existed but were little used. If no snow was on the ground, the fast-moving carriages might jolt one continually as one traveled over cobblestone or dirt roads. During the long hours of winter darkness, which could last from mid-afternoon to mid-morning, the street lights did not give off much light. Only a few gas lamps yet existed. Although it was the most industrialized of Russian cities, no more than one in twenty inhabitants worked in factories. About a third of the city's population were officially considered peasants, even though they worked in factories, shops, on the docks, in restaurants or bath houses, drove horse cabs, carted wood or ice, or peddled sweets, fruit or toys from the trays they carried as they walked along the streets. Even though residents dumped all types of waste into the city's canals and rivers they also used them for drinking water. In addition, unclean water often flooded basements in the low-lying capital. It was no wonder that in the 1850s deaths in St Petersburg outnumbered births.

In addition to Turgenev, from whose apartment he eventually moved when he found quarters of his own, Tolstoy met other important writers and spent many evenings with them. One of the most famous was Nicholas Nekrasov, a poet and the principal editor of *The Contemporary*. Tolstoy often visited Nekrasov's apartment on Little Stable Street, not far from the Tsar's Imperial Stables.

Nekrasov was a man of contradictions, almost a split personality. Like Tolstoy and Turgenev, he was from the landowning class. But unlike them, he had suffered poverty and hunger when as a youth of sixteen he had defied his father's wish that he enter a St Petersburg cadet corps and instead had begun preparing himself for entrance into St Petersburg University. Years of extreme poverty had followed, and he was never to obtain a university degree. For a while he had to rely on using the overcoat of his much larger roommate when he wanted to go out into the biting St Petersburg winter. He lived at other times with prostitutes and working girls. Although these difficult years had passed, Nekrasov maintained a strong sympathy for the poor and unfortunate. He had helped to discover and publish Dostoevsky's first major effort, *Poor Folk*, and many of his own poems reflected his identification with the sufferings of Russia's common people. Like Constantine Aksakov, but for different reasons, he worshiped at the altar of the Russian people (*narod*). But he also had the reputation of being a man much more concerned with making money than was the average poet or even editor. Some even considered him an unscrupulous wheeler-dealer. And his fondness for good food, drink and gambling, all of which he enjoyed at the exclusive English Club, contributed further to his janus image.

In recent years, although still only in his early thirties, Nekrasov had not been in good health. He was apparently suffering from syphilis and feared he might die. Never an imposing figure, the dark-haired, mustached Nekrasov was even less so now. His shoulders drooped and he walked slowly. At times he could not raise his high, squeaky voice above a whisper. His throat was constantly sore, and while Tolstoy was in the capital Nekrasov seldom left his apartment.

It was at Nekrasov's place that Tolstoy several times angered his new friends by his intemperate behavior. On one occasion he accused Turgenev of empty chattering and of lacking real convictions. The exasperated Turgenev, who normally had a rather high voice, whispered, "I can stand no more! I have bronchitis."[2] His large, soft body began striding back and forth through the three-room apartment. The shorter but more muscular Tolstoy lay on a morocco sofa and responded that bronchitis was an imaginary illness. While not true, it was not entirely inappropriate, for Turgenev was a bit of a hypochondriac. He also seemed excessively concerned with growing old. Nostalgia for youth and a sad resignation in the face of life had appeared with increasing frequency in some of his recent stories.

On another occasion at Nekrasov's, after being cautioned ahead of time to avoid the subject, Tolstoy attacked the French female novelist and advocate of women's rights, George Sand. He said that if her heroines actually existed, they should be tied to the hangman's cart and dragged through the streets of St Petersburg. Sand was a personal friend of Turgenev's and very close to his beloved Pauline Viardot, who some thought had been the model for Sand's famous heroine Consuelo.

Tolstoy's statement also no doubt offended Avdotya Panaeva, the wife of Nekrasov's fellow editor on *The Contemporary*, but Nekrasov's mistress. She often acted as the hostess at Nekrasov's gatherings. She was a great admirer of Sand and a writer herself who in her works dealt with injustices suffered by women. She also had collaborated with Nekrasov on several novels. She was small and attractive with dark hair and eyes and a velvety voice. Many writers praised her beauty. A decade earlier the young Dostoevsky had become infatuated with her. Nekrasov easily became jealous of her and the couple often quarreled. The past year or so had been especially difficult for them because of Nekrasov's illness and the death of an infant son.

Toward such liaisons as that of Nekrasov and Panaeva, Tolstoy was hardly more sympathetic than he was with some of the behavior of Sand's heroines. Sex with gypsies or peasant girls while still a bachelor was one thing, but to the early-orphaned Tolstoy, marriage and family life were sacred and eternal. And they would remain so for him in an age in which traditional ideas regarding women and the family would come under increasing attack.

While Tolstoy was in the capital a split was developing among the contributors to *The Contemporary*. It was precipitated by a radical young man of Tolstoy's age, Nicholas Chernyshevsky, who thought that literature should be subservient to man's social and political needs. Turgenev and several of his friends found this role too restrictive. Soon after leaving St Petersburg, Tolstoy wrote to Nekrasov and also criticized Chernyshevsky, referring to him as a "gentleman who smells of lice" with an "unpleasant, reedy little voice uttering stupid, unpleasant things."[3]

Although Tolstoy's description was hardly objective, Chernyshevsky was not an imposing-looking figure. His terrible nearsightedness necessitated glasses; and his delicate face, wavy hair and timid appearance had earned him the nickname "the pretty maid" when he was a seminary student in the Volga river town of Saratov. Nekrasov, however, would increasingly back Chernyshevsky and his young collaborator Dobrolyubov, both of whom were of more common origins than most older intellectuals. Turgenev labeled the pair the snake and the rattlesnake, and one senses in the attitudes of some of their noblemen critics, including Tolstoy and Turgenev, a touch of unconscious class snobbishness.

The differences which were now beginning to surface among the contributors to *The Contemporary* would become increasingly important. Just as Pogodin and Aksakov represented two forms of anti-Westernism, so Chernyshevsky and some of his critics such as Turgenev would come to represent two forms of Westernism, one radical and one liberal.

It would take, however, several years for some of Chernyshevsky's radical ideas to fully emerge. In 1856, he was still attempting, like a number of other thinkers, to be conciliatory. One of the most important conciliators of the day was Constantine Kavelin, whom Tolstoy met shortly before leaving the capital. He was a historian of law and a government official, who had earlier taught with Professor Soloviev at Moscow University. Early in 1855, he and one of his former students, Boris Chicherin, had begun a collaborative effort in behalf of Russian liberalism. The two of them wrote a number of works which circulated in manuscript and which early the following year they sent to the émigré radical journalist Alexander Herzen in London for printing. In one of them Chicherin wrote: "Liberalism! This is the slogan of every educated and sober-minded person in Russia. This is the banner which can unite about it people of all spheres, all estates, all inclinations. This is the word which can mold a powerful public opinion, if only we can shake off from ourselves self-destructive laziness and indifference to the common cause." Liberalism, he believed, was also the medicine Russia needed in order to cure its social ills and assume its proper place in the world. In this one word, he concluded, lies "all the future of Russia."[4] Chicherin identified liberalism with freedom – for example, freedom for the serfs, for religion, for the press and for teachers and professors. It also meant to him due process of law and the publicity and openness (*publichnost* and *glasnost*) of government and legal activities.

But the past of Russian liberalism seemed to portend that it had about as much chance for a fruitful future as an orange tree in Siberia. Whereas in the West liberalism was supported by a strong middle class wishing to limit governmental powers, in Russia the middle class was small and not always desirous of limiting the power of the monarch. Men such as Kavelin and Chicherin, as well as Professor Soloviev, who shared some of their important ideas, wanted a reforming monarch, but had no desire to weaken his authority. In fact, all three men wanted him to strongly pursue progressive policies while standing above class interests. Thus Kavelin could write, as he did in 1855, about the "complete necessity of retaining the unlimited power of the sovereign, basing it on the widest possible local freedom."[5] The inherent unlikeliness of any lasting marriage between autocracy and freedom, indeed the improbability of anything more than even a brief flirtation, does not seem to have occurred to Kavelin or his fellow moderates.

Nevertheless, in early 1856 there was considerable support among educated people for the type of changes advocated by Kavelin and Chicherin. In the capital the enthusiastic Kavelin was a whirlwind of activity. He was well thought of by the two most progressive members of the Imperial family, the Tsar's aunt

Grand Duchess Elena and his brother Constantine, and he was also friendly with a number of progressive bureaucrats. Furthermore, realizing that the times called for a unified public opinion, he tried to patch over past personal and intellectual differences and to create a consensus for moderate reform. In the material which he and Chicherin sent to Herzen, with whom Kavelin had once been close friends, the two liberals tried to persuade him to moderate his criticism of the Tsar and renounce what they considered his socialistic propaganda. Kavelin had recently also made overtures to one of his former teachers, the conservative nationalist Pogodin.

One of the subjects Kavelin had been most concerned with was the possibility of ending serfdom, and he had recently written a long "memorandum" suggesting how it could be successfully accomplished. Meanwhile, Tolstoy had been troubled by a guilty conscience because of his own ownership of serfs. Thus, he sought out Kavelin, who also contributed to *The Contemporary*, for enlightenment on how he might best improve their lot. After spending the evening of April 23rd with Kavelin, Tolstoy recorded in his diary that the serf question was becoming clearer, that Kavelin possessed "a charming mind and nature,"[6] and that he (Tolstoy) was now hopeful that he could return to his serfs with a written proposal.

Although Tolstoy shared some of Kavelin's enthusiasm for reform, he did not share his reconciling temperament. While Kavelin tried to appease and reconcile various groups, Tolstoy continued sporadically to antagonize or find fault with one after another. He believed that many of the liberal contributors to *The Contemporary*, i.e., most of those opposing Chernyshevsky, lacked moral depth. They in turn realized that, despite some liberal inclinations, Tolstoy was somehow essentially different from most of them. When one of the contributors wrote in a letter to Nekrasov that Tolstoy's sympathy with liberalism was insufficient, Tolstoy challenged him to a duel. Fortunately, Tolstoy's would-be opponent ignored the challenge.

During the first few weeks of May, Tolstoy's dissatisfaction targeted the Slavophiles and Pogodin. Earlier that year, he had visited Moscow and met with Constantine Aksakov and his father. Now in St Petersburg he met Constantine's younger brother Ivan and Ivan Kireevsky, another prominent Slavophile. In his diary, Tolstoy criticized their ideas for being too narrow and one-sided. Five days later after reading an article of Pogodin's about the honoring of the Sevastopol defenders in Moscow, he wrote: "I with pleasure would slap Pogodin's face. Contemptible flattery, seasoned with Slavophilism."[7]

Ironically, despite his critical disposition, he wrote in his diary for May 12th that the key to happiness in life was to dispense love in all directions. And a few months later when he wrote to Nekrasov criticizing Chernyshevsky, Tolstoy pointed to what he considered the radical's angry and bitter literary criticism.

Tolstoy thought that it reflected an absence of love and therefore could do only harm.

Already by the middle of April, with the first signs of spring in the air, Tolstoy was anxious to leave the capital and return to his lovely Yasnaya Polyana property. But first the military had to approve the leave which he had recently requested. Finally on May 16th, he received a long furlough, eleven months, from further military duties. The next day he boarded the train for Moscow en route to his estate.

6
THE TSAR, THE SERFS AND
THE CORONATION

In March 1856, a month after the Sevastopol sailors had left Moscow, the Tsar once again journeyed there by train. With the peace treaty having just been signed, those who concerned themselves with public affairs could now concentrate on other matters. And the old governor-general of Moscow had something other than war on his mind. Recently he had heard rumors that Alexander would announce the emancipation of the serfs during the upcoming coronation ceremonies. Although he himself might not believe such talk, some of his fellow nobles in Moscow were concerned. The governor-general asked the Emperor if he would reassure the nobles that their fears were groundless.

Even when primarily concerned with the war, Alexander had slowly begun to take steps to alleviate some of the more oppressive aspects of his father's rule. In addition to easing up on censorship, he lifted some of the restrictions on travel and on the number of students permitted into the universities. His manifesto announcing the peace also seemed to indicate reform. It spoke of a desire for strengthening Russia's internal well-being, for equal justice for all her people and for developing the urge toward enlightenment and useful activity.

But for many of the intellectuals of the day, the abolition of serfdom was the most pressing issue. From Alexander Herzen in his London sanctuary to more conservative thinkers like Constantine Aksakov and Pogodin in Moscow, there was general agreement among intellectuals that serfdom had to go. Many considered it a sign of backwardness and some a scandal that close to half of Russia's large peasant class and about two-fifths of its total population was comprised of serf families. Although the serfs usually lived in their own households and worked on strips of land whose produce they kept or sold, or even worked in the city if their owners approved, they all owed work or made payments on a regular basis to their lords. They could still be beaten, sent to Siberia or to the army for twenty-five years, or be compelled to marry by their masters. The nobles could still with impunity take sexual advantage of their female serfs. Regardless of how frequently or infrequently such abuses occurred, their mere possibility and the absence of legal safeguards for serfs seemed intolerable to such men as Herzen and Chernyshevsky.

To the governor-general of Moscow and to some of the area's less enlightened nobles, however, serfdom was not intolerable. For centuries the serfs had supported the nobility. (In the early nineteenth century the richest member of the Sheremetev clan owned about three hundred thousand male and female serfs and almost two million acres.) Many serf-owners could not imagine running their estates without serfs. Some "masters" were also convinced that serfdom was necessary, at least in their lifetime, for the good of Russia. Were not their serfs too ignorant, immature and indolent to operate on their own?

Despite some of the Emperor's other early steps in the direction of reform, the governor-general had some reason to hope that Alexander would not tamper with serfdom. Rulers from the time of Catherine the Great, almost a century before, had recognized some of the evils of the system, but had not dared to abolish it. Serf-owners were the backbone of the military and civilian leadership. The Tsar was dependent on them for carrying out his policies. Some thought that he could not afford to alienate this small but influential class. Moreover, as Tsarevich, Alexander had gained the reputation of being a supporter of the rights of the landowners.

Alexander's visit to Moscow was a short one, with the usual religious services, military ceremonies and governmental meetings. Since it was the Lenten season, however, the governor-general was not able to give a ball. The day after the Tsar arrived he received the representatives of the nobility of the Moscow province. While he spoke to them of serfdom, he was not very reassuring. Although he did not allow his speech to be printed nor its contents mentioned in the press, it nevertheless created a sensation. An underground text of it soon rapidly circulated. The Tsar told the nobles that while he did not intend to abolish serfdom immediately, eventually it must occur. He added that it would be better if it came from above rather than from below, an allusion to possible serf uprisings. Finally, he invited the nobles to give some consideration as to how serfdom might be ended.

After returning to the capital Alexander instructed his Minister of Interior to begin preparing a plan for the gradual liberation of the serfs. He also told him to speak informally about the subject to representatives of the nobility of various provinces when they convened at the upcoming coronation in Moscow. The Tsar hoped to obtain the co-operation of the landowners rather than forcing the emancipation of the serfs upon them.

During the war there had been scattered peasant disturbances, and some in the military believed that Russia's poor showing in the war was partly the result of serfdom. In the same month that Alexander spoke to the Moscow nobles, Dmitry Milyutin, a young general and friend of the liberal Constantine

Kavelin, composed a memorandum on army reform. In it he pointed to the necessity of creating a large trained reserve and reducing the size of the traditionally large standing army. But for a variety of reasons these steps were only feasible if serfdom was abolished. To the Tsar such military considerations were important. So also was the financial consideration that a smaller standing army would be more affordable. The Crimean War had strained the country's economy to a dangerous degree, and Alexander wished to reduce inflation and the threat of serious peacetime budget deficits. The peasant disturbances, public opinion, the aid of enlightened bureaucrats such as Milyutin's brother Nicholas (who served as deputy Minister of Interior), concern with its image at home and abroad, and Russia's industrial backwardness and sluggish economy also helped propel him toward emancipating the serfs.

Thus, in the first year of his reign, Alexander indicated that he could be more pragmatic and flexible than his father had been. What he wanted for his country was what most rulers wanted: strength and stability. He began to perceive that if Russia was to regain the status and power it lost during the recent war (an important consideration to Russia's ruling elite as well as to Alexander), it would have to reform and modernize. The trick was to do so while maintaining stability and without infringing upon his own autocratic powers. For he sincerely believed that in Russia's backward state only the Tsar could stand above narrower interests of class and ideology and rule in behalf of all.

Although Alexander thought that Russia must now concentrate on internal development and avoid costly foreign entanglements, he nevertheless had to take diplomatic steps to aid such a policy. A few weeks after his return from Moscow, he installed a new Foreign Minister. He was the vain, talkative Alexander Gorchakov, a distant relative of Leo Tolstoy. In domestic matters he supported reform, although always within proper bounds. He would prove to be a strong supporter of Alexander's emancipation efforts. Regarding foreign affairs, he was known for his anti-Austrian and pro-French sentiments. With his appointment the Tsar signaled a drastic change in Russian foreign policy. Turning his back on an Austria with which his father had allied himself, but which Alexander believed had betrayed Russia during the recent war, the Tsar now began moving Russia closer to France. In January 1857, after receiving a friendly letter from France's Napoleon III, Alexander would write to his brother Grand Duke Constantine: "I see union with France as a guarantee of future peace in Europe."[1] Alexander was no great admirer of Napoleon III, but he realized that the French ruler's ambitions conflicted with those of Austria. He hoped to take advantage of any estrangement between these two powers to regain, without undue risk, Russia's military rights in the Black Sea.

Moving closer to France, however, did not necessitate moving away from Russia's other pre-war friend, Prussia. Thus, in May 1856, Alexander traveled to

Berlin and Sans Souci to visit the Prussian monarch, Frederick William IV. He was met there by his mother, who was the sister of the Prussian monarch. The Tsar thanked Frederick William for not joining Russia's enemies during the war. Four days of cordial talks, parades and pleasantries followed.

On his way to Prussia the Emperor had spent six days in Russian Poland. Alexander had already shown signs of easing his father's harsh handling of the Poles, but while in Warsaw he warned Polish leaders not to dream of Polish autonomy. On the way back from Berlin, Alexander spent some time in Russia's Baltic provinces. As in Poland, he displayed there a firm resolve to hold together Russia's multi-ethnic empire.

He also wished to increase his hold on newly conquered border areas and to continue expanding the Russian empire. General Muraviev was tightening his control over former Chinese territories in Siberia. In the Caucasus Russian troops after two decades were still battling the legendary Shamil and his Islamic mountain forces. Many of the Tsar's advisors predicted the necessity of at least another decade of fighting before a Russian victory could be gained over Shamil. However, in the summer of 1856, Alexander placed a friend of his youth, Prince Alexander Baryatinsky, in charge of operations in the Caucasus. Within three years Baryatinsky would capture Shamil and break the resistance movement in the Eastern Caucasus.

As in his first year as Tsar, Alexander and his wife resided the greater part of that second summer in Tsarskoe Selo and then Peterhof. The planning for an August coronation was proceeding, and the family spent some happy moments together. One such time began with a trip on the Emperor's yacht from Peterhof to Gapsal, along the Estonian coast. The four sons were already at this seaside resort when their father and mother decided to pay them a surprise visit. The gulf waters were calm and the July weather beautiful. Although her constitution was not the strongest and she had not been feeling well before her departure, the Empress suddenly began to feel better. After a night at sea the yacht approached Gapsal, and the royal couple spotted their four sons out in a boat. A happy reunion followed, with parents, children and dogs all delighted to see one another. After some days together and receptions and festivities, the Empress kissed her boys on the forehead and blessed them. Then the parents said good-bye and once again boarded their yacht. That evening there was a beautiful sunset. As they sat on the deck the Empress told Anna Tyutcheva, that lady-in-waiting who had been so upset at Alexander's decision to end the war, that she loved the sea because to her it was a symbol of eternity. Their conversation then turned to St Augustine and his mother. Such religious topics were close to the heart of this pious, non-worldly Empress.

Another lady-in-waiting, the tall, slender, dark-haired and flirtatious Alexandra Dolgorukaya, also accompanied the couple on the trip. There were still rumors about her and the Tsar, and the Empress would become in-creasingly upset about such talk – Grand Duke Constantine's diary entry of November 22nd, 1859, indicated that three years later serious grounds for ru-mors still existed.[2] Nevertheless, a little more than nine months after these nights on the gulf waters, Empress Maria would give birth to another boy.

At the end of August, after more than a week's preliminary festivities, the coronation finally took place in Moscow's Kremlin. The ancient city was painted and cleaned in preparation. And one observer noted, perhaps with some exaggeration, that almost as much was being spent on coronation festiv-ities and preparations as on the costly Crimean War, and that this was being done partly to impress foreigners. People from throughout the empire streamed into the white-walled city, jamming the roads leading to it. The great variety of the empire's nationalities and costumes caught the eye. The weather was magnificent. On the day before the actual coronation, the Emperor's sub-jects joined foreign observers and diplomats along the city's roads and upon specially built platforms in order to watch the entrance of the royal procession into the city from a palace on the outskirts. Cossacks and elite cavalry units sit-ting upright on their horses, brilliantly decorated and colored uniforms, golden coaches and jeweled royalty, all captured the eye. The bells atop the hundreds of churches, the clatter of hoofs and carriage wheels, the music of the bands and the noise of the crowds created a cacophony of sounds. As a silver and glass car-riage, harnessed to eight gray horses, slowly passed by, people fell to their knees. Inside, alone and erect, sat Emperor Alexander II.

Among the diplomats in Moscow for the coronation was England's Lord Granville. His report to Queen Victoria spoke of the tremendous expense of the coronation festivities, but more importantly he briefly assessed the new mon-arch and the condition of Russia. Like Professor Soloviev and Anna Tyutcheva, Granville believed that the new Emperor did not possess a strong character, nor did he seem to have the ability to choose able ministers. And due to the oppres-sive nature of the reign of Nicholas I, Granville thought that the easing of re-strictions which was then occurring presented some danger for the new regime. On the future horizon, he believed, Socialism could pose a serious threat.

But on the morning of the coronation the sun shone brilliantly, and most Muscovites and visiting Russians from outside the city were in a joyous mood. Cheers, bells, cannons and the Russian national hymn greeted the Emperor as he descended the famous Red Staircase of the Great Palace and moved toward the Assumption Cathedral. Under a royal canopy, Alexander walked erectly next to his wife whose eyes only approached the level of his shoulders. He was in uniform, and it was not difficult to see why many considered him a hand-some man. He was a bit pale that day, but his sideburns curved around to meet his finely trimmed mustache and helped to give his face a regal appearance. The eyes of the Empress were downcast and she seemed withdrawn into her own inner world. Once inside the Assumption Cathedral, amidst its beautiful frescoes and icons, the ceremony continued for five hours. The Emperor's crowning of himself and his wife, as well as other aspects of the ceremony, symbolized the power of the Autocrat of the Russian Empire and the fact that he was responsible to no man, only to God.

On the days following the ceremony the pageantry and celebrations continued. Fountains flowed with wine. Soldiers served food to the people and coronation souvenirs were distributed. At night fireworks illuminated the sky, and the Kremlin towers could be seen reflected in the Moscow river below. Dinners, receptions and balls, where crinolined ladies danced mazurkas, polonaises, quadrilles and waltzes with their uniformed partners, followed one after another.

In general the coronation ceremonies seem to have been a smashing success. The Crimean war was a thing of the past. The coronation symbolized a new beginning, and in that spirit Alexander granted numerous amnesties to prisoners and exiles. He also ended some past injustices – for example, the practice of drafting selected young Jewish boys, who were subsequently pressured to convert to Russian Orthodoxy. But despite the euphoria of the day, there was one small incident which bothered the Empress, and that occurred during the coronation ceremony. At some point after the Emperor had placed the crown on her head, it had fallen off. She told Anna Tyutcheva: "It is a sign I will not wear it long."[3]

7

DOSTOEVSKY IN EXILE

While Alexander II was crowning himself in Moscow, far away in the in the Central Asian-Siberian border town of Semipalatinsk (present-day Seney) the non-commissioned officer Fedor Dostoevsky was languishing. He was thirty-four, about five feet six inches tall, with a pale freckled face and a receding hair-line. He smoked a lot and had a throaty voice.

He was the son of a Moscow doctor, whose mysterious death in 1839 left a permanent mark on the young Fedor. Hearing that his father had been killed by his own serfs, it is likely that the young man held himself partly responsible: he was then a student at the Military Engineering Academy in St Petersburg and repeatedly had requested money from his father, who was himself sliding towards impoverishment. Did not his requests contribute to his father's harsh demands on his serfs? Did they not indirectly help lead to the revenge thought to have been exacted by these peasants?[1]

Six difficult years later came Nekrasov's discovery of Dostoevsky's literary talent, and soon afterwards the publication of his first novel, *Poor Folk*. Subsequent events, however, soon deflated the spirits of this shy, awkward, nervous young man. Some of Dostoevsky's newly made friends, such as the more aristocratic Turgenev, began to tease and torment him because the success of *Poor Folk* had caused him to seem unduly vain. In addition, his new works failed to generate the enthusiasm of his first. Then he became involved with the Petrashevsky Circle. And his instincts for social justice, his hatred of serfdom (probably intensified by the circumstances of his father's death) and his utopian dreams for a golden age, all led him into trouble. Early one spring morning in 1849, Dostoevsky was awakened by a lieutenant colonel of the secret police and a local police official and led to a waiting carriage. He spent the next eight months surrounded by the damp, cold and moldy walls of his cell in the Peter and Paul Fortress.

A few days before Christmas he was taken to Semenovsky Square. There, amidst fresh snow and the newly risen sun, he and others who had once been part of the Petrashevsky group heard their death sentences read out in a hasty and indistinct voice. "Retired Engineer-Lieutenant Fedor Dostoevsky, twenty-seven, for participation in criminal plans, for circulating a private letter that contained infamous expressions about the Russian Orthodox Church and Supreme Authority, and for an attempt to disseminate writing against the government by means of a hand printing press – to be put to death by the firing squad."[2] Moments of agony followed as the first group of three were led forward, and he stood there in the second group. The troops assigned to this gruesome task loaded their muskets and took aim. But then came the deliberate last-minute arrival of the Tsar's reprieve, and instead of death, Siberia, where several wives of those Decembrists exiled a quarter century earlier met him in transit and gave him a copy of the Gospels. Following four years of prison in Omsk, in that "House of the Dead" as he would later describe it, he was assigned to the 7th Siberian Battalion of the Line in Semipalatinsk, a city about six hundred miles southeast and up the Irtysh River from Omsk.

It was a barren town of less than ten thousand inhabitants, even if one counted some three thousand Tatars, Kirghiz and other people of the steppe who lived on the western side of the Irtysh River. Its main section consisted of a long line of log houses and a few brick government and military structures, which were separated by a wide unpaved road from melon gardens along the eastern side of the Irtysh. Past the river and the Tatar village on the other side lay the treeless Kirghiz steppe. It stretched to the southwest for more than a thousand miles. Semipalatinsk was a military base from which troops could be dispatched to help keep the newly conquered, but still rebellious, Kirghiz in line. It was also a center for camel-caravaned and pack-horsed traders who departed and arrived from Chinese towns and also from cities like Bukhara and Tashkent, far to the southwest and not yet under Russian control. Sheep, horses, cattle and animal skins from the steppe also entered and left the town. It contained one Orthodox church, one district school, one hospital, seven mosques and many exotic shops. But there were no bookstores and no street lights. Mail came only once a week. Cards, gossip and drinking helped the townspeople to pass their spare hours.

After first arriving in early 1854, Dostoevsky lived in the barracks with most of the other soldiers, but soon he was renting a low-ceilinged, one-room cottage in a dreary part of town. He also acquired a new friend. This was a twenty-two-year-old newly appointed public prosecutor from St Petersburg, Baron Alexander Wrangel. He was familiar with Dostoevsky's writings and had been present five years earlier on the square where the writer thought he was to be executed. Wrangel was an intelligent, sympathetic young man who soon did all he could to help Dostoevsky. He brought the writer into the homes of Semipalatinsk's small Russian "elite" and during the extraordinarily hot summer of 1855, the men resided together at the dacha, or summer home, of a rich merchant. When Wrangel returned to St Petersburg in February of the following year, he interceded with officials in an attempt to improve the career of his good friend.

Dostoevsky himself had tried to better his own fate by displaying his patriotism in three poems he had written since arriving in Semipalatinsk. The first, "On the European Events in 1854," criticized Russia's enemies and stated that "God is with us." The second, which he dedicated to the widow of the Tsar who had sent him to Siberia, spoke of her just deceased husband as one "who illuminated us like the sun." The third, in honor of Alexander's coronation, spoke of the new Tsar as the "source of all mercy."[3] The poems were meant primarily for the eyes of high officials in the capital, and at least the second and third seem to have helped Dostoevsky improve his chances for an eventual pardon.

The poems were not as hypocritical as they might seem. Dostoevsky's Western-influenced utopian convictions had undergone a profound change since his arrest. At first in the prison at Omsk, the lonely writer observing the barbaric conduct of the common criminals had felt more isolated and cut off than ever. But he could not long stand this agony of isolation. Two experiences helped him to overcome it. The first was his participation one Easter week with these common prisoners at Orthodox Church services, and the second, occurring that same week, was a sudden long-forgotten recollection of the loving help one of his father's serfs had given him when he was nine years old. (Many years later Dostoevsky described this recollection in the short piece "Peasant Marey.") These two phenomena seem to have triggered in him an intense religious reawakening.

His vague religious beliefs, which had become amalgamated with his utopianism, were now replaced by a belief in the concrete Orthodox religion of the common man: the religion of Christ, of sin and suffering, of resurrection and redemption. And from this belief followed another: the only path for Russian intellectuals to follow was one that united them with the common people and their religious beliefs.

Yet, despite these beliefs, to which he would adhere for the remainder of his life, he did not completely abandon his earlier utopianism, but rather unconsciously merged it with his reawakened Orthodoxy. His youthful dream of creating a golden age would later be reborn in his hope that the Kingdom of God could be realized on earth. In general, his new faith was more optimistic and less fatalistic than that of the masses. He also remained much more concerned than most Church leaders about obtaining social justice and happiness for the masses on this earth, and not just in heaven. For these reasons, he never completely lost his sympathy for young people who dreamed of creating a more humane society.

Dostoevsky also shared the hopes of most educated society that Alexander II would be a great improvement over his father, that he would be a true reformer. After Wrangel wrote to him about the popularity of the new Tsar, Dostoevsky replied that the news greatly pleased him and that what was needed now was greater faith, unity and love.

Shortly after Wrangel left Semipalatinsk, Dostoevsky sent him a letter to be given to the hero of Sevastopol and now aide-de-camp to the Tsar, General Totleben. The general's brother, Adolf, had been a classmate and friend of Dostoevsky's when they had studied engineering together in St Petersburg. In the letter the ex-convict requested the general to ask the Tsar to release him from military service, allow him to leave Semipalatinsk and permit him to once again publish his works. Totleben agreed to help. But the Tsar allowed only the promotion of Dostoevsky to the officer rank of ensign. Permission for him to publish was to be granted only after continued surveillance had established his political reliability.

Although Dostoevsky and many other writers hoped for much good from the new Emperor, he never would reciprocate their confidence. When still a Tsarevich, he had criticized intellectuals who thought they were "more intelligent than everyone else" and who believed "that they should be able to do as they want."[4] For such false pride he had blamed foreign influences and some of Russia's professors. Later, a few years after becoming Tsar, he wrote to a friend: "I swear that I have never been greatly enamored of literary men in general, and in particular I have come to the unfortunate conclusion that they are a class of individuals with the most dangerous biases and hidden motives."[5]

The welcome news of Dostoevsky's promotion did not come until the fall of 1856. At the time of the August coronation, however, the exiled writer was a very unhappy man. Besides not being able to publish anything, he was in debt and his health was not good. He also missed his good friend Wrangel. Worst of all, he was in love with a woman five hundred miles away who, he feared, loved a younger rival who had the advantage of living in the same town with her.

The passion of his life at this time was Maria Isaeva. She was in her late twenties, of medium height, somewhat sickly, frail and thin, but capricious, high-strung and strong-willed. When Dostoevsky met her soon after arriving in Semipalatinsk she was married to a drunkard, who had lost his government position. She also had a seven-year-old son. Eventually an intimate relationship developed between the unhappy woman and the lonely writer who had been deprived of love for so long.

But then her husband found a new job in the distant town of Kuznetsk. When his wife left with him, Dostoevsky wept and became morbid. Nor did the death of her husband some months later greatly improve the writer's chances, for he was in no position to propose marriage. She herself was impoverished and unclear in her own mind as to her feelings about Dostoevsky or what she should do in the future. On a secret and unlawful trip to Kuznetsk several months before the coronation, the writer had met not only with Maria, but also with his young rival of twenty-four. He was a schoolteacher who, Dostoevsky had thought, had "seen nothing and knows nothing."[6]

Dostoevsky returned to Semipalatinsk in a state of nervous exhaustion. Several months passed, as did letters between Maria and Dostoevsky. She could not make up her mind, and Dostoevsky's health noticeably suffered from her indecision. Acquaintances found him on the verge of collapse.

Finally, after his promotion came, his odds with Maria shot up along with his salary and status. After another trip to Kuznetsk, he wrote to Wrangel in December that he hoped to be married before Lent of the following year.

Two months later, in February 1857, Dostoevsky and Maria were married at the Church of the Holy Guide in Kuznetsk. Only a few people were present including his rival, the young schoolteacher. On the way back to Semipalatinsk, the newlyweds stopped off in the town of Barnaul, where they visited a friend of the writer's, a well-known geographer and expeditionist, Peter Semenov. While there Dostoevsky fell to the floor, moaning and convulsing in spasms. His new bride was terrified. The doctor who was summoned diagnosed epilepsy. Maria had not realized that her new husband was an epileptic, and despite previous nervous attacks, he claimed that he had not known it either. He said that previous doctors had assured him that such attacks were not "true epilepsy" and that they might cease under more tranquil conditions.

After resting and recovering the couple moved on to Semipalatinsk and into four rented rooms in a square wooden house. They remained in the town for a little over two years; her son was sent to a cadet school in Omsk. Dostoevsky found time to write and renewed some of his literary contacts. A friend wrote that Nekrasov and Panaev would send money to help him until he could write something for them. He also read all that he could. He regarded Turgenev's works very highly and thought his *A Nest of the Landed Gentry*, which appeared in *The Contemporary* in early 1859, "extraordinarily good."[7] Meanwhile, the government finally allowed Dostoevsky himself to once again publish, and two of his stories and a novelette came out in Russian journals by the end of 1859. But before being published, his novelette, *The Village of Stepanchikovo*, was all but rejected by a disappointed Nekrasov. In general his return to literature was hardly noticed by the critics.

Nor was his life with Maria a great success. They were both often ill. She was in the early stages of consumption, a disease that had also taken the writer's mother when he was fifteen. They were both often jealous without reason and seemed to derive a perverse pleasure from inflicting or receiving pain and suffering at the hands of the other. Years later Dostoevsky wrote to a friend that they "were definitely unhappy together," but the more unhappy they were the more they "became attached to one another."[8]

Finally, in March 1859, the Tsar permitted Dostoevsky to retire from the army and live anywhere but St Petersburg or Moscow. The couple chose Tver, which was located between the two cities. But after several unhappy months there the writer, desperate to live in St Petersburg, wrote to the Tsar: "Your Imperial majesty, upon You my entire fate, health and life depend. Kindly permit me to go to St Petersburg to seek the advice of the capital's doctors [for epilepsy]. Resurrect me and by restoring my health give me the opportunity to be of use to my family, and perhaps in some way or other to my fatherland."[9] Dostoevsky sent this request to Alexander through the local governor, with whom he had become friendly. At the same time he once again wrote to General Totleben asking for his intercession.

Within a little over a month the Tsar responded favorably, but stipulated that even in the capital the writer was to be kept under surveillance. The Dostoevskys immediately planned their departure. In December 1859, almost exactly ten years after he had left the capital, he returned along with Maria and his stepson and was greeted at the train station by his brother Michael.

8
MICHAEL BAKUNIN

Two years before Dostoevsky arrived in Tver from Semipalatinsk, a prisoner arrived by sleigh at his family estate not far from that city. The prisoner was Michael Bakunin on his way to banishment in Siberia.

Premukhino was the name of the large Bakunin estate with its hundreds of serfs, and it was where Michael and his five brothers and four sisters had grown up. The family's big, one-storied, neo-classical house stood on a hill surrounded by woods and fields, and at the bottom of the hill was the river Osuga. After having to leave this estate to attend a military school in St Petersburg when he was fourteen, Bakunin always remembered it fondly.

While he was in prison, his father had died and long before that his sister Lyubov. But the rest of the family awaited him. How close Michael had once been to his sisters and brothers, especially his sisters, who were always falling in love with his friends! Bakunin's favorite, the blue-eyed Tatyana, had once loved Turgenev so ardently that she never really got over it. She was now in her early forties and still single.

When as a young man, Michael had returned home for a time from St Petersburg or Moscow, he had often defied his parents and acted as a champion for his brothers, all younger than he, or for his sisters. He was then a curly-haired, rebellious youth who disapproved of what he considered the superfluous world of the nobility. Neither military life nor civilian government service appealed to him, nor did dances, balls or drinking. Away from Premukhino he had been terribly lonely until he found within himself "something to fill the emptiness."[1] That something was German Romantic Idealism. It enabled him to justify his withdrawal from a society in which he felt uncomfortable and at the same time to convince himself that he was involved in a significant quest. It also brought him into close contact with a group of Moscow University students and other intellectuals who shared his enthusiasm for German thought. They included the radical Belinsky, Constantine Aksakov and the future journalist and editor Michael Katkov. Like many other intellectuals of his generation, Bakunin spent many years living in a mental world far removed from the practical realities of everyday life. But in a more profound psychological sense than most of them, he never matured.

In the beginning of the 1840s, he studied in Berlin, where he shared quarters with his friend and fellow student Ivan Turgenev. At about the time Bakunin arrived in the Prussian capital, Karl Marx, who was the same age as Turgenev and Alexander II and four years younger than Bakunin, was just completing five years of study at the University of Berlin. And Bakunin's intellectual development in the forties, the decade in which he became a political revolutionary, would closely resemble that of Marx. Both Marx and Bakunin were strongly influenced by radical German interpreters of the philosopher Hegel and then by French socialists. In 1848–9, with revolutions spreading across Europe, Bakunin took part in revolutionary or subversive activities in Paris and Prague, in Breslau and Berlin, and in Dresden, where he became friends with the composer Richard Wagner. He was finally arrested in 1849 in Chemnitz, not far from Dresden.

During the next two years Bakunin was twice sentenced to death, only to have the sentence commuted both times to life imprisonment, and then twice extradited to another country. He went from Saxon prisons to Austrian ones, and then to a cell in the Peter and Paul Fortress. He stayed there for three years until, fearing an English bombardment of the capital in 1854, the Russian government moved him to the Schlusselburg Prison on Lake Ladoga.

Now in 1857, after eight years in Saxon, Austrian and Russian prisons and seventeen years since he had last been home, Bakunin was allowed to spend one day at Premukhino. The man who alighted under guard from his sleigh that March day had aged greatly. Prisons seemed to have deprived him of his teeth and some of his hair, but surprisingly recompensed him with additional pounds. But it was undoubtedly the passing years rather than prison cooking which accounted for the more ample Michael who now stood before them. Prison life also seemed to have aged his spirit; he no longer seemed the same fiery rebel.

While in prison, he had written a "Confession" to Tsar Nicholas, and less than a month before finding himself at Premukhino he had sent an effective plea to Alexander II in which he expressed regret and sorrow for his past behavior.

After a rather subdued day with his family, the next morning he said goodbye to them. He was never to see most of them again. He settled his large body into the sleigh and still under guard set out over the snow towards Siberia. After a brief stop in Omsk, where Dostoevsky had spent four years in prison, Bakunin continued further east to the city of Tomsk, where he was to spend his next two years.

Tomsk at this time was a flourishing Siberian commercial center of about twenty thousand inhabitants. It was situated along the river Tom, a tributary of the Ob. With its unpaved streets, horse-drawn carriages and sleighs and wooden houses, it had the look of many nineteenth century Russian provincial towns. But its very cold winters, its substantial mixture of Asiatic natives and the rough, unrefined frontier look of some of its people all combined to indicate it was part of Siberia. While living there, Bakunin was restricted to a twenty-mile radius around the town, and the police kept him under surveillance.

He did, however, renew some of his political efforts, encouraging, for example, the radical views of the young Siberian Grigory Potanin, who later (in 1865) was arrested and subsequently sentenced to hard labor for supporting the formation of an independent Siberia. To supplement the money sent from home, Bakunin taught French to the daughters of a Polish merchant. Although some historians have claimed that Bakunin was impotent and fled from sexual involvement, he was now nevertheless a lonely man in his early forties.[2] He had also never minded admirers, male or female. One of the merchant's daughters, seventeen-year-old Antonia, seemed to be admiring enough, and Bakunin proposed marriage. The wedding took place in the fall of 1858.

One of the participants in the wedding was Nicholas Muraviev, the governor-general of Eastern Siberia (whose capital was Irkutsk). He was a famous and powerful man, capable of being dogmatic and dictatorial, but nevertheless with a reputation for advanced ideas. He was also Bakunin's second cousin. Five years older than Bakunin, he was a solid, energetic little man, with a well-kept mustache. By 1858, he had been governor-general for a decade, and earlier had fought against Shamil in the Caucasus. He was ambitious, confident and hardworking. He had exercised boldness and initiative in opening up the Amur River area to Russian exploration and colonization. Just that summer, provincial Chinese officials had formally ceded to Russia the whole northern bank of the Amur when they agreed in Muraviev's presence to the Treaty of Aigun.

Even before this, Alexander II had recognized the worth of Muraviev when at time of the coronation he had promoted and decorated him. Following the Treaty of Aigun, the Tsar bestowed upon him the title of count and the honor of having Amursky affixed to his name. Although Alexander was a more cautious man than the bold Muraviev, he was as imperialistic as most Western rulers of his time. He was apparently won over by Muraviev's stress on the economic gains to be won by wresting control of the Amur from the Chinese and by his warnings of British penetration of the area if Russia did not move soon. Strapped with insufficient government revenues and a high foreign debt, Alexander was anxious to increase trade with China. In the past it had been a good market for Russian textiles and a source of tea, some of which Russia then resold to other European countries. But since the Opium War of 1839–42 the British challenge to Russian trade had increased.

While in Moscow for the coronation, Muraviev also had the satisfaction of allowing his protégé, young Michael Volkonsky, to race to Irkutsk, the capital of Eastern Siberia, with the news that those Decembrists still in exile would now be allowed to leave Siberia. This was especially satisfying to both Muraviev and Volkonsky because Muraviev had befriended the parents of Michael, who were perhaps the most prominent Decembrist couple. Michael's mother had become a legend when, as a young bride, this tall, dark-eyed princess had defied her parents and followed her husband to the Siberian mines in Nerchinsk, where some of the Decembrists were first assigned. Just a year before the amnesty she had returned to European Russia due to poor health. But prior to that, her home in Irkutsk had become a prominent gathering place for Decembrists and other friends. Her husband, Prince Volkonsky, had taken up farming and associating with peasants. Some were impressed by his kindness and simplicity of manner and dress, others just thought him eccentric.

Muraviev was proud of the support he and his aristocratic French wife gave to these Decembrists. After most of them departed, he was friendly for a time in Irkutsk with Petrashevsky, the exiled leader of the group that Dostoevsky had become involved with in the late forties. At parties in the white colonnaded governor's mansion, which the Americanophile Muraviev labeled the White House, he enjoyed espousing progressive views. However, he could also be dogmatic and dictatorial when crossed or when it suited his purpose.

Thanks mainly to Muraviev's efforts, Bakunin's exile conditions were reduced, and in March 1859 Bakunin, Antonia and her family moved to Irkutsk. There Muraviev arranged for them to live comfortably. In exchange, Bakunin performed some light tasks as an agent for an Amur trading company. Bakunin, however, never cared for a steady job of any kind, no matter how undemanding, and after about half a year he resigned. But his boss knew that Bakunin's patron was the powerful Muraviev, and for almost two years he continued to pay him a salary, plus furnishing his house. Bakunin gladly accepted the payments and for the next two years resided mainly in Irkutsk.

It was not a bad Siberian city. About the size of Tomsk, it struck a number of foreign visitors favorably. It lay along the Angara river, not far from Lake Baikal, and possessed very fine churches and buildings and a hospitable population. Under Muraviev and with the aid of political exiles, whom he treated favorably, it maintained more of an intellectual and cultural atmosphere than one might expect in a Siberian town thousands of miles from Moscow.

Rather than becoming close to fellow exiles still in Irkutsk, Bakunin gravitated toward Muraviev and some of those around him. More significantly, he not only defended Muraviev, whom the émigré radical Herzen had criticized in his journal *The Bell*, but wrote to Herzen and others in glowing terms about his cousin. Bakunin referred to him as the "sun of Siberia," the "savior of Russia," "a firm democrat" and a "revolutionary" who was in favor of freeing the serfs, abolishing the class structure, and allowing a jury system and freedom of the press.[3] He indicated that in the beginning Muraviev would carry out these policies not by relying on a constitution or parliament but by establishing a temporary, rational dictatorship. Further, he could then be a focal point for Slavs everywhere, whom he would help liberate from the hated Austrians and Turks. In his earlier prison "Confession," Bakunin suggested a somewhat similar role for Tsar Nicholas. Bakunin believed that his ultimate goals had never changed, just the means of bringing them about. An enlightened dictator, Nicholas if he could have been persuaded, or now Muraviev, could be the new means of creating the good society.

As improbable as these hopes were, they were psychologically important to Bakunin. They reflected his desire to overcome a lingering sense of impotence and separation. Like Dostoevsky, but with a more exaggerated sense of self-importance, he thirsted to end his exile and to make his contribution to society. But only on his own terms. What better way then than to become a sort of ideological guru to a charismatic man of power. Bakunin's hopes for an enlightened dictator were also a reflection of the simple, almost patriarchal nature of the Russian state. Children of well-to-do nobles such as Bakunin were brought up on estates where their fathers ruled like little tsars. Not only did many of these nobles know individuals who had access to the Tsar or a member of his family, but when they got in political trouble the Tsar himself sometimes became involved. Nicholas I had sent his chief aide-de-camp to Bakunin's cell in the Peter and Paul Fortress with the request that the prisoner write a full confession to the Tsar as if he were a spiritual father. And when Bakunin complied, Nicholas read the document carefully. Educated Russians might read about parliaments and congresses, about representative governments, constitutions, and due process of law, but most of them had experience only with their own form of government. They might criticize the way it operated, they might hope for a more enlightened ruler, they might even advocate an end to the autocratic form of government, but few of them were capable of envisioning in any concrete sense how some other form of government might exist in the Russian Empire. It was just this condition which helps to explain the frequent letters of advice and appeal to the Tsar and the illusory hopes that many intellectuals, for greater or shorter periods of time, placed in him. He was after all the only concrete hope many of them could envision. And if radicals concluded he had to go, nothing was easier to imagine than a temporary dictatorship, as Bakunin suggested for Muraviev.

Bakunin's enthusiasm for Muraviev, however, was also influenced by the governor-general's willingness to help him. After arriving in Irkutsk, Bakunin was allowed to travel to other Siberian cities such as Krasnoyarsk and Kyakhta.

Both Bakunin and Muraviev hoped that come the spring of 1861, Bakunin would be allowed to return to European Russia. But for a variety of reasons, including his health, Muraviev resigned. By spring 1861, his former deputy, Korsakov, had taken over his post. Bakunin now saw his chances of obtaining permission to leave Siberia fading along with Muraviev's departure.

Although Bakunin's relations with Korsakov were not as cordial as with Muraviev, the new governor-general's cousin had just married Bakunin's brother Paul. When Bakunin asked for permission to travel on the Amur, Korsakov gave it to him. He also provided him with a letter requesting that ships on the Amur grant him passage. Bakunin's stated reason for wanting to travel was to act as a commercial business agent. His real reason was to escape from Siberia. In mid 1861, he said good-bye to his wife, Antonia, and headed for the Amur. At Kyakhta he received advances from several merchants. He then headed on toward the river's mouth at Nikolaevsk, where it emptied into the Tatar Strait, opposite the northern end of the island of Sakhalin. He arrived there four weeks after leaving Irkutsk. Legally, he could go no further. But luck and daring were on his side. After a couple of close calls, he made his way via a Russian and then an American ship to Yokahama, Japan, which due to America's Commodore Perry had recently been "opened" to foreign trade. Two weeks later Bakunin was on board the S.S. *Carrington* headed for San Francisco. At about the time Bakunin and Muraviev first met in Tomsk in late 1858, forty-year-old Peter Perovsky was in a country where the Emperor, residing in his Forbidden City, considered himself the son of Heaven and still surrounded himself with concubines and eunuchs. Perovsky was in Peking, and he was negotiating with the Chinese. He had been with Muraviev earlier in the year at Aigun on the Amur when the Russians had pressured Chinese officials to agree to Russia's Amur gains.

9

THE MURAVIEVS AND PEROVSKYS, SIBERIA AND CHINA

Between the Muravievs and the Perovskys, two important Russian clans, interesting relations had existed in the past and would continue in the future. The Muravievs were an outstanding example of how relatives in Russia were often on opposite sides of the political fence. Not only was the mother of the radical Bakunin a Muraviev, but in 1825 several Muravievs were implicated in the Decembrist revolt. On the other hand, even more Muravievs were important generals or officials. One of these, Michael Muraviev, who was now Minister of State Properties, once summed up the diversity nicely when he stated that he was "not one of the Muravyovs [Muravievs] who get hanged, but one of those who do the hanging."[1]

The first Perovskys were a notable group and were children of Alexei Razumovsky, a Minister of Education under Catherine II, and his mistress Maria Sobolevskaya. Under Imperial Order the children were legitimized and given the name Perovsky. Vasily and Lev, both born in the early 1790s, became the most famous. They took part in the wars against Napoleon and were influenced by the post-war reformist hopes that led some to the Decembrist conspiracy. But the two brothers stopped short of such radicalism, and by 1825 Vasily was an aide to the Tsar and stood with Nicholas I facing the revolting troops on the Senate Square on that cold December afternoon when the Tsar finally turned his cannon on them. Vasily later served as governor-general of Orenburg, from where he directed Russian advances into Central Asia. Lev became Minister of Interior under Nicholas and established a reputation as an efficient administrator who was not afraid to hire and encourage young men of talent. Nicholas Muraviev, the future conqueror of the Amur, was one such man who served under him, and Lev Perovsky eventually helped him to obtain his post as governor-general of Eastern Siberia. Both Perovsky brothers were strong supporters of Russia's advance along the Amur.

Peter Perovsky, negotiating in Peking, was the nephew of these two Perovskys. His father and their brother was a lesser public figure, but he had once been a governor in the Crimea. All three of these brothers had died in the space of a few years, Peter's father being the last to go in the month before his son accompanied Muraviev at Aigun.

Perovsky's main task in Peking was to see that the Chinese Emperor now ratified two treaties which his subordinates had signed with Russia, first at Aigun and then at Tientsin. The latter had resulted from military intervention by Great Britain and France, as well as diplomatic pressure applied by them and the United States and Russia. At Tientsin, Chinese officials had signed treaties with all four countries. They agreed to open more ports, to permit diplomatic legations in Peking, and to open the interior of China to trade and missionaries.

In addition, Muraviev bombarded Perovsky with mail suggesting additional concessions for which he should press. Although Perovsky was supposed to take his orders from Foreign Minister Gorchakov and not Muraviev, a fact that the latter resented, Muraviev knew from experience that a lengthy distance from St Petersburg allowed for some flexibility in negotiations. He hoped to influence Perovsky by his friendship.

It was not that there was any significant discrepancy between the goals of Muraviev and the Tsar or Gorchakov. Nevertheless, the latter two were more cautious men than the bold Muraviev, and more concerned with potential British and French reactions to Russian policies.

Perovsky's efforts in Peking did not go smoothly. There were reports and complaints that he visited taverns and brothels and allowed the small group of Cossacks who had accompanied him to act in a disorderly manner. One Chinese official even suggested he should be executed if the Russians' behavior did not improve. On one occasion some Chinese standing on one of the city's walls threw stones at him as he rode through the Ch'ung-wen Gate – when Perovsky complained, he was promised that if his men behaved properly, Russians would not be mistreated in the streets.

More importantly, however, the Chinese Emperor displayed little enthusiasm for ratifying either of the two treaties signed with the Russians. And further Muraviev incursions, this time into the Ussuri district, only reinforced Chinese hostility toward the Russians. Nevertheless, faced not only by pressures from the foreign powers, but also with a rebellion led by a man who claimed to be the brother of Jesus Christ, the young Chinese Emperor finally conceded and ratified the Treaty of Tientsin in April of 1859.

Unfortunately for Perovsky, however, his government had already decided to replace him with Count Nicholas Ignatiev, who although only twenty-six was already a major-general. He had served as a military agent in London and led a successful diplomatic mission to Khiva and Bukhara, two parts of Central Asia that Alexander II would later bring under Russian control. At about the time the Chinese finally ratified the Treaty of Tientsin, General Ignatiev arrived in Irkutsk, where he impressed the radical Bakunin as well as Muraviev. He and

Muraviev were soon on warm terms. Both were bold, dynamic men and ex-pansionists who especially resented British attempts to limit Russian expansion. Muraviev had grown dissatisfied with Perovsky's progress and had high hopes that Ignatiev could be more effective. After traveling from Irkutsk to Peking, Ignatiev was met on the outskirts of town by Perovsky and his men and escorted Chinese style in a sedan chair to his residence, a hostel of the Russian Orthodox Church near the Chien Men Gate. Three days later, at the end of June, Perovsky left for Russia.

Ignatiev remained in China for more than a year. He cleverly played off the English and French against the Chinese and even against each other, all to the benefit of Russia. When English and French troops entered Peking, the Chinese turned to Ignatiev asking for his help in lessening British and French demands. He stated that in exchange for his help he would expect Russian demands on China to be met. While getting no firm promises from the Chinese, Ignatiev did manage to gain a few minor concessions for China from the two Western powers before they signed treaties with China in October. The following month after wily negotiating and occasional threats, Ignatiev obtained Chinese acceptance of Russia's most pressing desires. By the Treaty of Peking, the earlier gains of Aigun were recognized and Russia received the large area east of the Ussuri and Amur rivers.

The treaties of Aigun and Peking added to the vast Russian Empire territories the size of France and Germany combined. This feat was carried out in part by outmaneuvering Great Britain: sweet revenge, it would seem, following the bitter conclusion of the Crimean War. The Tsar decorated General Ignatiev for his efforts and made him head of the Foreign Ministry's Asiatic Department.

Alexander II, however, received little credit for this triumph. Characteristic was the attitude of Prince Kropotkin, a former page to the Tsar who came to Irkutsk in 1862. He later wrote that the gains at the expense of the Chinese had been won by Count Muraviev "almost against the will of the St Petersburg authorities and certainly without much help from them."[2] The remarks of Kropotkin, a future revolutionary, suggest that Alexander followed the leadership of Muraviev rather than vice versa, and that the Tsar's ministers and generals lacked a firm sense of direction. This would not be the first nor the last time that Alexander was perceived in such a manner, but various evidence, including the Tsar's correspondence with Grand Duke Constantine and General Baryatinsky in the Caucasus, indicates that Kropotkin underestimated Alexander's intentions and determination to expand his empire.

The attitude of the Russian public toward the Amur gains was more complex. On the one hand, there were many educated Russians of various political hues who were enthusiastic about these advances. Supporters ranged from anti-Western nationalists such as Pogodin to radicals such as Bakunin and

Herzen. Coming shortly after the Crimean defeat, the gains helped assuage that humiliation to national pride. Many Russians were in favor of both reform and expansion, especially in Asia, where they could believe they were furthering the advance of civilization. The attitude of the idealistic Kropotkin, who decided after graduation from the Corps of Pages to serve in Siberia, is illustrative of such a viewpoint. He recalled in his memoirs that "the Amur region had recently been annexed by Russia; I had read all about that Mississippi of the East … I reasoned, there is in Siberia an immense field for the application of the great reforms which have been made or are coming." Not only was Muraviev known as an Americanophile, but the radical Alexander Herzen agreed with Muraviev and Bakunin that Amur acquisitions could be first steps in bringing Russia closer to the American republic across the Pacific.[3]

On the other hand, the educated public around 1860 was more concerned with internal questions, especially the fate of serfdom, than with the remote and sparsely populated areas along the Chinese border. Imperialistic rivalries had not whetted the appetite of public opinion to the extent they would later in the century, both in Russia and in the West. Michael Pogodin, perhaps exaggerating a bit, complained in 1859 that the public seemed more concerned with the battles going on to unify Italy and even with Tunisia – where the government had recently granted its people a constitution – than they were with the triumphs of Baryatinsky in the Caucasus and Muraviev in Siberia.[4]

Although Ignatiev was rewarded, Peter Perovsky by his relative failure had missed an important opportunity to further his career. He had an older brother, however, who still hoped to become an important figure in Alexander's bureaucracy. He too had not long before assisted a Muraviev, in fact the brother of the Siberian governor-general. This was when in the late 1850s Valerian Muraviev was the governor of Pskov and Perovsky was his vice governor. By the time Ignatiev had left Peking, Lev Perovsky had gotten himself transferred to the Crimea, where he was now the vice governor of Simferopol and of the Tavrichevsky Province. Decades before his father had been governor there and after his death, when Lev went to the Crimea to settle his inheritance, he had decided the family's standing in the area might prove helpful to his career. After Peter left China, he visited his brother at Kilburn, the family estate where his mother still resided near Simferopol. There Peter entertained his nieces and nephews with tales of exotic China. Kilburn was an appropriately romantic setting for such romantic stories. From the windows of the manor house one could look down at the Salgir River running through the valley below or look up and see, over a line of smaller mountains, the towering Chatir Dag (Tent Mountain).

The youngest of the four children was Sophia, born a year and a half before the start of Alexander's reign. She had bluish-gray eyes, and she already resembled her father with her small face, high forehead and weak chin. But for some reason she was able to avoid the sneaky, mouse-like look that character-ized her father's features. Her earliest memories were of her life in Pskov. She remembered their home there with a mezzanine and a big, neglected garden with a pool where the children sledded and skated in the winter. She also re-called a swing in the garden and how they climbed trees and battled with wooden swords in the summer. And she remembered, as did one of her broth-ers, the occasion on which Kolya Muraviev, the governor's son, who was three years older than she, had almost drowned. Along with one of her brothers and her sister, Sophia was over in his garden, which was divided from theirs by a wooden fence. In the garden he also had a pond, and they were out on a raft in the middle of the pond when Kolya fell into the water. Sophia recalled that his governess had just panicked and cried and shouted at the edge of the pond, but the Perovsky children had pulled him out of the water and onto the raft. Years later the fates of Sophia and Kolya Muraviev would once again intertwine in a dramatic setting; only this time the drama would revolve around Tsar Alexander II.

10
TWO NOBLEMEN:
TOLSTOY AND TURGENEV

During the late 1850s, Leo Tolstoy and Ivan Turgenev lived like the wealthy nobles they were. Turgenev owned a few thousand serfs, more than did ninety-nine per cent of the nobles in Russia, and even Tolstoy, with his few hundred, had more than at least eighty per cent of the nobles. Thus, they could afford, as only a small percentage of their class could, to divide their time between their estates, stays in Moscow and St Petersburg and travel abroad. They also tried to keep up with the latest news regarding plans for the emancipation of the serfs, a goal with which both men were more sympathetic than were most nobles.

Tolstoy had several properties, but the chief one was Yasnaya Polyana, which had once belonged to his maternal grandfather, Prince Nicholas Volkonsky. Tolstoy had been born there in a big columned house, which was later sold and dismantled to pay for his gambling debts. The estate was a hundred and thirty miles south of Moscow and consisted of about three thousand acres. The house where Tolstoy now lived had once been one of two smaller buildings on either side of the larger home. It was surrounded by woods and fields, birch and lime alleys, ponds and plants, flowers and fruit trees. It also contained huts for his serfs and their families and, near the edge of the estate, the small Voronka River, where a bathhouse stood. At night one could hear the frogs and nightingales. The still unmarried Tolstoy lived here with his old Aunt Toinette, who had helped raise him after the death of his mother. Numerous servants and at times relatives also helped fill the house.

After returning to his estate in 1856, he attempted to improve the conditions of his serfs. But the age-old distrust of peasants for their masters led them to suspect that he was trying to trick them. Their response disheartened and alarmed him. He feared that if the Tsar did not soon emancipate the serfs, they would rise up in massive revolt.

During this same period, he contemplated marriage with the twenty-two-year-old daughter of a local landowner. But after considerable agonizing, he decided she was not for him. Partly to escape local criticism, he left early in 1857 for a long-intended trip to Western Europe.

His first stay was in Paris, where he met Turgenev and Nekrasov, both of whom were moping about and complaining. Turgenev was then suffering from a painful disease of the bladder, but perhaps more distressing to him was Pauline Viardot's lack of attention. It was primarily to see her, whom he had not seen since prior to the Crimean War, that he had come to France. The relationship of this graying Russian writer and this intelligent, cultured, Spanish-blooded opera singer was certainly a strange one. She was dark-complected, with big dark eyes and a large mouth with dazzling white teeth. Not beautiful, she nevertheless possessed an exotic appeal, especially on stage, and she attracted many men. She was just a few years younger than Turgenev, but married to a French writer and former director of opera who was twenty-one years her senior. They now had three daughters, and Pauline was once again pregnant. There would later be rumors that the baby born that summer, a boy named Paul, was Turgenev's. But whatever intimacies Pauline had allowed years earlier – and nobody knows for certain what they were – Turgenev now seemed relegated to the role of a close family friend. Yet he still loved her so much that he told Nekrasov that he was "ready upon her command to dance on the roof, stark naked, and painted yellow."[1] He also made another unusual confession a short time earlier when he told the poet Fet that he was under Pauline's thumb and that he was only blissfully happy when a woman stomped her heel on his neck and pressed his nose into the dirt. To this lonely bachelor who complained that he was growing old without building himself a "nest," sadistic attention seemed better than little or none at all.

But if Turgenev was without a wife or lover, he was not without a child. Another, but less compelling, reason for his trip to France was to visit his daughter Paulinette. She had been born fourteen years before as a result of a brief liaison with one of his mother's seamstresses. Such affairs were not unusual for noblemen like Turgenev. Nor was generally ignoring one's illegitimate offspring, as he did the first eight years of her life. Then, however, his conscience pricked him and he sent her to France, where Pauline had agreed to look after her. When Tolstoy arrived in Paris she was going to school and living with her father and her governess on the Rue de Rivoli.

Like Turgenev, Nekrasov also had been having problems with his health and his love life. He had left Russia in the late summer of 1856 to consult a Viennese doctor and to meet his mistress Avdotya Panaeva, who had earlier gone abroad. In subsequent months, mostly spent in Rome, his health slowly began to improve. He also received the good news that a book of his poems which had just appeared was selling better than any poet's since Pushkin's. On the other hand, however, his life together with Panaeva began to deteriorate. The month before Tolstoy's arrival in the French capital, Nekrasov had decided he no longer needed her and had left Rome to come to Paris.

After arriving in late February 1857, Tolstoy remained in Paris for most of the next six weeks. Nekrasov soon returned to Rome, but Tolstoy saw more of Turgenev than anyone else and settled into a pension on the same street as the older writer's, which was across from the Tuileries Gardens. The relationship between the two continued to be as ambivalent as it had been in St Petersburg. While they admired each other's talent and at times got along well, they also each found fault with the other's personality. Tolstoy thought that Turgenev's chief problem was that he didn't believe in anything; Turgenev found Tolstoy too stubborn and mercurial to tolerate for very long.

During most of his stay, Tolstoy's impressions of Paris were favorable. Like his government, which was then improving its relations with its Crimean War enemy, Tolstoy bore little resentment against the French. Even though the enemies of the French emperor, Louis Napoleon, complained of his despotism, Tolstoy found the social freedoms enjoyed in France the main cause of its charm. He also enjoyed the usual tourist attractions. One day he would go to Notre Dame, Ste Chapelle or the Louvre, the next to Versailles or Fontainebleau. Or he would cross the Seine to hear lectures at the Sorbonne or visit the Cluny Museum. In the evenings he went along the gas-lit streets to concerts, operas, plays, or the theater of Offenbach for some light music. Although he did enjoy the French cafes and apparently a few brief encounters with French prostitutes, he spent most of his social hours with other Russians who were then staying in Paris.

In this period when money-making absorbed Parisians as perhaps never before, Tolstoy did criticize the Bourse, the Paris stock exchange. He shared the prejudice towards Western capitalism of many Russian intellectuals who saw only the numerous glaring defects of its early stages. But the future author of *War and Peace* reserved his strongest criticism for the Invalides, the tomb and monument of Napoleon Bonaparte. This conqueror's glorification, plus some disabled veterans Tolstoy saw on the way out, led him to the reflection that soldiers were "animals trained to bite."[2] Such complaints, however, were far outnumbered by more positive feelings for the city – at least until April 6th.

On that day Tolstoy witnessed an event that would transform his favorable impressions and leave a permanent impression on him. He saw a criminal's head severed from his body by means of the guillotine. It occurred early one morning after a crowd of some twelve to fifteen thousand people, including women and children, had slowly gathered during the pre-dawn hours. The nearby cafes had done a booming business throughout the night. The prisoner, a man named Frangois Richeux, was brought out on the square in front of the jail where a portable guillotine had been set up. He had a thick, healthy-looking, white neck and chest. A priest accompanied him until he was turned over to the executioner and his machine. Richeux's body stretched out on a board, and seconds later his bloody head was in a basket.

That same day Tolstoy wrote to a friend that the executioner had made an impression on him he would not soon forget. He had seen many things during his experience as a soldier, but nothing as revolting as the work of "this ingenious and elegant machine."[3] The cold, calculating, passionless nature of the execution, supposedly for the sake of justice and morality, troubled him deeply. He concluded that man-made laws and the governments behind them were shams, devices for exploiting and corrupting people. Tolstoy went on to relate that a plot had recently been discovered to assassinate Napoleon III, that arrests had been made, that more deaths would follow, but that he, Tolstoy, would never again witness such an execution or serve any government anywhere.

Tolstoy's hostility to the behavior of governments foreshadows here some of his later more developed ideas. But his thinking was still hazy. He was more of a moralist than a political thinker. And although the laws of politics all seemed horrible lies to him and he was privately critical of autocracy, he wasn't yet sure how societies should organize themselves politically.

Turgenev did not accompany Tolstoy to see the guillotine and French justice do its work, but years later he would also write a horrifying account of a similar occurrence when a man named Tropman was executed. The night after Richeux's death, Tolstoy had trouble going to sleep. Two days later, after he tearfully said good-bye to Turgenev, he left Paris.

Tolstoy traveled to Geneva, first by train and then by stagecoach. He would never be very fond of the former. After arriving in the Swiss city he wrote that "the railway is to travelling what the brothel is to love – just as convenient, but just as inhumanely mechanical and deadly monotonous."[4] He spent the next few months in Switzerland, including some time at a pension in Clarens. It was in this village that Rousseau had written *La Nouvelle Heloise*. As a young man Tolstoy had worn a medallion of Rousseau around his neck, and staying at this spot which looked out on Lake Geneva and the mountains beyond moved him deeply. During these months he saw a good deal of Alexandra Tolstoy. He jokingly called her "granny," but she was actually the daughter of his grandfather's brother. For more than a decade she had been a maid of honor to the Grand Duchess Maria, a daughter of Nicholas I. Although she was eleven years older than Tolstoy, he was strongly attracted to her. She was an intelligent and religious woman with beautiful gray eyes, a serene smile and a lovely low voice. If only she were younger, he thought.

Before returning to Russia, Tolstoy stopped at one of the Russian nobility's favorite spas, Baden-Baden. It was as famous for its gambling tables as for its mineral waters. Russian nobles were known for their improvident ways, and Tolstoy lived up to the tradition. He lost all his money in the casino, and

Turgenev, who was not too far away at another German spa, came to his rescue with a loan. And when he promptly lost that, Turgenev helped arrange another loan for him so that he could get back to Russia.

He spent most of the next year at Yasnaya Polyana, but was also frequently in Moscow and St Petersburg. In the two cities talk of emancipating the serfs bombarded his ears. By the end of 1857, Alexander II with a surprising show of determination had made clear his desire to accelerate the planning of emancipation; he had established a committee to oversee preparations for this complex social transformation.

In late December of that year, Tolstoy attended a dinner at the Moscow Merchant's Club, where the Sevastopol defenders had earlier been toasted. The reason for this gathering was to demonstrate the solidarity of intellectuals with the Tsar's aim of ending serfdom. Two of the men most responsible for organizing it were the St Petersburg liberal Constantine Kavelin and the Moscow editor of *The Russian Messenger*, Michael Katkov.

Possessing little tolerance of practical political questions unless approached from an ethical viewpoint, Tolstoy was privately critical of most of the banquet speeches for not focusing enough on the moral issue of serfdom.

Shortly after the banquet, he wrote to a friend that he was "tired of talk, arguments, speeches," and he proposed beginning a journal devoted to artistic enjoyment. It could be an island of truth and beauty amidst a world of sordid politics. He included with the letter a revealing sketch of a dream. In it he was mesmerizing an enormous crowd until he sensed a woman behind him and felt ashamed of his orating. He added that he didn't know if the woman was a "first vanished dream of love or a late memory of my mother's love – I only know that she had everything, and … I couldn't live without her."[5]

Tolstoy's own relationship to his peasants reflected a combination of sympathy for their misfortunes and vestiges of the ingrained habits of a master. In May of 1858, as Yasnaya Polyana came alive with greenery and the smells of spring, Tolstoy arranged a rendezvous in the woods with a big-breasted, bronze-skinned peasant woman named Aksinya. He wrote in his diary that he "was in love as never before" and could think of nothing else.[6] Although she was married, Tolstoy made love to her often, and eventually she had a son by him.

On occasion Tolstoy also worked with his peasants. He had always been fond of physical exercise, and when in Moscow or Petersburg he would often work out at a gymnasium. But plowing or scything filled an even deeper psychological need in him. It was related to his admiration of Rousseau and his desire to lead the good, simple life.

Since publishing his first two Sevastopol sketches, Tolstoy had seen a final one published. *Youth*, the third part of a trilogy based upon his early years, and several short works had also appeared. Now he was working on a couple of longer works, which would eventually appear under the titles *Family Happiness* and *The Cossacks*. In general, however, his literary work was not creating the excitement it once had, and he himself was beginning to wonder if the times were any longer favorable for his type of talent. Under the influence of critics such as Chernyshevsky, literature with more of a political slant than Tolstoy's was now in vogue. He was glad that he had not followed Turgenev's advice to devote himself completely to his writing.

Turgenev was exasperated with Tolstoy's ambivalence towards a full-time writing career. He wrote to him and, only partly in jest, said he could not figure out what he was if not a writer. Was he an "officer, landowner, philosopher, founder of a new religious doctrine, government official or businessman?"[7]

Turgenev had written from Rome. He himself was not writing much while abroad. He still suffered from a bladder disease, and from Rome he went to Florence, Venice and Vienna, where like Nekrasov he consulted a famous physician. After a brief stay in Dresden, he went to Leipzig just to see Pauline, who was performing there. Then back to Paris, over to London to see Herzen, back again to Paris, and finally on to Russia. By June 1858, he was once again at his estate, Spasskoe.

This was just one of the many properties his mother had left him upon her death almost a decade before. With its thousands of acres, Spasskoe contained some thirty acres of garden and park. An ardent lover of nature, Turgenev seemed happy to be back on this estate of lime, birch and oak trees, of lilac and honeysuckle bushes, of orchards, meadows and ponds, and of the birds he loved – the turtledoves, orioles, finches, thrushes, cuckoos and woodpeckers.

Like many country gentlemen, Turgenev was a passionate hunter. On his estate woodcocks, grouse, rabbits, snipe, partridges and wild ducks were plentiful. He could not, however, match Tolstoy's hunting story for that year, for before the year was out Tolstoy would be clawed by a wounded bear. The short, heavy-set poet Fet was with Tolstoy on that occasion. Fet also lived not far from Turgenev, and the poet often visited him at Spasskoe. Turgenev and Tolstoy both overlooked Fet's conservative and at times eccentric views. He opposed the emancipation of the serfs, and during one period of his life he used to put down a window of his carriage when passing by Moscow University in order to spit contemptuously in its direction. When Fet came to Spasskoe, Turgenev and he hunted together, and Fet later recounted how fond Turgenev was of a hunting dog called Boubou. She slept in his room at night under a quilt, and if it came off she would nudge Turgenev until he got up and placed it back on her. Turgenev was perhaps even more fond of her mother, Diane. When Diane died at the end of that summer, Turgenev buried her and cried.

Turgenev's memories of his past life at Spasskoe were strongly connected with images of his mother. She had been a cruel, domineering, possessive and sadistic woman, who mistreated her serfs and frequently tormented Ivan, even though he was her favorite of the three children. His later propensity for mixing love and suffering, seen especially in his relationship to Pauline Viardot, owed not a little to the strange relationship that his mother imposed upon him.

Although like Tolstoy, Turgenev had once had a peasant mistress, his own attitude toward his serfs was much more enlightened than that of his mother. While in Rome, he had frequently conversed with Russian supporters of emancipation, including the Grand Duchess Elena Pavlovna. This aunt of the Tsar, with the help of Constantine Kavelin and his friend Nicholas Milyutin, had just about completed a plan for emancipating the serfs on her own estate of Karlovka. Along with several others, Turgenev contemplated publishing a journal which would provide a forum for the discussion of various approaches to the emancipation. Although nothing came of the project, Turgenev left for home with the firm intention of quickly improving the lot of his own serfs. He soon did so by allowing them to pay rent for the land they farmed instead of paying him by means of laboring on land from which he kept all the profits. He figured that the new arrangement cost him about a quarter of his estate income. Feeling better than he had in some time, Turgenev spent part of the summer and fall working on a novel in his study, where his desk sat under a window looking out on an alley of lime trees. When the work, *A Nest of the Landed Gentry*, was published early the following year it would receive wide acclaim. And it would reveal Turgenev at his lyrical best. In it Turgenev painted such poetic scenes as the following:

> The tall reddish reeds rustled softly around them; before them the still water gleamed quietly, and softly they spoke. Liza stood on a small raft; Lavretsky sat on the bent trunk of a willow tree; Liza wore a white dress, tied at the waist, with a wide, white ribbon; her straw hat dangled in one hand, in the other with some effort she was holding up the bent fishing rod. Lavretsky gazed at her pure, serious profile, at her hair drawn back behind her ears, at her tender cheeks … and thought: "Oh how sweet you are, standing by my pond!" Liza did not turn towards him, but looked at the water either squinting or smiling. The shadow of a nearby lime tree fell upon them.[8]

As in many of Turgenev's short works of the mid- and late fifties, the novel was nostalgic about youth and love. Although in that summer Turgenev was only thirty-nine, he often lamented the aging process; and indeed, the gray on his head and in his beard was relentlessly taking over from the brown. It was as if his disposition and appearance had conspired to age him prematurely.

Spasskoe was only some seventy miles southwest of Tolstoy's estate and so in June, Turgenev visited Yasnaya Polyana for a couple of days. His host read to him a short story he had completed called "Three Deaths." In it Tolstoy contrasted the deaths of a peasant and a tree with those of a woman of the nobility. The first two died simple, beautiful deaths in keeping with the natural order, but the woman, despite her professed Christianity, feared death and died in a pitiful manner. Years earlier in a sketch called "Death," Turgenev had also written of the peasants' ability to die a natural and peaceful death. But the attitude of Turgenev himself towards death was more like that expressed by the narrator of his "The Diary of a Superfluous Man," which he finished at the beginning of the fifties: "I am terrified. Half bent over the silent, yawning abyss, I shudder and turn aside."[9] As a hypochondriac and more morbid personality than Tolstoy, such thoughts as these tended now to trouble Turgenev more than they did the younger Tolstoy.

A little later in the month Turgenev went to Pirogovo, not far from Yasnaya Polyana, in order to visit Tolstoy's sister Maria and two of the other Tolstoy brothers, Nicholas and Sergei. Turgenev had come to know and like both Nicholas and Maria shortly before he had met Leo. At Pirogovo both Maria and Sergei possessed estates, divided from each other by a wide, deep river. Sergei had been living at Pirogovo with his gypsy mistress for almost two decades. Maria and her three children had returned to Pirogovo only recently after she separated from her husband.

Maria was two years younger than her famous brother, and shortly after first meeting her, Turgenev had become infatuated with this young married woman. Despite his love for Pauline Viardot, Turgenev often developed close attachments to other women. He was very susceptible to feminine charm and to "affairs of the heart." Catching sight of a loved one walking in the garden with a long white dress and a parasol, seeing her blush, touching her hand, exchanging a brief kiss, Turgenev was a connoisseur of such moments. The sexual act itself was not as important to him as it was to the lusty Leo Tolstoy. And if a woman were married, or if there was a rival, it seemed to add an extra dimension to the romance.

Turgenev found Maria to be an intelligent, good and very attractive woman. He also was moved by her simplicity and her open, honest nature. She had large, dark, radiant eyes, dark hair and a youthful face, more sweet than beautiful. She usually spoke in a calm, even tone. She played the piano well – considerably better than Leo, who had once played for his fellow officers in Sevastopol – and on previous occasions when Turgenev had ridden over in his open carriage to visit her and her husband at their Pokrovskoe estate, she had played for him. Turgenev, like Maria and Leo, loved music. At times Turgenev with his thin, high voice would sing, his hand on her shoulder, as she played. Although he did not sing well, he felt deeply as he sang such songs as that of Glinka, put to the words of Pushkin:

I remember the wonderful moment:
You appeared before me,
Like a fleeting vision,
Like a spirit of pure beauty.
…
Years passed. The storm's turbulent gust
Scattered former dreams.[10]

While loving music, Maria did not care to read poetry. She thought it was un-realistic. Religion, however, did appeal to her, and she was much less skeptical about its mysteries than was Leo. Turgenev simply could not accept her attitude toward poetry and tried to change her mind. He read Pushkin's *Eugene Onegin* to her, and praised the poems of his friend Fet. Once he got so angry with her when arguing about the value of poetry that he grabbed his hat and without a word stormed angrily off of the veranda of her lovely old white stone house. She later remembered how he returned several days later and read to her a short story he had written called "Faust." In it he pictured a married woman who re-sembled Maria closely and who also did not care for poetry.

Maria liked Turgenev's "Faust," and her feelings for him seemed to grow stronger with time, especially after she separated permanently from her hus-band. Although Turgenev had gotten along well enough with him, he sympa-thized with Maria for breaking with her husband because of his many infidelities. In a letter to Pauline, Turgenev referred to him as a "rural Henry VIII."[11]

When Turgenev came to see Maria and her two brothers at Pirogovo in the summer of 1858, she had just been separated about a year. Leo was by now ap-prehensive about her feelings toward Turgenev. She had looked forward to Turgenev's return to Russia. When he finally returned and visited Pirogovo, ro-mance failed to blossom. Was it Maria's new position as a separated and now more available woman that scared Turgenev off? Or did some deep psycho-logical need lead him to prefer flirtatious relationships with women whose hus-bands were still around? Or simply, as he suggested in "Faust" and in a letter to Maria shortly after its publication, that his mind came to the realization that his chances for true happiness and love had, along with his youth, disappeared for-ever? Maria herself later thought that their relationship failed to develop fur-ther because of Turgenev's love for Pauline Viardot.

As Turgenev's feelings for Maria cooled, so did those of Leo for Turgenev. After visiting Turgenev at Spasskoe later in the summer, Tolstoy noted in his diary that Turgenev was treating Maria rottenly. Tolstoy thought that he was a worldly cad who had trifled with the heart of his more innocent sister.

In early September both writers came together at an assembly of the nobility of their Tula Province. The main purpose of this meeting was to elect delegates to a provincial committee which was to make recommendations on how best to carry out the emancipation of the serfs. Alexander had given the nobility of Russia's provinces an unprecedented opportunity to offer advice on a major piece of legislation. At this very time he was touring various provinces, attempting to demonstrate the mutual affection of a ruler and his people and talking to nobles. He was trying to convince them to come forward with suggestions that would be fair both to them and their serfs. While at the Tula assembly, both writers signed a request for the abolition of serfdom whereby the peasants would receive land and the owners compensation for it. The majority of the landowners refused to support the statement. Like the majority of serf owners throughout Russia at this time, those in the Tula Province were far from enthusiastic about the prospect of losing both serfs and substantial landholdings.

While Tolstoy and Turgenev agreed on the emancipation of the serfs, they became more disagreeable with each other. Turgenev's deteriorating relationship with Maria was certainly one of the main reasons. At the beginning of the following spring, Turgenev stopped at Yasnaya Polyana on the way back from wintering in St Petersburg. Tolstoy was not there, but Maria was. Turgenev no longer felt attracted to her and had little to say to her before moving on to his estate. Less than two weeks later he wrote to a friend that he would have no more to do with Leo Tolstoy, that they were created poles apart. "If I eat soup and like it," Turgenev wrote, "I already know for certain that for that reason alone Tolstoy will not like it, and vice versa."[12] In July, from Viardot's chateau-castle near Paris, he wrote to Fet, with whom Tolstoy was becoming ever friendlier: "He [Tolstoy] likes me very little, and I don't care much for him."[13]

11
HERZEN AND THE BELL
IN LONDON

While Alexander II encouraged the nobles to discuss the emancipation of the serfs and Tolstoy and Turgenev signed a petition in favor of it, and while Dostoevsky, Bakunin and Muraviev were all still in Siberia and Peter Perovsky in China, the aristocratic socialist Alexander Herzen edited *The Bell* from his London home. Smuggled into Russia, it rivaled Nekrasov's *The Contemporary* in popularity and influence. Herzen himself became a first class celebrity, and for about half a decade his successive London homes became beacons attracting progressive Russians traveling in Europe.

But when he first arrived in the bustling, noisy metropolis of London in the late summer of 1852, he was a sad and disillusioned man of forty. Within the previous year death had taken his mother, two sons and his wife, still leaving him the father of three young children. In addition to his personal misfortunes, the failures of the European revolutions of 1848–9 had left him depressed about the social and political future of Europe. How events had changed since the Herzen family had set out with such high hopes for Paris in 1847! Only the recovery from Russia of his considerable fortune, aided by the Parisian banker James Rothschild, prevented his lot from being worse.

Herzen spent much time in his early years in London among the various émigrés and political exiles. Rejecting many of the values of English capitalist society, he participated in and tried to strengthen the radical subculture which surrounded him. As part of this effort he employed radicals, including Polish democrats, to tutor his children and help print and distribute the works he published.

Among Herzen's favorite political exiles were the Italians. He was friendly with the prophet of Italian unity, Mazzini. For a while he was very close to Orsini, who in 1858 went to the guillotine for trying to assassinate Napoleon III. When the colorful Garibaldi sailed to London from South America in 1854, Herzen lunched with him in his cabin. Six years later Garibaldi and his red-shirted warriors would sail from Genoa to Sicily, lead an uprising in southern Italy, and help bring it into the newly formed Kingdom of Italy. Among

Herzen's least favorites were the German emigrants, of whom at least one, Karl Marx, reciprocated his feeling. Marx once refused an invitation to a gathering of revolutionary exiles because he did not wish to appear on the same platform as Herzen. Although Marx did not know Herzen personally, he was opposed to some of his ideas such as Herzen's belief, adopted after the failure of the 1848–9 revolutions, that the Russian peasants stood a better chance of creating a socialist society than did the Western European proletariat.

Upon hearing the news of the death of Tsar Nicholas I, Herzen celebrated with champagne and by throwing silver coins at some young boys and telling them to shout out in the streets the news of Nicholas's death. Shortly afterwards, he wrote an open letter of advice to the new Tsar and published it that summer in his *The Polar Star*, a forerunner of *The Bell*. "I am an incorrigible socialist," he wrote, "you are an autocratic emperor; but between your banner and mine there can be one thing in common, namely love of the people."[1] Herzen encouraged the Tsar to free the people from the horrors perpetrated on them by landowners and officials. And as long as the Tsar acted in such a way as to keep Herzen's hopes alive, Herzen promised to restrain his attacks.

Both the celebrating and the letter revealed much about Herzen. He was not a dour revolutionary ready to sacrifice all of life's present enjoyments for some hoped-for heaven-on-earth in the future. And although he was a committed socialist, capable as any of passionately denouncing the evils of autocracy, serfdom, or capitalism, he was also flexible regarding the means needed to evolve towards socialism.

In the spring of 1856, an event occurred which would have great consequences for Herzen's personal and political life. One day while the Herzen family was eating dinner, a horse cab drove up. Herzen soon heard the voice of his oldest and closest friend, and rushed out to meet him and a woman, who, like his friend and Herzen himself, was rather short. The friend was Nicholas Ogarev, with whom Herzen as a young teenaged boy had once sworn to avenge the Decembrists. The woman, Ogarev's wife Natalia, had in the revolutionary year of 1848 reciprocated a passionate friendship with Herzen's own wife. At that time the Herzens and Tuchkovs, the family of Ogarev's future wife, had spent considerable time together in Rome and Paris. Natalia Tuchkova was not quite twenty at the time, while Natalia Herzen had recently turned thirty. Soon after the Tuchkovs' return to Russia later that year, the young Natalia fell in love with Ogarev.

At that time he was a landowner of considerable property and serfs and had already published some poetry. He was sixteen years older than Natalia and estranged from his first wife, Maria, who had had a succession of lovers in recent years and was then living in Paris. He tried to get a divorce from her, but she would not agree. Therefore, until she died in 1853, Ogarev and Natalia lived together without being legally married. Only after Maria's death were they able to legalize their relationship.

Now in London, the Ogarevs soon moved in with the Herzen family. By the middle of the next year Natalia Ogareva and Herzen had become lovers. Ogarev himself knew of the relationship, suffered considerable pain as a result of it, but magnanimously refused to stand in Natalia's way. Suffering from epilepsy and alcoholism, Ogarev had at first improved in London. However, his wife's love for Herzen soon drove him towards more heavy drinking. Within a few years he had also established a lasting relationship with a small, dark-haired English prostitute named Mary Sutherland. It became the most satisfying relationship of his life. He became not only her lover, but her benefactor: he took her off the streets, established her and her five-year-old son in better quarters and helped educate both of them.

Despite his wife's relationship with Herzen, the two men remained close friends and collaborators. The radical Russian thinkers of the day, influenced by the views of George Sand among others, believed that love and marriage often did not go together. If one of the marriage partners fell in love with someone else, the radicals considered it "bourgeois" or "old-fashioned" for the other partner to be unreasonable and insist on fidelity. They were also critical of traditional family life, whether in Russia or the West. They often perceived it as a mechanism for the husband-father to exploit the other members of the family. Thus, their radical ethics predisposed husbands like Ogarev (and Nekrasov's friend Panaev) to tolerate and, in theory, even approve of what many others would consider scandalous behavior.

Although Herzen had already established what he called the Free Russian Press and published occasional pamphlets and irregularly *The Polar Star*, it was not until he was joined by Ogarev that together they began *The Bell*. That was in 1857. While Herzen was the more brilliant, visible, active and pragmatic of the two, Ogarev was the more revolutionary.

Initially a monthly, but soon a biweekly, *The Bell* was intended to be the free voice of progressive Russian opinion. Partly to maintain unity with those less radical than themselves, Herzen and Ogarev kept their demands to a minimum: the abolition of serfdom, corporal punishment and censorship.

The new journal was soon "must" reading for radicals and liberals in Russia. Even some government ministers read it and, some said, the Tsar. Although only a few thousand of each issue were smuggled into Russia, each copy seemed to pass in and out of countless hands. Since a wide variety of individuals sent Herzen information, including at times government employees or others wishing to expose corruption or incompetence, *The Bell* soon became a source of information that was nowhere else publicly available. On one occasion Nicholas Milyutin, a government official and the friend of Kavelin's who had worked with him on the plan for freeing the serfs of Grand Duchess Elena Pavlovna, sent to *The Bell* a scathing criticism of a minister he thought less liberal. On another occasion Alexander II forbade the lithographing of a memorandum for the members of his committee studying serfdom because he believed that no sooner would it be reproduced than it would appear in *The Bell*.[2]

Despite Herzen's great popularity among many educated Russians, he also had his detractors. He was still far to the left of the Tsar and most of his officials. Even some moderate liberals thought that much of his criticism was irresponsible and that he was helping to foment forces that might wreak havoc upon Russia. True, he might praise the Tsar on occasion – as he did with the words "Thou has conquered, Galilean,"[3] after the Tsar indicated his desire to abolish serfdom – but at other times Herzen's criticisms seemed too abusive.

One moderate who criticized Herzen was the liberal Boris Chicherin, who in the spring of 1858 had left Russia to travel throughout Europe. When he and Kavelin had sent some of their writings to Herzen in 1856, they had included an open letter to Herzen that criticized Herzen's socialist views. In response, over the next few years, Herzen not only published most of what they had sent him, but he and Ogarev also responded to some of their criticism of Herzen's ideas. In September 1858, Chicherin came to London, primarily to see Herzen and to try, as he and Kavelin had earlier done in their articles, to "direct him in a sense that would be useful for Russia."[4] Perhaps *The Bell* could help to guide a perplexed government and keep it on the correct path.

Chicherin's view of the government as "perplexed" was one shared by many intellectuals in 1858. True, the Tsar had decided that serfs must obtain their freedom, but he did not make it clear until the very end of the year that they were to be permitted to obtain land. Meanwhile, it became a central issue. While most landowners were determined to hold on to as much of their land as possible, most intellectuals were convinced that by some arrangement or other the peasants would have to receive enough of it to provide a means of livelihood. The key to victory for either side was, of course, the Tsar.

Throughout most of the year, Alexander II seemed indecisive on this central question. Meanwhile, progressive officials like the Minister of Interior Lanskoi and his assistant Nicholas Milyutin battled against other officials defending the interests of the landowners. Some of the most influential reactionaries sat on the Tsar's Main Committee to oversee the emancipation settlement. One of the most visible was the Minister of State Properties and a member of the large Muraviev clan, Michael Muraviev.

One of the reasons for Alexander II's indecisiveness on the issue of land was the difficulty of trying to bring about a fair and stable settlement, one that would balance off the interests of the nobility with that of their former serfs. In both the process of working towards emancipation and in any final arrangement, Alexander also risked threats to his own power. One was that the nobles might begin to push for the creation of permanent government bodies in which they could exercise some power over questions such as their landholding rights. A second was that the peasants, if displeased with the settlement, might revolt. Alexander could not easily forget the sporadic mass peasant revolts of earlier centuries.

Although the difficulty of obtaining a judicious compromise was no doubt great, that alone does not explain Alexander's indecisiveness. Time and again during his reign, he would allow his subordinates to battle over the direction government policies might take. While his tolerance for different viewpoints within his administration reflected a certain degree of pragmatism, it also indicated to some a lack of vision and leadership. The government official Nikitenko complained in May 1858 of the government's vacillation. He thought that of all systems the worst was to have no system at all. In his memoirs, completed in the late 1870s, Professor Soloviev criticized Alexander II for having no definite aims and for failing to exercise effective leadership. The historian also cited these failings as causes which contributed to the confusion and conflict which would increasingly characterize Alexander's era.

Liberals like Chicherin, Kavelin and Turgenev seemed to view Alexander II as a well-intentioned but ill-prepared ruler who was surrounded by many reactionary advisers. They were fearful in 1858 that reactionaries defending the landholding privileges of the nobles were gaining the upper hand. Turgenev and Kavelin cautioned Herzen not to criticize the Tsar personally and attempted to convince him that Alexander II needed Herzen's encouragement, understanding and help. In January, Turgenev wrote to Herzen that he was afraid that the Tsar might become too discouraged if badgered by both reactionaries and progressives.

Herzen's response to the wavering he thought he discerned on the part of the Tsar was characteristically sharper than that of Turgenev. He stated in *The Bell* that Alexander II had not justified his hopes, insisted once again that the emancipation settlement had to include sufficient land for the peasants, and printed an article from an anonymous contributor that called for the serfs to take up their axes in rebellion. Herzen's own position was that he preferred Alexander II to dispense a just settlement from above, but if he did not, the peasants would be justified in rebelling. He even stated in an article that appeared in September 1858 in an Italian publication that slavery and the agonizing uncertainty of the day were worse than a peasant uprising.

It was this increasingly truculent attitude of Herzen's that Chicherin hoped to alter when he visited the famous journalist in London that same month. Herzen was then living in Putney on the southwestern outskirts of the city.

From the center of London one could ride the train to Putney Station, from which it was only a very short walk to the Herzen residence. The ivy-walled house with its metal roof painted red sat amidst a garden, courtyard and empty stables and resembled more an English farmhouse than an urban dwelling.

In this house Natalia Ogarev was still recuperating, having recently given birth to a daughter called Liza who, although given Ogarev's name, was fathered by Herzen. Ogarev himself was sterile; and this was Natalia's first child. She had not, however, been ecstatic when early in that previous year she had discovered she was pregnant. By then feelings of guilt towards Ogarev had combined with increasing dissatisfaction with Herzen, who also had come to realize Natalia's many imperfections. As she became increasingly ill-tempered and emotionally overwrought, Herzen failed to be very compassionate and at times was petty and cynical in his behavior towards her.

Into this setting, the self-assured Chicherin entered on his self-imposed mission. He was from a distinguished gentry family, was the same age as Tolstoy and Chernyshevsky, and could be as dogmatic as either. The ideas of the German philosopher Hegel permanently influenced him and his attempts to apply them to Russia were often too schematic and unrealistic. While in London, he spent several days visiting and arguing with both Herzen and Ogarev. Although impressed by the brilliance with which Herzen intermingled stories, anecdotes and astute observations, Chicherin concluded that he had absolutely no understanding of the practical necessities of government. Herzen also was disappointed. In his Moscow days Herzen had been friendly with the younger man's father, and some of Herzen's old Moscow friends also thought well of the young Chicherin. But from their first meeting, Herzen tells us in his memoirs, he noted the cold light in his guest's eyes and the conceit in his voice.

Herzen's main complaint against Chicherin was that his Hegelian views had led him to worship a strong centralized government and look to it as a panacea for Russia's problems. Herzen also accused him of having too little faith in the individual and society. Unlike Chicherin and others such as Professor Soloviev, Herzen did not believe that Russia needed a strong ruler such as Peter the Great, but only one who would be guided by enlightened public opinion. Indeed, the ideas of Chicherin on government were almost diametrically opposed to those of Herzen. For despite the minimum program Herzen had insisted upon and his wavering willingness to give Alexander II a chance, his ultimate hope was to dismantle any centralized government in Russia. He thought such a feat possible because the Russian government lacked solid support from either Russia's educated minority or its peasants, who overwhelmingly farmed in peasant communes. This was true whether or not they were serfs, and Herzen saw the communes as embryonic democratic and socialist organizations. Did not the head of each household have a voice in how the commune was run? Did not most communes maintain some measure of equality among their members by the practice of redistributing land strips? Once serfdom and autocracy were removed, Herzen hoped that a system of federated and free communes could be established without a centralized government. He realized, however, that before the communes could become ideal bodies in an agrarian socialist society they would have to learn to respect individual freedom and dignity more than they had heretofore, but that could be accomplished with the help of educated individuals such as himself.

By the time Herzen and Chicherin finally parted at the Putney train station, about all they could agree on was their mutual respect for each other.

Within a few months of Chicherin's departure their differences became public when, at Chicherin's request, Herzen published a letter of his in *The Bell*. It repeated many of his earlier private criticisms: Herzen should emphasize reason, not passion; caution, not haste; evolution, not revolution. In his memoirs Chicherin claimed that the letter was the "first protest by a Russian against the political direction of the London émigrés."[5] Although an overstatement, his protest was significant because it loudly signaled the beginning of the end of the always rather tenuous unity of progressive forces.

About a year after Chicherin's September 1858 visit, the editor Michael Katkov, then also thought of as a liberal, called on Herzen. Katkov was an intelligent and patriotic man, but, some thought, overly ambitious. Not born into the gentry class, he had married a princess who possessed few noticeable attributes except her title. Meanwhile, Herzen, Ogarev, wife-mistress Natalia, the children and servants – Herzen always had several, including at different times a negro butler named George and an Italian cook recommended by Mazzini – had all moved to a larger dwelling in the nearby suburb of Fulham.

Little is known of Katkov's visit here, but it seems to have been no more successful than Chicherin's. And after returning from England, Katkov became increasingly critical of the views of Herzen. Since, however, the censors would not even permit Herzen's name to be mentioned in print, Katkov soon began polemicizing with a more convenient radical target, Nekrasov's *The Contemporary*. He especially disliked what he considered the journal's narrow view of what constituted worthwhile literature. And he also disagreed with its two main critics, Chernyshevsky and Dobrolyubov, as well as with Herzen, about the desirability of maintaining the peasant commune after emancipation. At this point in his life Katkov greatly admired much about the English, and like most Englishmen, he was a strong believer in the advantages of private, rather than communal, property.

While Chicherin and Katkov attacked Herzen from his right, Chernyshevsky and Dobrolyubov began thrusting at him from his left. Up until the previous year, Nekrasov's journal had assumed a position similar to that of *The Bell*.

Both Chernyshevsky and Dobrolyubov owed a considerable debt to Herzen's ideas. They had been inspired by Herzen's hope that someday members of the Russian radical intelligentsia and the Russian peasants might be able to show the world the way to socialism. But for a while they, like Herzen, worked for less utopian and more minimal goals such as a fair emancipation settlement.

But then in a January 1859 issue of *The Contemporary*, the twenty-two-year-old Dobrolyubov attacked the older generation of liberals. Already in the summer of the previous year in an article on France under Louis XVIII, Chernyshevsky had declared that liberalism everywhere would eventually become impotent due to its lack of concern for the real needs of the masses. Chernyshevsky was also becoming increasingly pessimistic about the chances for a fair emancipation arrangement. Alexander II's recent decision that the peasants would be allowed to purchase land did not appease him. He did not think that the peasants should have to pay for the lands they traditionally farmed and thought of as really theirs. Observing the behavior of the landowners who were discussing the proposed emancipation throughout Russia, he despaired of the serfs receiving a fair share of the land. He concluded that a social revolution would not come from above, only from below. Therefore, both Chernyshevsky and Dobrolyubov thought it was useless to work alongside liberals. Now was the time for a revolutionary front.

In the pages of *The Bell*, Herzen strenuously disagreed and claimed that attacks on liberals benefited only the reactionaries. He also defended his frequent exposés of abuses committed by government official and nobles – Dobrolyubov had charged that unless accompanied by a call to revolution such pieces merely aided the government to patch up the cracks in its decaying structure.

Although Nekrasov supported his two radical critics, he feared a widening breach between his journal and *The Bell*. For in addition to the growing ideological differences, there already existed a personal source of conflict between Herzen and himself.

Nekrasov's mistress, the beautiful Avdotya Panaeva, had been a close friend and confidante of Ogarev's first wife, Maria. After Ogarev had asked for and been refused a divorce, Maria sued him and won one of the properties he had inherited from his father. She continued living abroad, however, and asked her friend Avdotya to see to the running of the property, which she did until the estate was sold for 85,000 silver rubles. But little of the money ever reached Maria, and after she died in 1853, Avdotya refused to disgorge it until a civil suit forced her to turn it over to Maria's heirs in 1859. Despite Nekrasov's assurance that he had nothing to do with the whole affair, Herzen considered both Avdotya and Nekrasov swindlers and hypocrites. All of this occurred while his friend Ogarev had become a much poorer man as a result of Maria's suit and an ill-advised Ogarev transaction intended to lessen its consequences.

When Nekrasov had expressed a desire to accompany Turgenev to England to visit Herzen in 1857, Herzen had rejected the idea. Two years later, Nekrasov prevailed upon Chernyshevsky to undertake a trip to London in order to mollify Herzen.

The meeting between Chernyshevsky and Herzen occurred in the early summer of 1859, and it offered quite a contrast. The short, heavy-set, bearded Herzen was an illegitimate but aristocratic cosmopolitan who had lived abroad for better than a decade, a litterateur with a graceful style and sharp wit, and finally a man with a healthy dose of skepticism regarding the chances for European progress. Chernyshevsky was taller, thinner, clean-shaven and wore glasses. He was born and grew up the legitimate son of a priest in the Volga town of Saratov. He had never been to Europe before, was often ill at ease in public, and was a deadly serious man with little sense of humor. In the same year as his visit to London, Darwin's *Origin of Species* was published; and although Chernyshevsky would not become enamored of Darwin, the Russian shared the Englishman's enthusiasm for science. Chernyshevsky also was more knowledgeable about economics than Herzen, and although he was equally critical of capitalism, he was much more sympathetic to a Russian industrialization, which he, but not Herzen, envisioned as being capable of developing along socialist lines. Literature he valued only for its social usefulness, and his own writing style reflected his utilitarian view. Finally, he did not share Herzen's skepticism regarding Europe's potential for progress.

In their meeting neither man apparently impressed the other. Chernyshevsky thought Herzen was haughty and boring. Herzen could not help but think that the younger Chernyshevsky valued too highly his own opinions.

Although the editors of both *The Bell* and *The Contemporary* subsequently made an effort to minimize their differences, they continued to appear. A year after Chernyshevsky's trip, Herzen continued to insist that as long as there was still hope for the broom, it should be advocated rather than the ax. He also defended the writers of his generation against earlier attacks by Dobrolyubov. At least, said Herzen, most of them were honest men, not swindlers and cheats who stole from their friends.

12

TOLSTOY AND BAKUNIN
VISIT HERZEN

Two years after Chernyshevsky's visit, Tolstoy came to London and called on Herzen. Later that year a regenerated Bakunin arrived. Before leaving Russia once again, Tolstoy had begun teaching some of his serfs' children. Always the rebel and innovator, he disdained traditional educational methods. Memorization and threats went out the third-floor windows of the bedroom he converted into a classroom. He stressed instead freedom and the joy of learning. In the spring of 1860, he once again worked in the fields with his peasants and lay down in the woods with the peasant Aksinya. By now his original lust had developed into a more loving care for her. But, of course, she was not the type of woman he could marry.

Meanwhile, his oldest brother, Nicholas, was at Soden, a German spa, trying to alleviate his tuberculosis. His sister Maria, concerned about his health and perhaps also hoping to see Turgenev, who was also at Soden, decided to visit her sick brother, and Leo agreed to accompany her and her three children. Early in July they all left St Petersburg by steamship.

After arriving in Stettin and then moving on to Berlin, Leo decided to examine German educational methods. He did not arrive at Soden until the end of August. By then Nicholas's condition had worsened, and the weather in Soden had turned colder with frequent rain. Nicholas's doctors suggested wintering in a warmer climate. The two brothers and Maria and her children moved on to Hyeres, on France's Mediterranean coast. The climate, the view of the sea, and the orange, lemon and palm trees were beautiful. But it was a town for sick and dying people. About a month after arriving, Nicholas died.

The death of his brother stunned Tolstoy. Life now seemed absurd. Why work, why write, if death ended all?[1]

Before too long, however, Tolstoy recovered from his despair. He visited some schools in Marseilles, played with Maria's children, and began work on a new novel about a Decembrist. The idea for such a work first seems to have occurred to him in 1856, and that year he did begin a story he called "A Distant Field" that bore some resemblance to the new novel he now began in 1860. He began this new work by ironically sketching the atmosphere of 1856 under the new Tsar: the Moscow greeting of the Sevastopol sailors, the appearance of new journals and the animated discussions of the questions of the day. He then introduced his hero, an old Decembrist returning from Siberian exile.

A few months later Tolstoy was in Florence, where he met his "granny," Alexandra. He was also introduced to a distant relative of his mother, the old Decembrist Prince Volkonsky, and to his wife, Princess Maria Volkonskaya. Three decades earlier she had heroically followed her husband into Siberian exile and later in Irkutsk was helped by Governor-general Muraviev. Tolstoy was especially struck by the old man: "long gray hair … like an Old Testament prophet … a wonderful old man, the flower of Petersburg's aristocracy."[2] Tolstoy was already familiar with his life story and how in Siberia, following an earlier stint in the mines of Nerchinsk, he had taken up a simple life of farming and associating with peasants. And as the hero of Tolstoy's new novel evolved, his life came to resemble that of the old prince.

By February 1861, Tolstoy was once again in Paris, where he visited more schools and saw Turgenev, who had left Soden before Maria or he had arrived. Maria was no longer traveling with Leo, and Turgenev's infatuation for her was now definitely over. Nevertheless, he and Tolstoy got along well enough. Tolstoy read to him the first chapters of his new novel. Turgenev found him to be more mellow than usual, perhaps the result of his brother's death.

Tolstoy arrived in London in the beginning of March, accompanied only by a painful toothache. This bustling city, this center of capitalism and world trade, of fog and yellow gas-lights, of the Crystal Palace and East End slums, of Queen Victoria – who would be a grieving widow before the year was out – and of Dickens and Darwin failed to impress the count from Yasnaya Polyana. Nineteenth-century urban life, even in Russia, was never much to his liking.

He remained in London for a little over two weeks. Aided by Matthew Arnold, then an inspector of schools, Tolstoy visited some classrooms. He also attended a reading by one of his favorite writers, Charles Dickens, watched some cockfights and boxing matches, and was impressed by the Kensington Museum. He also went down to the Gothic-looking Houses of Parliament along the Thames and heard the Prime Minister Lord Palmerston give a long speech in the House of Commons. Perhaps partly because his comprehension of spoken English was weak, Tolstoy found it "boring and meaningless."[3]

But then, like many other Russian intellectuals, he was unsympathetic with parliamentary bodies. Slavophiles and other conservative nationalists disdained such institutions as part of a corrupt, egotistic Western world. Most radicals of Alexander II's reign believed, as one eloquent historian put it, that "salvation did not lie in politics or political parties: it seemed clear to them that liberal parties and their leaders had neither understood nor made a serious effort to forward the fundamental interests of the oppressed populations of their countries. What the vast majority of peasants in Russia (or workers in Europe) needed was to be fed and clothed, to be given physical security, to be rescued from disease, ignorance, poverty and humiliating inequalities. As for political rights, votes, parliaments, republican forms, these were meaningless and useless to ignorant, barbarous, half-naked and starving men."[4]

Nor did most Russian intellectuals value very highly two of the principles that underlie parliamentary bodies: compromise and toleration of opposing views. A belief such as Edmund Burke's that "all government, – indeed every human benefit and enjoyment, every virtue and every prudent act, – is founded on compromise and barter"[5] was foreign to the passionate Russian souls of most of them. Faced with the evils of autocracy and serfdom and unschooled in the real world of pragmatic politics, this failing is not surprising.

Being intellectuals, the Russian thinkers realized that the Russian ship of state needed new ideas if it were to progress, and most were willing to stoke these ideas with all the passion one could desire; but they failed to appreciate the complexity of running the ship. Some wanted to keep the captain and hope for the best, others to keep him only if he acted as they wished him to, and still others wanted to throw him overboard. But how the captain or they themselves could organize the crew so that it could at least agree and move forward in a common direction, while minimizing the hazards of storms and reefs, they had no more knowledge than that of contentious and inexperienced sailors.

Soon after arriving in London, Tolstoy called on Herzen. The editor was living then at Orsett House, Westbourne Terrace. It was a stone house of several stories with a pleasant tree-lined courtyard. Tolstoy was met by a servant who announced him to Herzen. The squat but quick-moving and energetic Herzen greeted the bushy-bearded Tolstoy, decked out in a fashionable Palmerston coat and holding a silk top hat; a scar on Tolstoy's forehead remained from his encounter with a bear. They went for a walk that day and stopped in a pub. Before he left London he spent much time in the home of Herzen and Natalia. He also met with Ogarev, whom he had known previously and who by now had moved into his own separate lodgings. Although Tolstoy was not sympathetic to Herzen's liaison with Ogarev's wife, he nevertheless liked Herzen. Tolstoy found him to be a friendly, open, brilliant, eloquent and witty man. Herzen wrote to Turgenev that he was seeing much of Tolstoy, that he was stubborn and impetuous and charged ahead in arguments as if on assault at Sevastopol. This, of course, was no news to Turgenev. Despite, Tolstoy's flaws and some political disagreements, Herzen thought him a good man.

In letters Tolstoy exchanged with Herzen after leaving London, the novelist praised a recent issue of the *Polar Star* devoted to the Decembrists – from the beginning this journal had displayed the profile of the five Decembrists who were hanged. From Herzen, Tolstoy asked for and received advice regarding the novel he had begun about a Decembrist. The new friends also exchanged photographs. In the one Tolstoy received of Herzen and Ogarev, the two editors look similar, both short, full-bearded and long-haired, though Herzen's was longer in back as if to compensate for his faster receding hairline.

The day Tolstoy left London he read that the Tsar had finally issued a manifesto abolishing serfdom. Actually Alexander II had signed it some two weeks earlier, but waited until the pre-Lenten drinking binge had ended before releasing it. After five years of the most persistent effort of his life, and thanks in large part to the work of liberal bureaucrats such as Nicholas Milyutin, Alexander had finally achieved a settlement that he believed was fair to both nobles and peasants.

But it was the type of pragmatic political compromise that one might expect from an English parliament, especially one still dominated by the upper classes, and it therefore failed to satisfy many of the Russian intellectuals, whose appetites for social justice had been whetted by unrealistic hopes. Despite some initial hurrahs for Alexander II and his efforts, it did not take many of them long to begin criticizing various aspects of the complex manifesto. The document was made even harder to read than necessary thanks to a final "polishing" given to it by Filaret, the Metropolitan of Moscow – his effort led Turgenev to note that the document looked to him as if it had been written in French and then translated into Russian by a German.

Nine days after leaving London, Tolstoy wrote to Herzen from Brussels that the peasants would not understand or believe a word of it and that it offered them nothing except promises. Two weeks later from Frankfurt-on-Main he wrote to Herzen that the emancipation statutes were "idle chatter."[6]

Although the serfs would no longer be the "baptized property" of their lords, as Herzen had once referred to them, they still would have to pay, one way or another, for the right to work what they always had considered their land. During a two-year transition period, gentry arbitrators appointed by the government were to assist in working out equitable terms so that the former serfs in a commune could purchase approximately the amount of land they had formerly tilled for themselves. The government was to provide most of the purchase price in the form of loans, repayable over a period of forty-nine years. Within the Russian part of the empire most of the property would be sold not to the individual, but collectively to the commune, within which the former serfs would continue to work.

At first many of the serfs were disbelieving – surely this was not the Tsar's final plan – or disappointed and confused because the expectations which they had developed in the last few years did not yet seem to be met. One noble recalled that his serfs responded with sarcastic laughter on hearing that they would have to pay for their land for almost half a century. Nevertheless, the peasants continued to believe, as they had for centuries, that the Tsar wished to deliver them from their many burdens, but evil officials and nobles kept him isolated and prevented his intentions from being fully carried out. Although this naive belief would infuriate many a radical, it was no guarantee of peasant stability. The former serfs could and did on occasion rebel against the landowners, charging that they were not carrying out the real will of the Tsar. Before the year was out landowners reported over a thousand disturbances, the great majority of which required soldiers to quell. And in the summer of that year Alexander felt compelled to tell a delegation of peasants: "There will be no emancipation except the one I have granted you. Obey the law and statutes! Work and toil! Be obedient to the authorities and to noble landowners!"[7]

Despite serious reservations concerning the manifesto's imperfections, Herzen's initial reaction was more positive than that of Tolstoy or many of the peasants. The serfs after all were now free, and Herzen's strenuous efforts had helped bring this about. He had always placed a great emphasis on human freedom and dignity, more it seems than did the serfs, who were more concerned with the size and cost of the land they would receive and with overcoming poverty.

Herzen decided to celebrate the news with a gigantic party at his house on April 10th. He bought champagne, hired an orchestra and arranged decorations. He invited all Russians who were or could be in London on the appointed day and who supported the emancipation. He also asked some other friends and acquaintances to come, such as Mazzini and the French socialist Louis Blanc. Originally, Herzen had planned to drink a toast to the health of the Tsar. But shortly before the festivities were to begin, Herzen received news that a riot had occurred in Warsaw and that Russian troops had fired into a Polish crowd. Since Herzen was a supporter of Polish independence, this was sad news. Although he went ahead with the party, he did not toast the Tsar.

In the days that followed, Herzen's disenchantment with the Tsar increased. In April, scores of peasants were shot by Russian soldiers in the province of Kazan. They were part of a crowd refusing to turn over a man who declared that the real manifesto of the Tsar allowed the people to take over the land immediately without payment. That same month, partly in an effort to overcome deep gentry discontentment over the terms of the emancipation, Alexander II appointed a new Minister of Interior who had been considered an enemy of the emancipation. He was the tall, intelligent but somewhat pompous Peter Valuev. Although his sympathies were thought to lie with the noble class, he was an ambitious man, pragmatic enough to shift with the Tsar's apparent zigzag approach to progress. Herzen's *The Bell* later would describe him as the "weather vane" of Alexander's administration, always indicating which way the court winds were blowing.[8]

Soon after naming Valuev to his new post, the Tsar appointed a new, more conservative Minister of Education and came out with new rules for Russia's five thousand university students. Alexander had come to the conclusion that the students, to whom he had already granted some new freedoms, were becoming too demanding and outspoken. New rules increasing students' costs and forbidding unauthorized meetings were enacted to help curtail such behavior. When students reconvened in the fall at St Petersburg University, they protested against the new regulations. The government responded by arresting some of the protest leaders and subsequently closing the university. It remained closed for almost two years. Less dramatic opposition also occurred at other universities including Moscow University, where according to information sent to *The Bell*, Professor Soloviev and Boris Chicherin, now a professor of jurisprudence, were among the leaders denouncing student demonstrations.

The Bell became increasingly critical of the Tsar, and Herzen moved closer to the position of Chernyshevsky. In November 1861, he declared that the government consisted of "riff-raff, swindlers, robbers and whores."[9] Ogarev, who had always been more revolutionary-minded than Herzen, encouraged the formation of revolutionary conspiracies.

The pressure on Herzen to encourage revolution was further accelerated in December when his old friend Bakunin arrived in London. He had spent only a short time in the not-so-United States – the Civil War had already begun – and then, having met a few interesting Americans, such as the poet Longfellow, he sailed for England.[10] Because he had written to Herzen and Ogarev requesting money, Herzen knew he was on his way, and two days after Christmas, when Herzen and Ogarev were just about to sit down for supper at the former's home, Bakunin arrived like a tornado. Herzen had not seen him for fourteen years. While Bakunin's body had noticeably aged, in spirit he still seemed a rebellious youth. He was forty-seven and had lost all his teeth. His six-foot-plus frame had ballooned to some two hundred and eighty pounds. With his unkempt thick curly hair, bushy beard and enormous round head, he looked like an aged Bohemian. But he was ready for action. He told Natalia, who was lying down on a couch recovering her strength after giving birth to twins five weeks before: "It's not good to be lying down. Get well! It is necessary to act, not lie down."[11] And when he asked Herzen where revolutionary activities were brewing and Herzen replied that except for some demonstrations in Poland all was quiet, he asked in amazement: "Then what are we to do? Must we go to Persia or India to stir things up? It's enough to drive one mad; I cannot sit and do nothing."[12]

Bakunin soon settled into quarters not far from Herzen. Amidst smoke, ashes and tea cups, he hosted an international group of revolutionaries at all hours of the day and night. When not talking he wrote, usually letters, often exhorting others from Belgrade and Bessarabia to Constantinople and Semipalatinsk. At times he would interrupt a letter to argue a point with one of his visitors. But his large sweating body and his active mind seldom rested.

13

TURGENEV AND DOSTOEVSKY VISIT HERZEN

In May of 1862, Turgenev arrived in London for a short visit. In the previous six years he had visited England and Herzen almost yearly. Unlike Tolstoy and Bakunin, the liberal Turgenev admired the British political system and appreciated its spirit of compromise and tolerance; and he had encouraged the political moderation that his good friend Herzen attempted to display prior to the emancipation.

But moderation, political or otherwise, was not a virtue that came easily to Russian intellectuals. In the face of provocations by some of his more abrasive countrymen, even Turgenev found it difficult to practice. Upset over criticism of his work by Dobrolyubov and Chernyshevsky, he had finally broken off relations with their chief editor, Nekrasov. In May of 1861, he had also quarreled so seriously with Tolstoy that the argument almost resulted in a duel. While at the poet Fet's estate one morning, Tolstoy criticized Turgenev for the way he was bringing up his daughter and, according to Turgenev, suggested that he would act differently if his daughter were legitimate. Turgenev later recalled threatening to slap Tolstoy's face if he continued insulting him. They soon parted, and a comedy of errors and delayed and misplaced correspondence followed. In these letters, Tolstoy was the first to insist on a duel. Turgenev was the more apologetic, but at one point he also stated he would demand satisfaction. Instead, they stopped seeing each other. A long interval would pass before they would meet again.

Early in 1862, Turgenev's novel *Fathers and Sons* appeared. In it he captured the spirit of young radicals, for whom he popularized the term nihilists, and the growing conflict between them and the older generations. This conflict was initiated by the radicals' rejection of all traditions they thought contrary to reason and their unconventional, uncompromising, some thought downright rude behavior. They thought of themselves as scientific, realistic and ready to act to change society. As the decade proceeded, they could increasingly be identified by their appearance: the men tended to let their hair grow longer, while the women cut theirs short, and both sexes cultivated a somewhat austere, unkempt look. An unflattering police report at the end of the decade described the typical nihilist woman in the following fashion: "She has cropped hair, wears blue glasses, is slovenly in her dress, [and] rejects the use of comb and soap."[1]

In Turgenev's central character, the brusque nihilist Bazarov, some observers thought they espied a composite of Chernyshevsky and Dobrolyubov, who had just died of consumption. Turgenev, however, stated that the character was based more on a doctor that he had actually met.

The novel produced an unprecedented storm. Some, including the editor Katkov, who published it in his *The Russian Messenger*, thought that Turgenev was too favorable towards Bazarov, others that he was too critical. Conservatives and radicals even disagreed among themselves, with some of the radicals going so far as to burn photographs of Turgenev. Actually, Bazarov reflected both Turgenev's attempt to describe objectively the rising radicalism of the day and his ambivalence toward radical youth.

While in London, Turgenev saw Bakunin as well as Herzen. Bakunin sought Turgenev's help in arranging for his wife, Antonia, to leave Irkutsk and eventually join him abroad. Turgenev contributed some money to the cause.

Although no record exists of the discussions of Herzen and Turgenev in London that spring, not long afterwards they aired their increasing differences in writing. Most of Herzen's letters appeared in *The Bell* addressed to an unknown correspondent who, many knew, was Turgenev. The novelist responded in private letters to Herzen. In these exchanges Herzen enunciated his view that the West was drowning in bourgeois materialistic satisfaction and that the uncorrupted Russian peasant was the socialist's hope for the future. He argued that Russia need not and should not take some of the erroneous paths traveled by Western Europe. Turgenev criticized Herzen for turning away from the West and making an idol out of the Russian peasant. Turgenev believed that only those who were enlightened, educated, reasonably moderate and sympathetic to the best of Western values could lead the Russian people toward progress. Herzen, however, detected that beneath Turgenev's lack of confidence in the Russian peasant lay a much deeper and more pervasive pessimism about life in general, fueled in part by Turgenev's affinity for the ideas of the German philosopher Schopenhauer.

A couple of months after Turgenev's departure from London, Dostoevsky arrived there. Since returning to St Petersburg at the end of 1859, he had begun, along with his brother Michael, a new journal called *Time*. The views he put forward there were somewhere between the radical ones enunciated in Nekrasov's *The Contemporary* and those of Slavophiles such as Ivan Aksakov and his brother Constantine, who had died the year after Dostoevsky's return. Although Dostoevsky praised Constantine Aksakov for an essay on the Russian peasant commune in which the Slavophile wrote of its basically

Christian nature, Dostoevsky did not share his almost completely negative view of Peter the Great and his westernizing fervor. Rather he believed that Russia was called upon to create a new culture that would be a synthesis of the best of Western learning and Russian native elements.

But to create this new culture, Russia first had to close the gap which still existed between educated society and the masses. In explaining the purpose of their new journal, Dostoevsky wrote about the necessity of unifying these two forces. "Union at any price, in spite of any sacrifices, and as quickly as possible – that is our foremost thought, that is our motto."[2] As much as anyone of his time, Dostoevsky desired and cried out for social unity, a unity and sense of community that would become increasingly difficult to experience in a turbulent age of social changes and modernization.

As to how this union would be brought about he emphasized, as did Tolstoy in his own unique manner, love and education. On the eve of the emancipation, Dostoevsky pointed to the loving work of Alexander II, which had almost removed the last barriers to this union and which was as great and sacred as any in Russian history. But now it was up to educated society to cease just chattering and get to work. He chided his fellow intellectuals who wanted immediate and grandiose results. He encouraged them to "teach just one boy reading and writing ... to walk a few inches instead of seven miles."[3] However, it was not just the masses who were to be taught. The educated class, so long alienated from the common people, could also learn from them.

Although Dostoevsky was a bit vague as to exactly what could be learned from the peasants, he no doubt hoped that more intellectuals would follow the path he himself had traversed in overcoming his alienation from the masses; for his return to a feeling of unity with them had also led him to a greater appreciation of their Orthodox religious beliefs and their traditional Russian ways. In addition to himself and his brother, several other chief contributors to *Time*, namely Appolon Grigoriev and Nicholas Strakhov, were also self-proclaimed "enthusiasts of the soil" (*pochvenniki*), who emphasized the importance of Russian roots and traditions.

In the year and a half following the emancipation, however, Dostoevsky witnessed little to encourage his hopes for social cohesion. The student demonstrators of the fall of 1861 were greeted at times with jeers from urban workers. When a series of mysterious and devastating fires broke out in the capital the following spring, many people, both educated and uneducated, angrily attributed them to radical students. When Turgenev returned at the end of May to St Petersburg, and incidentally dined with Dostoevsky at the Hotel Clea, an acquaintance stopped him on the street and said: "See what your Nihilists are doing! They're burning down Petersburg."[4] Ivan Aksakov even heard a St Petersburg peasant say "the *professors* burned this down."[5] In an article which greatly pleased the Tsar, the editor Katkov placed the ultimate blame for the St Petersburg fires on the London steps of Herzen and his émigré collaborators. Soon he was attacking Herzen in such virulent language that even some of Herzen's other detractors thought Katkov had gone too far.

The sense of alarm concerning the fires was heightened by a number of bloodthirsty pamphlets which appeared in this same period. One day in May 1862, when he opened the door of his apartment, Dostoevsky found one entitled "Young Russia." It called for revolution, socialism, the closing of monasteries, the emancipation of women and the abolition of marriage and the family. And if the defenders of the imperial party resisted, it proclaimed, "we will kill [them] in the streets … in their homes, in the narrow lanes of towns, in the broad avenues of cities, in hamlets and in villages!"[6]

The pamphlet seemed to bring together all the most radical demands of recent years and to crystallize for conservatives their worst fears. The radicals' challenge was not just to the political order, but to established society, even to its homes and families.

Concerned about the polarizing effect that the proclamation might have, Dostoevsky later recalled that he rushed over to see Chernyshevsky, who by now had become a hero to many young radicals. Dostoevsky showed him the proclamation and asked him to use his influence to help stop such writings. Chernyshevsky was not responsible for "Young Russia," nor was he especially happy about its appearance. But there is no doubt that the young man who wrote it had been influenced by some of the radical journalist's ideas. Chernyshevsky replied that occurrences such as the proclamation were unavoidable.

Within a few months *The Contemporary* was prohibited from continuing publication, and then Chernyshevsky was arrested. He was not the first major contributor of the journal to suffer that fate. In September of the previous year Michael Mikhailov, whose most valuable contribution had been a series of influential articles in behalf of the emancipation of women, was arrested for composing an illegal revolutionary pamphlet. He had managed to convince a reluctant Herzen to print it on his London press. Now Herzen played an even greater role in the events leading up to Chernyshevsky's arrest. Frightened by the most recent developments, the government arrested Chernyshevsky after discovering a careless Herzen letter which offered to continue abroad, in collaboration with Chernyshevsky, the publication of *The Contemporary*.

In June 1862, Dostoevsky left for Western Europe. It was his first trip abroad and one he had long desired to make. In ten weeks he visited Germany, still not a united country, France, England, Switzerland, Italy and Austria. One of the highlights of the trip was his eight-day stay in London, where he arrived in early July. He found it a huge, garish, noisy, bustling city with polluted air and water, with overhead railways and also the beginnings of underground ones. He visited the reconstructed Crystal Palace at Sydenham Hill in South London to view the 1862 World Exhibition and saw the products of human labor collected from all parts of the world. It seemed to symbolize the materialism which he felt had become the new god for Western man. But many of the poor who crowded London's slums seemed morose and somber to him as he wandered the crowded pavements, pubs and cafes. He observed large numbers of prostitutes walking the streets, and husbands and wives drinking to overcome their misery.

In his *Winter Notes on Summer Impressions*, which he wrote the following winter, he spoke of the egoism and absence of brotherhood which characterized Western peoples, or as such a critic might put it today, their "dog-eat-dog" philosophy. Of course, various Western thinkers had also decried the sharpened individualism and lack of social cohesion which they believed was increasingly rampant in the West, largely as a result of capitalism and rapid industrial growth. But to Russians such as Dostoevsky and Tolstoy, who in the 1857 story "Lucerne" had his protagonist refer to Western civilization as that "egotistical association of people" which was apparently destroying the "need for instinctive and loving association,"[7] the evils of this competitive economic individualism were undoubtedly magnified. Like almost all tourists, they could not help but contrast what they perceived abroad with what they were used to in their own country. The philosopher Berdyaev perhaps exaggerated when he claimed that "of all the peoples in the world the Russians have the community spirit,"[8] but certainly Russia and its vast peasant masses were characterized by strong traditions of communalism and a weakly developed individualism. And both Dostoevsky and Tolstoy feared any Western influences that might further erode this sense of community and brotherhood.

Soon after arriving in London, Dostoevsky called on Herzen. To Herzen he probably appeared as he did in a lithograph of 1862: with a short, neat beard and a receding hairline. The two men had first met sixteen years earlier in St Petersburg. Herzen appreciated Dostoevsky's radical past and his literary ability and had recently expressed interest in his recounting of prison experiences in his *House of the Dead*, which came out in 1861–2. Dostoevsky reciprocated the interest. He had closely read many of Herzen's pieces and undoubtedly appreciated Herzen's disillusionment with the West, his dislike of Western capitalism and materialism, his renewed faith in the Russian peasants and their sense of communalism, and his criticisms of the excesses of Chernyshevsky and Dobrolyubov. Dostoevsky also sympathized with the Herzen sentiment expressed in Herzen's *From the Other Shore*, in which the exile had written of the dangers of sacrificing individuals and their freedoms for abstract ideas or ideologies. In future years, Herzen's influence on Dostoevsky would be evident in such works as *Winter Notes on Summer Impressions* (1863) and *Notes from the Underground.*

Prior to leaving London, Dostoevsky visited Herzen at least one more time. Exactly what the two men talked about on these occasions is unknown except for the subject of Chernyshevsky – Herzen was more critical of his personality than was Dostoevsky – and most probably the "Young Russia" pamphlet, about which Herzen had just written a critical article.

Despite sharing a number of views and opinions about Russia and the West, the two men also had their differences. Perhaps most importantly, Dostoevsky had become a religious thinker, but Herzen rejected religious belief as dehumanizing. The former, unlike Herzen, also remained a strong supporter of the Tsar. Herzen found Dostoevsky naive and not altogether clear-headed, but a very nice person. The latter, like almost all visitors, found Herzen to be a brilliant conversationalist, but apparently also thought him, as he expressed it years later, too alienated from "his native land and its ideals," too much the cosmopolitan aristocrat.[9] While in London, Dostoevsky also probably saw Ogarev and, at least according to police reports, Bakunin.

In the late summer and fall of 1862, Herzen, Ogarev and Bakunin became increasingly involved in aiding the formation of a revolutionary organization that took its name, "Land and Liberty," from one of Ogarev's articles. It was not a very large society, but it did have members in a number of different Russian cities, and it included some army officers. Their demands were more moderate than those of the "Young Russia" pamphlet, but included among others the demand for a national assembly (*zemskii sobor*) and the freeing of Poland.

The call for the creation of a *zemskii sobor* had frequently been made by the editors of *The Bell*, especially by Ogarev, during the previous year. There was wide support among the gentry and some of the intellectuals for the establishment of some such body. Prior to Peter the Great, some of the Russian Tsars had turned to a similarly named council for advice; and in 1613 at the end of the chaotic Time of Troubles, a *zemskii sobor*, consisting of delegates from various classes including state peasants, had selected Michael Romanov to rule Russia. Thus, such an institution had Russian roots and could be readily accepted by those Russian nationalists who were wary of accepting Western innovations such as parliamentary bodies. In fact, Slavophiles such as Constantine Aksakov had long championed its appropriateness for Russia.

In 1861 and early 1862, some of the noble assemblies petitioned the Tsar to allow the creation of a national assembly to discuss further ramifications of the great change introduced by the emancipation. Conservative nobles wished for an assembly which they could dominate and in which they could air their grievances about the settlement. More liberal nobles desired an assembly representing all classes, and a small percentage of nobles were even willing to renounce any special class privileges. And while some insisted, as the Slavophiles generally did, that a *zemskii sobor* should do no more than offer advice to the Tsar, others hoped that it might, sooner or later, become more than just an advisory body. The most outspoken of these assemblies was that of the nobility of the province of Tver. In February 1862, the Tver nobles attempted to present an address to Alexander II calling for a number of measures including the "summoning of elected representatives from all the Russian land."[10] Alexander refused to accept it, and later that month he ordered the arrest of thirteen Tver emancipation arbitrators, including two of Bakunin's brothers, who declared that in their work they would be bound only by the convictions expressed by the Tver assembly. The "Tver Thirteen" remained in the capital's Peter and Paul Fortress until July, at which time they were sentenced to be held in a mental institution. Fortunately, however, the Tsar pardoned them before they were institutionalized.

At first Herzen had been skeptical about the Land and Liberty organization and about any chances of Polish independence, but he let himself be persuaded otherwise by Ogarev and Bakunin. The latter especially believed that revolution was imminent. But then as Herzen later wrote, Bakunin always "mistook the second month of pregnancy for the ninth."[11]

Poland had not existed as an independent country since the late eighteenth century when Austria, Russia and Prussia had divided it up among themselves. As a result of the defeat of Napoleon, Russia increased its share. The Poles in Russia revolted in 1830, but it only worsened their lot. Alexander II eased restrictions somewhat, but it was unlikely he would ever do enough to please radical Poles who detested Russian control over them. In January 1863, after several years of more minor disturbances, a full-scale rebellion broke out. Herzen supported it in *The Bell*. Bakunin lusted to participate. He still dreamed of a free union of federated Slavic states, and he hoped that the Poles might provide the spark which would eventually grow to inflame and destroy the autocratic powers of Austria, Prussia and Russia. In February he left by ship for Copenhagen, hoping from there to reach Poland.

Although many Russian intellectuals and students had been sympathetic with some of the Polish aspirations for more freedom, the events of January 1863 shocked many and hastened the movement of educated opinion further to the right. Such a shifting was already discernible during the previous year. Following the address by the Tver assembly, the nobility seemed to gradually simmer down – partly because they were mollified by some Tsarist concessions, including promises of judicial and local government reform, and partly because of a backlash against nihilism and the fears that it had aroused. Now in January, hearing that Poles in Warsaw had surprised and killed some Russian soldiers asleep in their barracks, public indignation arose to a fever pitch.

As indignation rose, the popularity of *The Bell* plummeted. Michael Katkov, who became a leader of public opinion by strongly attacking the Poles, pointed to Herzen and other Russian radicals who shared his beliefs when he wrote of those "prepared to sacrifice the interests of their native land and the unity and political significance of their people," of those that were "prepared to be Poles more than the Poles themselves."[12]

Thus, by the middle of 1863, Herzen had ceased to be a voice of authority, and the early hopeful days of Alexander's reign, the days in which Kavelin and others ardently hoped to unify public opinion and the Tsar around the banner of liberalism, seemed long gone. Progressive opinion had fragmented like chunks of ice on the Neva during the spring thaw.

The chief apostle of reconciliation, Kavelin himself, had by now become estranged from many he had formerly tried to bring together, including Katkov, Herzen, Chicherin, Pogodin and Soloviev. Chicherin, who along with Kavelin in 1856 had urged liberalism as a unifying banner, seemed increasingly less liberal himself as his passion for strong government led him to urge harsh measures against both student rebels in 1861 and Polish rebels in 1863. Turgenev's liberalism was also weak because, as Herzen correctly perceived, his pessimism drained him of the energy needed to battle for political convictions.[13] Katkov had attacked not only Herzen and *The Bell*, but had also polemicized in the last few years with the editors of *Time* and *The Contemporary* – although Chernyshevsky remained in prison, Nekrasov had once again been allowed to publish after an eight-month suspension.

But if events had indicated that the Tsar and educated opinion could not unite under a banner of reform and liberalism, the Polish crisis gave Katkov and others hope that Russia could rally around another banner, only this time one emblazoned with the symbols of Russian nationalism.

Part Two

Our administration does not enjoy our confidence … it is not surprising that society will try its best to weaken it.

A.V. NIKITENKO

That which thinking people have been afraid of has occurred: a time of turning backward, of reaction, is beginning.

A. V. NIKITENKO

Never had people considered themselves so intelligent and infallible … Never had individuals considered more unshakable their judgments, their scholarly conclusions, their moral convictions and beliefs … All were in a state of unrest and did not understand one another. Each thought that he alone possessed the truth, and looking at others, tormented himself, beat himself on the chest, cried and wrung his hands.

F. DOSTOEVSKY

14

A FATEFUL YEAR, 1866

The year 1866 was an eventful one for Alexander II. First, a man named Karakozov tried to assassinate him, and then he experienced sexual intimacy with a beloved young woman still in her late teens.

As the year began, the Tsar's subjects again were discontented. During the Polish rebellion the Russian public had enthusiastically cheered him, and many intellectuals supported his repression of the Poles. But the crisis was now over, and the public was concerned with other matters. The diary of the government official Nikitenko is illustrative of the mood of the times. He complains of the radical ideas expressed in *The Contemporary*, but also of government censorship policies. He fears that Russia is on the brink of anarchy, due in part to the lack of respect for authority, but he is also critical of a government which seems both weak and arbitrary, and which is apparently indifferent to public concerns.

Yet the educated public hardly spoke with a unified voice. While Nekrasov's *The Contemporary* attacked the government from the left, Katkov's increasingly conservative and outspoken newspaper, *The Moscow Gazette*, criticized government ministers and policies for being too liberal.

Dissatisfaction was compounded by the continuing economic problems of the empire. Alexander wished to modernize and strengthen Russia, especially to build up its railways. But how was he to pay the cost? And, despite occasional cautious words, he desired the continuing expansion of Russia's empire in places such as Central Asia, one reason that military spending continued to eat up about one-third of the government's budget. During a decade in which most Western European economies were booming, Russia produced insufficient capital, including bullion, goods for export and tax revenues. Despite the best efforts and reforms of his capable Minister of Finance, Michael Reutern, the government continued resorting to deficit spending and became increasingly dependent on foreign loans, while at the same time increasing taxes. Inflation outdistanced workers' wages in St Petersburg, the most industrialized city in the country; and peasants were increasingly hard pressed to pay their taxes along with their annual redemption payments. The condition of the nobles was also deteriorating. Even before the emancipation, the great majority of them could not make a decent living off of their land alone. And now they no longer had serf labor to rely on. Because many of them were indebted to the state prior to 1861, they received only a little over half the amount they had coming from the government's financing of the redemption settlement. And by the middle of the decade the government bonds which they had received could, according to a British report, be sold on the market only at a loss of between seventeen and twenty per cent of their face value.[1]

While some entrepreneurs and speculators grew rich, this only increased the unhappiness of many people. A special target of attack were the foreign capitalists and concessionaires involved in plans for expanding Russia's railways. Although making considerable profits, primarily at great government expense, they were only able to deliver a fraction of the promised new lines.

All in all, the situation in 1866 seemed so bleak that Reutern, who stated that "our whole future depends on the railways,"[2] offered to resign. In the following year, partly to pay for new railway construction, as well as to avoid any future costly conflict, Russia sold Alaska to the United States for a little over seven million dollars.

Meanwhile, Alexander's policy continued to be one of limited reform. In 1863, he permitted university faculty greater autonomy by allowing them to elect their own rectors and deans; he also allowed the first Diet to meet in Finland since it had become part of the Russian Empire in 1809. In 1864, he signed into law two of his most important reforms. The first created district and provincial *zemstvo* (land) assemblies and boards and gave representatives of the peasant communes, as well as the chosen spokesmen of independent property owners, the right to deal with a number of local needs. These included medicine, education, famine relief, accident insurance and the improvement of roads and agricultural techniques. The second reform modernized the antiquated and corrupt Russian legal system and furnished it with a degree of independence from government interference. The new law also introduced trial by jury for most criminal offenses and helped create a new class of lawyers.

However, Alexander was no more tolerant than ever of any talk suggesting limitations of his own powers. When an assembly of the Moscow gentry in 1865 called upon the Tsar to create "a general Assembly of elected representatives from the Russian land *for discussion of the common needs of the entire State*,"[3] Alexander dissolved their assembly and responded with a document which stated:

> The right of initiative ... belongs exclusively to ME, and is indissolubly bound to the autocratic power entrusted to ME by GOD ... No one is called to take upon himself before ME petitions about the general welfare and needs of the state.

Such departures from the order established by existing legislation can only hinder me in the execution of MY aims.[4]

At about the same time he told a Moscow nobleman: "I give you my word that now, on this table, I am ready to sign any constitution, if I were convinced that it was good for Russia. But I know that were I to do that today, tomorrow Russia would fall to pieces."[5] Earlier that year he had expressed a similar conviction to his twenty-one-year-old son and heir to the throne, Nicholas, stating that the adoption of Western-style constitutional forms would cause the disintegration of their country's multi-national state.

At the beginning of the fateful year of 1866, Alexander II was forty-seven years of age. With his mutton-chop whiskers and mustache and in the general's uniforms he constantly wore, he was still regal looking. His hair, however, had receded a little at the temples, and the asthma from which he suffered had grown worse. He no longer seemed to enjoy hunting or his game of whist. But then a decade of efforts which he believed were not duly appreciated and a tragic event the previous year had taken its toll on him. In April 1865, shortly after the assassination of America's President Lincoln, the Tsar's own son Nicholas had died of spinal meningitis while in Nice. By all accounts, he was a young man of great promise, and the death of the heir was a crushing blow to both parents.[6] When Nicholas's body was returned, Alexander once again walked behind the coffin in procession to the family vault at the Peter and Paul Fortress cathedral.

He was now left with five sons and his daughter Maria, who was his favorite. The oldest and new heir was Alexander, who was twenty at the time of his older brother's death. The relations of the Tsar with his wife, Maria, were no longer very intimate. Deeply grieved by the loss of her son, to whom she was especially close, this small, frail woman now seemed more reserved and religious than ever.

Although the Tsar's name was no longer linked to that of the flirtatious Alexandra Dolgorukaya, who had married an ambitious officer several years before, his attentions had recently turned toward a very distant relative of hers. Her name was Catherine (Katia) Dolgorukova. When Alexander began taking a romantic interest in her in the months following his son's death, she was still a student at the Smolny Institute. This was a finishing school for noble, but generally not rich, young ladies. She was of average height and possessed a well-proportioned trim figure. Her hair was chestnut brown, and her eyes and smile could be alluring and intriguing. No doubt the Tsar found them so. She soon withdrew from the Smolny and moved in with an elder brother who resided in the capital. She and the Tsar began meeting in the Summer Garden.

Alexander liked to walk and he frequently and freely did so in the capital, sometimes accompanied by his daughter or one or more of his favorite dogs.

The Summer Garden was not far from the Winter Palace and dated back to the early days of the city. It contained many statues, exotic trees, flowers and birds. With its shaded lanes, it was one of the favorite strolling places for ladies in their crinolined skirts and bonnets and men in their uniforms or top hats and frock coats. Alexander and Katia were usually both accompanied to the garden, he by an aide-de-camp and she by a maid. Once there, however, their companions left them alone. They discreetly met in an arbor by a picturesque fountain. But they soon feared that their meetings in the Summer Garden were becoming too obvious. They began meeting instead on some of the more distant islands of the city which contained summer homes and palaces. The more they met, the more Alexander became passionately attached to Katia. But during the first year of their meetings, she would not satisfy his growing passion.

One Monday afternoon, after the Tsar apparently already had transferred his place of rendezvous, he decided to take a walk in the Summer Garden. He was accompanied by his gordon setter Milord. It was a sunny day in early April, and most of the winter snow had already melted. After finishing his walk, he headed toward his open carriage, which was waiting near the garden gate. A small crowd had gathered around the carriage and its two horses, waiting for a glimpse of the Tsar. Suddenly a shot rang out. A man dressed in peasant clothes and holding a pistol darted out of the crowd and tried to run away. But two policemen on hand to keep undesirables out of the garden soon apprehended him. General Totleben, the hero of Sevastopol to whom Dostoevsky had turned for help, was also present at the scene. According to his testimony a peasant-born cap-maker named Komissarov had saved the Tsar's life by striking the arm of the would-be assassin just as he took aim at Alexander. Regardless of the accuracy of this account, it helped to reinforce the belief that the common people loved their Tsar.

The man apprehended was Dmitry Karakozov. He was a tall, sad, long-faced young man of twenty-five whose psychological condition in the months before the attempt was far from healthy. He had even thought seriously of suicide. Born into an impoverished noble family, he had spent the years since the emancipation growing increasingly hostile to the government. He had been expelled for radical activities from Kazan University, and more recently, suffering from a poverty that afflicted many university students, he was dismissed from Moscow University for not paying his tuition. He had also worked for a short time as a clerk for one of the local arbitrators assigned to work out the emancipation settlement. But he found his supervisor and the arbitrators in general indifferent to the needs of the peasants. Whether such an observation was accurate or not, many radicals were upset that in the working out of the settlement the former serfs as a group did not even receive the amount of land they had previously tilled for themselves.

While in Moscow, he had come under the influence of a cousin named Ishutin. Prior to Karakozov's departure for St Petersburg in the month before the assassination attempt, Ishutin had formed a revolutionary group called Organization and within it a smaller cell called Hell. The latter was especially interested in the use of terroristic methods. Ishutin's hero was Chernyshevsky, whom he considered, along with Jesus Christ and Paul the Apostle, as one of the three greatest men ever to have lived. Ishutin's group even planned to free Chernyshevsky, who in 1864, after almost two years in the Peter and Paul Fortress, had been sent to a Siberian penal camp. While Hell talked of assassination, Karakozov decided to act. He obtained not only a pistol, but also poison which he intended to take after committing his deed. He also wrote and distributed copies of a manifesto which claimed that the Tsar was the greatest enemy of the "simple people," that he enabled the idle rich to continue to exploit them, and that the writer of the manifesto had decided to kill him.

While Karakozov never succeeded in taking poison, the Tsar's government utilized another method to achieve the same end – hanging. After his arrest, he, Ishutin and others were tried in the Peter and Paul Fortress, in the same room in which the Decembrists had been convicted in 1826. Found guilty, Karakozov wrote to the Tsar, one Christian to another, appealing for forgiveness. Alexander replied that as a Christian, he forgave him, as Tsar he could not. Consequently, early one September morning Karakozov was taken to the Smolensk field. Amidst thousands of onlookers, including some groaning and crying women and many individuals who crossed themselves, he was hanged. His cousin and most of the others who were a part of the Organization ended up in Siberia.

Meanwhile, on July 1st, Katia had finally submitted to the Tsar's most ardent desire. Alexander and family had moved to the palace at Peterhof, which looked out on the Gulf of Finland. Katia, along with her brother and his wife, had moved into a nearby dacha. That Friday (July 1st) was the anniversary of the late Emperor Nicholas's wedding, as well as the birthday of his now widowed wife. For the occasion the grounds of Peterhof were opened up to thousands, and music and fireworks were provided. On this festive night, Alexander and Katia secretly met in one of the many structures on the large and beautiful grounds of Peterhof. It was called the Belvedere. It was a richly furnished little chateau in a remote park, a few miles behind the Grand Palace. There, as the Tsar later wrote to Katia, they "laid the foundation" of their happiness "and of the treasure" they both carried in their hearts.[7]

15

NEKRASOV AND MURAVIEV
THE HANGMAN

On a Saturday less than two weeks after the attempted assassination, the stoop-shouldered, goateed Nicholas Nekrasov approached the fat, bulldog-faced Count Michael Muraviev and asked if he could read him a poem. The scene was the exclusive English Club along the Neva, not far from the Winter Palace.

The previous five years had been difficult ones for Nekrasov. Due to differing ideologies and Nekrasov's contradictory personality, he had lost a number of old friends including Turgenev. Herzen was not the only one who came to think of him a hypocrite and swindler. How could he be a radical and sympathizer with the poor and at the same time ride in his carriage to the English Club and eat gourmet meals and gamble with the ministers and advisers of the Tsar? The fact that he was usually successful at cards and relieved such individuals as Alexander Abaza, a future Minister of Finance, of enormous sums of money did not seem to mitigate his guilt in the eyes of his critics.

Avdotya Panaeva was also no longer in his life. Perhaps she had hoped that after her husband's death in 1862, Nekrasov would marry her. Perhaps she grew tired of his sexual encounters with other women and his gambling. At any rate, she had moved out of the apartment they shared on the Liteiny Prospect. And two years after the death of her husband, she married someone else.

Then there were the losses by death and imprisonment. First was the death in 1861 of the young Dobrolyubov, of whom Nekrasov was very fond. For about a month in their apartment Nekrasov and Avdotya had watched this twenty-five-year-old slowly die from consumption. Then there were the arrests of several of the contributors to *The Contemporary*, most importantly that of Chernyshevsky in 1862. When he was sentenced to Siberia for life, even the moderate Professor Soloviev was incensed at the injustice of the sentence. How could the government allow him to preach his views for a decade and then suddenly send him to Siberia even though he had apparently committed no crime?

Although Nekrasov's journal was shut down shortly before Chernyshevsky's arrest, when it appeared again the following year it was clear that Nekrasov's radical sympathies were still intact. In the March, April and May issues he printed a novel which Chernyshevsky had written while in the Peter and Paul Fortress and which, incredibly enough, government censors permitted.

The novel was *What Is to Be Done?* It was not great literature, but it summarized Chernyshevsky's views, at least to the extent he could state them and still hope to get them through the censor. In it he portrayed characters he thought more appealing than the "sons" of Turgenev's *Fathers and Sons.* The novel preached enlightened, rational self-interest and radical views on love and marriage, and it hinted at the desirability of a socialist order by having its heroine establish dressmaking co-operatives. It also introduced Rakhmetov, an almost superhuman figure, a completely rational ascetic who trained himself by such feats as sleeping on a bed of nails. Chernyshevsky was confident his readers would realize that Rakhmetov was preparing himself for revolutionary activity. *What Is to Be Done?* soon helped to inspire a whole generation of radicals.

Nekrasov also continued writing his poetry, some of which appeared in *The Contemporary* and in new editions of his poems which appeared in the early sixties. At times he wrote satirical poems, critical of government policies and the behavior of society's elite, or poems expressing his own inadequacies, such as his "Knight for an Hour." But increasingly he wrote of the peasants and other poor suffering people such as Volga boat haulers and children in factories. In 1864 his journal earned an official warning for printing his poem "The Railroad," which deplored the oppression and suffering inflicted upon the railway workers who had built the St Petersburg-Moscow line. At times he even wrote for the literate poor; some of his poems or parts of them became popular folk songs. Like many intellectuals, he became increasingly interested in peasant folklore and tales. Although tending to idealize the poor, he also strove to picture them as they really were: often victims, but also at times victimizers; usually suffering, but also at times light and happy.

Less than a year after the emancipation of the serfs, Nekrasov bought a fourteen-hundred-acre estate, Karabikha, near the city of Yaroslavl, and not far from where he had spent most of his boyhood years. It became his summer retreat. His brother ran the estate for him, and it contained all the natural loveliness of a typical large estate: woods, ponds, parks, a wild-orange grove and greenhouses. A large central house with a belvedere atop and two wings, all of two stories, looked down on the lower park and woods and beyond them on the little Kotorosl River, which emptied into the great Volga. At Karabikha Nekrasov loved to hunt and swim, as well as write.

Both at Karabikha and at his apartment on the Liteiny Prospect he spent time with his new mistress, Celine Lefresne, a French actress from a St Petersburg acting company. While not a great beauty, she was attractive, dressed well, and possessed a lively disposition. Nekrasov loved to hear the French songs she would sing to him as she accompanied herself on the piano.

The man approached by Nekrasov at the English Club on that April day in 1866 was not only one of the "hanging Muravievs," he was "the hangman." He had earned this sobriquet by hanging Poles during the Polish rebellion. Although as a youth he had belonged to one of the secret societies which helped to produce the Decembrists, he soon got over such liberal inclinations. In the early years of Alexander's reign he acted as the Minister of State Properties and was one of the chief opponents of the proposed emancipation settlement. As the Polish revolt spread to the province of Lithuania, where Polish landowners predominated, Muraviev was appointed governor-general there. He soon unleashed a reign of terror on rebellious and suspected nobles and Catholic priests, restricted the use of Polish language and culture, and readjusted the land settlements between landowners and peasants in favor of the Lithuanian peasants. In addition to hanging a few hundred Poles, he also sent many thousands more into Siberian exile. Furthermore, Muraviev's methods were soon applied in Warsaw and other parts of Poland outside of his jurisdiction and gained in 1815 as a result of the war against Napoleon.

Angered by British and French popular and diplomatic support for the rebellious Poles and seeing the rebellion as part of a centuries-old conflict between Catholic Poland and Orthodox Russia, the Russian public, led by the journalist Katkov, cheered Muraviev on. They sent him letters, dispatches, deputations, flowers, icons and flags. He was met at trains by cheering crowds. Bells were rung in his honor. The Moscow publicist Michael Pogodin wrote: "Muraviev is a good man! He's hanging and shooting [the suspected rebels]. May God give him health!"[1]

Once the rebellion was firmly crushed and Muraviev's new policies enacted, the Tsar replaced him and he went into retirement. Alexander and his good friends and advisers in the capital did not care for Muraviev, even though the Tsar thought that under the circumstances Muraviev's extreme tactics were unfortunately necessary. Muraviev reciprocated the dislike of many of the Tsar's advisers. He believed they were too cosmopolitan, too influenced by European ideas.

In the relationship between Muraviev and Alexander one again sees that the Tsar was less a Russian nationalist than some of his subjects. In an age in which Bismarck in Germany and the Meiji leaders in Japan were skilfully orchestrating nationalist aspirations in order to better unite and modernize their nations, Alexander seemed little inclined to do likewise, for such a purpose. Perhaps he realized that as the ruler of a multinational empire, he could not rely on nationalism as a unifying force to the extent the rulers of more homogeneous populations could. He also distrusted any nationalist agitators, such as the editor Katkov, who might try to influence his thinking.

During the early stages of the Polish revolt, as Katkov and others beat the drums of Russian nationalism, even moderates such as Nikitenko criticized Alexander's government for being too pusillanimous and conciliatory towards the Polish rebels. Muraviev's bloodier tactics were more to the liking of an aroused Russian public.

Immediately following the attempted assassination of Alexander II, Russians once again reacted with a display of feverish emotion, this time out of gratitude that their Tsar had not been harmed. Despite dissatisfactions over conditions and government policies in Russia, many had still refused to place major blame on the Tsar. A British memorandum of the previous year had noted that "there is, perhaps, no country where the Sovereign is held by his people less responsible for the acts of his Ministers."[2] In St Petersburg crowds rushed along the streets yelling "hurrah" and headed for Palace Square, where they waited for the Tsar to appear on a Winter Palace balcony overlooking the square. In the days which followed cities, ethnic groups, professional and workers' organizations, students and even prisoners, poured forth telegrams and prayers of thanksgiving. Crowds on the streets and at concerts sang "God Save the Tsar." The man who supposedly had saved the Tsar's life became an instant hero. The Tsar made this cap-maker, Komissarov, a noble; and his picture, along with that of the Tsar, appeared on the streets.

Accompanying the outpouring of thanksgiving was another feeling, not nearly as intense, but yet present and disturbing. Who was this Karakozov who tried to kill the Tsar? Was he a Pole? A nihilist? Part of a larger conspiracy, possibly aided by revolutionaries abroad? An investigation was obviously needed and a tough investigator to head it. The Tsar called Michael Muraviev, now nearly seventy, out of retirement.

Many conservatives, such as Muraviev and Katkov, thought that the Tsar had listened too much to some of his more liberal St Petersburg advisers and that their liberal policies and permissiveness were partly responsible for such acts as Karakozov's. By mid April, Alexander had replaced a number of these "liberals" with more conservative-minded men. Thus, Alexander appointed a new Minister of Education, Count Dmitry Tolstoy, a new Director of the Third Division (security police), Count Peter Shuvalov and a new St Petersburg police chief, General Fedor Trepov. Alexander's behavior indicated, neither for the first nor the last time, that events and public opinion could strongly affect his policies and appointments.

The news of the new appointments helped to create a climate of fear among liberals and radicals in the capital. What would the "Hangman" do? Or the new police chief, Trepov, who had previously dealt severely with the Poles while holding a similar position in Warsaw? People became suspect if they seemed to lack enthusiasm when hurrahs were shouted for the Tsar or failed to remove their hats when passing a picture of Komissarov. Also suspect were women who wore no crinolines, but cut their hair short and wore dark glasses – later that year one governor ordered that such women were to be taken to police stations and given the choice of putting on crinolines or leaving his province. Those with scores to settle revenged themselves by denouncing their enemies. Arrests multiplied. So did rumors. One of the contributors to Nekrasov's journal later recalled that "all of these rumors, the constantly growing apprehension and the sleepless nights had so enervated me and brought me so near the point of complete prostration that I considered going and asking them to lock me up in the fortress."[3]

Amidst this reaction and fear, Nekrasov and his journal seemed destined to suffer. Despite his friendship and support for the likes of Chernyshevsky and Dobrolyubov, despite his own subversive poetry, he had up to now somehow avoided arrest. Meanwhile *The Contemporary*, according to conservatives, had continued to spew forth its poison. But then there was that other side of Nekrasov: he was a member of the English Club, where he ate, drank and gambled with Tsarist ministers. He also was conniving and had displayed an ability to do whatever was necessary to keep his journal running. Perhaps he could once again avoid the seemingly inevitable.

When the governor of the English Club asked him to prepare a poem for Komissarov at a banquet in the cap-maker's honor, Nekrasov agreed. On Saturday, April 9th, a week before he approached Muraviev with a poem, he stood up and recited his verse in his whispering, but husky voice. It was not his finest effort. He repeated a number of trite phrases that had already been attached to Komissarov's name in the press. Nekrasov called him "Son of the folk" and "the instrument of God."[4]

During the week that followed, Nekrasov heard that his poem had made a good impression on some high officials, but that his journal was nevertheless due to be shut down. He also was approached again by the governor of the English Club, who suggested he write another poem to be read at another dinner in honor of still another hero, Muraviev. Nekrasov now faced a terrible dilemma. If he said no, it would look like a protest against Muraviev and support for the would-be assassin, Karakozov. *The Contemporary* would then without doubt be terminated. But how could he who had exhorted the youth to "Go into the flames," "Go and perish," who had told them "You shall not die in vain: the cause is sure with your blood flowing under it,"[5] how could he, this same poet, now write a poem in honor of "the Hangman"?

The dinner for Muraviev was held the following Saturday. One can imagine the members and guests consuming in hearty Russian style the usual large quantities of food and drink that were served at such clubs. After dinner, coffee was served in the gallery near the entrance to the dining room. Muraviev sat in an armchair, the center of a small group. While he had the face of a bulldog, his bloated face and body also called to mind a hippopotamus. After another versifier had approached and read Muraviev a poem in his honor, Nekrasov walked up and asked permission to recite one. Muraviev continued smoking his pipe and contemptuously indicated his approval. The short poem was a shameless glorification of "the Hangman" who was now investigating the attempted assassination. It apparently concluded with the line "spare not the guilty ones."[6] Nekrasov had decided to degrade himself. His action and the reaction to it would scar him for the rest of his life.

16
THE PEROVSKYS AND HERZEN
IN GENEVA

The civilian governor of the St Petersburg province at the time of Karakozov's attempted assassination in 1866 was the mouse-like (in looks) Lev Perovsky, the brother of the former envoy to China and the father of Sophia Perovskaya, who would one day figure so prominently in the life of Alexander II. Earlier in the decade, Lev Perovsky had been transferred from the Crimea to the capital, first as vice-governor of the province and then as governor.

Although his career seemed to be proceeding well, his family life was not so satisfying. His wife, Barbara, was not as career minded as he. She was from the countryside and not especially at ease among St Petersburg's high society. As her husband nagged her about her social failures, a split developed in the family, with the children siding with their mother. Little Sophia (or Sonia as she was generally called) also resented her father's concern that she always appear as a well-bred young lady. She liked the woods and fields too much, especially in the summer, to be worrying about keeping her dress clean.

In 1865, when she was almost twelve, the family received a telegram from Geneva, signed by a man named Poggio. The telegram informed them that Sophia's uncle Peter was hopelessly ill. He had gone to Genoa as the Russian general consul several years after returning from Peking, but then became ill and had gone to Geneva for his health. Sophia and her mother left for Geneva and were soon at the sick man's side in this city on the lake with its beautiful mountains in the distance. While his sister-in-law cared for him, Sophia could not do much but be saddened by the condition of this warm, beloved uncle. He encouraged her to go play with his neighbor's daughter, Varya Poggio.

The girl's father was Alexander Poggio, a former Decembrist and close friend of old Prince Volkonsky, who had once so impressed Tolstoy. Poggio had also been very close, some thought a lover, to the prince's wife Maria. Like Volkonsky, he had left Siberia only after the amnesty of Alexander II. He was now an old, gray-haired man of medium height, but still energetic, handsome and majestic-looking. At least he was so in the eyes of a Geneva admirer, Alexander Herzen.

The fortunes of Herzen had declined considerably since his London heydays when *The Bell* had reverberated throughout Russia. His support of the Poles and of some of the Russian radicals, as well as his differences with other radicals, had led to a dramatic decline in the circulation of his journal. By 1864, only five hundred subscribers remained. Where he had once seemed to speak for many reformers, he now appeared to represent the thoughts of few beyond himself. In addition, he was troubled with family problems centering around his temperamental and moody mistress, Natalia Ogareva. At the beginning of 1864, he was depressed enough to write in his diary: "In general, there is only gloom, horror and blood."[1]

It was in these circumstances that Herzen decided to leave London, and eventually settled on Geneva as his new home. It was also perhaps because Natalia Ogareva was sick of London and because Herzen was being urged by some of the young Russian radicals to resettle his journal in Switzerland. There they hoped to have much more influence on it. Herzen hoped that such a move might regenerate *The Bell* and would at least move him closer to his two teenage daughters, who were living with a governess in Italy, and to Sasha, his oldest son, who had taken a position in Florence as a lecturer in physiology.

In December 1864, Herzen, Natalia and their three young children were in Paris. He intended to go on to Geneva to meet with some young radicals who were gathering for a congress there at the end of the month. There he could also lay the groundwork for the relocation of *The Bell* and what was left of his "family."

To move, however, was no easy task. It meant moving his printing press and several workers to Geneva. And it entailed not only moving Natalia Ogareva, himself and their three young children, but also Natalia's husband and Herzen's friend, Nick Ogarev, and his mistress Mary and her son, as well as a young woman named Charlotte and her son Toots, who had been fathered by Sasha. The group eventually moved in several stages – Charlotte and her son did not arrive until 1867, shortly after which she committed suicide. But before anyone reached Geneva, tragedy once again struck as it had more than a decade before. The three-year-old twins of Herzen and Natalia died in the midst of a diphtheria epidemic, and Natalia almost lost her mind. After temporarily settling Natalia and their daughter Liza in Montpellier, Herzen moved on to Geneva, where he arrived on December 28th, 1864.

Several days later, Alexander Poggio called on him. Herzen was staying at the Hotel Garni de la Poste when the old Decembrist stopped by late one morning. In the early part of the decade, Herzen had printed a reference to an injustice done to Poggio by relatives who refused to return the exile's property to him. The notice apparently helped the old man recover at least part of his property. Poggio was no doubt grateful to Herzen for his assistance. Herzen in turn was favorably impressed by the old man, but the two did not have long to become better acquainted before Herzen had to go back to France and England to complete arrangements for the move to Geneva.

By mid April 1865, Herzen and part of his "family" were back in the city of Calvin and Rousseau. The Herzens and Ogarevs moved into a magnificent rented chateau of more than thirty rooms. It was on the road to Chene, about a ten-minute tram ride from the center of Geneva. The two-storied chateau with its columns and terraces sat in the midst of a large shaded garden. Herzen's study was on the first floor, and here he wrote for *The Bell* and continued working on the memoirs he had begun writing and publishing years before. He remained in the chateau for about a year, after which further family changes resulted in another move for Herzen and his oldest daughter to less grandiose lodgings.

Once back in Geneva, Herzen renewed his acquaintance with Poggio, and they sometimes talked politics in the presence of Poggio's young daughter. In that year before the Karakozov assassination attempt, Poggio still had faith in the reforming tendencies of the Tsar who had granted him and the other Decembrists an amnesty. Herzen thought such hopes were misplaced. However, this did not prevent him from writing Alexander II yet another open letter and printing it in the first Geneva issue of *The Bell*. He was prompted to do so by the death of the Tsar's oldest son. Herzen believed it a proper occasion to encourage Alexander to fulfill the early hopes of his regime, but the tone of the letter reflected more Herzen's disenchantment with the Tsar than any real hope that his words of advice would be followed. Some of Herzen's critics believed him insensitive for addressing the Tsar at such a time of personal suffering.

Meanwhile, Varya Poggio was becoming a close friend of Sophia Perovskaya and was telling her of the heroic Decembrists and also probably about those who presently opposed the Tsar, such as her father's friend Herzen. But Sophia's informal lessons soon came to an end when her uncle Peter died at the end of August 1865. Her mother had informed her father that his brother's health was fast deteriorating, but when he arrived in Geneva his brother was already dead. The Perovskys, therefore, prepared to go back to Russia. Sophia and Varya Poggio posed for a photograph before they parted. In it they stand, Sophia's arm firmly around the shoulder of her friend. They are about the same size. Sophia has a large forehead, small mouth and a weak chin; she has a serious look on her face.

After the Perovskys left Geneva, it continued to be the home of the Poggios and Herzen. Natalia Ogareva, however, soon tired of it. In September, after quarreling with Herzen's teenaged daughters, who temporarily had joined the family, Natalia took Liza and set off for Montreux at the other end of Lake

Geneva. She never recovered from the shock of the twins' death. Only her obsession with finding adequate schooling for the high-strung Liza kept her going. But she was never satisfied, and moved from city to city. Only in Nice, where the twins were buried in the Herzen family plot, did Natalia seem to find a tortured comfort. The relations between her and Herzen continued to be stormy whenever he visited her and Liza. "Intimate relations" between the couple seemed, in his words, to "put her right for the time." But he thought it was "an awful remedy"[2] : whether for him or for her or for both is not perfectly clear.

In early 1866, upon hearing of Karakozov's assassination attempt, Herzen criticized him and stated that "only in savage and decrepit nations does history proceed by assassinations."[3] Within the next year, his criticism of Karakozov led to open warfare between the radical young Russians in Geneva and himself. Already resentful of Herzen, his chateau and his unwillingness to support and bankroll more of their radical projects, they became increasingly critical. One of the leading Geneva nihilists was Alexander Serno-Solovievich. The curly, dark-haired Serno-Solovievich, along with his older brother, had helped to found the radical Land and Liberty group, which had been supported by Ogarev, Bakunin and Herzen. His brother had been arrested thanks in part to the same Herzen letter which had played a role in Chernyshevsky's arrest. The younger brother had been in London when he heard of his brother's arrest, and later moved on to Zurich and Geneva.

Now after Herzen printed an article in *The Bell* in which he praised Chernyshevsky and claimed that the editors of *The Bell* and the radical jour-nalist complemented each other, Serno-Solovievich printed and distributed an open letter to Herzen. This occurred about a year after both the Karakozov at-tempt and the death of his own exiled brother in Irkutsk. The piece was filled with hatred and contempt for Herzen and maintained that he had nothing in common with Chernyshevsky. "You, Mr Herzen, are a dead [i.e. no longer rele-vant] man,"[4] was Serno-Solovievich's conclusion.

While Herzen bemoaned these nihilists, the "syphilis of our revolutionary lusts,"[5] as he called them, his own health and vitality were beginning to wane, and he no longer had much energy left to fight them.

After the Perovskys returned to St Petersburg, the life of the governor's fam-ily continued in ways appropriate to his status. Sophia's older sister, Masha, had made her debut, and her oldest brother, Kolya, was also of an age to mix with the opposite sex. So the governor arranged dances in his home. As the finely dressed young men and women whirled around amidst the music and the lights of the candelabras, Sophia and her sixteen-year-old brother, Vasya, stood around and watched or made their way to the buffet table. They both thought that the dancing, curtseying and other mannerisms were incredibly stupid.

When a woman sitting near Sophia's mother looked at Sophia through her lorgnette and asked why she wasn't dancing, she said she did not like to dance. Her mother explained that she would much rather read. A colonel in the gendarmes overheard the remark and said she would be better dancing more and reading less. Reading, he explained, was leading many of the young to revolutionary ideas. Vasya later told Sophia that the colonel was a typical gendarme and that in the Third Division a special room existed where they tortured people.

On the day of the Karakozov attempt, Sophia's father was riding in his carriage along the Nevsky Prospect when he noticed several carriages and crowds of people hurrying to Palace Square. He was told at the commandant's entrance of the Winter Palace that someone had shot at the Tsar, but that he was alive. But before Governor Perovsky could join other officials wishing to express their happiness that Alexander II was still in good health, he thought it necessary to go home and change into more appropriate attire. When he returned to the palace, Governor-general Suvorov was there accompanied by the "savior of the Tsar," Komissarov. Soon the Emperor and Empress and the rest of the imperial family appeared, with pages carrying the trains of the dresses of the Empress and Grand Duchesses.

As hurrahs arose amidst the sparkling halls, Suvorov was in tears because he had been unable to prevent the attempted assassination. He soon went into retirement. In late July, Sophia's father joined the growing list of ministers whom the Tsar had decided to replace following Karakozov's attempt.

17

DOSTOEVSKY AND ANNA SNITKINA

Several months after the replacement of Perovsky, an attractive twenty-year-old woman walked up the steps to Dostoevsky's apartment. It was about 11:30 in the morning, and the young woman's name was Anna Snitkina. She had gray eyes, a broad forehead and a firm chin. Although she was a bit apprehensive about the coming encounter, her face normally reflected a certain resoluteness. For a woman so young, she was well educated and possessed an unusual degree of common sense mixed with intelligence. She had completed a secondary education and had also enrolled in a Pedagogical Institute recently opened for women, but she dropped out after a year to help care for her dying father. She still, however, had time to take a stenography class at night. It was due to this training that she was now on her way to begin working for a novelist whose works she had read and enjoyed.

Most recently she had read the first parts of his *Crime and Punishment*, which had been appearing serially that year in Katkov's *The Russian Messenger*. In fact, the big stone corner building in which she now found herself, with its many small apartments, reminded her of the one lived in by Raskolnikov, the hero of Dostoevsky's new novel.

Indeed, much of the story was set in the writer's own neighborhood, not far from the Haymarket Square and about a mile south of the Winter Palace. In his novel he wrote of Sonia, a good-hearted woman forced into prostitution by poverty and the irresponsibility of her alcoholic father, Mr Marmeladov. The author also described the miserable, crowded conditions of the Marmeladovs and of Raskolnikov, who lived by himself in a small attic room. In this part of the city and in the capital generally, prostitution, alcoholism, overcrowding and crime were growing problems. There were many men in St Petersburg without their families. When they could afford it, lonely soldiers or peasants performing temporary or seasonal work in the city often turned to prostitutes, alcohol, or both. Syphilis rates climbed sharply. So did the number of illegitimate children, many of whom were turned over to a foundling home. Unsanitary conditions, caused especially by overcrowding and polluted water, continued to kill more people each year than were born in the city. The past year or two had been especially bad because of a cholera epidemic. This was the St Petersburg of Dostoevsky, the city in which his hero decided to kill an old pawnbroker for her money.

When Anna Snitkina reached apartment 13, she rang and the door was opened by a maid. Such help was cheap in those days and normal for a man of Dostoevsky's standing, even though he was then in a precarious financial position. After the maid had led her into a dining room and she had waited a few minutes, Dostoevsky appeared and invited her into his study. When she first looked at him he seemed rather old, but once he began speaking he seemed younger than his forty-four years. She noticed that his dark blue jacket was stained, that his brown-reddish hair was heavily pomaded, that one of his eyes was so dilated that its iris couldn't be seen, and that his face was pale and unhealthy looking.

After offering her tea, he began nervously pacing around the overheated room, smoking one cigarette after another. His talk was disjointed. He mentioned an epileptic attack that had struck him several days before. Finally, he asked her to take some dictation. It was obvious that he still had doubts about how effective any stenographer could be. After looking over what she had transcribed and finding two small errors, he rebuked her. Soon he told her he was in no mood to dictate and asked her to come back that night. She left feeling depressed.

At 8:00 p.m. she returned. Dostoevsky had her sit at his study desk, gave her some tea, and began talking. He told her of that day on Semenovsky Square when he thought he would be executed by a firing squad. They talked of other things, and finally he began dictating the novel which he would call *The Gambler*. At 11:00 p.m. she left, promising to transcribe her shorthand and return the following day at noon. When she returned the next day about half an hour late, he was agitated, having feared she would not return. He had explained to her the previous night that he must finish the novel by November 1st, less than a month away. Economic necessity had driven him to sign a contract with an unscrupulous publisher. If the novel was not completed by the promised date, Dostoevsky would forfeit all rights to his own works, without any compensation, for the next nine years.

The death of his brother Michael and the collapse of a new journal, both within the past two years, had helped to trigger a whole series of financial obligations and debts for which he now was responsible. Thus, when Anna met him he was trying to stay out of debtor's prison by writing two novels at once, and he had arranged for her help in order to expedite the process. In the days ahead as she continued to work for him, she sometimes noticed that a vase or silver spoons were missing, and discovered that, like his hero Raskolnikov, he had resorted to pawning his valuables.

She came almost every day at noon or in the early afternoon, always in a black mourning dress for her recently expired father, and left at about four. Soon he began writing at night so he could dictate to her from his manuscript, as opposed to composing on the spot. Dictation was interspersed with tea or coffee, sweets and talk. She found out that the portrait of the emaciated woman which hung in a walnut frame above a couch in his study was that of his wife, who had died the same year as his brother. Dostoevsky also told her of an eighteen-year-old woman, to whom he had proposed not long before. He was speaking of the beautiful, well-born Anna Korvin-Krukovskaya, who had submitted several stories to *The Epoch*. Dostoevsky had fallen in love with her, but his possessiveness and their differing political views – she was a radical – prevented them from marrying. As Anna Snitkina worked over *The Gambler*, she must also have wondered about the novel's heroine, Polina. She knew that the hero, Alexei, was partly based upon Dostoevsky himself, and she must have speculated about the extent to which the relations of Polina and Alexei mirrored those of Dostoevsky and her real life model. Eventually, Anna was to find out quite a bit about the "real" Polina.

Apollinaria (Polina) Suslova first came into Dostoevsky's life in the early sixties. She was an aspiring writer in her early twenties and sympathetic to the radical views of the day, especially regarding women. Since he was a former political prisoner and well-known writer, Dostoevsky had a special appeal for her. She was a striking, strong-looking young woman of common origins. She had reddish hair and a low voice. Dostoevsky became strongly attracted to her, and they soon became lovers. His wife, Maria, was still alive at that time, but ailing. Several tempestuous years, both in Western Europe and Russia, followed. After giving herself to the writer, Polina came to believe he was insensitive to her needs. Although they both inflicted pain and suffered at the hands of each other, Polina seemed more sadistic and Dostoevsky more masochistic. One time while traveling in Europe together – the year of his wife's death – she denied him sexual intimacy, at the same time inflaming his passions with her mixture of sensuality and cruelty. One night in Baden-Baden she got in bed and asked Dostoevsky to sit close to her while she held his hand. Before he left she allowed him an ardent kiss, but nothing more. Later she confided to her diary that she neither wished him to "cherish hope nor be quite without it."[1]

As Anna Snitkina sat in her house at night near the Smolny Convent and Institute, the school that Katia Dolgorukova had recently attended, one wonders what she thought as she transcribed Dostoevsky's sentences from her shorthand notations. When Alexei confessed his lust, his self-contempt and willingness to do anything, even kill, for Polina, what thoughts ran through the mind of this young woman? She liked neither the hero nor the heroine, but what did either of them tell her about the man with whom she was now working so closely – this strange, irritable, but somehow likable man who bared his soul to her?

As the days of October moved quickly forward, the pages of the novel accumulated and Dostoevsky's mood improved. Actually, there was something about the audacity of writing a novel in less than a month, about the intense pressure of time, that he enjoyed. A little earlier that year he had even bragged about being unique among Russian writers in being able to write under such conditions. Turgenev, he stated, "would die from even the thought" of it.[2]

The pressure of time seemed to somehow intensify experience for him, to make it richer and more full of meaning. No moments of his life had been more significant than those few minutes he had once stood on Semenovsky Square waiting to be shot. He sometimes experienced similar intense moments just before an epileptic attack. He would later describe the experience in his novel *The Idiot*. "His self-awareness increased almost ten-fold ... all his anxieties, all his doubts, all his worries seemed at once to be pacified, resolved into some sort of higher serenity, full of clear, harmonious happiness and hope, of reason and final cause."[3] Roulette had also furnished some intense moments for him when he risked everything on one spin of the wheel.

Between dictations, tea and talk continued in the smoke-filled study. Since all the experience which he related to her seemed sad, she asked him to tell her about some of his happy times. He replied that he had not had any happiness yet, at least of the type he dreamed. Once he told her that three paths lay open before him: to go East to Constantinople and Jerusalem, to go abroad and play roulette, or to marry again and seek happiness in family life. She probably understood that the first choice would reflect a religious quest, but his addiction to gambling and other intense experiences she probably did not yet fully understand. Regarding the third path he asked her whether, if he chose it, he should try to find a wife who was intelligent or kind. When she replied, "an intelligent one," he said no, that he would pick a kind one who would take pity on him and love him.[4]

As they worked and talked, he became more affectionate and she more relaxed. Although he kept forgetting her name, he began calling her *golubchik* (little dove) or "my dear." She wondered if he might propose to her and if he did, what she would say. Despite his irritability, the ardent, although always well-behaved and self-possessed, Anna was growing increasingly fond of him.

At the end of October, Dostoevsky dictated the final words of *The Gambler*. On the 28th, the capital celebrated the marriage of the new Tsarevich Alexander, who had inherited his older brother's fiancée, Dagmar of Denmark. The 30th was Dostoevsky's birthday and a Sunday. On the following day, Anna appeared in a long, lilac dress with the final transcription. Dostoevsky greeted her warmly and, seeing her for the first time in a dress other than black, told her that she looked nice. They talked; he showed her a picture of Polina Suslova, and he asked her if anyone had yet proposed marriage to her. Several days earlier he had told her he would miss her when their work was finished and asked if he might call on her. On this Monday before she departed, they agreed that he would come to her home the following Thursday evening. When he did so and talked with her and her mother, he requested Anna's help in completing the final chapters of *Crime and Punishment*.

November 8th was a frosty, brilliant day. Anna walked the two miles from her home to Dostoevsky's apartment. When she arrived, he helped to undo her hood and take off her coat. He seemed happy and excited. The light streaming through the windows seemed to brighten his study. He told Anna that he was thinking of a plot for a new novel and wanted her advice. It was about a man of his own age who had fallen in love with a woman of about Anna's age. As he described the hero it was evident to Anna that he was describing a character very much like himself.

What he wanted Anna to tell him was whether it would be realistic, psychologically true to life, to have an exuberant young woman fall in love with a hero who was elderly, sick and debt-ridden. Anna insisted it would be possible. Then in a trembling voice he asked her to put herself in the heroine's place and himself in place of the hero. Then what would she answer. Anna later recalled that she said: "I would answer that I love you and will love you all my life."[5] Before they parted that day they decided that as soon as circumstances permitted, they would marry.

The next month was full of happy anticipation. Only a continued shortage of money and problems with those dependent on Dostoevsky punctured from time to time the spirits of the couple. The author's stepson from his first marriage lived with him, and neither he nor the widow of Dostoevsky's brother seemed happy about the marriage plans of the man upon whom they depended.

Meanwhile, *Crime and Punishment* had to be completed. He once again began dictating to Anna, sometimes in her two-story stone house near the Smolny and sometimes in his apartment.

Since the beginning of the decade, Dostoevsky had become more and more alarmed at the thinking and behavior of the nihilists, and the news of Karakozov's attempted assassination upset him to the point of trembling. He became especially critical of several journalists, including Dmitry Pisarev, who wrote for *The Russian Word*. As compared with Chernyshevsky and *The Contemporary*, Pisarev and *The Russian Word* were more elitist and less concerned with the masses. The main character of *Crime and Punishment*,

Raskolnikov, not only reflected portions of Dostoevsky's own youthful turmoil, but he also symbolized the bankruptcy of this latest development in nihilistic thought. He believed in rational self-interest and had cut himself off from ordinary people and from his religious roots. He reasoned that he could kill the useless old woman pawnbroker and put her money to good use. He also believed that some people, Napoleon for example, were not bound by traditional ethics, and he wanted to see if he, Raskolnikov, were such a superior individual. But little went as planned. He also had to kill the pawnbroker's sister; he obtained little of value; and he never spent the stolen money. Instead he was tormented with guilt.

Only in the previous instalment which had appeared in *The Russian Messenger* had Raskolnikov finally confessed his crime to the loving prostitute Sonia. Now, in the last part dictated to Anna, Raskolnikov haltingly continued his way back from the depths of nihilistic thinking and individual isolation. He allowed Sonia to put a wooden cross, the kind the common people wore, around his neck. He went out to the crowded Haymarket Square and following Sonia's advice, he kissed the earth, since he had sinned against it. Finally, he confessed to the police and was sent to Siberia. There he had a feverish dream in which Europe was stricken by a plague, but one of a unique type. It caused all men to have confidence only in their own particular ideas, to come into conflict with everyone else. Soon only bloody anarchy reigned. Only after this dream did Raskolnikov throw himself at the feet of Sonia, who had followed him into exile. Only then did he fully cast aside his false pride and rationalism, legacies of his radical, Western type thinking. Only then did he fully believe that he might share the simple Russian beliefs of the humble Sonia.

In depicting the isolated Raskolnikov, cut off by his Western views from the Russian masses until he is resurrected by suffering, guilt and the love of Sonia, Dostoevsky captured well one of the central motifs of the times: the alienation of intellectuals and their longing, often subconsciously, for community.

The novel was completed in December. At the end of the month Dostoevsky took the train to Moscow to see his editor, the nationalistic Katkov, for an advance on a new novel. Katkov promised that he would receive it in January. Anna and he were now able to begin planning a pre-Lenten wedding. On February 15th, 1867, at about 8:00 p.m., an hour later than planned, they were finally married in St Petersburg's Izmailovsky Cathedral.

18
PROFESSOR SOLOVIEV AND HIS FAMILY

During the year following the death of the Tsar's oldest son, Professor Soloviev gave lessons in history to the new Tsarevich Alexander, just as he had earlier done for his older brother. The selection of Soloviev reflected the outstanding reputation the historian had by now achieved.

The professor spent part of his summers during the mid sixties at Pokrovskoe, an area of pleasant summer dachas on the outskirts of Moscow. There he continued working on his *History of Russia from Ancient Times*. Despite administrative and teaching duties at Moscow University and his occasional tutoring of a Tsarevich, he had managed since 1851 to continue publishing his history at the rate of a volume per year. During the mid-sixties he was writing several volumes on the reign of Peter the Great, an era like his own, full of great changes. After rising at 6:00 a.m. and a long morning walk in this area dotted with trees, dachas, peasant huts, ponds, a small river running under a precipice and a green cupolated village church, he would come back to his study and work on the reign of the man he thought the greatest leader in history.

In his memoirs, Soloviev would compare Alexander II unfavorably with Peter the Great. As the historian saw it, they both held the reigns of power in a period of transition; but whereas Peter's strong hands had directed a successful transformation, Alexander's weak hands allowed the carriage of state to rush ahead toward its destruction. Soloviev, who favored modernization, industrialization and the growth of a middle class, believed that Russia required another Peter the Great, but feared that fate had brought his country another Louis XVI of France.

Although the natural sciences were now in vogue with young radicals, some of their leaders and the educated public in general also took an increasing interest in history. One historian and publicist noted, perhaps with some bias, that "with each decade, and lately almost with each year, Russian history gains in interest, significance and importance."[1] Soloviev and others gave public lectures on history, which were well attended. Plays and operas dealing with historic themes became increasingly common. In the fall of 1866, Dostoevsky and Anna Snitkina had gone to see Count Alexei Tolstoy's play *The Death of Ivan the Terrible*. By the end of the decade Mussorgsky would begin working on his majestic historical opera *Boris Godunov*. The Russian historical periods which fascinated people the most were those like their own, ones of great historical changes. In addition to the era of Peter, another favorite was the one in which Boris Godunov had lived, the Time of Troubles. It was a period of problems with Poland, and more importantly to the radicals, of peasant rebellions.

While some of the radicals such as Chernyshevsky respected the work of Soloviev and thought it important, the historian was also charged with ignoring the historical role of the common people. The Ukrainian historian Kostomarov was more to the radicals' liking for his extensive treatment of the common Russian and border peoples.

In recent years the Soloviev family had continued to grow. By the summer of 1867, his wife had given birth to twelve children, but by then only eight were still alive, five girls and three boys. The baby, who would prove to be the family's last child, named after her mother, Poliksena. The latter, dark-haired and attractive, was quite a bit younger than her husband, who was now in his late forties, with his blond receding hair growing increasingly gray. Her life revolved around him and their children. Along with a number of servants, she tried to shield him from noise and irritation as he worked at his desk on his historical writings. Not only did his work require quiet, but he was thought to have a weak heart, and Poliksena did not want him to suffer undue stress. During his working hours at home no one was allowed to disturb him.

During the academic year, he usually worked at home in the early mornings before leaving to do historical research at places such as the library of the Rumyantsev Museum or seeing to his duties at the university. For a while in the mid-sixties, the family was furnished with a large apartment in one of the university buildings. After returning home late in the afternoon, having dinner, and enjoying a brief rest or some light reading, he would return to his desk and his research and writing. Only on weekends did the regime vary. Occasionally on Friday nights he might have friends over, but even then Poliksena would remind him at 11:00 that it was time to retire. On Saturdays he might dine out at Moscow's English Club and then go to the Italian opera. His fondness for opera, as well as for poets such as Pushkin and Goethe, revealed an emotional aspect of his character which was usually not apparent. Sundays he spent with the family, first at church and then amidst talking, singing, reading aloud, or game playing. In some ways he was an old-fashioned father. Except for Sundays, he did not spend a great deal of time with his children. But in his own way he loved them, and he encouraged their intellectual development, that of his girls as well as his boys. At times he let them sit around and listen as he talked with friends. The children in turn greatly respected their father.

His lectures at the university were characteristic of his temperament. His tall, solid body entered the lecture hall promptly on time, and he would lecture for forty minutes, mainly with his eyes closed. His tone was even and unhurried. He did not try to entertain or dazzle his students with colorful images, but spoke on a clear intellectual level, attempting to point out the connection of one event to another. He believed in historical laws and patterns and that God stood behind history, guiding it forward. Although his defense of strong Russian governments and rulers did not appeal to some of his more radical students, they were more sympathetic to his view of Russia as an integral part of Europe.

In addition to teaching, Soloviev also had administrative duties. He had been selected by his colleagues to be Dean of the Historical-Philological Faculty, and from time to time during this period he also assumed the responsibilities of rector of the university. He brought to these administrative tasks, his solid, hard-working, prudent approach. He could display flashes of temper, and he did not tolerate fools easily, but generally he was restrained and had little appetite for dramatic confrontations. He tried to settle disputes without a great deal of fanfare. For the radical students of the decade he was too conservative, and for some St Petersburg reactionaries in the Ministry of Education, too liberal. In fact, he had always been a moderate but independent man, confident of his own political view that Russia needed a strong but enlightened government based on sound rational and moral principles.

During the summers, he had more time for writing. At Pokrovskoe he worked in his study, which possessed a big window looking out on a winding country road. If he wished a break from his efforts, he could look out and watch carriages carrying dacha owners, peasants on foot, or children at play. Once when his second son, Vladimir, and several friends constructed a zoological station under his window, he said with a flash of humor that Vladimir and his friends would be good subjects themselves for zoological investigation.

Vladimir (or Volodya as he was more commonly called) was in fact an interesting young boy. He had been born prematurely and was never in robust health. Although thin and pale, with dark hair like his mother's, his mind and imagination were exceedingly active. Like his father, he was interested in foreign countries, but more inclined towards the romantic and mysterious in life than was his more sober father. Spanish knights, saints who practised severe asceticism, military heroes and the more enchanted writings of Gogol and Pushkin captured his fancy. His mother and a short, stout, bossy governess named Anna, whom Volodya credited with prophetic dreams, seemed to have encouraged some of his appetite for the marvelous in life.

When he was nine, in 1862, he experienced an event that would leave an indelible mark on him. As he recalled it many years later, it was Ascension Day, and he was in church. He was still in bitter agony over discovering that a girl to whom he had confessed his love preferred a rival. The odor of incense filled the church. The priest proclaimed "Let us banish earthly cares."[2] Suddenly there was azure all around and his torments disappeared. All he saw was azure and a beautiful lady bathed in a golden blue light. She stood with a radiant smile on her face and a flower in her hand. She nodded to him and then vanished in a mist.

When Volodya was eleven he entered the same Moscow gymnasium where his father and older brother Vsevolod had prepared for college. He would remain there five years. It was an excellent school with a tough curriculum. In his third year there, for example, he took religion, Russian, German, French, Latin, Greek, math, physics and history. He was a good student and learned well. But he was also a passionate and mischievous boy. In the summers at Pokrovskoe he and a couple of his young friends would go down to the river where the women bathed and scream in disguised voices, "fire, fire, Pokrovskoe burns."[3] They would then hide in the bushes as the women emerged from the river or bathhouse in a state of disarray and panic. Or the boys would wrap themselves in sheets, make scary noises, and come charging out of a graveyard adjacent to a park as people walked by at night. They especially tried to provoke three actresses staying at Pokrovskoe. Volodya was so eager for their attention that he would have welcomed a beating from them, but unfortunately they would not respond. His parents discovered some of these exploits and scolded him, but Volodya was not easily discouraged.

In the mid- and late 1860s, while still in his early teens, he gradually lost the Orthodox faith that was so dear to his parents. His now deceased paternal grandfather, the priest, had dedicated Volodya to the service of Orthodoxy. Volodya's parents had named his two older sisters Vera (faith) and Nadezhda (hope) and the sister born after him, Lyubov (charity or love). Icons had an honorable place in the family's rooms, and the family observed church fasts to the extent that health permitted.

But influenced by the heroes of the radical youth in the 1860s, Volodya renounced it all. The Russian nihilist Pisarev, Darwin and others became his guides. Like the heroes of Chernyshevsky, he believed that science and socialism would lead man towards a better future. In the style of the radicals of the day he let his hair grow long and espoused nihilist views. His father apparently thought it was just a phase the boy was going though and did not become overly troubled.

19
TOLSTOY: A MARRIAGE AND
A MASTERPIECE

While Professor Soloviev was writing about Peter the Great, Leo Tolstoy was at his estate working on a different type of historical work, *War and Peace*.

In the years since the emancipation of the serfs, Tolstoy had married and by the summer of 1866 had three children, Sergei, Tatyana and Ilya. His wife was Sonia Bers, the daughter of a government physician who worked in the Kremlin. Sonia's mother, Lyubov, was only a few years older than Tolstoy himself and as a young boy he apparently had once been infatuated with her. Sonia's father had met Lyubov in the early 1840s when he had interrupted a trip to Turgenev's in order to attend to her when she fell ill. Turgenev's mother had once been his mistress, and they apparently even had an illegitimate child.

In the early and mid-1860s the large Bers family, like the Solovievs, spent their summers in Pokrovskoe, and many a morning in the summer of 1862, Leo Tolstoy walked the eight miles from his rented apartment in Moscow to the Bers' dacha. One of his rivals for the affections of Sonia was a Moscow history professor, Nil Popov, who years later would marry the oldest of the Soloviev girls, Vera.

The young Sonia had rosy cheeks, dark hair and eyes, and was inclined to be serious and introspective. Tolstoy was sixteen years older than this teenager, still had his dark beard, and feared that he was too old and ugly. But she was awed by this famous writer who was also a count. The fact that her father was not born a noble and her mother was only an illegitimate daughter of a princess both seemed to contribute to Sonia's infatuation for someone with a solid and legitimate aristocratic background. The Bers' parents hoped that Tolstoy, a family friend, might be most interested in the oldest daughter, Liza. This probably only increased the desirability of the count for the younger Sonia. In the idyllic, romantic setting of Pokrovskoe the romance proceeded, and in September 1862, Tolstoy and Sonia were married in the Kremlin's Church of the Nativity of the Blessed Virgin.

Following the marriage the couple settled down on his estate, Yasnaya Polyana. Tolstoy's shriveled-up Aunt Toninette and her companion Natalia, plus maids and cooks, a housekeeper, coachmen, seamstresses, laundry women and other servants were all part of the household. Tolstoy rose early, dressed in work clothes, and spent his days supervising the estate. He planted fruit trees, imported Japanese pigs, took up beekeeping, built a distillery, and for a short while continued teaching in the school for peasant children which he had enthusiastically started before his marriage. Sometimes he went hunting or retired to his study to write.

For Sonia life on a large and somewhat isolated country estate was quite different from her active life in Moscow and at Pokrovskoe. While there certainly were happy times and she expressed a strong love of her husband, she also brooded. She wrote in her diary in November 1862:

> It isn't hard to find work [here], but before doing anything one has to create some enthusiasm for breeding hens, tinkling the piano, and reading a lot of silly books and a very few good ones, or pickling cucumbers and what not. All this will come in time when I forget my lazy old life and get used to the country.[1]

Ten days later she wrote:

> He disgusts me with his People [peasants]. I feel he ought to choose between me, i.e. the representative of the family, and his beloved People. This is egoism, I know. But let it be. I have given my life to him, I live through him, and I expect him to do the same. Otherwise the place grows too depressing; I ran away to-day because everybody and everything repelled me – Auntie and the students and N.P. [his aunt's companion] and the walls and the whole life here, so that I laughed for joy when I ran quietly away from the house. L. did not disgust me, but I suddenly felt that he and I were miles apart, i.e. that his People could never absorb *all* my attention, while I couldn't take up all his attention, as he does mine. It's quite clear. If I am no good to him, if I am merely a doll, a *wife*, and not a *human being* – then it is all useless and I don't want to carry on this existence.[2]

There was also Sonia's jealousy. Shortly after she had agreed to marry him, Tolstoy had insisted that she know the whole truth about what he considered his immoral past. He had handed her his diaries. Among his erotic adventures, she had discovered his liaison with the peasant Aksinya, who now still lived in a hamlet at Yasnaya Polyana along with her illegitimate son by Tolstoy. Sonia could not forget what Tolstoy had written in his diary of his feelings for Aksinya in 1858: "I am in love as never before … the feeling is no longer bestial, but like a husband's for his wife."[3] In her diary Sonia wrote: "Some day I shall kill myself with jealousy."[4]

Tolstoy's feelings towards his new wife were also full of ambivalence. He had long dreamed of family happiness, but he was a perfectionist and dogmatic. Therefore, he was not an easy man to live with, unless a wife was willing to be molded according to his views. The age difference between them, as well as

Sonia's awe of him in their brief courtship, no doubt led him to believe she would follow his guidance. But her dissatisfaction and the couple's detailed analyses and revelations of their feelings – they openly read each other's diaries – often led to further mistrust, suspicion and quarrels.

With the birth of Sergei in the summer of 1863, a new source of both happiness and tension appeared. Sonia became a proud and loving mother, and Tolstoy had always thought that mothering was a woman's chief obligation in life. However, they soon quarreled when because of painful breasts Sonia had to employ a wet-nurse to feed the baby. To Tolstoy the employment of wet-nurses represented the type of dereliction of duty that he expected of society women or of those with "emancipated" views. He contrasted such a practice with the more natural, healthy way of the peasant women who breast-fed their own children. During this same year he also lashed out, in a play called *The Infected Family*, at the types of emancipated women and nihilist views pictured in Chernyshevsky's *What Is To be Done?* But when he tried to get his play produced in Moscow the following year, he was unable to do so.

Despite some dissatisfactions in the years which followed, the couple gradually adjusted to each other. With the arrival of Tatyana in 1864 and Ilya in 1866, Sonia took on increasing responsibilities. Tolstoy, on the other hand, allowed some of his to lapse. Not long after their marriage he lost his enthusiasm for educating the peasant children, and before too long he also turned over more of the management of the estate to hired help.

Instead he took up in earnest the writing of what he eventually would call *War and Peace*. Like Poliksena Solovieva, Sonia supervised the household staff and tried to see that her husband was undisturbed as he wrote. He did so in a large former storeroom on the ground floor. Heavy rings from which hams had once been hung still were affixed to the ceiling. Sonia was happy that he was busy on the novel, and she helped him greatly by laboriously copying over and over his scrawled and at times almost illegible drafts.

From time to time trips to relatives or friends or welcoming them to Yasnaya Polyana also helped to fill Sonia's days. Tolstoy's sister Maria was one guest, along with her two daughters, the last fathered by a Swedish nobleman whom Maria had recently lived with but not married. More frequently members of Sonia's family visited them, especially her younger sister Tanya, who was two years younger than Sonia. She was bubbly, enthusiastic, mercurial and mischievous. Tolstoy jokingly referred to her as "Mme Viardot" (Turgenev's love) because of her fine singing voice. Family members believed that she was a model for the enchanting and appealing young Natasha of *War and Peace*.

For several years there had been some hope that Tanya would marry Tolstoy's brother Sergei, despite the fact he was twice her age and had a gypsy mistress and illegitimate children. A wedding was actually planned, but Sergei finally decided he could not desert his mistress. It took Tanya some time to recover.

Occasional flashes of jealousy still infected Sonia. In the summer of 1866, shortly after giving birth to Ilya, Sonia was jealous of a new steward's pretty young nihilistic wife. Despite Tolstoy's disapproval of nihilism, he always seemed eager to discuss such ideas with enthusiastic young exponents of them. While teaching the young peasants on his estate, he had hired a number of young radicals to teach in neighboring villages. He soon converted them to some of his own views, and perhaps he hoped he could do the same with this nihilist woman. But Sonia feared that Tolstoy was interested in more than the young woman's views. She wrote in her diary that she wished the woman "every misfortune."[5]

Such times of trial for Sonia, however, alternated with days of happiness. An especially memorable one was her name day, September 17, 1866. As family and guests sat down for dinner on a terrace flooded with sunshine and at a table decorated with flowers, an army band hidden in the garden began to play one of Sonia's favorite pieces, the overture from the opera *Fennella ou La Muette de Portici*. Sonia beamed at this surprise arranged by her husband. After dinner there was dancing. Tolstoy enthusiastically directed the fun and danced along with Sonia and the guests. Tanya danced a Russian folkdance while others clapped, and Tolstoy observed the scene and later transformed it into Natasha's country dance in *War and Peace*. At one in the morning, beneath a luminous moon and starlit night, the band along with some officers left to the beat of a marching tune.

Ironically, the band's appearance was accompanied and arranged by a colonel who several months earlier had condemned to death a man Tolstoy had defended. This unusual incident had occurred as a result of a slow-witted enlisted man named Shibunin striking his sadistic commanding officer. Such an offense was punishable by death. A couple of young officers of this unit, which was stationed nearby, appealed to Tolstoy to defend the man. Tolstoy agreed and proposed a defense based on Shibunin's abnormal mental state at the time of the offense. A majority of the court, however, ruled against him. Tolstoy appealed the decision, but the execution was carried out.

Meanwhile, Tolstoy had his writing to do. In 1865 and 1866, after numerous reworkings, the first part of *War and Peace* was published under the title *1805*. It appeared in five instalments in Katkov's *The Russian Messenger*, the same journal that was publishing Dostoevsky's *Crime and Punishment* and had first published Turgenev's *Fathers and Sons*. Only in 1869 would Tolstoy complete the entire manuscript.

The idea for the novel began with Tolstoy's earlier desire to write about a Decembrist returning in 1856 from Siberian exile. Tolstoy believed that certain resemblances exited between 1856 and the years that gave birth to the Decembrist ideas and revolt of 1825, and he kept pushing back the beginning date of *War and Peace* until he finally arrived at 1805, when Russia first entered the war against Napoleon. As the novel progressed, Tolstoy's artistry demanded a different approach than he had begun with, and the novel never reached 1825.

Many of Tolstoy's critics were puzzled by the nature of the work. It was certainly not a conventional novel, nor according to some was it accurate history. Tolstoy used historical events and characters such as Napoleon and General Kutuzov, but he transformed them according to his artistic and ideological intentions. He also invented scores of characters, and he wove a story around their interactions with historical events, personages and one another. And at times he interrupted the flow of the story to discourse on such topics as war and history.

Most of the characters were from the aristocracy, and Tolstoy's sympathies with old noble families such as his own come through clearly in the novel. Two of the chief figures, Pierre Bezukhov and Andrei Bolkonsky, reflected different aspects of Tolstoy's own personality. While in *The Cossacks* Tolstoy's hero had hoped to find the meaning of life among the spontaneous Cossacks, Pierre learned wisdom from the humble peasant Platon Karataev. The good people in his book were those who rose above individual egoism, found meaning in something larger than themselves, and were in harmony with nature. Despite their many differences, Tolstoy's central theme in *War and Peace* was similar to Dostoevsky's in *Crime and Punishment*: the necessity of overcoming egoism, of restoring unity, community and harmony.

For Tolstoy the orphan, family life was a central part of the harmony which he craved. In *War and Peace* two noble families figure prominently, the Rostovs and the Bolkonskys. By the end of the novel the once lively Natasha Rostov is married to Pierre and has four children. Tolstoy painted her as almost an ideal wife and mother, one devoted to her husband and children, and caring little for society or appearances, Tolstoy wrote:

> There were then as now conversations and discussions about women's rights, the relations of husband and wife and their freedom and rights … but these topics were not merely uninteresting to Natasha, she positively did not understand them.
>
> These questions, then as now, existed only for those who see nothing in marriage but the pleasure married people get from one another, that is, only the beginnings of marriage and not its whole significance, which lies in the family.[6]

Tolstoy's women in *War and Peace* led Turgenev, who was still estranged from Tolstoy, to ask a friend: "Why is it that all his good women are unfailingly not only females – but fools? And why does he try to convince the reader that if a woman is wise and cultured she is without exception a phrasemonger and a liar?"[7]

While Tolstoy was dogmatic about the proper role of women, he remained ambivalent about his attitude towards war. In 1863, in the midst of his troubled adjustment to marriage, he had expressed an interest in running off to help put down the Polish rebels. A few years later he wrote to his "granny" Alexandra, who that year would become the tutor to Alexander II's daughter Maria: "it's a matter of complete indifference to me who suppresses the Poles, or captures Schleswig-Holstein, or delivers a speech at a *zemstvo* meeting."[8]

When it came to history, *War and Peace* indicated that Tolstoy differed in many respects from the views of Professor Soloviev. Years before beginning the novel he had stated: "History is nothing but a collection of fables and useless trifles, cluttered up with a mass of unnecessary figures and proper names."[9] Later he read in the *Russian Messenger* Soloviev's "Historical Letters," in which the historian defended "progress" and urbanization. Like a number of European historians of his time, Soloviev believed that history was a story of gradual progress. Tolstoy, however, was much more suspicious of such developments. While engaged in running his school for peasant children, he wrote that while historians talked about a law of progress, they seemed to ignore all the non-Europeans who had not progressed according to the criteria of these historians. Further, Tolstoy accused historians of unclear thinking when they talked of progress. While he would equate progress with an overall improvement of well-being, they seemed to emphasize more the development of such phenomena as printing, railways and the telegraph, and to take it for granted that such developments arbitrarily contributed to an improvement in the overall well-being of the individual and nation.

But Tolstoy was convinced that "progress on one side is always paid back by retrogression on the other side of human life."[10] For him the growth of cities and newspapers, gas-lighting, railways and sewing machines were all either regressive developments or not worth the cost of destroying forests and peoples' sense of simplicity and moderation. He believed that the railways, for example, brought the peasant only what he did not need: an increase in the temptations of the city, the destruction of the forests, the carting away of laborers and an increase in the price of bread.

Between the views of Tolstoy and Soloviev there were many other differences. Whereas Soloviev strongly emphasized the role of governments in history, Tolstoy thought it should be the people who were stressed; while Soloviev thought history was a science and that the historian could discover historical laws, Tolstoy ridiculed the historians' claims to scientific validity and believed that the causes of any one historical event were so many that historians could never discover them all; while Soloviev had written of the tremendous changes in Russia brought about by Peter the Great, Tolstoy in *War and Peace* minimized the effect of so-called "great men" on history. And perhaps most importantly, whereas Soloviev tended to see life and society from an historical perspective, Tolstoy was more concerned with such eternal questions as "How should one live?" and "What is the good life?" Before, during and after writing *War and Peace*, it was the answer to such ahistorical questions that Tolstoy sought. In fact, this historical novel was really anti-historical in the sense that Tolstoy wished to show that the activities of the great historical figures were insignificant as compared to the daily life and aspirations of ordinary people such as Pierre and Natasha.

It was this view of life that also contributed to Tolstoy's relative indifference to many of the political debates of the sixties and to his unwillingness to side with liberals and radicals who claimed to be on the side of progress. Just as he thought that what happened to Pierre and Natasha was more important than the activities of Napoleon and Alexander I, so in the 1860s he was more concerned with his own search for meaning and truth than with the activities of Alexander II.

Despite Tolstoy's views on history – he even stated in 1862 that it would be harmful to have children study history prior to entering a university – he himself benefited from the ideas of several historians. One such was Professor Soloviev's old rival, M.P. Pogodin. While Tolstoy was working on *War and Peace*, he occasionally came to Moscow and received help and advice from the older Pogodin.

After finishing *War and Peace*, Tolstoy was prepared to continue his battle with historians such as Soloviev. Tolstoy now contemplated a novel set in the age of Peter the Great. He read Soloviev's volumes for background and came to the conclusion that the professor had greatly overemphasized the positive role of Peter and had neglected the people's life, those who "made the brocades, broadcloth, clothes and damask cloth which the tsars and nobles flaunted, who trapped the black foxes and sables that were given to ambassadors, who mined the gold and iron, who raised the horses, cattle and sheep, who constructed the houses, palaces and churches and who transported goods."[11] Whereas Soloviev criticized the Cossacks of the seventeenth century for what he considered their anti-government, anti-peasant, destructive activities, Tolstoy praised them.

Tolstoy believed that only an artist, like himself, could present historical life as it really was. Soloviev he thought dealt not with the real texture of history, but with governments and pseudo-scientific, abstract historical laws, such as the law of progress.

In his new novel, Tolstoy paradoxically hoped to teach historians how to recreate a true portrait of past life. He was not completely satisfied with his efforts in *War and Peace*, and he now hoped to better integrate the historical with the fictional, the public events with the private lives of his characters. He thought that in the novel he could also deal with such fundamental questions that still troubled him and his contemporaries as the attitude of noblemen to government sponsored changes and to the peasants. The significance of war and of foreign influences were other topics which he contemplated treating.

But this new effort of Tolstoy's occurred only in the early seventies. By this time Sonia had given birth to several additional children and important events had occurred to the Tsar and some of Tolstoy's former friends and acquaintances.

20

A SHOT IN PARIS

Late in the afternoon of Saturday, June 1, 1867, the Tsar and his entourage arrived at the Gare du Nord in Paris. He was met there by the French Emperor, Napoleon III, who was a smaller and older man than the Tsar and sported a goatee and a mustache with long waxed ends.

Their personalities were as different as their appearances. While Alexander cared little for ideas, Napoleon III was somewhat of an intellectual who had written a number of books. His two-volume *History of Caesar*, published just two years earlier, had been a sensation and led to a European-wide debate on the role and ethical rights of great historical figures, a subject, as we have seen, of interest in different ways to Dostoevsky, Professor Soloviev and Tolstoy. While Alexander was bred for autocracy and, following Karakozov's assassination attempt, was becoming more isolated from the Russian public, Louis Napoleon had to first be elected president and then later confirmed as Emperor and was an early master at manipulating public opinion. And while Alexander expressed only disdain for radicals, Napoleon III had once flirted with some of their ideas and still attempted to depict himself as a champion of social justice.

Now with a cavalry escort, the two monarchs rode together to the Emperor's Tuileries Palace. The French Emperor was tactful enough to avoid the route which would have taken them down the recently constructed Boulevard de Sebastopol.

The French ruler probably was hopeful that the Tsar would be in a forgiving mood, especially regarding Poland. Four years earlier, during the Polish revolt, Napoleon III had made requests and demands in behalf of the Polish rebels. He had joined with Great Britain and Austria to put pressure on Russia, and it had proved fruitless. It had only angered Russia and cooled the more cordial relationship that had been developing between Russia and France.

If Napoleon III wished to ignore the subject of Poland, some of his people did not. The cause of rebellious, Catholic Poland was one championed by many Frenchmen of both the Left and the Right. Some of the capital's newspapers reminded the public that the visiting Tsar was the oppressor of Poland. The many

Polish émigrés in Paris also served as a constant reminder. As the two sovereigns proceeded toward the Tuileries, some among the crowds shouted out the names of Poland, as well as that of the persecutor of Poles, Muraviev, who had died at the end of the previous summer. In the days which followed his entrance into the city, Alexander would more than once hear "Vive la Polonge." If any positive effect was produced by the news that the Tsar had just recently decreed a partial amnesty for Poles, it was not very evident in the capital.

After a brief reception at the Tuileries, the Tsar was escorted down the Rue de Rivoli and the Champs Elysées in the direction of the Arc de Triomphe. His final destination was the Elysée Palace, where his uncle Alexander I had once stayed after entering Paris in victory. The palace remained at Alexander II's disposal during his stay. That same evening the Tsar and two of his sons who had accompanied him to Paris had the opportunity to sample one of the pleasures of the city, Offenbach's operetta *La Grande Duchesse de Gerolstein*. More than ever, Paris was a city of pleasure and excitement, of crazes and courtesans, of glitter and luxury – at least it was for the well-off. Offenbach and his light, jaunty music reflected this spirit well. In the role of the Grand Duchess the captivating Hortense Schneider charmed her audiences.

Although some Russians found Offenbach's operettas decadent, neither the Tsar nor his sons were the type to be easily scandalized. Alexander, for example, was an appreciative admirer of the erotic drawings of his court artist Zichi. From all accounts, the royal party seemed to enjoy the performance.

The Tsar's mood was perhaps also affected by the realization that he was once again to spend some private moments with Catherine Dolgorukova. After the consummation of their love that July night in Peterhof, many other similar nights followed. The sexual satisfaction he experienced with Katia seemed to increase his love for her. He pledged his eternal love. When parted for a while, they wrote to each other, almost always in French. "I shall now live only in the hope of our meeting again,"[1] he wrote to her at the end of the previous August. In early October she wrote to him, her "adored angel,"[2] complaining of boredom without him and mentioning her yearning for him. Occasionally she was jealous of the attentions she thought he was paying to other women, but her fears were groundless. As their affair developed, gossip intensified, and to avoid inflaming it more, Katia left for a trip to sunny Naples. When the Tsar was invited to Paris he arranged for Katia to visit him there. Whereas he arrived at the Elysée Palace with all of the pomp of a great visiting ruler, she quietly checked into a nearby small hotel in the Rue Basse du Rempart.

In the days which followed they spent spare moments together riding horses in the picturesque Bois de Boulogne, where men could be seen riding in frock coats and top hats and the women sitting sidesaddle in their long, elegant, riding-habits. Or open carriages might speed by with liveried drivers and finely dressed women holding their parasols to protect them against the rays of the June sun. Gardens, foot and bridle paths, lakes and waterfalls, cafés and outdoor restaurants, hot-houses and a zoological garden, all of this and much more had made this newly transformed government property into one of the outdoor centers of fashionable Paris.

After riding together on the Wednesday after his arrival, he wrote to Katia a brief note saying how he loved the Bois de Boulogne and concluded by saying: "You have driven me completely insane. I am happy to love you, and belong to you forever."[3] When Alexander was free from his busy schedule, Katia also contributed to his delirium by entering through a secret garden gate into his private quarters at the Elysée Palace.

Meanwhile the Tsar had numerous official functions to attend: gala dinners, opera, the horse races at Longchamp in the Bois de Boulogne, a visit to St Cloud, one of the French Emperor's warm-weather retreats, trips to the Cluny Museum, Ste Chapelle and the tomb of Napoleon at the Invalides, which a decade earlier had disgusted Tolstoy. In the middle of the week some more distinguished visitors entered Paris by train. They were King William of Prussia and his tall, bald and wily Foreign Minister, Otto von Bismarck. Again Napoleon III was on hand to greet them. Alexander knew that they were coming, and in fact desired that his visit coincide with that of his uncle King William. The Tsar had always been friendly with the Prussian monarch, and Bismarck had been favorably treated when he had been the German ambassador in St Petersburg at the turn of the decade. When Napoleon III and others had tried to pressure Russia regarding Poland and when the danger of French military intervention was taken so seriously that the Russians called up reserve battalions, Prussia had given diplomatic support to Russia. Bismarck no more wished for an independent Poland than did the Tsar. Following the Polish crisis, Alexander provided limited but important support to his uncle as he strengthened the Prussian state, first in a war with Denmark and then, just the previous year, in one with Austria. Not many members of the Tsar's family supported his policy. The Tsarevich especially was anti-Prussian, even before his marriage to the vehemently anti-Prussian Danish Princess Dagmar. Many other members, including the Tsarina, had connections with smaller German territories which had either recently been annexed or feared being so in the future. Although concerned about such developments, Alexander was soon mollified by arguments that a strong conservative Prussia was in the interest of Russia. He was also influenced by suggestions that Prussia would support future Russian efforts to end the restrictive Black Sea clauses imposed at the end of the Crimean War.

Alexander supported a stronger Prussia because he feared that otherwise France, with her Polish sympathies, would dominate the continent. Napoleon

III had given other countries good reason to be wary of his ambitions. He had led France into war against the Russians in the Crimea, against the Austrians in Italy, while obtaining Savoy and Nice as his price for helping the Italians, and had maintained French forces in Rome to protect the Pope. Like several other European rulers, he was also adventuresome outside Europe. French troops had subjugated Algerian and Senegalese tribesmen and parts of Indochina; they had fought in China and been sent to protect Christians in Syria. Napoleon III's most disastrous adventure had been sending troops to Mexico and helping to install the Austrian Archduke Maximilian as Emperor of Mexico. French troops had only departed Mexico several months before the Tsar arrived in Paris, and while Alexander was still there rumors circulated that the now deposed Maximilian had been put to death. The rumors proved to be premature, but only by a few weeks.

Before arriving in Paris, the Tsar had stopped at Berlin and spent several days at his uncle's palace at Potsdam. There both monarchs talked about how they could maintain the peace in the light of French ambitions. Just a month or two before, there had been danger of a Franco-Prussian war over France's desire to take over Luxembourg. Although the immediate danger now seemed to have passed, thanks in part to Russian and English efforts at mediation, the Russian and German monarchs both still feared that France might have future territorial designs along her eastern border. One of Alexander's purposes for the trip to Paris was to convince the French Emperor of the necessity of peace in Europe.

Recent events in the Ottoman Turkish Empire provided another reason for the trip. Foreign Minister Gorchakov had become concerned with the Muslim Turks' treatment of Christians on the island of Crete and with rumors of a possible revolt by some of the Balkan Christians against the Muslim Turks. General Ignatiev, who had so successfully negotiated for the Russians at Peking, had just been upgraded from envoy to ambassador in Constantinople and had let the Turkish Sultan know that Russia expected the Turks to treat their Orthodox population in a decent fashion. For some months Gorchakov had been trying to get the French to go along with increasing the pressure on the Sultan and with demanding the cession of Crete to Greece. But he had little luck, perhaps because Russia offered little in return for French help. Gorchakov hoped to be more effective in Paris.

Once in Paris, however, neither the Tsar nor Gorchakov was offered much opportunity for serious discussions. Napoleon III seemed to think that he had little to gain from such talks. He had invited Alexander not for serious conversations but, along with a host of other royalty that year, primarily to witness the Paris Exposition. Napoleon III also wished to show off the wonders of his capital, which he took such pride in transforming and refurbishing.

On the Tuesday after his arrival Alexander took part in a military review at Longchamp in the Bois de Boulogne. Along with his uncle William of Prussia and Napoleon III, Alexander reviewed tens of thousands of colorful French troops. Amongst their aides, accompanying family members and some hundred thousand other spectators, the three sovereigns reviewed cavalry, infantry and artillery. It was a colorful show. Amidst the sun and the dust, eyes feasted on the blues, reds, greens, yellows and whites of uniforms and epaulets, on glittering breastplates and plumed hats, on lances and sabers, on rifles and bayonets, on staffs and flags, on campaign colors from the Crimea and Italy, from China and Mexico. And, of course, there were the military bands and the sounds of trumpets and drums.

In the last decade and a half the call to war had once again come frequently to Europe and the Americas. At Sevastopol and Solferino, at Shiloh and Sadowa, young men died in alarming numbers. Sometimes they gave their lives for national unity, sometimes for national or personal glory, sometimes for racial or economic reasons, and sometimes, as Herzen and Tolstoy suggested about war in general, for irresponsible or power-hungry rulers and because the masses felt helpless to prevent war. Although many did not yet perceive the full implications of recent developments in industry, in communication and transportation, in the invention of new guns and explosives, and in a changing intellectual climate that glorified science, technology and various applications of Darwin's ideas, nevertheless the future offered little promise for a reduction in bloodshed. France and Prussia especially seemed headed for an eventual collision. Therefore, Bismarck and General von Moltke, who accompanied their monarch to the review, certainly had more than a passing interest in the state of French military preparedness.

Although no major war clouds appeared on Russia's horizon, Russian troops were conquering new parts of Central Asia, and Alexander continued to improve his army. Alexander's able War Minister, Dmitry Milyutin, believed that Russia had become a major European power thanks to its military might, and to retain its status Russia would have to remain abreast of the other powers as they modernized their armaments and techniques. But the cost of such competition was steep indeed for a Russia that was much poorer and less modern than other major European countries. Russia's military expenditures in recent years had consumed about a third of all government spending, and yet the Russian army was still backward in many ways.

When the review was over, by which time a few drops of rain had fallen, the Tsar left in an open carriage with his two sons and Napoleon III. He had not gotten very far in the Bois de Boulogne when at the crossroads near the rocks of the Grand Cascade, the carriage slowed down due to the crowds. A young Pole named Berezowski stepped forward in the crowd with a double-barreled pistol in his hand and aimed at the Tsar. Before he could fire, one of Napoleon's men riding near the side of the carriage, moved his horse between the pistol and the carriage. The bullet went through the nostril of the horse and missed the Tsar. Only the horse's blood sprayed into the carriage. According to reports, Napoleon said: "Sire, we have been under fire together," and the Tsar replied: "Our destinies are in the hands of Providence."[4] The only fatality was the horse; it died that evening.

As a teenager Berezowski had taken part in the Polish revolt four years earlier and then came to Paris to escape the Russian authorities. He had never forgiven Alexander for crushing the Poles. After his first shot at the Tsar, he tried again, but the pistol burst in his hands. Some of the men among the crowd hit him with their canes and wanted to kill him. He was arrested and grilled by the French police and by Shuvalov, the head of the Tsar's secret police who had accompanied him to Paris. Berezowski refused to express remorse for his action and spent the next four decades on an island penal colony.

Although some of the Tsar's advisers recommended that he leave Paris, he decided to continue his visit. However, he rearranged his schedule. The next day he attended a Thanksgiving service at the Russian Orthodox Church on the Rue Daru. He had just been there the morning before to celebrate the Orthodox Ascension Thursday. While William of Prussia arrived in a closed carriage, Alexander still utilized an open one. Later that day the Tsar, along with the French Emperor, drove to the Paris Exposition, where they were surrounded by a great crowd and warmly cheered.

The exhibition was another of the type that Dostoevsky had been critical of in London five years before. They had become increasingly popular since the first Great Exhibition in London in 1851, and Paris had hosted its first one in 1855. This second French international exhibit was more ambitious and grandiose, more in keeping with Napoleon III's sense of imperial grandeur and the Parisians' love of the new, the exotic, the pleasurable. As in the other exhibits, the latest machines and products from around the world had a central place in the glass and iron Palace of Industry and in national pavilions constructed on the Champ de Mars. Some fifty thousand firms from around the world exhibited their wares. Military equipment was also on display, including a fifty-eight-ton Krupp gun sent by Prussia. The millions of fair-goers that year, including the American writer Mark Twain, who would later that summer meet the Tsar in Yalta, could sample food and drink from Tunisia, Persia, China, Russia and a host of other countries in cafes, restaurants and kiosks.

The Goncourt brothers, French writers and acquaintances of Turgenev and Herzen, wrote that the exposition was "the final blow levelled at the past, the Americanization of France, industry lording it over art, the steam thresher displacing the painting – in brief, the Federation of Matter."[5] At about this same time Herzen wrote that an International Exhibition was a "fashionable mus-tard-plaster"[6] that people utilized in their quest for external distractions, to keep busy, to avoid serious thinking. He predicted that when people grew sick of exhibitions, they would take to war and be diverted by heaps of corpses, any-thing to avoid being reminded of the "emptiness and senselessness of their lives."[7]

As Alexander viewed some of the latest civilian and military marvels of Western technology, one wonders if he was tempted to despair: How was his poor Russia ever to catch up with the more modernized Western Europe, where economic growth and industrialization continued to speed ahead?

Alexander did not leave Paris until the following Tuesday. Napoleon III and the French people tried to make amends for the attempted assassination. Both privately and publicly, individuals and groups, including Polish imigris in Paris, expressed their outrage at the attempt. There were gala balls and dinners at the Tuileries. Baron Haussmann, the architect of the new Paris and its wide boule-vards, hosted a ball at the Hotel de Ville, and another was held at the Russian Embassy. The Tsar also visited Versailles and Fontainebleau, and when time al-lowed he continued seeing Katia.

However, except for his moments with Katia, the trip was not a success. After the assassination attempt a certain tenseness prevailed, and neither the Tsar nor Gorchakov was able to obtain either of their diplomatic goals: a French prom-ise to keep the peace with Germany or French assistance in pressuring the Turkish Sultan. In the days ahead, the Tsar would think more than ever before that Prussia was Russia's only real European friend, and within a few years Alexander's sympathies would indirectly assist Prussia in the completion of its unification of Germany. Only after two wars in the next century would the full consequences of the Tsar's benevolent attitude toward Prussia become clear.

21

TURGENEV AND DOSTOEVSKY IN BADEN-BADEN

After leaving Paris, Alexander II stopped off in Baden-Baden, a lovely German resort town. One of the little city's most prominent residents, Ivan Turgenev, joined other Russians in going to the train station to welcome the Tsar. The author wrote to a friend telling him that Alexander seemed thinner and suggested that the loss of weight was connected with the vile act of the would-be assassin in Paris.

About a month later another Russian visitor came to Baden-Baden, and one hot stifling day at about noon, he walked up to a pleasant but modest two-story house, sitting in a courtyard, a stone's throw away from the little Oos River. The visitor was Dostoevsky, and the man who lodged in the top story of this house on Schillerstrasse was Turgenev, who was at that moment having lunch.

Turgenev had been residing here, no more than a ten-minute walk up a slight hill to the Viardot villa, ever since following Pauline Viardot and her family to Baden-Baden four years earlier. The Viardot house, along with its separate concert hall and theater buildings, was one of the social centers of this internationally famous resort and spa. Royalty and distinguished men and women of the arts frequently visited the Viardots, and Turgenev himself had already arranged to have his own villa constructed on property which he had bought next to that of Pauline.

He was now reconciled to his role of being no more than a good friend to Pauline and the Viardot family. Indeed Louis Viardot and the four Viardot children were all dear to him. After Pauline, his favorite was Claudie or Didie, who in 1867 turned fifteen. Turgenev spent many hours at the Viardots, and he encouraged and often worked with Pauline in the composing of songs. Although his taste in music was not always the same as that of Pauline – she, for example, loved Wagner much more than he did – he nevertheless was very fond of music.

When he had first moved to Baden-Baden, he had brought his illegitimate daughter Paulinette with him, but she did not get along with Pauline and soon returned to Paris. A short time afterwards she married, and Turgenev provided a substantial dowry. Despite his great landholdings in Russia, which remained substantial even after the loss of some land in the emancipation settlement, Turgenev was troubled by financial concerns. His uncle who managed his estates for him was both incompetent and dishonest. Turgenev himself made only occasional visits to Russia and even then did not always visit his Spasskoe estate.

One of his trips to Russia, in the beginning of 1864, was in answer to a summons to appear at a Russian Senate hearing. The Russian Senate had no legislative powers but acted as part of the Tsar's bureaucracy; it was the highest court of appeal and conducted some investigations. It wanted to know from Turgenev what his connections were with some of the radical exiles. In an earlier letter to the Tsar, Turgenev had apparently persuaded his sovereign to allow him to answer the Senate's questions by mail, but after receiving his answers the Senate still wished to question him further. His two visits to the Senate in January added little to his written testimony, in which he had played down his closeness to any of the exiles. Indeed, he had not been close to Bakunin for decades and was not as friendly with Herzen as he had once been. The Senate apparently believed him, and took no action against him.

In *The Bell*, however, Herzen soon alluded to Turgenev's denials. He wrote that a correspondent had reported about a "grey-haired Magdalen (of the male sex) who wrote to the Emperor that she had lost sleep and appetite, her rest, her white hairs and her teeth"[1] because the Emperor did not know of her repentance. Turgenev protested to Herzen at the injustice of the attack, sent him a copy of his letter to the Tsar, and wrote of his increased gratitude to Alexander II for treating him as an honest man. Herzen countered by also finding fault with Turgenev for pledging money to help Russian soldiers who had been wounded putting down the Poles. The charge was true, but reflected more Turgenev's sympathy for the wounded than any type of strong nationalistic impulse. Nevertheless, the two men ceased communicating for a few years until Turgenev cautiously resumed their correspondence several months before Dostoevsky's visit.

Until he began writing a new novel called *Smoke* at the end of 1865, Turgenev's creative energies seemed to have waned. He had written only a few short stories in the previous three years, and none of them had generated much enthusiasm. They reflected his basic pessimistic outlook and his fear of aging and death. His comment to a friend that he was making a little nest for himself in Baden-Baden where he could "await the coming of the inevitable end"[2] was typical of his disposition. Ironically, his physical condition was fairly good in these years.

For Turgenev his relationship with Pauline and her family was bittersweet, bitter because of the absence of romantic love and sweet because the presence of the Viardots was more satisfying to him than their absence. At times while playing games or listening to music in the bosom of the family, he could seem genuinely happy. For some deep reasons, which he himself probably did not fathom, his unusual relationship with Pauline and his closeness to her family were necessary to him.

Although his recent short stories had not created much excitement, *Smoke* did. Even before it appeared in *The Russian Messenger* in April 1867, the journal's conservative editor had been upset. Katkov thought that this story, set primarily in Baden-Baden, depicted visiting Russian officers and conservative landowners too critically. He also disliked the immoral behavior of the novel's self-willed heroine, Irena. In addition, Katkov feared that she bore too much of a resemblance to Alexandra Dolgorukaya, once the Tsar's rumored favorite. The fact that Irena's husband, General Ratmirov, resembled Dolgorukaya's husband, General Albedinsky, did not help matters. Katkov wanted Turgenev to alter Irena so that her prototype would not be so obvious. Turgenev made some, but not all, of the alterations requested by Katkov, but then restored the novel more to its original form when it was published as a separate volume the following year.

Once published, more criticism was showered upon him, for in the novel he satirized both radicals and conservatives. While the former criticized him for his unflattering depiction of radicals, including one called Gubarev, who bore some resemblance to Ogarev; the latter group did not care for the westernizing anti-Slavophile views of the character Potugin. Like his creator, he expressed the belief that only by learning from the West, only by utilizing and applying its positive tendencies, could Russia hope to become a truly civilized nation. One Russian who could not agree with such a viewpoint was Dostoevsky. He thought that Russia with her Orthodox Church and peasant population was already better off than the decadent West. Too much emphasis on Western ideas only led to the actions of Karakozov or to those of Dostoevsky's fictional Raskolnikov.

On this stifling Wednesday in Baden-Baden Dostoevsky was calling on Turgenev because he thought he should. He owed him money, borrowed to pay gambling debts, and did not wish to seem hesitant to visit Turgenev. Although both writers had admired some of each other's earlier writings, they had been more critical of each other's recent efforts. Whereas Turgenev's prose was more lyrical, nostalgic and laconic, Dostoevsky's was more intense and frenzied, more psychologically probing and dramatic. Even though Dostoevsky had told Turgenev of his enthusiasm for his story "Phantoms" and requested it for his journal *The Epoch*, he privately found it sickly, senile and lacking in faith. Turgenev thought the last parts of *Crime and Punishment* seemed like a "prolonged colic."[3] As Dostoevsky's anti-Western, Slavophile sympathies became increasingly pronounced, the ideological gap between Turgenev and himself increased accordingly. On a personal basis, they had never been very close, even in the late forties when Dostoevsky had briefly been awed by the more established Turgenev.

Upon meeting that noon, the large gray-haired and bearded Turgenev apparently bent over and embraced Dostoevsky with his auburn beard and pale complexion. The latter reported that he did not like the "aristocratic" way that Turgenev embraced one and then offered his cheek to be kissed.[4] Since embracing and kissing on both cheeks was a typical Russian practice, it must have been the manner and not the act itself which upset Dostoevsky.

The conversation which followed was unpleasant. Dostoevsky's version of their meeting was that Turgenev was in a bad mood and bitter about the critical reviews *Smoke* had received. He stated that he was an atheist, and Dostoevsky spoke sharply and satirically to him, advising him that since he had exiled himself he should obtain a telescope if he wished to see what was going on in Russia. When Dostoevsky complained of the Germans, Turgenev took offense saying he now considered himself a German, not a Russian, and that if Russia disappeared the world would not miss it and that any attempt to create a Russian culture separate from the West would be folly. Although upset by Turgenev's perceived aristocratic airs, vanity and traitorous views, after about an hour and a half Dostoevsky politely said goodbye.

Turgenev's account of their meeting was somewhat different. According to him, Dostoevsky condemned *Smoke*, Turgenev and the Germans, but Turgenev chose not to argue with him. He considered Dostoevsky a sick, deranged person. Besides, Dostoevsky left him little time for reply and left after no more than an hour.

After leaving Turgenev, Dostoevsky headed for the gambling tables, no more than a ten minute walk from Turgenev's. He was probably in no mood to observe the beauty along the way. But Baden-Baden had its charms. It was set in a cozy valley not far from the Rhine. Way up on a distant hill, surrounded by greenery, could be seen the ruins of the "old castle." Below it and off to one side was the "new castle" where the Margraves of Baden-Baden had once resided. Well-kept lawns and paths were shadowed over by poplars, chestnuts, pines and other magnificent trees. The Oos River ran pleasantly through the town. Royalty or finely dressed ladies and gentlemen from Berlin, Paris, St Petersburg, or scores of other cities and landed estates came here to drink or bathe in the medicinal waters of this famous German spa. Others came to gamble or, like some of the French prostitutes, to make money from the wealthy of Europe. The gambling tables were in several opulent, ornate and gilded rooms of the Conversation House, a long building with a frescoed corinthian colonnade. The previous night the Dostoevskys had listened with great enjoyment to the band in its garden play Rossini's *Stabat Mater*. At other times a military band played lighter, more lively songs or marches. Inside the Conversation House, as well as in its garden, food and drink were served, or one could read in its library. But Dostoevsky's passion was for the hall with the large roulette table and six croupiers.

While in Dresden earlier that spring, he had left Anna for over a week while he had taken a train to Bad Homburg in order to play roulette. He had lost the money he had taken with him, twice wrote Anna for more, and pawned his watch. Since arriving in Baden-Baden the previous week, he had often placed his francs or thalers on red or black, odd or even. He was not like the wealthy, finely dressed men and women who sat or stood around the table and who could afford to lose. Rather he was one of the intense, desperate gamblers who was willing to risk all of the little he had left on the little spinning ball. As the days passed, so did the couple's resources. On the day before his visit to Turgenev, he had pawned his wedding ring and lost what he received for it. Only after Anna had provided him with more money was he able to redeem it.

On this hot Wednesday afternoon he had five gold pieces in his pocket. Back at their two small rented rooms Anna had only ten more. She had gone to the post office and then returned and started to read a volume of Soloviev's history, only to be interrupted by the German maid, who wished to clean their rooms. Anna was already pregnant and was not feeling well. Finally, Dostoevsky returned in a bad mood, announced that he had lost his five gold pieces, and blamed it on his inability to concentrate due to the jostling and bustling around him at the table. He asked for five more gold pieces, which she gave him, and hurried back to the casino. She lay down on the couch and thought.

Perhaps she recalled some of their moments together in these last few months of European wanderings: how they had left Russia to get away from his relatives and creditors, gone to Berlin, and then to Dresden; the hours together in the art gallery of Dresden, where he pointed out to her some of his favorite paintings – Raphael's "Sistine Madonna," Titian's "Christ with the Tribute Money" and Claude Lorrain's "Acis and Galatea," a portrait of idyllic beauty, of sun, sea and woods, of joy and innocence; the times spent at the "Italian Village" restaurant, whose windows looked out on the Elbe, or just strolling or sitting at another restaurant in the large park where concerts played that spring in Dresden; and, of course, the loving and sexual moments spent together which, despite many of her husband's fetishes, she seems to have accepted and to some extent even welcomed from the beginning. But there had been painful times also: those lonely days when he had gone off to Bad Homburg; the almost constant worry over money; the fright of a false rumor that the Tsar, whom they both loved, had been killed in Paris; the epileptic attacks of her husband; picking up a letter Polina Suslova had written Fedya, as Anna called him, and wondering if he might leave her for Polina; listening to his frequent complaints about waiters, clerks, attendants and Europeans in general, or to his criticisms of her or the way she acted or dressed. But whenever he offended her, he was usually soon sorry and asked her forgiveness. And she in turn, a combination of loving wife, mother and child to him, was more than willing to quickly patch up any quarrel.

When Dostoevsky returned to her later that Wednesday afternoon, he announced he had won forty-six gold pieces at the casino. He then went out to get coffee, candles and wine and also bought a basket of fruit and a bouquet of flowers for Anna.

For the next six weeks their days centered around his gambling. Although he won and they celebrated on occasion, more frequently he lost, and Anna usually tried to console him. They pawned, redeemed and at times repawned almost everything they possessed, including her wedding ring and earrings and a brooch he had given her. She was reduced to wearing one drab black dress when they went out, and was therefore reluctant to be seen in the casino or in many of the other areas where more fashionable women appeared or promenaded. He was often irritable. The blacksmiths that worked beneath their rooms bothered him, as did their landlady's children, various people around the roulette table, and an assortment of others of varying occupations and nationalities, including Poles and Jews, for neither of whom he much cared. He had several epileptic fits, and the couple quarreled on occasion. But he was usually grateful to her for being so understanding of his defects, especially his gambling fever. Finally in late August, after receiving some money from her mother and after he even lost some of that, they boarded an afternoon train headed for Geneva.

22
THE DOSTOEVSKYS IN GENEVA

A few weeks after arriving in Geneva, the Dostoevskys attended a session of the Congress of the League of Peace and Freedom, which had been called together amidst the fears of a possible Franco-Prussian war. What a contrast it offered to the military review presented by Napoleon III to Alexander II and William of Prussia at Longchamp just a few months earlier! Instead of monarchs reviewing troops, its leading luminaries were revolutionaries condemning militarism and war.

The most famous of them was Garibaldi, the romantic fighter for Italian independence and unity and a symbol of hope for oppressed nationalities throughout Europe and even beyond. On the day on which he entered Geneva, the Dostoevskys were among the large crowd that waited along the wide and straight Rue du Mont Blanc, down which Garibaldi was scheduled to ride en route to his hotel near the northern side of the Mont Blanc Bridge. Flags and bunting decorated some of the hotels and other buildings along the street. Finally, a cannon shot was heard and the whistle of the locomotive. After some time Garibaldi appeared amidst a large procession of guilds, societies and organizations that had marched to meet him and accompany him to his hotel. The groups had their colorful flags and banners, and some bands played. The sun had already begun to set over Lake Geneva.

Garibaldi rode in an open carriage drawn by four magnificent horses. Both of the Dostoevskys, who were in separate places among the crowd, thought that he had a kindly, sympathetic face. The sixty-year-old revolutionary dressed in his own unique style: red shirt, blue pants and striped poncho. In response to the cheering crowd, he stood in the carriage bowing or waving his hat from one side to the other.

The next day at the Electoral Palace on the Place Neuve, Garibaldi addressed the Peace Congress. He called on all peoples to overthrow despotism and establish democracy and stated that only democracy could end war. The most harmful of sects he declared was the Papacy, which still prevented a completely united Italy. In the future he hoped that democratic nations would elect delegates to the Congress and that it would end war by acting as an arbitrator of all quarrels.

The following day, Tuesday, a huge, bearded man addressed the thousands of listeners. The previous day when this carelessly dressed giant walked up the steps to take his place on the platform among the executive committee of the Congress, Garibaldi had embraced him. He was one of the two Russian representatives on the committee. He was the legendary Michael Bakunin.

Since leaving London more than four years earlier and after being unable to reach Poland, Bakunin had spent some months in Stockholm, where his wife, Antonia, had finally rejoined him. Then they had gone to Italy, where with his acquiescence and in keeping with the revolutionary principles which he espoused, Antonia took as a lover one of her husband's Italian friends. In 1866 he outlined the following as one of his revolutionary goals:

> Religious and civil marriage to be replaced by *free* marriage. Adult men and women have the right to unite and separate as they please … With the abolition of the right of inheritance and the education of children assured by society, all the legal reasons for the irrevocability of marriage will disappear … In marriage, man and woman must enjoy absolute liberty.[1]

On this second day of the Peace Congress, Bakunin spoke rapidly in French without notes. He told his listeners that peace could only come after the destruction of large centralized states, for they fostered nationalism and militarism. Upon their ashes a system of free federated communes could then be established. The communes could form themselves into provinces, the provinces into nations and the nations into a loosely federated United States of Europe. His speech was warmly applauded.

On the same day that Bakunin was delivering his speech, Dostoevsky ran into Nicholas Ogarev, who was now living in a suburb of Geneva with his mistress Mary Sutherland. Several months earlier Ogarev had agreed with Herzen's idea to suspend *The Bell* for six months, and Herzen had left to join Natalia Ogareva and their daughter Liza in Nice. Herzen had been encouraged to take part in the Congress by its organizers, but decided to remain in Nice. Among other reasons, he believed that those at the Congress would be too hostile towards not only the Russian government, but the very nation itself. He also still believed that the socialist potential of the Russian people was greater than that of the masses in the West. Ogarev, however, did take part in the Congress, and along with Bakunin was elected as one of the two Russian representatives on the executive committee. Ogarev encouraged Dostoevsky to attend the Congress.

The next day Dostoevsky and Anna set out for the Electoral Palace. Their apartment at this time consisted of several rented rooms on the second floor of a corner, five-storied building not far from the Rue du Mont Blanc. From one of its windows they could see the Island of Jean-Jacques Rousseau. To the left of the island there was the lake and to the right the swift blue waters of the Rhone, which flowed from it. To get to the Congress, they had to cross one of the bridges spanning the Rhone and then head up along the western edge of the oldest part of Geneva.

The inside of the large Electoral Palace was decorated with flags and coats of arms of the Swiss Cantons. Since there was a separate place for women to sit, the Dostoevskys separated. He thought the speeches that day were incredibly stupid. He was especially upset by those who wanted to bring about peace by destroying the Christian faith and the governments of the Great Powers. He decried the "rabble" that wished to stir up the working class, abolish capital and declare all property in common. Anna also did not care for the speeches. Later the couple quarreled, and Dostoevsky attributed it to their attending the Peace Congress, where delegates argued and revolutionaries talked more of war on churches and governments than they did of peace. Whatever the cause or causes of the couple's fight, Anna cried. All in all it was not a very pleasant day, especially considering that it was her twenty-first birthday.

Dostoevsky's view of the Congress was hardly an objective, dispassionate one, but others were also critical. Some of the delegates and observers, like many Genevans, were Catholic and were upset by the attack on the Papacy by Garibaldi, who had already left town and before the year was out would lead his troops against those of the Pope. Others at the Congress were upset at the socialistic and anarchistic tone of the speeches.

One who was much more pleased with the Congress was Bakunin. During the year that followed, he worked hard as a member of the central committee of the League to bring it over to his views. He enunciated these in a piece he wrote at that time entitled *Federalism, Socialism and Anti-Theologism*. He and Antonia settled on the other side of Lake Geneva, first at Vevey and then at Clarens, where Tolstoy had stayed a decade before. In both places, the Bakunins benefited from at least one wealthy Russian benefactress. From time to time he travelled to Berne for meetings of the Leagues' central committee.

He also joined Karl Marx's International Worker's Association; and he tried unsuccessfully to challenge Marx's leadership in it by suggesting that the International ally itself with the League. But at the second Congress of the League in September he himself, along with some of his followers, including Antonia's Italian lover, resigned from the League. The majority of the Congress had not accepted Bakunin's radical views, and he concluded that it was useless to belong to any organization that would not accept the abolition of classes and the economic and social equality of mankind.

The Dostoevskys remained in Geneva about nine more months, but they seem to have seldom come across Bakunin. Ogarev, on the other hand, despite his radical political views, was a welcome visitor. He sometimes brought them books or newspapers, and he took a special liking to the pregnant Anna and treated her with fatherly warmth. He lent them money on occasion and gave them advice on a variety of practical matters, including which doctor to visit.

Outside of Ogarev, the Dostoevskys had no real friends in Geneva. They liked their spinster landladies, but not Genevans in general. In his letters to friends in Russia Dostoevsky complained of the self-satisfied and proud nature of the inhabitants of the city, but also of the town drunks. Herzen also had not cared for the citizens of Geneva. He found them too cold, too full of the spirit of Calvin, too occupied with saving their souls or money, too bourgeois. He lamented Geneva's churches without adornment, its democracy without equality, its women without beauty and its beer without taste. Both men no doubt exaggerated and suffered from a homesickness for the more expansive, emotional Russian way of life.

Dostoevsky also complained of the weather and the *bises*, or cold winds, that blew down from the mountains. Used to the warmer apartments of Russia, their rooms seemed frightfully cold that autumn. In mid December they moved to a warmer apartment on the Rue du Mont Blanc, next to the English Church.

Despite finding Geneva boring, gloomy, ugly and depressing, Dostoevsky had chosen it partly because of Anna's condition. It seemed a safe place, free from any threat of war, and one where his French would suffice to communicate, especially in any emergency necessitated by Anna's pregnancy. He also eventually found the city conducive for writing. But it took him a little while before he could produce anything he considered of value. In late October he was still complaining of frequent epileptic attacks which left him unable to work well for days afterwards. By early January, however, the attacks had become less frequent, and he had completed and sent off to his publisher, Katkov, the first part of a new novel, *The Idiot*. In the book he hoped to portray a "positively first rate man,"[2] a humble Christ-like figure, but one that some of the other characters in the novel would consider a fool. This was his Prince Myshkin, the "idiot" of the title.

Despite Dostoevsky's fascination with moments of intensity and with unusual, bizarre behavior, he generally appreciated and needed for his writing a regular, ordered routine. Anna, with her steady, dependable personality, proved to be a great help in this regard. He wrote late into the night, awoke late in the morning, had breakfast with Anna and then worked again until later in the afternoon when they had dinner. After eating he often went by himself to a cafe to have coffee and read the newspapers, including several from Russia. He was especially interested in Russian news relating to the new jury system and to the progress of the railways, both developments which he strongly supported. In the evenings they sometimes looked in the expensive shops of the city, and he pointed out what he would buy her if he were wealthy. Unfortunately, however, the opposite was the case, and many a day they went to the post office hoping for money from Russia. At night in their apartment, he would light a fire, they would drink coffee, and he would dictate *The Idiot* to her, or they might read, especially French authors. Hugo, Balzac and George Sand were some of his favorites, and he guided Anna's reading.

Their baby was due in late February, and both of them looked forward to the event with great anticipation. He longed to be a father and to experience what he hoped would be the warmth of family life. Anna made clothes for the baby; and after he finished reading the newspapers, he would walk up through the old part of town, located across the Rhone, to the street of the midwife that was to help Anna. He wanted to be sure that he could find the house when the time came for his wife to have the baby. To get there he would have to climb a steep hill, and this seemed to have exacerbated his asthma, which just recently had begun to trouble him. The fact that he was a heavy smoker also no doubt contributed to his problem.

In early March, on a rainy, windy night, Anna began to experience labor pains, but Dostoevsky was sleeping and was still recovering from an epileptic attack. He was in no condition to go for the midwife. Anna felt helpless and alone. She prayed. The trees outside rustled violently. By morning Dostoevsky was well enough to go out, but her labor was to be a long one, thirty-three hours. Dostoevsky managed to see that the midwife and nurse were available during the crucial final hours. At about five in the morning of March 5th, a girl was born. They named her Sophia, but used the more common nickname, Sonia, after both the heroine of *Crime and Punishment* and Dostoevsky's favorite niece, the daughter of his sister Vera. The midwife said she had never seen such a distressed and agitated expectant father. But once Anna's ordeal was over, he doted on his new baby daughter, rocking and singing to her, and helping Anna bathe her.

About two weeks before the birth of little Sonia, Nicholas Ogarev had an epileptic attack while out one night and fell into a ditch and broke his leg. Herzen returned to Geneva from Nice for a few months to be with his friend. Ogarev still lived with Mary Sutherland in the nearby suburb of Lancy. In January, Herzen had resumed publication of *The Bell*, but few people any longer seemed to care.

On the second of April, Dostoevsky wrote to a friend that he had run into Herzen on the street and that they had talked and bantered for ten minutes in a "hostile but polite tone."[3] Since Dostoevsky had visited Herzen in London six years before, they had met only once more, in the year following the London visit. It was on a steamboat from Naples to Genoa. Dostoevsky was with

Appolinaria Suslova and Herzen with several of his children. Appolinaria already knew some of the younger Herzens. The next night Dostoevsky and Appolinaria dined with the Herzens in Genoa.

In the years since that meeting Dostoevsky's ideas had become increasingly hostile to views such as those of Herzen. While they both valued the Russian peasant and were critical in many ways of Western societies, Dostoevsky had become more nationalistic than ever. He wrote to his friends about the superiority of Russian Orthodoxy and of the necessity for bringing about Russia's supremacy over the entire Slavic world and about the military-political necessity of Russia's developing railways and new guns. And he praised the greatness of Alexander II – "he has done almost more for Russia than all of his predecessors put together"[4] – and stressed the absolute importance of the love that the Russian people had for him.

Thus, it was not surprising that he could no longer talk to Herzen without feeling hostile to this man who was a critic of autocracy, of a strong centralized Russian government, of Russian Orthodoxy and Russian militarism. What was unusual was that Dostoevsky felt some affection for Ogarev, whose views were even more radical than those of Herzen. But then the epileptic and alcoholic Ogarev – that "gentle, kind, affectionate old bear," as Natalia Herzen described him[5]- was someone to whom it was hard not to feel kindly. The wealthier, more aristocratic-mannered, more cynical Herzen, was easier for Dostoevsky to dislike.

During May the Dostoevskys often crossed the bridge to walk in the Jardin des Anglais, a pleasant public garden on the southern shore of the lake. Little Sonia was in her carriage and the weather was usually beautiful. Despite their continuing financial worries, homesickness, and the problems he was having completing *The Idiot*, they were happy on these fine days to have such a wonderful baby. Anna was also especially happy because her mother came from Russia that month for Sonia's christening.

One day during the family's stroll in the Jardin des Anglais, the winds suddenly sprang up and Sonia apparently got chilled. That evening she started coughing and her temperature shot up. Her parents hastened to find a doctor. He visited Sonia every day for almost a week, and assured her anxious parents that she was getting better. But she did not. On May 24th, 1868 she died. Dostoevsky wept uncontrollably and covered the dead Sonia's face and hands with kisses. A few days later after a church service in a small, recently built Russian Orthodox church, they buried her at the Plainpalais cemetery dressed in her little white dress. After a few weeks, in which they took flowers to her grave and cried, they could bear Geneva no longer. They left for Vevey on the other side of Lake Geneva.

23

NECHAEV, BAKUNIN AND THE
LAST DAYS OF HERZEN

Some nine months after the Dostoevskys' departure from Geneva, a twenty-one-year-old Russian radical named Sergei Nechaev arrived in the city. He was of medium height and weight and possessed an abundance of nervous energy. To some his compressed lips and the look in his dark eyes hinted at the sinister nature of the man. Unlike Ogarev and Bakunin, both of whom he would soon meet, he was not from the noble class. His father worked as both a waiter and a painter of signs in and around Ivanovo, a small Russian textile town. Already hostile to the local nobility, he left his hometown in 1865 and went to Moscow. There he briefly worked as a copyist for the historian Pogodin before moving on to the capital, where he obtained a teaching position.

For almost three years St Petersburg was his home. He witnessed the reaction symbolized by Muraviev's investigating commission and the appointment of several new men to key posts. One of these was the new Minister of Education, Dmitry Tolstoy, who in the year following his appointment issued new rules further restricting students' rights. Partly in reaction to these further restrictions, students, who had quieted down a bit during the middle of the decade, once again became more active in 1868 and 1869. The number of illegal circles and meetings increased significantly, and Nechaev, who enrolled as an auditing student at St Petersburg University, became active in the midst of them.

By this time his resentment towards Russia's privileged class and his thirst for knowledge, along with the radical influences of the capital, had helped lead him to revolutionary ideas. Through his reading and personal contacts he became familiar with revolutionary literature and with the Russian revolutionary tradition of the Decembrists, the Petrashevsky Circle, Herzen, Ogarev, Bakunin, Chernyshevsky, Dobrolyubov and Karakozov. Despite Herzen's disapproval of Karakozov's attempted assassination, the writer and editor had contributed to his enshrinement in the pantheon of revolutionary martyrs by printing several stories of his heroism while in prison. Nechaev read these articles in *The Bell*. And it was to the more conspiratorial and violent type of revolutionary activity that Nechaev was especially attracted. He wanted to be a man of action, not just talk.

In early 1869, after becoming aware that the police knew of some of his radical activities, which included circulating a petition, Nechaev decided to leave Russia temporarily. However, before illegally leaving the country, he expended considerable effort to leave his radical acquaintances with the impression he had been arrested.

At the end of March, Ogarev opened a letter requesting that Herzen print a message to Russian students from someone who had just escaped from the Peter and Paul Fortress. The message called upon the students, allied with other radical forces, to engage in a continual struggle against the forces of reaction. It promised that whatever the sacrifice, eventually they would have their vengeance. The letter was from Nechaev, who soon afterwards arrived in Geneva himself and repeated to Ogarev and Bakunin the lie that he had been incarcerated in the Peter and Paul Fortress.

By the time Nechaev arrived in Geneva, Ogarev and Mary Sutherland had moved out of Lancy to a small house and garden on the Rue des Petits Philosophes in Geneva. From there Ogarev had written to Herzen on 28th March: "All is white. The snow falls as in Russia. Lovely."[1] The mountains, roofs, trees and streets were all covered with snow. In addition to his epilepsy and alcoholism, Ogarev still had a bad leg, although by now he could get around with a cane. Despite his infirmities, however, he still maintained youthful revolutionary hopes. After meeting Nechaev, Ogarev took up his cause. So did Bakunin, who along with Antonia had moved back to a Geneva apartment not far from the railway station. Nechaev told both of the old radicals that he was a representative of a significant Russian revolutionary committee, and he gave them an overly optimistic picture of Russia's readiness for revolution. Soon the three of them were working together sending revolutionary proclamations to various addresses in Russia. Ogarev even printed a poem about a young revolutionary and dedicated it to his "young friend Nechaev."[2] The poem was distributed widely in Russia and contributed to Nechaev's reputation in revolutionary circles.

Bakunin was even more enthusiastic about Nechaev than was Ogarev. During the previous half year, following his resignation from the League of Peace and Freedom, Bakunin had formed a new rather amorphous organization of his own, the International Social Democratic Alliance. In the beginning it appears not to have possessed more than about a hundred members. He had also become more active among Swiss members of the Marx-led International Working Men's Association. He hoped to bring many of them into his Alliance, while simultaneously he and they would remain in the International, which he would attempt to bring more under his influence. But despite some successes, he decided that Swiss youth were too reactionary and the workers too bour-geois. Where was the fire of revolutionary youth? Just then Nechaev appeared.

To the fifty-four-year-old Bakunin, he seemed fearless and full of youthful energy. To a thinker such as Bakunin, strong-willed men of action that might help fulfil his aspirations had always had an appeal, as his earlier infatuation in Siberia with General Muraviev-Amursky had indicated. Bakunin now hoped that through Nechaev he could help from afar in directing the revolutionary movement in the land of his birth. Nechaev revitalized, personified and sym-bolized Bakunin's own revolutionary aspirations. "How deeply, how passion-ately, how tenderly," according to Bakunin, he came to "love" and trust this young radical.[3]

One old radical who was not impressed by the "boy," as Ogarev and Bakunin affectionately referred to Nechaev, was Herzen. From Ogarev's articles and let-ters which he received in Nice, it was clear to Herzen that Nechaev was prompt-ing his old friend to more extreme rhetoric. In early May, Herzen arrived in Geneva himself to see Ogarev and some of his other friends. For most of the next month and a half, he resided there, first at the Hotel de la Couronne and then at a pension. He discovered that Bakunin, although still sufficiently en-dowed, had lost some weight, and was working like a locomotive, albeit a de-railed one. Herzen also met Nechaev and found him dislikable; later he even referred to him as a reptile.

By 1869, Herzen was more wary of Bakunin's radicalism than ever and was fearful that Nechaev's influence would only further widen the gap between them. Bakunin already desired a general uprising of the Russian people, to be led by brave young men who would abandon Russia's universities and their pseudo-learning to become brigand-rebels among the peasant masses. He was confident that out of the destruction of the old society and the government which supported it a new, free, egalitarian order, without any centralized gov-ernment, could be created. But Nechaev's Geneva proclamations not only sug-gested that blood had to flow, they seemed to relish the idea. "Poison, the knife, the noose ... revolution consecrates everything equally in this struggle,"[4] he wrote. Herzen thought that such ideas of Bakunin and Nechaev were nonsense. He now believed that if the old order of his day, whether in Russia or Western Europe, was ended by violence, then the new order would have to be instituted and maintained by violence. The socialist society which he wished to see con-structed could only come about after gradual preparation, after the innate con-servatism of the masses was overcome by education and time. More than ever, he now advocated reason and understanding, not destruction and blood-letting.

Herzen, however, was not able to convince either Bakunin or Ogarev of the dangers of Nechaev's influence. All he could do was to prevent Ogarev from sounding too radical in the pages of *The Bell*. Nevertheless, he feared an open break with his two old friends. And when Ogarev, influenced by Bakunin and Nechaev, pressed him for some money out of a revolutionary fund which had been given over to him and Ogarev a decade earlier, Herzen agreed. He knew much of it would end up in Nechaev's hands, but he apparently thought he could not deny Ogarev use of part of the fund.

By August, Nechaev was ready to sneak back into Russia. In about five months he had accomplished much in Switzerland. From being just one of the radical student leaders in St Petersburg, he had become an issuer of proclamations and a collaborator of Bakunin and Ogarev. He had obtained money for his work, and Bakunin had issued him a document which stated: "The bearer of this is one of the accredited representatives of the Russian section of the World Revolutionary Alliance, No. 2771."[5] It was signed "Michael Bakunin" and on it was a seal of the European Revolutionary Alliance: Central Committee. Of course, there were no such organizations, unless Bakunin was thinking of his International Social Democratic Alliance. And by the time Nechaev left for Russia, that organization was composed of a little more than a hundred members who lived in and around Geneva. Nevertheless, the document signed by Bakunin would seem impressive to student radicals back in Russia.

With Nechaev when he left was another interesting document, written in code. It was "The Catechism of a Revolutionary." It reflected the ideas of both Bakunin and Nechaev, and Bakunin possibly collaborated with Nechaev in the writing of it. It was meant as a guide for the members of the revolutionary organization which Nechaev intended to form once he was back in Russia. It especially spelled out the attitudes the true revolutionary should have. He should be one who breaks all his ties with conventional morality and totally dedicates himself to one goal: the merciless destruction of the government and the old class structure. In the process he should be willing to do *anything* for the sake of the revolution, including partaking in the killing of any who might hinder its success.

Aided by some Bulgarian revolutionary connections of Bakunin, Nechaev was able to sneak back into Russia and eventually make his way to Moscow. Arrests earlier in the year of student dissidents had considerably weakened the leadership of the radical movement, both there in Moscow and in St Petersburg. Nechaev set out to create a new organization of revolutionaries in Moscow. He worked primarily among students and former students, including those of the Petrovsky Agricultural Academy and a number of students who were expelled from Moscow University in October. He told them various stories, many untrue, about his past involvement in revolutionary circles in Russia and abroad. He said he was a representative of "The Committee of the People's Revenge of February 19th, 1870." The date, the ninth anniversary of the emancipation manifesto, was to mark the hoped-for beginning of a general uprising against the government and the class society which it supported. The committee itself was nonexistent.

Nechaev played upon his new followers' genuine sympathies for the plight of the peasants and urban poor and upon their guilt for being more privileged. He stressed and exaggerated his own humble beginnings. His strength of will, apparent self-assurance and incredible energy also impressed some of his new acquaintances.

One student of the Agricultural Academy who joined Nechaev's new revolutionary organization nevertheless refused to be completely subservient to his will. His name was Ivanov, and he often disagreed with Nechaev. But Nechaev would always claim the support of the revolutionary "Committee," which he said he represented and under which the new Moscow organization was to work. Perhaps Ivanov came to suspect the very existence of the Committee. At any rate, after a heated disagreement with Nechaev over the distribution of propaganda, Ivanov declared he would not go along with Nechaev regardless of the wishes of the Committee. Shortly afterwards he resigned from Nechaev's organization. Nechaev decided to kill him.

Whether Nechaev was motivated by hatred of someone who would dare to oppose him so completely, or by fear that Ivanov would inform upon him to the police, or perhaps by some combination of these and other motives, it is difficult to say. But on Friday, November 21st 1869, Nechaev and some of his followers gathered together in the park belonging to the Agricultural Academy. A century before, Catherine the Great had given the land to Count Cyril Razumovsky, the grandfather of the first Perovskys. Only at the beginning of the sixties had the government repurchased the land and made plans to open the new Agricultural Academy. At the entrance of a grotto near a pond, Nechaev and his followers beat, strangled and shot Ivanov and then pushed his body through a hole in the ice. Amidst his own curses, Nechaev directed the operation and did most of the work. Before succumbing, Ivanov managed to bite Nechaev's hand several times. Nevertheless, Nechaev fired the shot that went through the skull of Ivanov's prone, twitching body. It was a little past 5:30 in the evening. It was hardly a professional job. Four days later the body was discovered with some implicating evidence left on it.

Nechaev remained in Russia about four more weeks. He kept on the move and avoided arrest. Many of his fellow conspirators were not so lucky. They were rounded up before he left the country with a female revolutionary who had become attracted to him and his message.

In early January he turned up once again in Geneva and resumed contact with Ogarev, who had moved into new quarters, this time on the Route de Carouge. Bakunin had gone to Locarno. Short of money, as was usually the case unless he found a wealthy benefactor or benefactress, Bakunin decided life was cheaper there. It was also more private, and Antonia could have the baby she was expecting without as many questions being raised as to whom the father was. Bakunin "jumped for joy"[6] when he heard from Ogarev that the "boy" was safe and back in Geneva. He tried to convince Ogarev that Nechaev should come to Locarno, where he could lie low for a while. Ogarev also informed Herzen of Nechaev's escape, but Herzen was less enthusiastic and continued to consider Nechaev's actions and those of his two elder supporters as "positively harmful."[7]

Herzen was living in Paris at this time on the Rue de Rivoli, the same street where Tolstoy and Turgenev had lived in 1857. The previous year and a half had not been an easy time for him. He suffered from diabetes and continued to have family problems, and not just with his still emotionally distraught companion of many years, Natalia Ogareva. In addition to a host of more minor problems, his oldest daughter, Natalia (Tata), suffered a nervous breakdown in Florence, where he had gone to take care of her before bringing her back to Paris.

One day in the middle of January, Turgenev came to call on him. It was the first time the two had met since Turgenev visited Herzen in London eight years before. As the giant Turgenev greeted him, Herzen undoubtedly noticed that the hair and beard of the fifty-one-year-old Turgenev were now almost completely white, much more so than his own, even though he was six years older. Turgenev found his host vigorous and full of life. The two men chatted pleasantly for a time and Turgenev promised to call again.

Later that evening while in their apartment, Herzen complained to Natalia Ogareva of pains in his chest and side. He spent a restless and feverish night; a doctor was summoned the next day. Herzen's lungs were inflamed. For several days he remained sick. But on the 20th, he had his oldest daughter send a telegram to one of his Geneva friends. It read: "Great danger past. Dissatisfied with the doctors ... Will try to write tomorrow."[8] But that same evening Herzen became delirious and early the next morning he died.

After Ogarev and Bakunin heard the news, Bakunin wrote to Ogarev from Locarno that words failed him except to say: "We shall die in action."[9] Along with Nechaev, who came to visit him in Locarno in February, Bakunin began to discuss ways to get their hands on some funds to continue their revolutionary work and existence. They thought of the remainder of the revolutionary fund which had been left to Herzen and Ogarev. Bakunin pressed Ogarev to obtain what remained of it from Herzen's estate.

In Geneva that March, with Natalia Ogareva, Natalia Herzen, Bakunin and Nechaev all present, Herzen's son, turned over ten thousand francs to Ogarev. The poet in turn made most of it available to Nechaev for his revolutionary purposes. By this time the young revolutionary had also enlisted the help of

Natalia Herzen in a variety of secretarial and other tasks. He played upon her guilt, called her a spoiled parasite and bullied her into helping the revolutionary cause. She knew that he had murdered a man, but Nechaev assured her that Ivanov had been working for the police. She wondered if Nechaev was after the money she had inherited, and she became upset and suspicious when Nechaev told her that he loved her. But she continued to help him. In early April, *The Bell* came out under new management. Although Ogarev and Bakunin collaborated, its driving force was Nechaev. The journal that had once made Herzen famous was now in the hands of a plebeian man whom he had considered reptilian. Perhaps this was not a completely inappropriate irony for Herzen, who had once written that "history is the autobiography of a madman."[10]

PART THREE

Fate did not send him [Alexander II] a Richelieu or a Bismarck; but the point is that he was incapable of using a Richelieu or a Bismarck; he possessed pretensions and the fear of a weak man to seem weak … respect for the authority of the autocratic state collapsed: no type of system, no type of general plan … complete discord.

S. SOLOVIEV

The definitions and boundary lines between good and evil have disappeared … disintegration is everywhere, for everything has come apart, and no bonds remain.

F. DOSTOEVSKY

They did not know whom and how to judge, they could not agree on what was evil and what was good. They did not know whom to accuse and whom to justify. People killed each other out of some sort of senseless evil anger.

F. DOSTOEVSKY

I felt that if I wished to live and understand the meaning of life, I must seek it amongst … the simple, unlearned and poor men.

L. TOLSTOY

Another remedy presents itself … Why not try it?

L. TOLSTOY

24
THE TSAR VISITS LONDON, 1874

On a sunny but cool Wednesday in the middle of May 1874, Emperor Alexander II of Russia was in the English Channel on his yacht *Derzhava*, headed for Dover. Accompanying him was an entourage of more than a dozen aides and officials including his oldest son, the Tsarevich Alexander, by now himself the father of two boys. The Tsar's wife, Maria, was not with him. She seldom was any more, and the emotional ties which once bound husband and wife had long since come undone.

As far as the Tsar was concerned his true wife was Catherine Dolgorukova, whom he still loved passionately eight years after first consummating his love with her that July night at Peterhof. After their rendezvous in Paris and return to Russia, their lives became more and more intertwined. Although he tried to remain discreet, his love for Katia was not easily hidden. He provided her with an apartment in the capital and arranged for nearby quarters for her when he was at Tsarskoe Selo, Peterhof, Livadia in the Crimea, or Bad Ems in Germany. In 1870, she had become a lady-in-waiting to the Empress and therefore had an excuse often to be around the royal family. Her duties, however, did not oblige her to travel with Maria when she went off, as she often did, to take the cure in Europe. On such occasions Alexander could arrange their rendezvous a little more easily. In recent years Katia occasionally had even surreptitiously made her way into the Tsar's quarters at the Winter Palace. There, in May of 1872, she gave birth to their first child, George. A year and a half later a girl, Olga, followed.

A week before boarding his yacht for the Flushing-Dover crossing, he had written to Katia from Stuttgart, that she was his "idol," his "treasure," his "life." He also wrote: "Oh, my Angel, I cannot bear it any longer, I do so yearn for you and would so like to be warmed by you, my adored little wife, and I feel more than ever that my whole life is in you – May God continue to watch over us four." It was not at all unusual for Alexander to write to her, as he also did from Stuttgart, that "all my life is left in you, and yours in me. We want each other and nothing else." Although he fulfilled to the best of his abilities his duties as

Tsar, his heart was no longer in his work. It belonged to this young woman still in her mid-twenties, with whom he loved to "clench" together "like hungry cats."[1]

While attractive, Katia was not a great beauty, nor was she a woman of great refinement or culture. She could be possessive, jealous and shallow. But like most men in love, Alexander either did not notice or did not care about most of her imperfections. She was his island of rest and pleasure in a life otherwise full of duties and cares. And he was sure, as perhaps fitted a ruler who crowned himself, that God was with him and Katia and blessed their relationship. Once this visit to England was completed, she was to meet him in Bad Ems, where he would take the waters for a month.

As the white cliffs of Dover came clearly into view for the Tsar, and the early evening sun shone on the water, his daughter, Maria, waited on shore to greet him. Recently married to Queen Victoria's second son, who had joined the Tsar's party in Flushing, she was now the Duchess of Edinburgh. After some initial reservations on the part of both Victoria and Maria's parents, the couple had been allowed to marry in St Petersburg that previous January. Although Queen Victoria awaited the Tsar at Windsor Castle, her oldest son, the portly Prince of Wales, was on hand to welcome him officially to English soil. Although Alexander had not been to England for thirty-five years, his son the Tsarevich, whose wife was the sister of the Princess of Wales, had visited London just the previous year.

When his daughter came into view the Tsar, dressed in military uniform and maintaining his royal bearing, threw kisses to her. By the time the yacht docked tears were in his eyes – she had always been his favorite. After words of welcome, embraces and a booming salute from the guns of the castle on the hill, the Russian guests and English hosts boarded a train. As the crowd watched and the band played, the train headed out, bound for Windsor.

At Windsor Castle, Queen Victoria waited impatiently. The Tsar had been scheduled to appear much earlier that day, but his yacht had been delayed. She had last seen him when she had first turned twenty and he was twenty-one. She was then already the Queen and he but a Tsarevich. But they were both unmarried. She had written in her diary: "I really love this amiable and dear young man," and a little later, "he is so frank, so really young and merry, has such a nice open countenance with a sweet smile, and such a manly, fine figure and appearance."[2] Only the Queen knew in what sense she "loved" this young man. And despite the fact that he was already smitten by his future wife, Maria of Hesse-Darmstadt, whom he had met shortly before coming to England, he also seems to have enjoyed the company of the young Queen. But regardless of how deep (or shallow) their feelings towards each other were, reasons of state would have prevented them from ever coming closer.

Now, thirty-five years later, Victoria waited in the Waterloo Gallery of Windsor Castle until finally at 10:15 p.m. word arrived that the train had pulled into Windsor Station. All was ready for the Tsar: a guards' unit and flowers on the Grand Staircase, a band, finely dressed ladies and gentlemen of the court; and at the Grand Entrance, the queen herself. His carriage came up the hill escorted by a guard of honor. Several minutes later he got out and reached down to embrace the Queen and then gave her his arm. She noticed that night how much he had changed since she had last seen him. She thought him "terribly altered," with a face that looked "old, sad and careworn."[3] She also thought him thin, but that was perhaps because when he was young he had been on the stout side. Victoria, on the other hand, was considerably heavier than when they had last met: she was now a very matronly-looking woman with fat jowls. Less than an hour after arriving, the Tsar sat down to dinner in the Oak Room between the Queen and his daughter. A band played in the quadrangle, beginning with "God Save the Tsar" and ending with "God Save the Queen." Finally, at about midnight, the exhausted Tsar parted from the Queen and retired to his rooms.

The next evening there was a state banquet in the long oak-paneled St George's Hall. The Tsar, towering over the Queen, escorted her into the hall. He was in a Red Guards' uniform and she wore a coronet of diamonds to match the diamonds on her dress. He sat between Victoria and his daughter, who was wearing the brilliant sapphire stones he had given her. This set of earrings, necklace, bracelet and brooches had once belonged to Catherine the Great. Although Victoria had at first opposed her second son's marriage to Maria, she had since grown fond of this pleasant young woman who spoke English well and possessed, according to her new mother-in-law, beautiful eyes, a nice nose, a pretty bust, but too short a chin and too long a neck. As they ate and the band of the Coldstream Guards played selections from Glinka, Schubert, Meyerbeer and others, Alexander talked with Victoria of his previous visit. Speaking in French, he recalled how he had loved England, but then how his feelings had changed as a result of the events which brought about the Crimean War. He suggested that the Queen had been poorly served by the former Prime Minister, Palmerston, but he saw no reason why their two countries could not now be on the best of terms. But both he and Victoria knew very well that potential sources of conflict still existed between their two countries. In 1870, with the Franco-Prussian war sill in progress, the Russians had declared that they would no longer be bound by the hated Black Sea clauses of the Treaty of Paris. Victoria found this behavior outrageous. Like many of her realm she was fearful of any strengthening of Russia at the expense of the Turkish government. British power in the eastern Mediterranean might thereby be adversely affected. This was especially important now that the Suez Canal had been completed.

There was also the question of Central Asia. During the past decade British diplomats had watched, often with alarm, as Tashkent, Kokand, Samarkand, Krasnovodsk and other cities had fallen to Russia and as the Russians moved closer to British India. Like the American white men taking over the Native American Indians' territory as they moved toward the Pacific Ocean, so the Russians continued taking over the smaller khanates of Central Asia and seemed destined to continue their forward movement until they also met a more formidable barrier, whether geographical or human.

Some Russians such as Ignatiev, still ambassador to Constantinople, or the War Minister, General Dmitry Milyutin, believed that Russia owed Great Britain no apologies for her advancement. Milyutin noted that the British did not consult the Russians when they wished to expand their empire. Others like Foreign Minister Gorchakov were more concerned with the opinion of other governments. He often advised caution in the Tsar's councils, but when further advances occurred he did his best to justify them. A decade earlier he sent out a circular dispatch to Russian representatives abroad; it urged them to justify Russian advances by pointing to the necessity of advancing against barbarous peoples in order to safeguard Russia's frontiers. It also indicated that the United States government in America and the British in India, as well as other colonial powers, had faced similar problems in attempting to maintain and advance the cause of civilization. When Russia's forward thrusts seemed to go beyond what Gorchakov had led the British to expect, he misleadingly downplayed the Tsar's responsibility and blamed it on insubordinate generals. Finance Minister Reutern's concerns about the costs of continuing expansion and military spending generally – still about one-third of the government's total expenditures – seemed no more capable than British verbal opposition of halting the Russian advance.

Yet, just the previous year, Alexander had sent to London Peter Shuvalov, the head of the Third Division (secret police) and a longtime friend. His mission was not just to help arrange the wedding of the Tsar's daughter, but also to assure the British government that the Tsar did not intend to conquer Khiva. After it fell a little later that year, Shuvalov also blamed it on the generals. With a base now in the Turkoman steppes, some British diplomats feared Russia was in a better position than ever before to threaten the independence of Persia and Afghanistan and pose a heightened danger to British India.

Perhaps having in mind Constantinople or Central Asia, Alexander at the banquet that night asked Victoria if he could write to her directly if difficulties arose. She agreed. Then Alexander changed the subject, and with tears in his eyes he thanked Victoria for all of her kindnesses to his daughter and expressed the hope that Maria would always prove herself worthy of favor. Victoria herself was touched and reached out to take Maria's hand.

One of the guests that evening was the Prime Minister, Disraeli, who had just recently come to power and who had been critical of his predecessor Gladstone for not being sufficiently concerned with Great Britain's international and imperial role. He found the Tsar to be dignified but "soft in his manners," unlike the Tsarevich whose manner seemed more that of a soldier.[4] The following day the sixty-nine-year-old Prime Minister had an audience with the Tsar at Buckingham Palace, which had been made available for Alexander for the remainder of his stay. The Tsar expressed his friendly feelings toward England, but nothing of substance was discussed. Disraeli thought that the Russian Emperor was gracious, but that his face, with its muttonchop whiskers, was a sad one, probably habitually so. What Alexander thought that afternoon of the old Prime Minister who was also a novelist, a Jewish Christian and a wily politician much appreciated by Queen Victoria, we do not know.

Alexander remained at Buckingham Palace for six days. Victoria stayed at Windsor Castle while her oldest sons and their wives escorted the Tsar around London, by now an enormous city of four million people. He visited the Houses of Parliament and Westminister Abbey; he went in procession, surrounded by cheering crowds, flags and bunting and ringing bells, to Guildhall, where he was officially greeted by the city officials. In the evenings, he attended banquets, balls and concerts. He also went to the Crystal Palace, the reconstruction on new grounds of the iron and glass structure that had been the centerpiece of the first great international exhibition in London in 1851. There, thirty thousand people were on hand, and he enjoyed a concert and fireworks.

To many, including the critical Dostoevsky, the Crystal Palace symbolized the spirit of England in the midst of its prosperity. But a quarter century of almost unimpeded growth and unchallenged economic dominance was coming to an end for the island kingdom. The years 1873 and 1874 witnessed the beginning of a recessionary period for Western economies. In addition, in the years ahead Great Britain would face increasing competition from the newly united Germany, which was just now in the process of surpassing Queen Victoria's country as Russia's chief trading partner.

Alexander's own economy would not be as seriously affected by the recession as that of Victoria's, and his modernization process would be able to continue despite various obstacles. In the last five years alone he had overseen the doubling of his country's railway tracks. Nevertheless, serious economic problems continued to plague his administration. Despite increasing exports, especially of grain, they continually lagged behind imports. The government also constantly spent more than it received, and its foreign debt over the past decade was in the neighborhood of one billion rubles. Yet despite this indebtedness, Russia remained far behind the more industrialized Western countries.

One morning the Tsar took a brief train ride out to Chistlehurst to visit the former Empress of France, Eugenie, widowed since the previous year. She and Napoleon III had settled on an estate here after he had been ousted from power in the wake of defeats at the hands of Prussia.

On the two days before he left London, the Tsar attended the inevitable military reviews that monarchs and rulers were so fond of putting on for one another. The first was on the dusty fields of Aldershot, which lay to the southwest of London. There in a dark green and gold uniform with a plume of feathers on his helmet and sitting atop a gray charger, the Tsar reviewed thousands of the Queen's best Dragoons, Hussars, Fusileers and Scottish Highlanders. The next afternoon, on the first really bright sunny day since he had arrived in London, he reviewed six horse batteries and ten of field artillery on the fields near the royal Arsenal at Woolwich.

In the past year the Tsar had been very concerned with his own military. He had finally taken the advice of his reform-minded Minister of War, Dmitry Milyutin, and introduced a new conscription law. Among other provisions, it made all classes, and not just the poorer ones, liable for military service, and it shortened the terms for active duty. Milyutin was a cultured, intellectual man, noted for his industriousness and his reserved and unpretentious demeanor. Although he had been at his post since 1861 and had been responsible for gradually improving the education, training, and treatment of Russian soldiers, the appointment of Peter Shuvalov as head of the Third Division in 1866 had prevented Milyutin from being more influential than he was. Instead, for almost eight years the influence of this chief of the gendarmes seemed to increase steadily until he was the second most powerful man in Russia. He usually sided with the interests of the large landowning class, who resisted any reforms which they thought would weaken their power and privileges. He was Milyutin's chief antagonist and opposed the War Minister's new conscription proposals. Milyutin blamed the suave Shuvalov for over-emphasizing the personal and political dangers facing Alexander and for being the man most responsible for stemming the Tsar's earlier sympathy for reform.

But finally Shuvalov let his success go to his head. He became increasingly arrogant and also became critical of the Tsar's beloved Katia. After Alexander approved the military reform legislation at the very beginning of the year, he became more attentive to Milyutin and seemed to listen less to Shuvalov. Not long after leaving London, the Tsar would announce that Shuvalov was to take up a new post, and he was replaced as the head of the Third Division. The new position for this friend of the Tsar's youth who had accompanied him to England and who was at the review with him that day was to be that of ambassador to Great Britain.

On the day after the review at Woolwich, the Tsar, his daughter Maria and the Tsarevich attended an Orthodox Church service on Welbeck Street. Then accompanied by Maria's husband and the Prince and Princess of Wales, they took a train to Gravesend. There, amidst the pomp of a military escort and the firing of guns, he said goodby to his daughter and hosts and steamed away on his yacht.

25
DOSTOEVSKY IN BAD EMS

About a month after the Tsar's departure from London, Fedor Dostoevsky arrived in Bad Ems. His Tsar had left this famous health resort less than a week before, seen off at the train station by his uncle Kaiser William, the Emperor of Germany. A reporter stated that the Tsar seemed to have benefited from the waters. But it is more likely that he looked healthier just being with Katia in this lovely valley town.

It was a beautiful sunny day close to noon when Dostoevsky's train pulled in from Berlin. At first, as he wrote to his wife Anna, he found Ems to be a beautiful place. The narrow, gentle Lahn River flowed through the town, which squeezed itself in between high hills which overlooked it on both sides.

Ems was then one of the most famous spas in all of Europe. As in Baden-Baden, the cream of European society could be seen walking its promenades or sitting in its gardens. Kaiser William went there regularly, as did the Russian Tsar. In 1870, the two monarchs, along with Bismarck and Gorchakov, met there. Shortly after the Tsar returned to Russia that year a famous meeting occurred at Ems between Kaiser William and the French ambassador to Prussia. It was utilized by Bismarck to provoke France into a war which would help to complete the unification of Germany. Alexander at that time gave diplomatic support to his uncle by pressuring Austria not to become involved against Prussia.

Several days after he had arrived, Dostoevsky came across Emperor William, now, thanks to Chancellor Bismarck, the head of a united and strong Germany. Dostoevsky thought that the tall old monarch was an imposing-looking figure. He wrote to Anna that when the Emperor passed by, everyone stood up, took off their hats, and bowed or curtsied. The Emperor on the other hand didn't bow to anyone, but sometimes waved his hand. Dostoevsky, always the nationalist, contrasted the German Emperor's behavior to what he had heard of that of his own ruler, who in Ems had graciously bowed to others in return.

Dostoevsky was undoubtedly among the minority in Ems who admired the Russian monarch more than his German uncle. Even many Russians abroad tended to be critical of their Tsar. William I and Bismarck, on the other hand, despite conflicts with German Catholics and economic problems characteristic of the European recession, remained popular with most educated Germans, who were still flush with the excitement of German victories and nationhood. The support of liberals and university students and professors for the German government especially contrasted with the situation in Russia, where little such support was forthcoming.

For some five weeks Dostoevsky wrote to Anna about life in Ems, about his literary work, the weather, his health and the progress of his cure, and about how he loved and missed her and their two children.

Thanks in part to Anna's thriftiness and good business sense and to his having finally given up his gambling mania, the Dostoevskys were now better off financially than they had been in the first year of their marriage. But the income of a writer was still unsteady, and they both watched their expenditures closely. Dostoevsky thought that Ems was terribly expensive. Over the course of several weeks, he bargained hard with two different landladies, and he managed to pay only twelve thalers a week for his modest rooms at each lodging. He preferred the second place, the Hotel Ville d'Alger, run by a French woman from Algiers. Here his two rooms were larger and better furnished than at the first pension where he stayed, and he had a balcony. This small hotel was at the eastern edge of town and faced the Lahn river, which was a stone's throw away.

Like almost everyone taking the cure, Dostoevsky arose at 6:00 a.m. in order to go to one of the springs in the center of town and line up for his glasses of mineral water. By 6:30 some two thousand people would be lined up with their glasses. When their turn came they would hand them to young girls who would give them the prescribed amount from the springs. Just as at the gambling tables in Baden-Baden, Dostoevsky often got angry when jostled or nudged in the crowd. As the patients drank their water, which smelled just a little like rotten eggs, a band played in the garden. Much to the Orthodox Dostoevsky's chagrin, it often opened with a Lutheran hymn.

After having his morning coffee, he often tried to work in his rooms. After leaving Geneva six years earlier, he had finished *The Idiot*, and in Dresden written another novel, *The Eternal Husband*, and worked on still another, *The Devils*. The last work evolved to a large extent out of Dostoevsky's fascination with Nechaev's murder of Ivanov on the grounds of Moscow's Agricultural Academy, an event he had read about in the newspapers. His interest in the case might also have been heightened by the fact that Anna's brother Ivan was a student at the Agricultural Academy and had visited his sister and Dostoevsky in Dresden shortly before the murder. He told the couple something of the political atmosphere at the Academy.

Raskolnikov in *Crime and Punishment*, influenced by Western secular ideas, had reasoned that murder was permissible, and then with Nechaev, reality

seemed to copy art. Nechaev became the prototype for one of the main characters of *The Devils*, Peter Verkhovensky. Although Nechaev was not brought to
trial in Russia until January 1873, five months after his arrest by Swiss police,
some of his co-conspirators were tried earlier in the summer of 1871. The
government publicized the trial, and the Dostoevskys happened to return to
Russia, after four years abroad, just as the lengthy trial was in its beginning
stages. Dostoevsky followed it closely and was especially horrified by "The
Catechism of a Revolutionary." In his novel he hoped to demonstrate the harm-
fulness of Western atheistic and socialist ideas. But he also wished to display in
a more accurate fashion than he thought Turgenev had done the true relationship between the liberal "fathers" and their radical "sons." He wished to show
that the "fathers" bore a heavy responsibility for helping to infect their "sons"
with false Western ideas, for leading them away from true Russian ideas, including Russian Orthodoxy, and for acquiescing in their radicalism. One minor
fictional character of the older generation was especially mocked and attacked
in the novel, and that was Karmazinov. Dostoevsky clearly meant him to be
a reflection of Turgenev. But as with Verkhovensky's likeness to Nechaev,
Karmazinov was more of a caricature of Turgenev than a fair, objective portrait.

Now in Ems after his morning coffee, he was planning still another novel,
one that he thought would mirror the true condition of a turbulent modern society, as opposed to one of those idyllic works of landowner literature sometimes written by his more acclaimed rivals for fame, Turgenev and especially
Tolstoy. At first he contemplated entitling it "Disorder," but would eventually
call it *A Raw Youth*. Surprisingly, he had promised to deliver it to Nekrasov. For
the last six to seven years, following the government's indefinite suspension of
The Contemporary, Nekrasov had edited the leftist *Notes of the Fatherland*. A
few months before Dostoevsky had left for Ems, the enigmatic Nekrasov had
come to him with a generous offer. When the conservative Katkov and his *The
Russian Messenger* could not match it, Dostoevsky decided to accept Nekrasov's
overture. But he was a little concerned about editorial tampering on the part of
the radical staff of the *Notes of the Fatherland*.

He had already jotted down various ideas in his notebook. Among them:
"Children. A mother who has married a second time. A group of orphans ...
The foundations of society have cracked as a result of the revolutionary reforms ... The definitions and boundary lines of good and evil have disappeared." Now in Ems, he continued writing down pertinent material. "Most
Important. The idea of disintegration is everywhere, for everything has come
apart, and no bonds remain."[1]

He also made many other notes including ones on abandoned children,
about children murdering and robbing their father, and about a predatory type
character who seduces his stepdaughter and plans to murder his wife. During

his weeks in Ems two central characters gradually evolved in his mind. One was the predatory individual already mentioned and the other a youth, who for a while Dostoevsky envisioned as the younger brother of the predatory man. Eventually they would become father and illegitimate son. Dostoevsky thought of the first as an atheist, a shameless man, but already in his Ems notes a complex figure bearing some resemblance to the now deceased Alexander Herzen. The second, like some of the characters in the author's earlier works, dreams of making money, of becoming a Rothschild. When the older man treats this dream with disdain, the youth asks him to point out a better ideal. But his request is left unanswered. Once again, as in *The Devils*, Dostoevsky was pointing to the responsibility of the older generation for the behavior of the misguided youth.

In Ems, homesick for his wife and two young children and for Staraya Russa and the summer house they rented near a river lined with elm trees, Dostoevsky was afraid that many of Russia's educated minority were leading his country away from all that he loved. He planned to have one of his characters say: "The idea of children, the idea of the fatherland, the idea of integrity, of a future ideal – all these ideas no longer exit; they have been smashed, undermined and ridiculed."[2] Like Tolstoy, he placed the highest emphasis on marriage and family life and disagreed fundamentally with the radicals who advocated free love. He believed that relationships like the ones Nekrasov and Herzen had had with their friends' wives were unnatural. Did he know or suspect that the Tsar himself had two families and had often slept with Catherine Dolgorukova at the villa she rented in Ems?

During 1873 and early 1874, Dostoevsky had edited the conservative journal *The Citizen*, owned by a friend of the Tsarevich. He also had become increasingly friendly with the Tsarevich's chief tutor and adviser, Constantine Pobedonostsev, a tall, thin, dour man who also contributed to the journal. It is possible that in his talks with such individuals who were close to the Tsarevich, Dostoevsky might have heard of some of the details of the Tsar's private life. By 1874 the Tsar's relationship to Katia was common knowledge at court and was probably among the reasons that some, such as Pobedonostsev, placed increasing hopes on the Tsarevich, who was faithful to his wife and in general behaved more as conservatives believed a good and upright Tsar should.

To someone such as Dostoevsky the number of children given up to foundling homes, often by mothers of illegitimate children, would also be alarming. Dostoevsky tended to attribute the break-up of family life, as well as most other evils, to Western influence. In the westernized St Petersburg, for every three births in the city one child was left, usually by city residents, at the city's Foundling Home. A majority of these infants would die during their first year, either at the Home or in the nearby peasants' households to which they were sent.[3]

In addition to radical Western ideas which challenged marriage, the family, religion and monarchical rule, Dostoevsky was also opposed to the materialism and capitalist spirit he had witnessed in Western Europe and which he feared were becoming increasingly prevalent in Russia. Not only does his "raw youth" wish to become a Rothschild – the anti-Semitic Dostoevsky would also increasingly blame Jewish acquisitive influences for polluting the true Russian spirit – but in the author's Ems notes he has one of his characters bemoan the deforestation of Russia and the exhaustion of her soil by those interested only in immediate profit. Although a strong supporter of modernization efforts needed for Russian military strength, Dostoevsky never outlined how they could be carried out without encouraging the capitalistic spirit which distressed him.

When it was not raining, and it often was that summer in Ems, Dostoevsky would go out for a walk before he ate dinner at 1:00 p.m. He complained in his letters to Anna that besides a crowded garden and park there was nowhere else to go. Climbing the nearby hills would be too exhausting for an asthmatic like himself. He also complained of the Germans and of most of the Russians who came to Ems. He had never felt especially comfortable among the wealthy classes. And here in fashionable Ems, where some of the ladies walked about as if dressed for a ball, he worried about the adequacy of his white waistcoat and the calamanco suit he had had made in Ems. As the weeks succeeded each other, he spent a little time with a few Russian acquaintances, but mostly he stayed to himself and concluded that Ems was a vile place, even worse, he wrote to Anna, than his Siberian prison experience!

When he failed to receive letters from Anna as frequently and regularly as he would have liked, he scolded her, but more frequently he expressed his love and his ardent longing for her. After she had mentioned some dreams in a letter to him, he wrote: "I strongly kiss you, and as for the account of your indecent dreams, my little dove, if you could only know what I see. For a woman, however, it is not so proper. Never mind, never mind. Hush! On the contrary, I am very happy. I kiss you passionately all over."[4] He also frequently mentioned his children: Lyubov, who was not quite five, and little Fedor, or Fedya, who celebrated his third birthday during his father's absence that July. When one of Anna's letters was delayed, he often worried that perhaps something had happened to one of his precious little ones.

He put up with this and other anxieties and dissatisfactions caused by his stay in Ems only because he hoped to improve his health. So in addition to planning his novel and reading Pushkin or various newspapers at the Kurhaus, he occasionally went to the magnificent quarters of his doctor, a man named Orth. And he wrote to Anna about the progress of his "cure." He reported on which springs he drank from and whether or not he mixed his mineral water with milk. He also informed Anna that Dr Orth told him to eat meat with fat and more acidic things. During one of his subsequent visits to Ems – he would come again in 1875, 1876 and 1879 – Dr Orth would forbid most fruits and greens. But Dostoevsky continued to smoke heavily, and Dr Orth apparently never saw any significant connection between his patient's coughing and wheezing and his smoking habit. But then most other doctors of his day probably would not have either. After his first three weeks in Ems, Dr Orth listened to his chest and told him it was completely healed in three places, but not yet in two others.

On the first of August Dostoevsky wrote to Anna that despite a cold and some hoarseness in his chest, he felt incomparably better than he had before arriving in Ems. And if it had not been for a couple of epileptic seizures, he was sure that the cure would have done him even more good. Not too many days after writing this letter, he left Ems and returned to Russia. But only after he had first gone to Geneva to visit the grave of his first daughter, Sonia.

26

SOPHIA PEROVSKAYA, RADICALISM AND THE RUSSIAN PEOPLE

In the same month that Dostoevsky arrived in Bad Ems, Sophia Perovskaya was released from five months in prison. What crime had merited such treatment for this little twenty-year-old whose father had once been governor of St Petersburg and who was now still a member of the Council of Ministers of the Ministry of the Interior?

Not long after her father had lost his job as governor in 1866, she had gone with her mother and sister to Kilburn, the family estate in the Crimea. There they lived for over two years. In the summers, and once in the spring after a two-month university suspension for taking part in student disorders, her brother Vasily came down from St Petersburg armed with radical literature. The young Sophia longed to know more. And at the end of the sixties she got her chance. In the summer her father came to the Crimea with the news that it was necessary to sell Kilburn to help pay for his debts. The family returned to the capital, where he found a place for them, while he continued to live in his own apartment. Sophia enrolled in the newly begun classes for women being offered at the Alarchinsky gymnasium, which was located near her new lodgings on the western side of the city.

Soon she was spending hours in rooms with other women discussing the position of women in society and other social questions. Amidst heavy cigarette smoke, Sophia looked almost like a child. She seemed oblivious to her appearance. The look of her gray-blue eyes and the way she held her mouth indicated that she was a most serious woman. She often sat in the corner. She seldom talked for long in these sessions, but when she did speak she was not hesitant to present her views forcefully and sharply. She argued, for example, that the women should keep their discussion circles limited to women. If they merged with those of young men, the better educated men would make it difficult for them to come up with their own independent ideas.

Within a couple of years, however, young Sophia changed her mind. Along with several other women, including her good friend Alexandra Kornilova, she joined a circle headed by a young Jewish medical student named Mark

Natanson. For several years he had opposed Nechaev's violent, hurried, elitist approach to change. Instead he emphasized a more gradual method which stressed the enlightenment of the self and of the masses. At the end of 1871, however, Natanson was arrested, and the circle was eventually referred to as the Chaikovsky Circle, after one of its other members. By the fall of 1873, it would have about thirty members in the capital and slightly more spread out in other areas of the country.

Despite its name, the men and women who made up the circle in the capital were opposed to having a single leader. Reacting in part against Nechaev's elitism and criminal behavior, they thought of themselves as a group of friends working honestly and forthrightly together for their own improvement and for the good of the people. One of their later members, Prince Kropotkin, said he never again met "such a collection of morally superior men and women."[1]

At first the circle's main task, in addition to their own enlightenment and improvement, was the distribution of important books to various parts of Russia. Among these were works of Chernyshevsky, Lavrov's *Historical Letters*, a translation of Marx's *Das Kapital* and Bervi-Flerovsky's *The Situation of the Working Class in Russia* and his *Alphabet of Social Sciences*. The circle also distributed pamphlets that were printed by circle members who had gone to Switzerland. These pamphlets were designed especially for propagandizing among the peasants.

Like other members of her group, Sophia was heavily influenced herself by these works, especially by those of the Russian writers. Chernyshevsky's feminist heroine Vera in *What Is to Be Done?* was an early model for radical young women, and his superhuman Rakhmetov became a model for both sexes. Lavrov was a middle-aged former artillery officer and mathematics instructor who had been arrested and exiled following Karakozov's attempted assassination of Alexander II. He had recently escaped and turned up in Paris. Along with Bakunin he would be the leading imigri influence on young Russians in the early seventies. In his *Historical Letters* young radicals read that the comforts and privileges which they enjoyed, including education, were made available to them as a result of the exploitation of the masses. Therefore, they had a heavy debt to repay to the people. The educated minority who realized their obligation had to help bring about social and economic justice. However, unlike Bakunin, who hoped for an immediate revolution, Lavrov thought that one could only come about after a great deal of preparation and education. Sophia reflected his influence when she thought, as she did in the early seventies, that it might take a couple of generations before a revolution could occur.

Bervi-Flerovsky's *The Situation of the Working Class in Russia* (1869) was based partly on his own experiences in exile in Siberia and other places within Russia. He wrote of both peasants and industrial laborers. He began his book with a quote from a peasant woman: "O, wretched is our life, little our land, great are our taxes, and we do not know what to do."[2] He rejected the argument that the poor's poverty was due to laziness and vice. On the contrary, he attributed it to the high redemption payments that peasants had been making for their land since the emancipation and to high taxes; and in the case of industrial workers, it resulted from low wages and their exploitation by the upper classes and the state. The Russian workers, Bervi-Flerovsky thought, were even worse off than those in capitalistic countries. And he was no doubt correct. While the conditions of both Russian peasants and urban workers had apparently deteriorated during the previous decade, the ten years prior to the economic downturn of 1873 had witnessed real economic gains for workers in the more industrialized western countries of Europe. Nevertheless, Bervi-Flerovsky did not want to see capitalism develop in Russia. Like Herzen and Chernyshevsky, he hoped that Russia could achieve socialism before capitalism became fully developed.

Sophia and her young friends shared both this hope and his vagueness about the role of industrialization in any future socialist society. In addition, they were not especially interested in achieving a constitution for Russia. If one could be achieved, and that was doubtful, they thought it might end up benefiting only the upper classes while increasing the exploitation of Russia's vast poor and illiterate masses.

No, their concerns and obligations were for the welfare of "the people" – thus the confusing term "populists," which some radicals would soon adopt and which historians would later use to tag most radicals of the 1870s. In keeping with this spirit, in the spring of 1872, Sophia decided to go out and directly help them. She went to the Samara Province, located just east of the Volga river. There she assisted a school teacher, but then, after a few months, learned to give smallpox shots and went to administer them in the villages. That same summer Leo Tolstoy lived further south in the steppes of the same province on thousands of acres he had recently purchased.

In the villages Sophia slept in the small huts of the peasants, just as they did, on a bench or on the floor. Three-generational families, although beginning to break up, were still common then, and it was not at all unusual for ten to fifteen people to be living together in a single room. Despite the appallingly high death rate of the Russian peasants – syphilis seemed to be the most recent scourge – she often had a difficult time convincing her superstitious villagers of the necessity for smallpox inoculations. As she talked to them she learned first hand how they felt about their lives. They complained of high taxes, too little land and too many dishonest officials. But they did not blame the Tsar, and they continued to hope that he or one of his successors would someday deliver them from their crushing burdens – they paid taxes and redemption payments to the state at a rate of about ten times as much per acre of land owned as did the nobles. In the meantime, the peasants seemed to believe that there was little they could do about their fate, and nothing this earnest little teenage girl said seemed to have much effect. Despite Sophia's efforts, their religion or vodka probably continued to offer them more solace than any revolutionary hopes.

The winter after she arrived in the Samara Province, there was a famine there, but by then she was gone. She had left to go to a village in the Tver Province, the same province in which Bakunin had grown up. She had a friend there who taught in a village school, and Sophia assisted her. Not many Russian peasants or their children were yet literate, but thanks to the *zemstvos* and the peasants' desire for literacy for their children the number of schools was increasing. In the evenings Sophia and her friend, Alexandra Obodovskaya, taught some of the children's fathers to read.

After the formal lessons the two young ladies read to the peasant men from the writings of Nekrasov and Gogol, from stories about Ivan the Terrible and the old town councils of Novgorod, and about the folk rebels that Bakunin admired, the seventeenth-century Stenka Razin and the eighteenth-century Emelyan Pugachev.

Sophia was happy and content that winter and spring. She felt useful and healthy. She lived simply in a log hut in the snow-covered village. But then her friends in the capital wrote to her of their educational and propagandistic work among St Petersburg workers, and she decided to go back to the capital.

She soon settled into quarters in the Vyborg District, north of the Neva River. From here she worked along with others at propagandizing among workers and helping to send out books and pamphlets to various parts of Russia. When the gendarmes began to watch too closely the little house where she stayed, she left it and settled into a house on the southeastern side of the city beyond the Alexander Nevsky Monastery. There in a gloomy unattractive house, divided into two parts by a dark narrow corridor, she lived with several other members of her circle.

On one side of the corridor lived the thin, gray-eyed Sergei Sinegub and his wife Larisa. Following the example of one of Chernyshevsky's heroes, he had married the young Larisa purely to assist her to obtain a life of her own free from parental interference. He understood that in keeping with the revolutionary ethics of the day, he obtained no rights over her as a result of the marriage. However, when he needed the presence of a wife to obtain a village teaching job, she had volunteered to accompany him. While in the countryside love had bloomed, and the merely legal marriage had turned into a real one. Now back in the capital, Sergei, a wealthy nobleman by background, was one of the organizers of the circle's educational and propagandistic work among St Petersburg's workers.

On the other side of the corridor, which contained two rooms and a kitchen, Sophia lived along with Dmitry Rogachev. According to her false internal passport, she was the wife of a worker. Although Rogachev was a former artillery officer, he looked the part of a worker and in fact had taken a job in the Putilov factory at the smelting furnaces. He was a strong, powerful man, who later on worked a stint as a Volga barge hauler. Unlike the Sinegubs, Sophia and Dmitry never became romantically interested in each other. At this time in her life, Sophia seemed not the least bit interested in romantic love or sex. She was very critical of "ladies' men" and wanted only to devote herself to the cause of the people.

Sophia cooked and washed clothes for the group. Dressed in a cotton dress and men's boots, and with a kerchief on her head, she could also be seen supporting a yoke on her small shoulders as she brought two buckets of water back from nearby Neva. When her friends tracked in mud from the streets, she would scold them with a severe look on her girlish little face. But despite her rebukes and her serious nature, she was a general favorite among her circle.

In the evenings she now taught geography and geometry to some of the weavers and textile workers that the circle had attracted. After the lessons she talked with them about the evils of the government, the needs of the people and about socialism.

Although industrial workers still comprised only a little over five per cent of the city's population, they were growing rapidly in this the most industrialized city of Russia. Government sponsored railway construction had been one of the reasons for the growth. It had led to a considerable expansion of the metal-working industry and to the development of such metal-working plants as the large Putilov one where Dmitry Rogachev worked. Sophia and her friends, however, preferred working with some of the textile workers, who were more poorly paid than the metal workers and who were more peasant-like in their mentality. In fact, in the summers many of them, some infected with syphilis contracted in the city, still returned to work and to see their wives and families in their native villages. They did not need Sophia and her friends to tell them about their miserable urban conditions that often included thirteen- or fourteen-hour work days for subsistence wages that enabled them to live together ten or more crowded into a room or two. If their employers mistreated them, for example failed to pay them on time, they had little legal recourse. Unions and strikes were forbidden. Then there were the noisy and unhealthy factories where not only men, but large numbers of women and children, put in their long days. Yet these textile workers knew they were better off than many others in the capital, those without regular work, those in lower-paying industries, or some of those living in factory-owned dormitories. And, of course, life in the countryside had been no better, or many of them would not have come to the capital in the first place.

No, in regard to their lot in life and that of the workers and peasants in general, Sophia and her friends could not teach them much. But they could teach them how to read and write. Through history and geography they could give them some sense of their place in the world. Some of Sophia's friends told them about the activities of workers in Western Europe. Peter Kropotkin, a prince and former page to the Tsar, who often visited a friend in the Tsar's Winter Palace, would change into peasant work clothes and tell the workers about the labor movement aboard. He had been especially impressed by some of Bakunin's worker friends in Switzerland. Some of the St Petersburg textile workers now became convinced that their fates were not inevitable, that they could work towards changing their conditions. Kropotkin incidentally also hoped to move some of his fellow propagandists more towards the less patient revolutionary methods of Bakunin.

The activities of the Chaikovsky Circle, however, were not going unnoticed. One night when Sophia was out, the gendarmes came, searched the house and arrested Sergei Sinegub. Several months later when she was at Alexandra Kornilova's, the gendarmes once gain burst in. They found a letter in code, some revolutionary books and songs and a French dictionary with Sinegub's name on it. The two young women, along with one of Alexandra's sisters, Lyubov, were arrested. This was in the beginning of January 1874.

Sophia was taken that night to a three-story building behind the Summer Garden. It had bars on the windows. Two helmeted gendarmes with sabers drawn, met her gendarme escorts and herself as their carriage came to a halt in a courtyard. She was led into the three-storied building. In her boots and old dress, this little young woman must have looked rather helpless that night, standing there surrounded by the bigger and uniformed gendarmes. She was taken up a staircase to the third floor, where a sentry unlocked iron bars and led them into a corridor. On one side was a blank wall, on the other a series of doors. Sophia was led through one of them into a fairly large room. A gendarme sentry then locked the door; she was now incarcerated in the Third Division's own special little prison.

Her room contained an iron bed, a blanket and a little table and stool. The walls were ocher. The top part of the door was made of glass, covered on the outside by a green blind which the sentry would lift from time to time. She realized that although she was cut off from her friends, she would have little privacy. At first, between the morning's tea and roll and a dinner probably brought from a neighboring tavern, there was nothing to do. Nor was there any activity for her from dinner until more tea and a roll in the evening. But soon a friendly gendarme, who for some time had been secretly aiding the prisoners, saw to it that Sophia received a roll with a little writing paper and graphite in it. She was able to sneak messages out and, shortly afterwards, to receive, openly this time, books and clean clothes.

Once she was called before a gendarme colonel who sat behind a green table and asked her questions. The questions, however, seemed to indicate that he really did not have much incriminating evidence against her. She was returned to her room, and the months dragged slowly on.

One night she heard commotion in the corridor and found out later that Kropotkin and other friends had been arrested. After a short time in the Third Division's prison, he and some of the others were transferred to the Peter and Paul Fortress. A similar fate had earlier befallen Sinegub.

It was a year in which there would be many more arrests. In the spring and summer of 1874, over a thousand individuals, mostly young, "went to the people." From St Petersburg and Moscow, from Kiev, Kharkov, Odessa and other university cities, they went to work (for example, giving smallpox inoculations and teaching literacy) and to propagandize among the people. Some had been part of the Chaikovsky Circle or one of its branches, most had not. Some following the ideas of Bakunin, hoped to start a fire that would soon lead to the type of massive conflagration that Razin and Pugachev had led in earlier centuries. Others, more influenced by Lavrov, stressed a more gradual education of the people. Almost all believed that they owed a debt to the peasants, and many thought they could also learn from the peasants. Some students left their universities shortly before they would have received their degrees. The movement was a manifestation of the dominant quest of the seventies: the desire on the part of Russian intellectuals to overcome their alienation and to achieve a sense of community and oneness with the people.

Yet the youths' propaganda had little effect. The movement was not well coordinated, and the peasants were naturally wary of the young outsiders and of becoming involved with them. Other rural elements such as the local gentry often reported these outsiders to the police. Before the year was out, over seven hundred of them were arrested, and more than two hundred of them would be held in prison for several years awaiting trial.

Meanwhile, that June, Sofia was led into a big room and found to her surprise that her father was there. The two of them had seldom seen each other in the last five years. There had been a brief period a year after Sofia had first returned to the capital when the family had all lived together in a crowded apartment on Little Meshchanskoi Street. Her father, however, was sickly and irritable at the time, and he objected to her radical, short-haired female friends. He told his daughter to tell them that he did not wish them to come around anymore. Shortly after this, she replied that she would live separately from the family. Her father raved at such a reply from his seventeen-year-old daughter.

But that evening she left home. Her father asked her brother Vasily if he expected him, her father, to allow Sophia to destroy herself. Vasily replied that if he attempted to force his will on her, she might kill herself. Days passed and she did not return. Her father informed the authorities. Her mother went to Alexandra Kornilova and pleaded with her to tell her where Sophia was. But Alexandra would not. Without an internal passport, Sophia could be arrested as a vagrant and put in prison. Before too long, she left by train for Kiev. Finally, on his doctor's advice her father, whose health had grown worse, decided to allow Sophia to live separately. She returned to the capital, but did not go to see her father. For years he could not bear to hear her name mentioned.

Now, however, upon seeing his daughter in prison, Lev Perovsky bent down and kissed her. They both wept. He told her that Shuvalov, who had served in the same regiment as he, had promised to release her on bail. Not long after this meeting, Sophia was released, and Shuvalov took up his new post as ambassador to London. Not for three years would Sophia be brought to trial along with many others arrested in 1874 but, unlike her, kept for the entire three years in pre-trial detention. For a short time in 1874, Sophia lived with her father and Vasily. Her brother had by now himself become involved in her circle, which had been depleted by arrests and departures. Their father no longer pried or interfered in their lives. But that summer as arrests continued around them, Sophia and her brother decided to go and stay temporarily with their mother, who was living in the Crimea. After obtaining permission from the authorities, they left by train: from St Petersburg to Moscow, and then, on recently opened lines, from Moscow via Kiev to Odessa. From there they went by steamboat on the Black Sea to Sevastopol, where they transferred to the other side of the bay and climbed a hill in a rented cart. Before too long they reached a little isolated house and a happy reunion with their mother. After a winter and spring locked up inside prison, Sophia was now free to enjoy herself in this picturesque retreat. She went riding in the hills, picked grapes, read books, and went down to the seashore to swim.

27
A MYSTIC IN THE DESERT

At the end of 1875, a young Russian the same age as Sophia Perovskaya found himself alone in the Egyptian desert. He was wearing a top hat and a long black coat. He was taller than average, pale and thin. But his dark blue eyes were what people noticed. Beneath his thick, dark brows, they seemed both penetrating and mysterious. The young man was Vladimir Soloviev, the son of the historian.

Although as a young teenager he had rejected the religious beliefs of his parents and become an atheist and a nihilist, he by now had given up such views. He still sought the transformation of society, but now by the workings of both God and man. Only gradually had he worked out this religiously oriented philosophy. At sixteen, he entered Moscow University, where his sober hardworking father continued to serve as dean of the Historical-Philological faculty and then, after 1871, as rector of the university. But the learning that was most important to the young Vladimir was not that dictated by his professors, but by his own inner search for truth.

From his preference for reading Darwin, the nihilist Pisarev and the German materialist Büchner, he passed on to the philosophers Spinoza, Feuerbach, Mill, Kant and, especially, Comte and Schopenhauer. The latter helped lead him to other German philosophers such as Hegel and Schelling. He also became interested in Eastern religions and in mystical writings. After graduating from the university in 1873, Vladimir went to the Moscow Theological Academy at the Trinity Monastery of St Sergius. The monastery was one of Russia's most cherished holy places. Vladimir, however, did not intend to become a monk, as some rumors stated. He merely wished to attend lectures and study religion and philosophy. While there that year, he wrote an article on primitive religious beliefs and worked on a thesis, *The Crisis of Western Philosophy*, which would earn him a Master's degree at St Petersburg University in 1874.

In his thesis he surveyed the development of Western philosophy and found all of its manifestations incomplete. Scholasticism, rationalism, materialism and positivism all contained some truth, but also serious limitations. Finally, he thought that in his own day Schopenhauer and Eduard von Hartman had begun to move Western philosophy back in the direction of the truths long proclaimed by Eastern faiths. Also influenced by some of the works of the Russian Slavophile thinkers, the young Soloviev suggested that the world was now ready for a new synthesis. It would be one of science, religion and philosophy, and one which would incorporate the truths and discard the falsehoods that all three had manifested in the past.

His thesis was not just a manifestation of abstract thinking, but also reflected his deepest feelings. As he indicated to his cousin Katia, he thought himself called to help bring the desired synthesis about. It in turn would help bring about the Kingdom of God on earth, "the kingdom of internal spiritual relations, of pure love and happiness."[1]

Although he certainly had a head for abstract philosophical thinking and seemed often to have it in the clouds, he was not a dry, pedantic person, but an ardent young man strongly attracted to feminine beauty. The jealous pangs over a young girl and the vision of a beautiful lady that he had experienced when he was nine had been an early indication of his complex personality.

In the summer after his eighteenth birthday, he went south to visit his grandmother Romanova in the Kherson province. Her husband, the old Sevastopol hero, had been dead for seven years, but staying with her was a niece and a granddaughter, both of whom Vladimir found attractive. His feelings for the granddaughter, his cousin Katia, proved to be the longer lasting.

Her parents had separated years earlier, and for a while in the sixties she had lived with Vladimir's family in Moscow. But that summer as they read poetry together on his grandmother's estate, they became more intimate, and when he returned to Moscow they wrote to each other. Katia was sixteen that summer, and was a lovely dark-eyed, dark-haired girl who resembled her aunt, Vladimir's mother.

The following May he again went south to see her, but a strange event occurred on the train from Moscow to Kharkhov, where she was now staying with an aunt. Years after this event of 1872, he wrote a story about it. What parts actually happened and which ones were later figments of his imagination no one can say for sure. Nevertheless, the story relates how as the train moved southward towards Tula, he noticed a slender ash-blonde woman who, while not beautiful, seemed to him very appealing. To the thin, pale, nineteen-year-old Vladimir it seemed that after a while she began glancing at him with a friendly and encouraging smile. But he was too awe-struck to approach her. At the Tula station, however, some sort of troupe of loud French men and women entered their car and settled in near the slender blonde. She soon became upset by their disruptive and drunken behavior and came and sat next to Vladimir. Before long she was speaking frankly and openly of herself. She was married, with several children, but often fell in love with other men. As he was then still under the influence of Schopenhauer, he replied that love was an illusion, but one to be preferred over marriage, which entangled one too much in a corrupt world.

On tracks completed only three years earlier, the train rolled southward. It became dark outside. The exhausted French troupe fell asleep, and it became quiet in their second-class car. She took off her hat and let down her hair. A woman's hair falling on her shoulders had always had an irresistible appeal for him. And her thick luxurious hair now seemed the most beautiful he had ever seen. It induced in him an almost trance-like condition. Time seemed obliterated.

He began kissing her hair and then covered her arms with kisses. "How strange you are! Who allows you to do this?"[2] she asked. He whispered some naive apology, but then felt on his lips a long, hot kiss. Other kisses and embraces followed.

The next morning he felt guilty for violating his philosophic principles and for betraying his cousin, whom he was on the way to see. His companion no longer seemed so appealing, and he was a bit abrupt when he spoke with her.

In Kursk, they changed trains. She went to a first-class compartment and he went to a second-class seat, where he struck up a conversation with a radical medical student from Kiev University. The student took him for a fellow radical, perhaps because of Vladimir's long hair and unkempt appearance.

After they had talked a while, the slender blonde appeared in his car and invited him into her first-class compartment. She told him she was alone in it and bored; they could ride together all the way to Kharkhov. Although reluctant, he agreed. As they stepped out of the car to cross over to another one, he fainted. He discovered later that she had grabbed him and prevented him from falling between the cars. When he regained consciousness lying on the platform of his car, all he saw was clear sunlight, a strip of blue sky, and a beautiful woman with wonderful familiar eyes and a rosy light about her face. She was bending over him and whispering something soft and tender. It was his blonde friend but somehow transformed. And he felt himself also transformed. All his thoughts, feelings and inclinations had dissolved into this sweet, light, calm, almost mystical, vision before him. In it he felt all the beauty and wonder, all the fullness and meaning of the universe.

Later, after he had returned with her to her compartment and kissed the edge of her dress and her legs, he told her that she had awakened in him a love in which he had completely forgotten himself, that only now did he really understand the workings of the divine in man and what goodness and true happiness were. He no longer felt guilty, but only filled with a pure love.

After he promised to visit her and her husband in Moscow, he departed at the train station at Kharkhov. As the train began to pull off into the night, she reached her hands out the train window to him and he felt warm tears in his eyes. Upon meeting his cousin Katia, he was disappointed. She appeared less tender and heavenly than he had remembered her.

At least that was the way he told it all twenty years later. In the two years which followed this memorable trip, his feelings for cousin Katia fluctuated. At one point, the two of them considered marriage. She was by then in St Petersburg a good part of the time, and he became very jealous of the attentions directed towards her by one of his uncles and by his older brother Vsevolod. But at about the time that he was preparing to live at the Moscow Theological Academy, she apparently became upset with his reclusive ways, and their relationship soon cooled.

After receiving his Master's degree in the fall of 1874, the young Soloviev was befriended by some conservative Slavophiles and criticized by some Western-oriented thinkers who were upset with his thesis. One of his new Slavophile acquaintances was Ivan Aksakov, the brother of the deceased Constantine, who had once polemicized with his father. At the beginning of 1875, Vladimir was appointed a lecturer of philosophy at Moscow University, where his father was still rector and still completing each year a volume of Russian history. At the same time, Vladimir gave lectures at the Moscow Higher Courses for Women, which his father had helped to begin – women were not yet permitted to enroll in Russia's universities. In spring, however, Vladimir took leave to study Gnostic, medieval and Hindu philosophy. By the end of June, he was in London.

At this point in his life he was still trying to integrate his abstract rational philosophizing with his deeper mystical inclinations. Before leaving for London he had become very interested in certain mystical writings, and at the British Museum he continued to seek out such works. He became especially interested in the Jewish Kabbala and in the works of the mystical German writer of the early seventeenth century, Jacob Boehme. Boehme emphasized the universal role of the Divine Wisdom, "Sophia" in Greek. Divine Wisdom or the Wisdom of God had also been written of in the Bible and in Kabbalistic texts and depicted in Russian icons. Churches, the various St Sophias, had also been dedicated to it in Soloviev's native land.

This concept of Sophia now became for the young Soloviev his lodestar and a key to integrating his philosophy and his mysticism. He came to think of Sophia as the universal oneness, the oneness of God with creation. He began to see history as a process of man and nature falling away from God and splintering into separateness and then eventually reuniting in a higher synthesis. Sophia symbolized that potential synthesis. And for Soloviev that all-oneness with God became the goal of history.

At the same time, however, Sophia had a more personal meaning. Like others before him, he perceived Sophia in feminine form and now identified her with the beautiful lady who had appeared to him in church when he was nine. In the reading room of the British Museum, also then a favorite haunt of Karl Marx's, he read all that he could in the mystic literature which related to her. Then one day when he longed to personally experience her, as he thought he had in childhood, he once again sensed her presence. As he later wrote:

> All was filled with a golden azure,
> And before me she once again shone.
> Only her face – it alone.[3]

When he complained of seeing only her face, a voice within him told him to go to Egypt. By the end of October he had left London. By way of Paris, Lyon, Turin, Parma, Ancona and Brindisi, where he boarded a steamboat, he finally one morning reached the port of Alexandria. That same evening he arrived by train in Cairo.

It had been a good trip ever since he had avoided seasickness crossing the English Channel. The train ride through the Alps and Italy was pleasant, as was the Mediterranean voyage. The weather was clear and warm, the sea blue and the nights moonlit.

Upon arriving he checked into the Hotel Abbat on the Station Road, not far from the railway station. It was a comfortable hotel which catered to European tourists, of whom the number had increased significantly in recent years. The Suez Canal had opened just six years earlier in 1869, and British and French influence had been increasing in Egypt, which in theory was still part of the Ottoman Empire. Compared to most Middle Eastern cities, Cairo was large, but its population was still only half that of St Petersburg and one-tenth that of London.

In his hotel, the young Soloviev met a retired Russian general who was advising the Egyptian khedive, Ismail, on the reorganization of his army. The general and Ambassador Ignatiev in Constantinople hoped that it might eventually be utilized against the Turkish sovereign, to whom Ismail still had to pay tribute. The general was the well-known Russian nationalist Rostislav Fadeev. A veteran of the wars in the Caucasus and the Crimean War, he also had written the official history of the Caucasian wars. But he had been forced to resign from active service because of his opposition to the proposed reforms of Minister of War Milyutin. At the very end of the sixties, Fadeev's *The Eastern Question* had appeared. In it he argued in behalf of Russian policies which would lead to the creation of a pan-Slavic federation. Such a grouping would unite all Slavs, as well as the Greeks, Rumanians and the city of Constantinople, under the leadership of the Russian Tsar. Fadeev was not foolish enough to think such a dream could come about without a war or wars with Germany, Austria and the Ottoman Empire. He believed, however, that with the help of other Slavs,

Russia could prove triumphant. No wonder he wished to help improve Egyptian forces and to strengthen the khedive's ties with Russia. Egypt might prove helpful before too long against Turkish forces. Soloviev often ate meals with Fadeev at the hotel and found this fifty-one year old general to be quite loquacious, full of opinions and risqué anecdotes.

During his first week in Cairo, Soloviev took in some of the sights of the city. He went up to the twelfth-century Citadel, which sat on a high rocky plateau at the eastern edge of town. It offered a wonderful view of Cairo. The colorful domes and minarets of the city's mosques, often red and white, were interspersed with acacias and palms, stone buildings and narrow streets. From the Citadel he could also see the Nile valley stretching north and south, a green strip of fertility between brown desert sands. He also examined some of the city's mosques, visited the Museum of Egyptian Antiquities – which he thought marvelous – and went out to bathe in the Nile and see the Great Pyramid of Cheops at Giza. Nearby, he viewed the great Sphinx, with its body of a lion and head of a human. It was about an hour and a half carriage ride from his hotel, much of it via a new road into the desert and up to the rocky platform on which this and several other pyramids stood. In addition to climbing up the pyramid of Cheops, he also visited the burial chambers within it. Unlike many other tourists he did not complain, at least in his letters to his mother, of the local Egyptians who pressed their services upon foreigners and demanded a tip (*baksheesh*).

Soloviev remained in Egypt until March and seemed to enjoy his stay. Before the new year had begun, he had moved out of his hotel to live in quarters with the family of a photographer. By early February, a good friend, Prince Dmitry Tsertelev, had come to join him and moved into the same building with him. On the warm spring evenings they would sit on the roof and look out at the city and the sky above.

Sometimes, the tall, thin Soloviev would travel on the back of a donkey through the city's colorful sights. He especially liked to ride on a big white one who was guided through the narrow streets by a man named Tolbi. In these streets were turbaned men and veiled women, some dressed magnificently in a variety of colors, but also poorer people, often barefooted and wearing only simple gowns. Young children of both sexes sometimes wore nothing at all. In crowded bazaars one could buy almost anything from yellow slippers to green vegetables, from gold bracelets to camels, and one could see jugglers and barbers plying their trades.

In addition to its colorful, exotic aspect, Cairo also had a more modern side. French and English influence had increased in recent years. Khedive Ismail had been educated in France, and on a trip to Paris at about the same time that Tsar Alexander had visited there, he had been impressed by Baron Haussmann's wide new boulevards. He came back to Cairo and began imitating Haussmann. By the time Soloviev arrived in the city, the Esbekiya quarter had become the modern showpiece of the city. Here a military band played in a public garden. Cafes and clubs, a white opera house and French theater, European-style hotels and houses, gas lighting and broad streets, all set this quarter off from the rest of Cairo. In the Esbekiya one saw fewer turbans and more European attire. One might even see some American officers, for the khedive had purchased American weapons and employed some US Civil War veterans, including several generals, in his effort to strengthen his army.

One day while Soloviev was in the Esbekiya and, in spite of the heat, dressed in a long black coat and tall black hat, he met Ferdinand de Lesseps, the builder of the Suez Canal. De Lesseps was already seventy, but still an energetic, lively Frenchman with a talent for making friends. He brought Soloviev back with him to his quarters, and there Soloviev met the French writer M. de Vogue. In the course of their conversation, Soloviev told him that once in the same clothes he was then wearing he had gone into the Suez desert looking for a tribe that guarded certain secret Kabbalistic teachings. But he had not found the tribe. Instead he had been discovered by some Bedouins who relieved him of his watch.

Although Soloviev probably told the story with a touch of humor, for he often had a way of dealing with his deepest experiences in a light joking manner, his trip into the desert was one of the most serious events of his life. It had occurred just a few weeks after he had first arrived in Cairo, and within just a few days of a day that in retrospect would prove important to Egyptians and Europeans alike, a day on which occurred, according to Leopold II of Belgium, "the greatest event of modern politics."[4] The event was the sale by the deeply indebted Ismail of his 177,000 shares in the Suez Canal to the British government under Disraeli. While not completely indifferent to such international occurrences, Soloviev was much more concerned with his own spiritual quest. Whether or not Soloviev told De Vogue his real reason for going into the desert is not altogether clear. Years later he wrote that the voice of the mystical Sophia had told him to seek her in the desert. At any rate, he set out in his tall hat and long black coat, but without food or money. About thirteen miles from Cairo the group of Bedouins who were to take his watch mistook him in the night for a devil. They tied up his arms and led him off further into the desert. Luckily, however, they soon released him. Exhausted by the walk and ordeal, he decided to lie down and sleep. With the stars shining above, he stretched himself out on the desert sands. Despite the heat of the day, the night was cold and he had trouble sleeping. He thought he heard a jackal howling, and then after a while, a voice saying "sleep, my poor friend."[5] When he awoke it was to a mystic vision of Sophia, the Eternal Feminine.

Years later in words influenced by the symbolic language of the mystics and by the description of Wisdom in the Book of Proverbs, he would try to describe that indescribable experience. In the poem "Three Meetings" he would write of his desert vision of Sophia, her eyes full of azure flame, appearing amidst the purple of heavenly splendor and the smell of roses. The image of her filled his being. Only she existed. Past, present and future were all encompassed in her gaze, as were the blue "seas and rivers," the "distant forest" and the "heights of snowy mountains," all of which Soloviev stated he saw stretched out before him.[6]

Before leaving Cairo he would write a poem about Sophia, his "queen," as he called her. It helps to fill out his image of her. He wrote of her palace with its golden pillars, her jewel-filled crown and her garden full of roses and lilies and a silvery stream. But when far below she sees her desolate friend, she comes to him bathed in light and full of quiet tenderness. She covers him with her radiance.[7] For Soloviev, Sophia represented not only the mystical oneness of the universe, but also a tender, loving, maternal force.

Thus, a year after thousands of his contemporaries sought, whether consciously or unconsciously, a sense of community and oneness by going to the people, the young Soloviev believed he had twice experienced a oneness much more profound than any earthly manifestations of it.

After his vision of Sophia in the desert, Soloviev followed the sun back towards the west to Cairo and arrived at his hotel in the evening. He told General Fadeev of his trip, but not of the vision. The general, who incidentally was the uncle of the theosophist Madame Blavatsky and thus would have been no stranger to unusual spiritual tales, advised him not to say anything more of his excursion unless he wanted to be thought a fool or a madman.

28

THE TSAR AT THE FRONT

At the end of June 1877, the Tsar was in Simnitza, Rumania with his soldiers. Russia was again at war with Turkey, for the tenth time in two centuries. The day before his arrival in this little town, Russian troops had crossed the Danube under Turkish fire and successfully secured the opposite Bulgarian bank and surrounding heights. Before the day was over, they had also taken over the small town of Sistova, which lay a few miles south of the great river. After arriving in Simnitza, with an entourage that included the Tsarevich and Minister of War Milyutin, Alexander visited the wounded and established his quarters at a nearby country house which sat up on a hill overlooking a wide stretch of the Danube below. Later that same day he and his retinue rode down to the river and were transported to the southern bank. His soldiers greeted him with cheers and a regimental band. Then flanked by two solid rows of soldiers, his party rode up into the hills to congratulate the generals and troops now situated near Sistova. As the Tsar strode up on this hot sunny day to shake the hand of one of his victorious generals, an English war correspondent thought that he looked younger than his fifty-nine years and every inch a majestic ruler.

At the entrance of Sistova the Bulgarians welcomed him warmly. He was met by a crowd led by clergymen carrying banners, the gospels and a cross. Alexander told them to lead him to their church. Along the route, the Bulgarians showered him and his men with flowers. The women and children seemed especially happy, and the old people crossed themselves. When he entered the crowded church some people kissed his hand, others applauded. Many Bulgarians thought of Alexander as the "divine figure from the north"[1] who had come to liberate his co-religionists and fellow Slavs from the hated infidel Turk. Already the windows of Turkish houses and shops in the town had been broken, some had been looted, and Turkish inhabitants had fled before the approaching Russians. Near one of the town's mosques the street was strewn with the pages of torn-up Islamic books.

The Bulgarian hatred of their Turkish masters was understandable. In the spring and summer of the previous year, the Turks had put down a Bulgarian rebellion with the utmost severity. Thousands of defenseless peasants were massacred and about sixty villages destroyed.

In a proclamation issued at the beginning of Russia's involvement, Alexander himself told the Bulgarians that Russia was called upon by the "decrees of Providence" to assist the Bulgarians, to deliver them from the "arbitrary rule" of the Muslims.[2] Nevertheless, almost a full year had passed after the Bulgarians had first risen against the Turks before Alexander had answered the call of Providence. Many of his Russian subjects had hoped he would act sooner.

In fact, the Bulgarians were not even the first Orthodox Slavs to revolt against the Turks. A year before their revolt the Christians of Herzegovina and then Bosnia had begun an uprising against them. The following year, shortly after the Bulgarians had arisen, Serbia and Montenegro declared war on Turkey. In Russia during the summer of 1876 enthusiasm for the heroic battle of the Slavs against the Turks spread like a contagious disease. An unsympathetic Leo Tolstoy described the fever in *Anna Karenina*, which he was then writing.

> Among the people to whom he belonged, nothing was written or talked about at that time except the Serbian war. Everything that the idle crowd usually does to kill time, it now did for the benefit of the Slavs: balls, concerts, dinners, speeches, ladies' dresses, beer, restaurants – all bore witness to our sympathy with the Slavs … The massacre of our co-religionists and brother Slavs evoked sympathy for the sufferers and indignation against their oppressors. And the heroism of the Serbs and Montenegrins, fighting for a great cause, aroused in the whole nation a desire to help their brothers not only with words but by deeds.[3]

Tolstoy made it clear, however, that he did not believe that the average peasant had any desire to fight for his fellow Slavs.

Some Russian radicals, though, did go off to help the Slavs, and a number of leftist journals supported the cause. It was, after all, a revolt against oppression, and some liberals and radicals hoped it would lead to more progressive policies in Russia itself. The leaders of public opinion, however, were primarily more conservative journalists such as Ivan Aksakov, the brother of Professor Soloviev's old critic, and Michael Katkov, the influential editor of *The Russian Messenger* and *The Moscow Gazette*. Dostoevsky in his popular *The Diary of a Writer*, issued on a monthly basis in 1876 and 1877, also strongly supported the panslavic cause. All three men were also members of the Slavonic Benevolent Committee, which reached the height of its influence in these years. By 1877 the Moscow Committee and its branches in St Petersburg, Kiev and Odessa possessed over a thousand members. For over a decade before his death in 1875, the conservative panslavist M.P. Pogodin had been the president of the organization, and Ivan Aksakov took over the position after his death. General Fadeev, whom the young Vladimir Soloviev had met in Cairo, belonged to the St Petersburg branch. Copies of his *Eastern Question*, with its call for Russia to battle her enemies and unite the Slavs, were now distributed widely. Another St Petersburg member was N. Danilevsky. His *Russia and Europe* (1869) contained a message very similar to that of Fadeev's, but dressed up in more scientific garb.

The committee played an important role in 1876 in channeling aid to the Slavs. The Tsarina and Tsarevich, both aggrieved by the Tsar's continuing relationship with his beloved Katia and both more conservative nationalists than he, were ardent supporters of aid. Important churchmen also helped, as did various volunteers including Russian officers permitted to volunteer in the Serbian army. The general who soon became the head of the Serbian army was the semi-retired Russian M. Chernyaev, whose earlier conquests in Central Asia had earned him the sobriquet "Lion of Tashkent."

From Constantinople, Russian ambassador Nicholas Ignatiev also encouraged Russian aid to the Slavs. The successful negotiator of the Treaty of Peking almost two decades earlier, Ignatiev was an ardent panslav and a member of the Slavonic Benevolent Committee. It had been Ignatiev who had persuaded the khedive in Cairo to accept General Fadeev's offer of help.

Although Ignatiev was fated to witness Egyptian troops enter the fight on the side of the Turks, first against the southern Slavs and a year later against the Russians, his schemes were usually more successful. To many British diplomats this mustached ambassador, with his mocking smile and wily seductive wife, was the devil incarnate.

While Alexander still was discouraging the Serbs from taking up arms against Turkey, Ignatiev encouraged them to believe that Russia would aid them in case of a conflict. Shortly after the Serbs declared war, he suggested to his government that Russia send an army of two hundred thousand men to aid the Serbs. Later, in the late summer and fall of 1876, after the Serbs had suffered a series of defeats, he joined other Tsarist advisers at Alexander's Livadia estate in the Crimea. Here amidst the semi-tropical vegetation, with the waves of the Black Sea below and the mountains behind them, he again urged the Tsar to fight. Although War Minister Milyutin and Finance Minister Reutern urged caution – the latter was especially fearful that a war would wreck his fifteen-year effort to stabilize Russian finances – the Tsarina and Tsarevich sided with more bellicose advisers such as Ignatiev. Alexander decided on a partial mobilization and on an overall campaign plan. But cautious as always about heeding the voices of extreme Russian nationalists eager for battle, he still hoped to avoid war.

Since late 1875 he had cooperated with other European rulers to solve the problem of the Turkish treatment of its European Christians. The major European governments, except Great Britain, agreed on Balkan land, tax and religious reforms that Turkey should carry out. British Prime Minister Disraeli, however, encouraged Turkish resistance to these efforts. He distrusted Russian intentions and hoped to sow dissension between the members of the Three Emperors' League – Austria, Germany and Russia – who since 1873 had agreed to consult together if war threatened in Europe. After Turkish military successes in the middle of 1876, and shortly after the Livadia decisions, Russia unilaterally sent an ultimatum to the Turks. Coming right after a Turkish victory that opened the way to Belgrade, Alexander believed that only this demand for an end to hostilities could save Serbia from another rout and possible Turkish massacres. Turkey agreed to a six-week armistice.

In the months that followed, Alexander continued to seek a diplomatic solution that could be imposed upon the Turks. He assured the British ambassador to Russia that British fears of Russian intentions regarding Constantinople and India were ludicrous. But Disraeli remained uncooperative. Alexander continued to feel pressure from ardent nationalists. He complained of being reproached for his "passive attitude," and foreign observers wondered how long he could resist "the national conscience." After several more months of futile diplomatic efforts, Russia decided to act alone. First, however, Alexander obtained Austria's assurance of neutrality, but only by assenting to a future Austrian occupation of Bosnia and Herzegovina. Finally, in April 1877, by which time Serbia had made peace but Turkish-Montenegrin talks had broken off, Russia declared war on Turkey.

In the Russian cities public opinion was enthusiastic. Police reports indicated approval of the declaration of war by all classes. But it is difficult to say how the average peasant felt because no one paid much attention to peasant opinion, despite the fact that the peasants still made up more than eighty per cent of the population. Among the educated public there were some exceptions to the general clamor of approval. As the Russian government and conservatives had become more bellicose, some of the radicals became increasingly disenchanted. Tolstoy remained bitterly opposed to Russian involvement. But Dostoevsky's enthusiasm was much more characteristic of the spirit of the times. He believed that Russia was fighting for a holy cause and that the struggle would help unite Russia around its true Orthodox roots.

Another enthusiast for the war was the young mystic, Vladimir Soloviev. His father, despite his differences with Pogodin and the Aksakovs, had been a charter member of the Slavonic Benevolent Committee. In 1877, the old historian published a book on Alexander I; and in it he justified the past Tsar's policies toward Turkey and his sympathies with the Orthodox Christians then controlled by the Ottomans. Vladimir thought about volunteering but finally set off for Rumania and Bulgaria as a war correspondent for Katkov's conservative newspaper – about thirty Russian correspondents covered the war. On the road to Bucharest, he ran into his cousin and former loved one, Katia Romanova, who had volunteered as a nurse. It was later recounted by a family friend how during the war the beautiful Katia caught the appreciative eye of the Tsar him-self when he visited an aid station where she was working. The young Soloviev, however, for some unknown reason, returned to Russia before ever reaching the front.

Meanwhile, the Tsar spent the last days of June and the first part of July in the hot and dusty little town of Simnitza. He watched his engineers build a narrow pontoon bridge over the Danube and his men and supplies cross it in a steady stream; he visited the sick in the hospital station set up near his lodgings; he read telegrams from his generals who had moved further into Bulgaria or who were engaging the Turks in the Caucuses; he met with his ministers and advis-ers; and he visited his troops on both sides of the Danube.

The Tsar usually dined with his entourage under a tent cover set up on the lawn of his "borrowed" estate. One day while dining he heard a funeral knell from a nearby church. Realizing that it was the service for an officer killed in the Danube crossing, he got up and went into the decrepit, dark Rumanian Orthodox church, where an old priest officiated. His ministers and generals fol-lowed. He remained for the whole service, lasting about an hour, and then had engineers prepare a grave under the peristyle of the church, and watched as the body was lowered into it.

The next day Alexander decided to visit two mutilated Bulgarians in the hospital set up near his quarters. He also invited the British military attaché to come along and "admire the work" of his government's Turkish "protégés."[4] By the time of the royal arrival, one of the mutilated, his head having been split open by a Turkish saber, had died. His widow was grieving at his side.

That same day Alexander wrote to his beloved Katia that part of the British Mediterranean fleet had received an order to move closer to the Dardanelles and Constantinople. The British government feared Russian designs on Constantinople and the vital straits, the Bosporus and Dardanelles, leading from the Black Sea into the Mediterranean.

Two months earlier, Disraeli (now a "swine," according to the Tsar[5]) had threatened to go to war if Constantinople or the Straits were endangered. Having witnessed continued Russian expansion in Central Asia, in spite of earlier promises, Disraeli and Queen Victoria were wary of Alexander's new as-surances regarding Constantinople. And indeed some of the Tsar's advisers rec-ommended the establishment of Constantinople as a "free city." Dostoevsky had gone even further when in the spring of 1877 he had written: "Constantinople must be ours."[6]

Despite being near the front, Alexander did not intend to command the Russian troops. Instead, he made his younger brother Nicholas the commander-in-chief. He, the Tsar, was to be a spectator, and hopefully an inspiration for his men. He called himself a "brother of mercy"[7] (nurses were referred to as "sisters of mercy"), and when he visited the hospitals he told the doctors and nurses to carry on as if he were not there. Once again, as had happened more frequently early in his reign, he and others could see him as the benevolent, loving Tsar looking out for the welfare of his subjects. Although he was eager to cross the Danube and set up quarters closer to his troops who were pushing forward in Bulgaria, he temporarily allowed his brother to dissuade him from doing so.

At first the news was good. A week after his arrival, he wrote to Katia that the initial crossing of the Danube at Simnitza and the securing of Sistova had only cost the Russians a few hundred lives, whereas he had feared losing at least ten thousand. After receiving a favorable telegram from one of his advancing generals, he would frequently read it to his staff and some of his soldiers, who often greeted the news with cheers and thanksgiving services. With perhaps as much anticipation as for these military dispatches, Alexander awaited letters or telegrams from Katia. His passion and love for her was as strong as ever. At the beginning of the previous year when she was five months pregnant, he wrote to her as follows: "I enjoyed our love-making madly, and am still all steeped in it. You are so tempting, it is impossible to resist! There is no word for this delirium."[8] The day before that, she had written to him that she could not be without his "fountain," which she loved so.[9] Now at the front, he longed to hear of her and their children. George (or Gogo as they called him) was five and Olga (or Oly) three and a half; another boy, Boris, born a year earlier, had died soon after birth.

As the year went on, his letters to Katia reflected the changing fortunes of the Russian army and his changing locations in Bulgaria. He frequently mentioned Plevna, a Bulgarian town some forty miles southwest of Simnitza. There the Russians were twice repulsed by Turkish forces. Many young Russian soldiers with their bayonets affixed to their outdated rifles lost their lives in these attacks. And in September, although aided by the Rumanians who were now pressed into a more active role, the Russians were again repulsed and suffered about sixteen thousand casualties.

Despite some victories to counterbalance the defeats at Plevna, the war was not yet the rout that many Russians had expected. Some of the Russian deficiencies included the use of old-fashioned artillery, as well as rifles, failures in the organization of supplies and medical treatment, and a poor and disunified leadership. The presence of the Tsar in Bulgaria, accompanied by War Minister Milyutin, meant that there were really two command headquarters. Despite his intentions to remain a spectator and leave the command to his brother, it proved impossible. Confusion and recriminations often resulted.

The English war correspondent who had been impressed by the Tsar's appearance in June at Sistova found him in August to be gaunt, haggard and stooped, with a "hunted expression" in his eyes.[10] During this Englishman's interview with the Tsar at Gorny Studen, a village in the hills south of Sistova, he also noticed that the Tsar's asthma was bothering him terribly, as he gasped for air in spasms. His doctor, Sergei Botkin, was deeply concerned with his patient's asthma, as well as with the insomnia that often troubled the Tsar. Botkin tried to persuade him to leave his troops and return to Russia. But his sense of duty kept him in the field.

In September he wrote to Katia that it was unbearable to be separated from her and that on one occasion he "cried like a child"[11] when reading one of her letters and a dictated letter from their son, Gogo. Later that same evening he had to inform her of the death of her younger sister's husband at the battle of Shipka Pass. Casualties, he reported, had been high on both sides. He told Katia that he prayed God would come to Russia's aid and put an end to the "odious war, for the glory of Russia and the good of the Christians."[12]

Whether or not God came to Russia's aid, by January of the following year it looked as if Russian troops might soon be in Constantinople. In the preceding month, they had finally taken Plevna. In January several more important victories followed, and before the end of the month Russian troops were in Adrianople. By this time, Alexander was back in St Petersburg, having returned in December to a tumultuous reception of ringing church bells, booming cannons and shouting crowds. For a brief time, it seemed almost like the first few years of his reign when he had more freely traveled through Russia encouraging his troops during the Crimean War, coming to Moscow for the coronation, or trying to convince nobles to support the emancipation of the serfs. Then newspapers had reported on the mutual love of ruler and people, and Alexander had apparently hoped to use such a perception to rule more effectively. But too much had happened since then to undercut the confidence of both the ruler and ruled in each other, and matters would just get worse in the few years that remained of Alexander's reign. For now, Pobedonostsev, the chief adviser of the more nationalistic Tsarevich, noted the applause for the Tsar, but faulted him in letters, including some to the Tsarevich, for his military appointments and his lack of a firm will.

The day after the capture of Adrianople, the Tsar's brother Nicholas wrote to Alexander that it was necessary to take Constantinople. But fear of English and Austro-Hungarian intervention restrained the Tsar. He ordered his brother to advance without attempting to take either Constantinople or Gallipoli, which overlooked the crucial Dardanelles. On January 30th, the Turks accepted Russian conditions for peace negotiations, and the following day an armistice was signed. The Russians were to halt at a line which at its nearest point was only some thirty-five miles away from Constantinople.

Alexander sent Ignatiev to Adrianople to negotiate a treaty. Ignatiev and the extreme nationalists in Russia had wanted Russia to continue advancing towards Constantinople. But others like Foreign Minister Gorchakov, always mindful of British and Austrian fears, advised caution. Indeed, Disraeli and Queen Victoria, whom Alexander the previous year had referred to privately as "that old madwoman of a Queen,"[13] were both determined to resist what they considered excessive demands on Turkey. Even after the armistice they continued to fear a Russian advance on Constantinople. In the middle of February, British ships entered the Dardanelles and advanced to within a few miles of Constantinople. Russia countered by demanding and obtaining Turkish acquiescence in the occupation of the little village of San Stefano, located on the Sea of Marmara, only about six miles from the walls of the capital.

It was in this picturesque site that the Russians and Turks finally signed a peace treaty in early March. It created a large autonomous Bulgaria with a large Aegean coastline; provided for Russian territorial gains in the Caucasus and a Turkish indemnity to Russia; stipulated some territorial gains for Serbia and especially Montenegro; recognized the full independence of Serbia, Montenegro and Rumania; and mandated Turkish reforms in Bosnia and Herzegovina.

Russian nationalists and panslavists were in general happy with the treaty. Some thought, however, that it was the very minimum that Russia could be expected to accept. But Alexander was worried, and with good reason. He feared that London and Vienna would find the treaty unacceptable. For a variety of reasons, not the least of which was the already strained national budget, Alexander did not wish war against these two European powers. Consequently, within the next few months he succumbed to Austrian and British diplomatic pressure and agreed to some modifications. After months of complex negotiations, the concerned major powers agreed to meet in Berlin in an attempt to finalize a mutually acceptable postwar settlement.

The Congress of Berlin opened in the middle of June 1878 and lasted for a month. Alexander's Foreign Minister, the vain Gorchakov, was the head of Russia's delegation. But, almost eighty years old and not in the best of health, he had neither the energy nor the desire to undertake much of the arduous but inevitable give and take. Instead, Alexander's ambassador to England, his old friend Shuvalov, undertook the task of maintaining whatever war gains were possible in the potentially hostile atmosphere of the conference.

Shuvalov was probably the most able man for the job. Having just turned fifty the previous year, he was a dignified, aristocratic and conservative gentleman, whose balding white hair and mustache made him look much older. Nevertheless, he had a reputation as a lover of wine and women, and he mixed easily in fashionable London circles. Despite Disraeli's distrust of Russia and his determination to best the Russian negotiators at the conference, the old Prime Minister had private praise for the aristocratic Shuvalov's considerable abilities. Bismarck, with whom Shuvalov was on excellent terms and who kept the Congress sessions on track, also thought that he performed admirably.

The Treaty of Berlin was nevertheless a grave disappointment to many Russian nationalists. The large and grateful Bulgaria that Russia hoped to create was greatly reduced in size; Austria-Hungary obtained the right to occupy Bosnia and Herzegovina and Britain to administer the island of Cyprus. In Asia Minor, where the British feared any Russian advance so near to Persia, Russia retained most of its gains. The powers also recognized Russia's right to annex Bessarabia. Although territorial gains, an indemnity, expanded rights for the peoples of the Balkans, and a weakening of the Ottoman Turkish Empire remained as real accomplishments, nationalists like the panslav leader Ivan Aksakov were bitterly disappointed with Alexander's compromise. When Aksakov openly criticized Russian actions in Berlin, the government exiled him to the countryside and closed the Moscow Slavonic Committee.

When Gorchakov told Alexander that the Berlin Treaty was "the darkest page in my life," the hapless Tsar replied, "And in mine too."[14]

29
THE DEATH OF NEKRASOV

During the period that Alexander II was in the Balkans, a man who especially epitomized the alienated intellectuals' agonizing quest to serve the common people was slowly dying of cancer. He was the poet and editor Nicholas Nekrasov.

The decade following that infamous night at the English Club, when he had read his poem of praise to Count Michael Muraviev (the Hangman) had been a difficult but productive time for Nekrasov. He was often in poor health, and poems with titles such as "I Shall Soon Die" (1867) and "Despondency" (1874) reflect the bleak mood that often struck him. In 1871 he turned fifty. As his hair continued to recede and along with his goatee showed signs of graying, he thought more and more of the past.

He could never forget his "fateful blunder" at the English Club, and although he lashed back at the many hypocritical voices that had mocked him for his performance that night, he never could quite forgive himself. He continued to live two lives, that of a wealthy landowner with a penchant for hunting, gambling, gastronomy, servants and carriages, and that of a radical editor and poet. He was almost like one of Dostoevsky's fictional split personalities, and like some of them, he often berated himself for his sins. The radical poet in him did not much care for the wealthy landowner.

Although he had taken over and remade the *Notes of the Fatherland* into the most successful radical journal of its day, the running of it was often an agonizing job. He used all of his wiles and connections to keep the censors from emasculating it. And although he sometimes lost a battle with them, he was generally successful. He indicated to one of his friends that he also kept the journal going by financing it in part with his gambling winnings.

By the end of the sixties Nekrasov had parted with the French actress Celine Lefresne; and after a brief affair with another woman, he took as his mistress a nineteen-year-old prostitute whose name he changed from Fekla to Zinaida (or, more commonly, Zina). She was a good natured, full-faced and full-figured young woman from the lower class. She had little education, but Nekrasov arranged language and music lessons for her and she often went with him to the theater. She also accompanied him and his sister Anna abroad when he went in 1873 to drink the waters at Bad Kissengen and to bathe at the resort town of Dieppe on the French coast of the English Channel. The spring before the trip, Nekrasov had complained of listlessness and loss of appetite, and so his doctor, like so many of this time, had recommended "taking the waters."

Nekrasov also usually took Zina with him when he went to his Karabikha estate near Yaroslavl or to a hunting lodge he bought at Chudovo, some seventy-five miles south of the capital by train. Once while hunting there with him on a May morning, she accidentally shot and killed his favorite dog, a black pointer called Kado. When they went to Karabikha, as they often did in the summers, they lived in the east wing while his brother and his family, to whom he transferred control of the property, resided in the main house. In addition to hunting and swimming there, he enjoyed walks in the parks on the estate. Sometimes he was accompanied by friends or family. At other times wearing only a dressing gown with a tasseled fez on his head and shoes but no socks, he would walk with his dogs.

At Karabikha he worked on some of his most famous poems. He often paced back and forth, repeating lines to himself, until he was satisfied enough to jot down a line or two From a second-story balcony he could look down at the lower park and beyond on the Kotorosl River, on fields and forests, on meadows and on villages with little white churches.

On one occasion, after several days of especially intensive work, he went out to the lower park and under a huge cedar tree read aloud to his brother and his wife the best part of his poem "Russian Women." It was about two of the Decembrist wives. Like Tolstoy and so many others of their generation, Nekrasov was especially fascinated with Prince Volkonsky and his wife Maria. Whereas Tolstoy had once begun a novel about a man much like the prince, Nekrasov had completed a narrative poem about a character also much like Volkonsky and entitled it "Granddad." During the following two years he completed "Russian Women." It was about Princess Trubetskaya and Princess Maria Volkonskaya and their heroic acts of joining their husbands in Siberian exile. Although naturally allowing himself some artistic license, Nekrasov first researched his two subjects thoroughly and consulted closely with Michael Volkonsky, the son of the Volkonsky couple.

Now an important official in the Ministry of Education, but one who admired Nekrasov's poetry, Michael Volkonsky reflected well the often tangled ideological strands of nineteenth-century Russia. Although the son of a political criminal, he also became a protégé of his parents' benefactor, Muraviev-Amursky. After leaving Siberia, he married one of his cousins, Elizabeth, who was the granddaughter of the head of the Third Division at the time the sentences of the Decembrists were being carried out.

While working on "Russian Women" the poet finally persuaded Volkonsky, with whom he sometimes hunted, to share with him the unpublished memoirs of his now deceased mother. Since they were written in French and Nekrasov's French was poor, Volkonsky spent three nights with him orally translating the work into Russian as Nekrasov took notes. On one occasion, Nekrasov was so touched by the memoirs that he jumped up, said "Stop," walked over to the fireplace, sat down, and began to cry like a baby.

By the summer of 1876, Nekrasov was suffering from agonizing pain, but it would not be until December that doctors would finally diagnose it as cancer of the rectum. Among the doctors whom he consulted that summer was the well-known Sergei Botkin, who, as we have seen, looked after the Tsar in Bulgaria during the following year. This physician was also the brother of a former non-radical contributor to *The Contemporary*, Vasily Botkin.[1]

At the end of the summer of 1876, Dr Botkin was going to Yalta with the imperial family. Not yet knowing for certain what was troubling Nekrasov, he suggested that the poet also come to Yalta for the warm sea air and Crimean grapes. Nekrasov agreed. He and Zina spent September and most of October at the Hotel Rossiya, which was located near the main quay in the center of town. In front of the hotel, across the terrace and the quay, stretched the beautiful deep blue waters of the Black Sea. Behind the hotel, not far away arose the mountains. While he continued to suffer from pain and sleeplessness and remained thin and haggard, he felt that his condition was improving a little. He wrote to his sister that Botkin looked in on him almost every day and was very attentive to him and that the sea and the lush Yalta setting provided him with some peaceful moments. At times he would ride in a carriage into the hills or down past the Tsar's Livadia Palace to the royal grounds of Orianda, which at this time were open to the public. While the Tsar met with advisors, diplomats and generals at Livadia and contemplated war with the Ottoman Empire, the sickly Nekrasov, only a mile away, wandered among the rare flowers, trees and cascades of Orianda, which like Livadia sat up on a hill overlooking the sea.

While in Yalta, Nekrasov wrote the last part of the long narrative poem "Who Is Happy in Russia?" and dedicated this last section to Dr Botkin. He had been working on the poem off and on for over a decade. It depicted seven peasants wandering around Russia trying to discover who in their country could be happy and free. It presented a lively and realistic view of the difficult life of Russian peasants, but yet it pulsated, especially the last part he wrote in Yalta, with hope for the future. The peasants and the young intelligentsia dedicated to their service would yet win out over injustice and the miserable conditions of the peasants. The more miserable Nekrasov's own life, the more he suffered from physical and psychological pain, the more important it seemed to him to be the poetic voice of the people (*narod*). In 1874 he had written:

> My soul is sick, my sorrow grows.
> *Narod*! *narod*! Heroic in your service
> I've not been, bad citizen that I am,
> But a burning, holy anxiety
> For your fate I've carried to the end.[2]

Shortly after the Tsar had issued his ultimatum to the Turks in order to save the Serbs from being routed, Dr Botkin advised Nekrasov to leave the vulnerable Crimean area. Nekrasov took his advice, and by the end of October he was back in the capital. To his friends his condition appeared worse that ever. One of them, a co-editor of the *Notes of the Fatherland*, the satirist Saltykov-Shchedrin, noted that Nekrasov was now in almost constant pain, had lost his appetite, and had great difficulty sleeping. His thinning body and face contributed to the alarm which his friends felt for him. Nekrasov grew increasingly despondent and thought of suicide. Difficulties he had that fall with the censors contributed to his gloom, and they would not let him print the final portion of "Who Is Happy in Russia?"

In December, after his disease was finally diagnosed as cancer of the rectum, his doctors recommended an operation. Nekrasov said that he would rather die than subject himself to one. Nevertheless, his sister wrote to a famous surgeon in Vienna asking whether he would be willing to come to St Petersburg in order to operate. Meanwhile her brother's suffering continued. Neither the opium, which he took three times a day, nor the loving care which she and Zina competed with each other to lavish upon him could do much to alleviate the pain. One December night he captured the suffering and Zina's tender, caring love when he wrote:

> Already two hundred days,
> Two hundred nights
> My suffering continues;
> Night and day
> In your heart
> My groans resound;
> Already two hundred days, two hundred nights!
> Dark winter days,
> Clear winter nights …
> Zina! Close your weary eyes!
> Zina! Sleep![3]

In February and March, the Russian painter Ivan Kramskoi came to Nekrasov's Liteiny apartment. He was commissioned to paint the dying Nekrasov by one of Russia's new breed of wealthy businessmen, the deeply nationalistic art lover and collector Paul Tretyakov.

Fourteen years earlier in the name of artistic freedom, Kramskoi had led a protest of fourteen art students against certain restrictions of the government-run Academy of Arts. He and the other artists then formed an artists' cooperative. At the beginning of the seventies he played an important role in helping to give birth to another organization, the Association of Traveling Art Exhibits. He and the other "Itinerants," as the members of this group called themselves, did not all share the same political ideas. Like Nekrasov, however, most of these gifted artists were sympathetic with the suffering masses and devoted to a realistic depiction of Russian life. Their paintings would become the best of Alexander II's era.

In early April, just eight days before the declaration of war on the Ottoman Empire, Nekrasov took a step he had never cared to take before. He got married. It was a sign of his appreciation and love for Zina and perhaps of his desire to make her future more secure after his death. The ceremony occurred at Nekrasov's apartment. Since the only legal marriage that could be performed was a religious one, Nekrasov's friends arranged for the presence of an Orthodox priest. And through the War Department, they obtained and set up in Nekrasov's reception room a portable church tent. The pale, suffering, barefooted, gray-goateed Nekrasov wore only a long white shirt-gown.

One week later the famous Viennese surgeon Bilroth arrived in St Petersburg in order to operate on Nekrasov. The poet had finally agreed. The following day the doctor came to Nekrasov's at 8:00 in the morning and checked him over. At 1:00 p.m. Bilroth performed a colotomy, but the patient had received chloroform and felt no pain during the operation.

Less than two months later, apparently in the beginning of June, Nekrasov had another well-known visitor, Ivan Turgenev. Since breaking off his relationship with Nekrasov in the early 1860s, Turgenev had remained hostile to his former editor and friend and to most of his poetry.

During recent years Turgenev had spent most of his time in and around Paris. In the city, he lived in Montmarte in four rooms above the quarters of Pauline Viardot and her family. And in Bougival, about an hour from the city on a bank overlooking the Seine, he and the Viardots in 1874 bought a large estate. Although Turgenev had a separate Swiss chalet constructed for himself on the property, he remained almost a member of the Viardot family. His life with the Viardots, as well as some of his stories of the early and mid-seventies, indicated that he had still not outgrown or resolved some of the fears and passions of his childhood. Despite being three years younger than Turgenev, who would be sixty in 1878, Pauline must have continued on his unconscious level to remind him of his mother. Once in the early part of the decade when she was on concert tour, he wrote to her: "Your absence causes me physical anxiety, as if I didn't have enough air. It is a secret and obscure ennui from which I cannot escape … When you are here, I experience a calm joy, I feel at home, I wish nothing more."[4]

In Paris, Turgenev frequently associated with other writers, including George Sand, Flaubert, Zola and the American Henry James. He and Flaubert became especially close. The Frenchman nicknamed his Russian friend the "soft pear"[5] due to his weak-willed nature and apparent lack of backbone. Although the "gentle giant," as some called him, was not always accommodating – he had after all quarreled with Tolstoy and Dostoevsky as well as Nekrasov – he had a reputation for being a man who found it difficult to say "no" unless an important principle was at stake. Some thought that on occasion the Viardots took advantage of his unwillingness to refuse a favor. He was frequently seen on the Paris streets running errands. And for the many Russians who for one reason or another turned up at his Paris address and besieged him with a variety of requests, he almost inevitably did what he could. He read manuscripts for them, wrote letters of recommendation, even lent them money. Most years, he also spent a month or two in Russia, and there were also occasional trips to London, Karlsbad, or other parts of Europe. But France had become his home base.

In January and February 1877, Turgenev's novel *Virgin Soil* appeared in the Russian journal *The Messenger of Europe*. Except for the short novel *Spring Torrents*, it was the first novel he had published since *Smoke* had appeared a decade before. In his new novel he depicted two young idealists, Nezhdanov and Marianna, who wished, like the radical Populists of the mid-seventies, to "go to the people." But for his spokesman in the novel, Turgenev turned towards a new type of individual: the sober factory manager Solomin, who had received scientific and technical schooling in England. Like Turgenev, he sympathized with the revolutionaries' desire to overcome Russian backwardness, but felt that revolutionary activities would prove fruitless. Only patient hard work among the peasants and their gradual enlightenment would bring positive results. Unlike Turgenev, Solomin came from a humble background, perhaps reflecting Turgenev's increasing doubts that any real reform would come from the efforts of his own class. Neither the Right nor the Left liked this new novel. Half of the government's censorship committee had voted against allowing the publication of the second part of it. Only the Minister of Interior's convoluted political reasoning had permitted the latter portion of *Virgin Soil* to appear. On the Left, Nekrasov's co-editor Saltykov-Shchedrin was very critical of Turgenev's portrayal of young radicals. Nekrasov himself stated to a friend that he thought that the second part of the novel was not very good. Nekrasov thought that Turgenev was not objective enough, that he was too critical of the Populist movement.

At the end of May, while in the capital, Turgenev apparently received a note from Nekrasov in which the poet expressed his kind feelings towards Turgenev and his desire to see him. Knowing that Nekrasov was dying, Turgenev was willing under the circumstances to forget their past differences.

Death and the thought of dying continued to haunt Turgenev as it had for many years. The older he got, the more he heard about the deaths of friends and acquaintances of former days. The previous summer the frazzled but still rebellious Bakunin had died in a Berne hospital. The two men had once been close when they had studied together in Berlin twenty-five years earlier, but in the sixties and seventies Turgenev grew increasingly critical of the gigantic, slovenly rebel and his influence on Russian youth. Although Turgenev was not yet aware of it, at about the same time that he heard from Nekrasov, another old rebel, Nicholas Ogarev, was on his deathbed in Greenwich, England. At the time of Herzen's death Bakunin had promised Ogarev: "We shall die in action."[6] But then Bakunin had never been a very accurate prophet. In the same year as Bakunin's death, George Sand had died. This woman, whom Tolstoy had once so vehemently criticized in Nekrasov's old apartment, had become an especially close friend of Turgenev's during the seventies.

Just two months before hearing from Nekrasov, Turgenev had written in his diary: "My soul is darker than a dark night. It is as if the grave is hurrying to swallow me up."[7] Except for the gout and a few minor ailments, Turgenev was not really in bad health for a man close to sixty, but the idea of visiting a dying man three years younger than himself was probably not one that Turgenev entertained with enthusiasm.

Nevertheless, accompanied by a mutual acquaintance, Turgenev came to the poet's apartment on the Liteiny Prospect. As Zina remembered the event many years later, she went to her husband's bedroom, helped him put on a dressing gown, and assisted him into their large dining room, where he sat down at the table. Turgenev approached from the reception room, through the poet's study, to the door of the dining room. He was carrying a top hat in his hand. His tall, full physique and full gray beard were quite a contrast to the smaller and emaciated Nekrasov. In a prose poem written about the meeting Turgenev wrote: "Yellow, wrinkled, completely bald, with a thin gray beard ... he stretched out to me this terribly thin hand that looked as if it were gnawed upon."[8]

Turgenev's account and that of Zina differ somewhat, but the composite picture they present is a scene in which Nekrasov did not feel up to conversing with his former friend, and so no conversation took place. But the faces of both men revealed strong emotions. Turgenev was moved by the pitiful, hideous condition of Nekrasov and stayed only a minute or two. Zina says that he silently blessed her husband before leaving. Turgenev suggests that he took Nekrasov's hand and in the face of death was reconciled with his old friend.

Neither account is very explicit as to the thoughts or exact emotions experienced by Nekrasov.

Overcoming some reservations about the bumpy carriage ride that would be necessary, Nekrasov rode out to spend July and August in a countryside dacha along the little Black River. At times he dictated to his sister or brother Constantine portions of memoirs he hoped to complete.

Back in the city during the fall, his condition continued to worsen. By December his appetite had almost disappeared; he usually felt too weak to move about, even with assistance, and his face had taken on a pale green pallor. Nevertheless, during these fall months he followed the news of the war in the papers, wrote some short poems, and in his weak, almost whispering voice talked occasionally with family or friends.

In a few of his poems he bemoaned the suffering which the war was causing both to the soldiers at the front and to their families and friends back at home. In the last poem he ever wrote, he spoke, as he often had before, of his past failings and guilt. In the final months of his life, his 1866 poem to Muraviev "the Hangman" and other transgressions continued to haunt him. He hoped his love and poetic service to the people would make up for his sins, but he could not be sure.

In November one of his friends briefly cheered him up when he conveyed to him a message from the still exiled Chernyshevsky. From a miserable Siberian village several hundred kilometers from Yakutsk, this hero of the radical Left wrote to their mutual friend. "Tell him [Nekrasov] that I have always dearly loved him ... that I thank him for his kindly disposition towards me ... that I am convinced that his fame will be immortal and the love of Russia eternal towards him, the greatest and most valuable of Russian poets. I weep for him."9

Nekrasov had not forgotten the man whom it had once cost him so dearly to support. Earlier that year he had made provisions in his will for Chernyshevsky's family. And now when he received his message, he told his friend to write to Chernyshevsky, thanking him and telling him that his words were a great comfort.

It was apparently a few weeks after hearing the comforting words of Chernyshevsky that Nekrasov received his last visit from still another old acquaintance – Dostoevsky. Despite their considerable ideological differences, Dostoevsky never forgot Nekrasov's enthusiastic "discovery" of him in 1845 when they were both young men of twenty-three. In the January issue of *The Diary of a Writer*, Dostoevsky recalled how the young editor Nekrasov had come to his apartment shortly after 4:00 a.m. one warm, beautiful, bright-as-day St Petersburg morning. He had come to give the young Dostoevsky the news so dear to every aspiring young writer – that he (Nekrasov) had read Dostoevsky's first novel, *Poor Folk*, and considered it a triumph. In true Russian style, the usually reserved Nekrasov, had embraced him and been close to tears of happiness. Dostoevsky referred to this experience as part of "something so youthful, so fresh and good which is forever preserved in the hearts of those who have lived through this experience."[10]

In addition to this fond memory, Dostoevsky greatly appreciated much of Nekrasov's poetry. He especially liked that which reflected the poet's love of the people and his recognition of their suffering, goodness and wisdom. Nekrasov had also once written a poem called "The Unfortunates," in which he depicted a brave political exile. When Dostoevsky returned from Siberian exile, Nekrasov told him that when he wrote the poem he was thinking of him. After Nekrasov had begun publishing Dostoevsky's *A Raw Youth* in the *Notes of the Fatherland*, they met on occasion. When Dostoevsky heard that Nekrasov was seriously ill, he visited him from time to time. Sometimes they talked about the past. At other times Nekrasov would read to him one of his latest poems. Sometimes, if Nekrasov did not seem up to a visit, Dostoevsky would just ask one of the family or servants to convey his warm greetings. When Dostoevsky visited him late that fall, he thought that he looked like a corpse. A few weeks later Nekrasov suffered a stroke which paralyzed the right side of his body. He grew still weaker, complained of pain in his head and throat, and on December 26th 1877, in a barely distinct voice, he seemed to say farewell to his wife and sister. He died the following evening.

Dostoevsky heard the news the next morning and went to Nekrasov's apartment that same day to pay his respects. He thought that the corpse's face looked disfigured as a result of his suffering, and he recalled the psalmist reading over him the words, "There is no man who has not sinned."[11] After returning home, Dostoevsky picked up Nekrasov's collected poems and read one after another until 6:00 a.m. Early on the morning of December 30th, Dostoevsky and his wife Anna returned to Nekrasov's apartment to take part in the funeral procession. It was clear, cold and frosty, and the late-rising winter sun still had not appeared. A crowd of young people, some carrying wreaths, were already there. At about 9:00 a.m. the coffin was carried out into the street, and the procession began. It headed southwest for the Novodevichy Convent, about four miles away. Across the Nevsky Prospect and past the Technological Institute, and then due south across the Obvodny Canal, the procession of thousands slowly made its way. The closed casket was supported on the shoulders of willing youths and friends. In front of the coffin others carried laurel wreaths bearing such inscriptions as "From Russian women," "To the poet of the people's suffering," "To Nekrasov from the students." Others in the procession heartily led the singing of a traditional hymn.

Dostoevsky allowed himself to be persuaded by the always solicitous Anna that it was too cold for him to accompany the crowd for the whole distance. So after a short time, he and Anna returned home. A few hours later they went to the church of the Novodevichy Convent. The procession did not arrive until close to 1:00 p.m. Between those waiting at the convent and those who had accompanied Nekrasov's body, the crowd now swelled to about five thousand. Writers and other members of the intelligentsia, members of other professions, workers, students and professional revolutionaries were among the crowd.

One revolutionary organization, Land and Liberty, decided to take part openly in the funeral. The group had been formed the previous year, due in large part to the efforts of a friend of Sophia Perovskaya, who herself at present was among those being tried in the "Trial of the 193." The organization prepared a wreath reading "From the Socialists." Some of its members carried revolvers and were prepared to use them should the police try to seize the wreath.

After the service in the overheated church, into which only a small portion of the crowd could fit, the coffin was taken to the convent cemetery. Within its walls the crowd pressed against each other. The coffin was lowered into its grave; the last hymn was sung, and some of Nekrasov's friends and admirers spoke of him to those assembled. Dostoevsky was one of the speakers. He spoke of Nekrasov's love for the people, especially for the suffering and unfortunate. Dostoevsky said that the poet followed in the footsteps of Pushkin and Lermontov in introducing a "new word" into Russian poetry.[12] One of the radical youth interrupted him and yelled that Nekrasov was greater than Pushkin or Lermontov. Others repeated the cry, but then allowed Dostoevsky to finish his remarks. By the time the crowd dispersed, the brief St Petersburg daylight hours of this cold winter day had ended, and the sun had been replaced by the stars.

30
A VISIT TO A MONASTERY

Less than five months after the death of Nekrasov, Dostoevsky was crushed by the death of someone much closer to him, his two-year-old son Alyosha. One May morning in 1878, shortly before the family was to leave the capital for their summer retreat at Staraya Russa, Anna noticed that her little Alyosha's oval face began to twitch. She called the children's doctor, who came over, gave her a prescription, and assured her that the twitching would soon cease. But since it continued, she awoke Dostoevsky, and they decided to seek out a specialist in nervous disorders. The specialist promised to come as soon as possible and arrived early in the afternoon. By that time the infant was unconscious, and his little body convulsed sporadically in spasms. The doctor told Dostoevsky, but not Anna, that the boy was near death. Dostoevsky knelt down next to the couch where they had placed Alyosha. Anna knelt beside him, not knowing what the doctor had told her husband. About an hour later, after the convulsions had begun to occur less frequently, the infant stopped breathing. His father kissed him, made the sign of the cross over him three times, and let out his grief in sobs and tears. Anna and the other children, their eight-year-old daughter Lyubov and the six-year-old Fedor, also cried.

A few days later, after a church service, the family stood in the Great Okhta Cemetery on a beautiful May day and watched Alyosha's little white coffin being lowered into the ground.

Both father and mother were deeply distraught by the unexpected death. Dostoevsky was especially troubled by the thought that his boy had died of epilepsy, which he had inherited from him. Anna grew apathetic and her head swam with memories of her toddler. Each of the spouses tried to comfort the other. Anna asked a young friend of Dostoevsky to persuade her husband to accompany him to a monastery that he was planning to visit that summer.

The young friend was Vladimir Soloviev, the son of the historian. Dostoevsky had first met both Vladimir and his older brother Vsevolod in 1873. But in the beginning it was the older brother, a minor writer and government official, who became friendliest with Dostoevsky. It was not until Vladimir's return from Egypt, and his acceptance in early 1877 of a position on the Academic Committee of the Ministry of Education, that he settled in the capital and became a close friend of the older Dostoevsky.

Vladimir reminded Dostoevsky of a friend of his youth, a certain Shidlovsky, who had had a great influence on him. Anna, like many others, noted Soloviev's laughter. She thought it gay and infectious. But at least one society lady thought it repellent. It seems to have been loud and uninhibited, at times preceded by a shriek. (In the first lecture that he gave at the Higher Courses for Women in Moscow in 1875, Soloviev had stressed the ability to laugh as one of human nature's most important characteristics.) Anna also noted Soloviev's other-worldly, absent-minded nature, especially when he failed to notice that she was much younger than her husband. Soloviev's face reminded Dostoevsky of one of his favorite paintings, the "Head of the Young Christ" by Carracci. By the time they became close friends, the young man's pale face was framed against long, dark, wavy hair, accompanied by a mustache and beard which grew longer towards the end of the decade. But his deep, dark, penetrating eyes, under thick dark brows, remained his most notable feature. While many believed it the face of a mystic or holy man, others detected a certain sensuality in it. He was indeed a man of strong erotic tendencies, but an almost obsessive fear of venereal disease, coupled with his ethical principles and mystical inclinations, enabled him to sublimate these tendencies into his mystical doctrine of Sophia, the vision of whom he had experienced in the Egyptian desert.

Despite the differences in age between Dostoevsky and the young Soloviev, the two men had a great deal in common. Both believed in a Russian messianic mission and in Russia's central role in helping to bring about a religious renaissance in the world. Dostoevsky tended to be more hostile to the West and its influences than did the young Soloviev, but at times the novelist also acknowledged the positive aspects of Western civilization and Russia's indebtedness to it. Soloviev, on the other hand, like Dostoevsky, spoke of the West's recent degeneration into egoism and anarchy, into a condition of godlessness and the worship of money.

In April of 1877, just as Russia was preparing to go to war with the Ottoman Turks, Soloviev spelled out some of these ideas in a public lecture entitled "Three Forces." At this time he shared Dostoevsky's hope that the coming war would help to awaken the Russian nation to its religious mission in the world.

At the beginning of the following year, with the war still in progress, Soloviev began a series of twelve talks entitled "Lectures on Godmanhood." They continued into the spring. Soloviev decided that the proceeds from the lectures were to go to the Red Cross and for the restoration of the Church of the Holy Wisdom (Sophia) in Constantinople. Despite their rather abstract, philosophic nature, these lectures held in a lecture hall along the Fontanka Canal were well attended. Among the thousands who came to hear one or more of the twenty-five-year-old philosopher's lectures were Dostoevsky and Anna; Princess Volkonskaya, the daughter-in-law of the now dead Decembrist; Pobedonostsev, the chief adviser of the Tsarevich Alexander; and Leo Tolstoy.

On the only night Tolstoy attended, Soloviev read his lecture to a hall so packed that even women in their evening clothes were sitting on the window-sills because there were no more empty chairs. The central theme of the lectures was the falling away of the world from the Divine and then the gradual incarnation of the Divine into the world. The appearance of Jesus Christ was the most perfect expression of this incarnation, but it was up to humanity to help bring about the more complete worldly incarnation of the Divine. Soloviev's idea of Godmanhood was closely related to his mystical visions of Sophia, or Holy Wisdom. He stated in one of the lectures that "Sophia is the ideal or perfect humanity, eternally contained in the integral divine being or Christ."[1] Both Godmanhood and Sophia represented for the young philosopher and mystic his utopian desire to bridge the gap between heaven and earth and to create a universal oneness. As he had indicated years earlier to his cousin Katia, he hoped to help bring about the Kingdom of God on earth, "the kingdom of eternal, spiritual relations, of pure love and happiness."[2]

Although Tolstoy had found Soloviev's ideas stimulating when the young man had come to visit him at Yasnaya Polyana three years earlier, his private reaction now was "childish nonsense."[3] But many others, including Dostoevsky, would have strongly disagreed had they known Tolstoy's reaction. Nevertheless, the Dostoevskys would very much have liked to have met Tolstoy that night all three of them attended the same lecture. Despite being critical of Tolstoy for his hostility toward Russian involvement in the war against the Turks, Dostoevsky greatly admired Tolstoy's just completed novel, *Anna Karenina*. But only later did the Dostoevskys discover that Tolstoy was at the lecture with a mutual friend. The friend was the critic Strakhov, who told them that Tolstoy had asked him not to introduce him to anybody. That was as close as the two great novelists ever came to meeting one another.

In addition to attending Soloviev's lectures, Dostoevsky was also present at a famous trial during the spring of that same year. This was the trial of Vera Zasulich, who was charged with shooting and wounding the head of the St Petersburg police, General Trepov. Although not a disciple of Nechaev, Zasulich had known him and been arrested following the investigation of his murder of the student Ivanov. Now almost a decade later, after years of prison, exile, and more revolutionary activity, she heard that Trepov had had a young political prisoner flogged. She also knew that many of those who were being tried in the Trial of the 193 had already been in prison without a trial since being apprehended after "going to the people" in 1874. The injustice of it all, the thought of what these young people had to endure in prison, outraged her. Then on the day after verdicts had finally been reached in the Trial of the 193 – almost half of the defendants including Sophia Perovskaya were found not guilty – Vera Zasulich walked into the office of Trepov, pulled a revolver out of her muff, and shot him.

Dostoevsky was fascinated with trials and managed to obtain a press pass to Zasulich's trial; it was held on the last day of March at the district court on the Liteiny Prospect, not far from the Neva River. Zasulich's defense attorney did not deny she had shot Trepov, but he pleaded with the jury to understand that she did it for a noble reason. After hearing all the testimony, the jurors withdrew to consider the verdict. Dostoevsky himself had mixed feelings, but this defender of Orthodoxy and Autocracy and critic of leftist radicalism was more pleased than upset when the jury returned with a verdict of "Not Guilty." The verdict and relieved reaction of some observers were bad omens for the government and another indication that support for Alexander II and his policies was weakening.

Dostoevsky's reaction was also indicative of a certain ambivalence that he, as well as many other intellectuals, had about the youthful revolutionaries. His feelings about them, however, were perhaps more unusual than that of liberals such as Turgenev. In a letter to a group of Moscow students a few weeks after the trial, Dostoevsky criticized young radicals for adopting Western ideas and trying to convert the Russian people to them. The youth, he thought, should be learning from the people, especially from the people's fundamental principle, Russian Orthodoxy. Yet he blamed not so much the young, but rather Russia's educated society that had earlier turned its back on the peasants and their truth. He believed that never before had so many young people been "more sincere, more pure hearted, more thirsting for truth and justice, more willing to sacrifice everything, even their lives, for truth."[4] Dostoevsky never forgot his own youth and how he had been filled with noble desires, but misled by Western ideas. He no doubt now hoped that he could help the young radicals of the 1870s to realize the errors of their ways without having to experience all the years of imprisonment and exile which he had.

Two years later, after the detonation of a bomb in the Winter Palace, he confessed that even had he somehow heard about this failed plan to blow up the Tsar, he would not have informed on the would-be assassins. He said it was because he did not want to be regarded as an informer, but it certainly was also an indication of his ambivalence toward young revolutionaries.

Although now a conservative in many ways, in others he continued to have more in common with young radicals than with old reactionaries. His utopianism (though now of a religious nature similar to that of the young Soloviev's) and his concern with improving the lives of the masses were two such ways. In

1875, he had noted in one of his notebooks that General Fadeev, whom the young Soloviev had met in Egypt, treated the socialist followers of Fourier too condescendingly. And a little later he included Fadeev among conservatives about whom he stated: "Our conservative part of society is just as shitty as the others."[5] Overall, Dostoevsky remained a difficult man to label. Although his convictions were strong, they were often complex.

About a month after the death of his son, Dostoevsky left his wife and two children in Staraya Russa, located in the province of Novgorod, and took a train to Moscow. He intended to meet the young Soloviev there and go on with him to the famous Optina Monastery. But he also wanted to talk to the editor Katkov about a new novel he was planning and about a possible advance on it.

He arrived at about midnight on a Monday in late June. He was tired and exhausted and had been bothered by a cough on the train. He told the driver of his horse cab to take him to the Victoria Hotel, but the driver told him that men took prostitutes there, and it was not fit for a decent person. The driver advised the Hotel Europe across from the Little Theater, about a quarter of a mile north of the Kremlin. There, as Dostoevsky wrote to Anna, he took a room for two and a half rubles – they both still watched their money carefully.

He did not sleep well that night. A choking cough tormented him. At about noon he went to see Katkov at his office on Strasnoi Boulevard. Considered a liberal until the early 1860s, Katkov had emerged after the Polish crisis and the Karakozov attempt as Russia's leading conservative nationalistic journalist and editor. He had also published in his *The Russian Messenger* most of the best writings of Russia's great novelists, although Turgenev finally broke off relations with him after the publication of *Smoke* and in 1874 referred to him as "the most disgusting and dangerous man in Russia."[6] At about the time Dostoevsky met with Katkov, pictures depict his long-face ending in a neatly trimmed graying beard and his receding gray hair being combed straight back from his high forehead. His small pale blue eyes were a lusterless contrast to his spirit, which had earned him the sobriquet "Thunderer of Strastnoi Boulevard." Appropriately enough, a genuine thunderstorm erupted as he and Dostoevsky talked about the latter's projected novel, but nothing definite was settled. As the storm temporarily subsided, the novelist drove off to visit his oldest sister, Barbara, who lived in Moscow. After returning to the hotel for dinner, he set out at about 7 o'clock that evening to visit Vladimir Soloviev.

The Solovievs were staying, as they had in recent summers, at a cottage in the Neskuchny Garden. This was a beautiful park owned by the government which spread out over many acres on the southern bank of the Moscow River. The privileges of residing there with his family went to Professor Soloviev for his years of service to the state. Up until the previous year, he had continued to serve it and his fellow professors as rector of Moscow University. He had also been selected in 1870 to be the director of the Armoury Chamber, a Kremlin historical museum. For a time he also made special trips to the capital to give history lessons to the Tsar's youngest sons, Sergei and Paul.

Although a loyal, patriotic man, Professor Soloviev by now was privately very critical of the Tsar, who by sins of commission and omission had contributed to the deterioration that Soloviev now thought he saw all around him: the government had changed the liquor laws in 1863 and drunkenness had increased significantly;[7] so had syphilis, as peasants moved back and forth from the city to the countryside; the gentry class was declining, as was respect for authority and the cohesiveness of family life; inflation, materialism and greed, on the other hand, were increasing, along with deforestation, as trees were chopped down to feed the expanding network of railways.

According to Soloviev, the problem was not that Alexander had been mistaken to try by his early reforms to transform and modernize Russia, but that he was a weak man who feared to seem weak. Therefore, even if fate had been kind enough to send him a strong, capable minister, such as a Russian Bismarck, he would have dismissed him. Yet the Tsar himself did not provide a cohesive sense of direction to his generally incompetent ministers. Although Soloviev's assessment of his times was perhaps overly bleak, his characterization of the Tsar was echoed by many others who had had personal contact with their sovereign.

Soloviev considered one of the Tsar's ministers an especially "vile figure."[8] This was Dmitry Tolstoy, the Minister of Education. Named to his post after the Karakozov attempt on the Tsar's life in 1866, this Tolstoy did not take long to incur the wrath of many professors. On one occasion in the late sixties, Soloviev resigned his position at the university because of Tolstoy's interference in its dealings. The Tsar, however, persuaded Soloviev to remain. In 1877, Soloviev again decided to resign due to a controversy which grew out of a proposed plan of Tolstoy's to revise the relatively liberal university statute of 1863. This statute in the eyes of Tolstoy and in the lackluster eyes of Katkov, who exercised considerable influence over him, allowed too much autonomy to the universities. Perceiving that he could no longer honorably remain as rector under these circumstances, and perhaps beginning to detect a deterioration of his health, Soloviev left the university.

One of his former colleagues who had resigned from the university in the late sixties, Boris Chicherin, later summed up Soloviev's career by saying that he was universally respected for his high sense of duty, his moderation and his complete lack of arrogance or pettiness.

The controversy over the proposed educational changes had also earlier led to a resignation by the young Vladimir. After returning from Egypt, he had once again briefly resumed his teaching of philosophy at Moscow University.

But he did not wish to get involved in a controversy with on the one side Katkov, who had befriended him after the defense of his Master's thesis, *The Crisis of Western Philosophy*, and on the other side, his father. It was this resignation that had led to his acceptance of a position in the capital.

When Dostoevsky arrived at Neskuchny Garden, he found the young Soloviev tired and gloomy. They agreed to leave for the monastery on Friday. During the next few days, Dostoevsky again talked to Katkov, who now agreed on a two thousand ruble advance. The novelist visited several others including the editor, journalist and rabid panslavist Ivan Aksakov, who, like Katkov, had encouraged and praised the young Soloviev after the defense of his Master's thesis. While in Moscow, Dostoevsky also prayed before the icon of the Iberian Virgin in a chapel near the Kremlin and wrote to Anna about his activities, his lack of sleep and his troubled nerves. As usual, he asked Anna to convey his love and kisses to his children.

On Friday he and Soloviev left by train for the Optina Monastery. They headed south past Tula, not far from where Leo Tolstoy's estate lay, and on towards Orel, near which stood Turgenev's property. Before reaching Orel, however, they got off the train and travelled west by carriage for two days over bumpy roads. Finally, they could see across a river, against a background of large pine and fir trees, the white monastery buildings and the blue-cupolated churches, with their golden crosses thrust into the air.

This monastery was one of the most famous in all of Russia. Countless Russians had visited it, many seeking help for their physical or spiritual maladies. Decades earlier the novelist Gogol had come. And just the previous year Tolstoy and Strakhov, who was also on friendly terms with Dostoevsky and Soloviev, together made a pilgrimage to the monastery. Many came in hopes of gaining a hearing from the Elder Ambrose. Some thought him a miracle worker and a saint, others just a wise man of God.

After settling into a small hut, Dostoevsky and Soloviev managed to see this holy man. According to Anna, Dostoevsky was able to twice talk to him alone. The elder resided in a little house with windows looking over a flower bed. There the novelist told the frail old man with kindly eyes about the death of his son and the grief it had caused him and especially his wife. The elder responded with words meant for both Dostoevsky and his wife. Not only did Dostoevsky convey them to Anna, he also repeated their substance in the chapter "Peasant women who have faith" in his novel *The Brothers Karamazov*.

This was not the only passage of the recently begun novel which would be affected by his trip to the monastery. Both his friendship with Soloviev and his experiences at Optina would leave strong traces on it. The saintly monk of the novel, Zossima, and the monastery where he and the youngest Karamazov, Alyosha, reside are based in large part on Ambrose and Optina. When the novel appeared, some thought Alyosha was based partly on Soloviev and that the affection Zossima felt for the young monk mirrored that of the novelist for the young philosopher. Certainly Alyosha's dream of the coming of the Kingdom of God on earth was one that was shared by both Dostoevsky and his young friend. They also both believed, as Dostoevsky stated several months before, "in a real, literal and personal resurrection" that would "come about on earth."9

Perhaps, however, the middle Karamazov brother, Ivan, bore an even greater resemblance to Soloviev. At least Dostoevsky's wife thought so.10 Like Soloviev, Ivan is a brilliant philosopher with a strongly rational mind. Early in *The Brothers Karamazov*, in the chapter "So be it! So be it!," Ivan's ideas about the relationship of church and state are discussed. Although not absolutely the same as Soloviev's, they clearly reflect the influence of Soloviev's second lecture on Godmanhood. The key difference between Ivan and Soloviev was that the former's rationalism was not harnessed by faith and mysticism the way Soloviev's was.

While on the trip the two friends talked, at least briefly, of the new novel. They remained at Optina for two days and nights, then returned for two days along the same dusty, bumpy road, stopping in villages at night. Finally, they reached the train station and returned to Moscow.

31
TOLSTOY APOLOGIZES

In August 1878, several months after Dostoevsky and Soloviev returned from the Optina Monastery, Tolstoy and Turgenev rode together in Tolstoy's carriage over a dirt road heading for his estate at Yasnaya Polyana. It was the first time the two had been together since they had quarreled seventeen years earlier. The initiative for reconciliation came from Tolstoy. That April he had written to Turgenev: "Let us shake hands and, please, forgive me thoroughly for all that I was guilty of towards you … If you can forgive me, I offer you all the friendship of which I am capable. At our age, there is only one good – loving relations with people."[1]

Tolstoy had been prompted to write the letter by the effects of a prolonged spiritual crisis which he was then undergoing and which he later described in detail in his *My Confession*. At the very end of the previous decade, while in a strange town one night, he had experienced a horrifying fear of death. There seemed to be no specific cause for this night of anxiety and fear, spent in a strange inn, and after returning to Yasnaya Polyana he seemed to regain his inner balance. But gradually by the middle of the seventies the fear of death began to haunt him more and more, and it gradually transformed his life. Three months after his forty-seventh birthday he wrote to a friend that he felt old age had begun for him. He defined this as an "inner spiritual condition in which nothing from the outer world has any interest, in which there are no desires and one sees nothing but death ahead of one."[2]

Perhaps the deaths during the previous two years of three Tolstoy infants and his old aunt who had helped raise him contributed to his anxiety and fear. Perhaps he no longer felt like striving for anything except inner peace because he had obtained so much. His income from royalties and his properties made him financially secure. The estate on which he lived was a lovely place, resplendent with the glories of nature. *Anna Karenina*, which he was then writing and sharing with readers in Katkov's *The Russian Messenger*, was a success, and he had achieved all the fame one could reasonably desire. Despite the deaths of three children, he and Sonia still had five healthy children, three boys and two girls. Sonia, who was only thirty-one, was a capable and devoted wife and mother. He himself was in good physical condition.

But, he thought, what good was any of this when one realized that sooner or later the "dragon of death" awaited everyone. "So what?" was the response that came from deep within him whenever he thought of his accomplishments, "why?" or "for what reason?" whenever he contemplated a new activity. Life had become meaningless for him.

It was not that he gave up and did not search ardently for the meaning of life. He did, but like a man lost in a dark forest, for a long time he could find no exit. The Orthodox faith in which he had been brought up had not had any real meaning for him since his teenage years. Nor did philosophy now offer him the answer he was seeking. For years the German Schopenhauer, who had also influenced Turgenev and the young Vladimir Soloviev, had been his favorite philosopher. But like Socrates and Buddha, Schopenhauer seemed to be saying to Tolstoy that death was better than life. Tolstoy recalled the German philosopher's words that "the passage into nothingness is the only good of life."[3]

Even though at this stage he could not envision anything after death but nothingness, he was strongly tempted to end his own life. His fear of death and his mental anguish seemed greater evils than death itself. He was not the type to wait patiently for his end to come some day. Yet, despite the darkness within him, he could not quite make up his mind to kill himself. Perhaps he had overlooked something. So as not to succumb to temptation in one of his many moments of despair, he removed a rope from his study and stopped taking his gun out to hunt.

Finally, he began to detect a glimmer of light in the dark forest of his mind. And he found that light among the simple peasants of Russia. Like some other intellectuals who had rejected their Orthodox roots, he could not find a satisfactory answer to the meaning of life in Western philosophies. Some, such as Turgenev, never found a satisfactory answer to this ultimate question. Others, like Dostoevsky, had already returned to a belief in the faith of the Russian people and never tired of suggesting that only by rediscovering the truth of the people (*narod*) and their Orthodoxy could the intellectuals find meaning and happiness.

While Dostoevsky discovered religious truth among the people, others found other truths among them. Herzen, Bakunin, Nekrasov, composers like Mussorgsky, painters like Kramskoi, many of the radicals who went to the countryside in the summer of 1874, all of them thought they had discovered some important virtues and truths among the Russian peasants.

Tolstoy later described his own condition as that of one who had cast off from shore in a boat and unknowingly headed for rapids which would kill him, until he finally came to his senses and rowed in the correct direction toward

God. He was not the first nor the last intellectual of that period to envision himself searching for new shores. And the shores, boats and water were interpreted in different ways. But the fact was that many of Tolstoy's intellectual contemporaries had initially set out from the shores of Russian tradition, rejecting Orthodoxy, Autocracy and the backward ways of the peasant. They metaphysically or actually visited foreign lands and imbibed foreign ideas, but eventually grew nostalgic for "mother Russia." Therefore they returned in spirit or in fact and went among the people. Some tried to enlighten them, to educate them away from loyalty to church and state. Others returned to learn from the people. Some, like Tolstoy, would try to do both. But the deepest and most essential need seemed to be overcoming, one way or another, the separation from the people.

Tolstoy had remained closer to the peasants than most of his educated contemporaries, but he had rejected the Orthodoxy so dear to them, and now finally it seemed to him that it was their faith that gave meaning to their lives and which enabled them to face death without fear. His mistake he believed had been to think that he could find the meaning of life through reason. But on the other hand, how could he accept religion if he thought it contrary to reason?

By the beginning of 1878, after his trip the previous summer to the Optina Monastery, he had worked out a solution and was once again following Orthodox practices. He prayed, went to church and fasted. The answer he arrived at was that the important truths of religion were not accessible to reason, but beyond its powers to fathom. He no longer would attempt to hold up each church tradition and ritual to the test of reason, but would just swim along "like a fish in water."[4] This did not mean he would accept all the pronouncements of the Orthodox hierarchy. If they were contrary to the voice of his heart, if they told him for example to pray for Russian successes in the war against Turkey, he would reject such teaching.

Tolstoy's solution, however, was a precarious one. In his own unique way, he had always been rebellious and rationalistic. Only his despair and his deep-seated desire to be united with the Russian people led him to forge such an answer.

During the winter preceding his letter to Turgenev, Tolstoy was working on a new novel. He had finished *Anna Karenina*, in which he had had his character Levin agonize over some of the same questions that were troubling him. (See Part VIII, chapters 8–13.) His thoughts now turned, as they had several decades earlier, to the subject of the Decembrists and their exile. He thought of having a Decembrist from the noble class come into contact with Russian peasants in the area around Irkutsk or in the Samara-Orenburg region. This would have enabled his Decembrist to discover the simple and good life of the peasants.

The Tolstoys owned considerable territory in the province of Samara, and Tolstoy went there annually and was fascinated with this primitive area and its mixtures of peoples.

Not far east of Samara was Orenburg, and Tolstoy thought of using the military governor of that region during part of Nicholas I's reign as one of his chief prototypes. The man was Vasily Perovsky, the great uncle of little Sophia Perovskaya, the radical. Although preserving some liberal inclinations himself, Perovsky had stood with Nicholas against the Decembrists in 1825. What Tolstoy had read and heard about the man impressed him. Tolstoy asked his aunt, still in service to the royal family and one-time friend of Perovsky, to send him all she could about him.

For the purpose of gathering materials for the novel he made several trips to Moscow and one to St Petersburg. He talked to former Decembrists and their relatives, including a few of the Muraviev clan. In the capital, he visited his aunt, talked religion with her and received from her letters written by Perovsky. He also visited the Peter and Paul Fortress, where the Decembrists had been imprisoned, and where he received a guided tour from the prison commandant. He left indignant with Nicholas I for being so harsh with the rebels. It was just a few days later that Tolstoy went to hear one of Vladimir Soloviev's lectures, the one in which both he and Dostoevsky were in the audience.

One of Tolstoy's sons later recalled that at about this time, his father ran into Alexander II on the steps of a photographic shop. As he let the Tsar pass, Tolstoy noticed the fear in his eyes, as if he thought that Tolstoy, who he did not know by sight, might be an assassin.

On the same day that Tolstoy wrote his letter of reconciliation to Turgenev, he wrote to his aunt about Vera Zasulich, her attempted assassination of General Trepov and her trial. He believed that the animosity of the radicals and conservative government officials towards each other had reached "bestial proportions."[5] Soon afterwards he wrote to a friend "the Zasulich affair is no joke. These people are the first terms in a series which we don't understand, but it's an important folly. The Slavonic business was the precursor of war, this could be the precursor of revolution."[6]

When Turgenev received Tolstoy's letter he was in Paris. He responded cordially and suggested that they might be able to see each other when he visited Russia that coming summer. In early August, just back from his Samara property, Tolstoy received a telegram from Turgenev announcing that he would come to see him at Yasnaya Polyana. Tolstoy took along his brother-in-law and went by carriage to Tula to bring Turgenev down to his estate.

Since Turgenev had last visited him, Tolstoy had enlarged the main house to make room for his ever-growing family. A sixth child, Andrei, had been born the year before, and a large household staff assisted husband and wife. The children were educated at home. Their mother and father gave them some lessons, and others were given by a whole array of tutors. Tolstoy, who had taught himself Greek, worked with his children on that subject. Among the teachers whom he hired was one young man named Alexeev, who had once been part of the Chaikovsky circle, the same radical group to which Sophia Perovskaya had belonged in the early seventies. But with Chaikovsky and a group of other Russians, Alexeev became converted to a new religion based on Christian teachings and left Russia for the United States. In Kansas they established a commune based on their beliefs, but after about two years he returned to Russia. By the time of Turgenev's visit he had settled in at Yasnaya Polyana with his common law wife and baby. His gentle religious ways endeared him to Tolstoy and the family.

Turgenev remained for two days. Both men were careful not to strain their fragile relationship. Sonia and the children were fascinated with the new arrival. Next to Tolstoy, who was of average height, he seemed a giant. Even though he was only a decade older than their father, to the children he seemed much older. His hair and beard were white, while Tolstoy's short hair and big bushy beard were still predominantly dark. In contrast to their father, who always liked to dress simply, Turgenev wore a silk shirt and tie and matching velvet coat and vest. He had a pair of beautiful gold watches and a magnificent snuff-box. In his high-pitched voice, which always seemed rather out of place in such a giant of a man, he told the Tolstoys that he had given up smoking because two nice Parisian women refused to kiss him unless he stopped. Such talk usually irritated Tolstoy, but if it did now, he refrained from saying so.

During the visit the two men spent some time in Tolstoy's study, where they apparently talked mainly of literature. The room was in a part of the house which had been added since Turgenev's last visit almost two decades earlier. It was here that Tolstoy had written *Anna Karenina*, a work about which Turgenev had mixed feelings.[7] As with most of the rooms in the big house, this one seemed light and airy and was decorated rather modestly, with no hint of ostentatious display.

The two men also took long walks amidst the beautiful estate with its linden and birch alleys, its ponds, orchards, woods and meadows. Both writers loved nature and hunting and were marvelous observers of the wonders of the countryside. Turgenev could tell the birds by their song. On one occasion Tolstoy stopped to stroke an old horse, whispered something to him, and then recounted to Turgenev what the horse was feeling. Turgenev was amazed at his ability to get inside a horse and told him that he must have been a horse himself in a previous life. Some years later Tolstoy would complete a story called "Kholstomer," which he told from a horse's point of view. Once while outdoors Turgenev settled his large body on one side of a see-saw, the smaller but more muscular Tolstoy straddled the other side, and to the delight of others they began bouncing up and down.

Sonia thought Turgenev gentle, kind and charming. She could see that compared to her husband, he was a softer, less decisive man, almost childlike in some ways. He played chess with their fifteen-year-old son and told of past experiences. Sonia thought his descriptive powers were wonderful. Switching back and forth from Russian to French, he talked with animation. He also spoke of the French people, described the villa that he and the Viardots possessed outside of Paris, imitated a hen and the pointing of his gun dog, and admitted he had a deathly fear of cholera.

At dinner when thirteen people sat down at the table, they joked about who would die first. In the past year Turgenev had not written much except some "Poems in Prose," many of which reflected his fear of aging and death. He now requested that those who were afraid of death should raise their hand, and he immediately raised his own. No one else joined him except a reluctant Tolstoy, who after a moment stated in French "Oh well, I also do not wish to die."[8]

When Turgenev prepared to leave to go to his own estate, he probably cheered Sonia further when he told Tolstoy that he had done well in marrying her. He departed cordially and promised to return soon.

Less than a month later, after leaving his estate, he stopped at Yasnaya Polyana on his way to Moscow. He spent three days there, and again left with good feelings towards the Tolstoys. Turgenev believed that Tolstoy had mellowed and matured with age. He also thought him Russia's greatest living writer. At least that is what he wrote to the poet Fet several weeks after the second visit. Tolstoy also wrote to Fet, but sounded a bit more skeptical. He said that Turgenev was the same as ever and that he (Tolstoy) had no illusions about how intimate they could become. To another friend he wrote that Turgenev was as kindly and brilliant as ever, but like a fountain, he might go dry at any time.

Turgenev did not see Tolstoy again for almost two years, but they occasionally wrote to each other. Turgenev enthusiastically recommended to his Parisian friends some of Tolstoy's works, including *War and Peace*, which appeared in a French translation at the end of the decade. In his letters to Tolstoy, Turgenev mentioned his efforts to spread Tolstoy's fame, and he also passed on favorable comments, such as those Flaubert made about *War and Peace*. In one letter Tolstoy displayed his old irritability when he unjustly suggested that Turgenev was making fun of him. But he ended this letter to Turgenev in an amicable fashion.

Although Turgenev did not write much of substance in this period, he did experience some triumphant moments. In early 1879, his brother's death led him to return to Russia, and he was lionized in both St Petersburg and Moscow. He was especially moved by the reception given him by students in both cities.

They cheered him at lectures and streamed to his lodgings. In his speeches, he defended liberal ideas, but even some radical students looked upon him with favor. The arch-conservative Pobedonostsev wrote of him: "This grey-haired madman Turgenev, like the crow praised to the skies by the fox, dissolves with emotion, and makes speeches in which he bows down with enthusiasm before the younger generation."9

Later that year Turgenev, who was the best-known Russian writer abroad, received an honorary degree from Oxford University. Although he did not think that the red gown and black mortarboard hat were particularly suited to his Russian face, he was delighted. Since he was the first novelist of any country to be so honored by Oxford, he had good reason to be.

But perhaps sweetest of all his experiences in this period was a new love. He had always been a connoisseur of the bittersweet delights of "falling in love." They appealed to some deep emotional need within him. Now slightly over sixty, he fell in love with a Russian actress in her mid-twenties. Her name was Maria Savina, and in early 1879 she was playing the role of Vera in his *A Month in the Country*, a play he had written three decades earlier, but which up to now had hardly ever been performed. Savina had been primarily responsible for this new production, and she arranged for the author to be present one evening in the director's box at the capital's Alexandrinsky Theater. He was fascinated with this lively young woman of dark hair and dark eyes who played the role of a seventeen-year-old girl, and she at first was somewhat in awe of the famous author. But it probably did not take long for the resourceful and energetic Savina to feel completely at ease with the kindly and complimentary old man.

They saw each other several more times before he left the capital for Paris, but it was only after he returned to St Petersburg the following winter that he gradually began to express deeper feelings toward the young actress. After two months in St Petersburg he wrote to her from Moscow that he loved her and that his dearest and best memories of the capital were of her.

In late April 1880, having been informed she was going to Odessa to perform, he made plans to come up from his estate and meet her train at Mtsensk. From there he would travel with her as far as Orel, or better yet, bring her to his estate for at least a one-day visit before she resumed her journey. First, however, he had to leave Moscow and go down to his estate. He decided to visit Tolstoy on the way.

During the twenty months since their last meeting, Tolstoy's religious seeking had continued. But it had not solidified his Orthodox beliefs. His restless, questioning mind could not long accept Orthodox teachings that seemed senseless to him. While continuing to revere Jesus and the Gospels, he came to reject many of the teachings of the Orthodox Church, including the doctrine of the Trinity. He also became critical of church-state relations in Russia. He believed that religion should negate temporal authority, not try to buttress it up. Prior to Turgenev's spring visit, Tolstoy had begun work on a book he would entitle *A Critique of Dogmatic Theology*.

On the novel he had planned about Decembrists, however, he had given up. Instead, for a brief time he contemplated writing a novel which would begin in the reign of Peter the Great. The novel he had begun working on in the early seventies set in Peter's era had never gotten very far. In March 1879, he went to Moscow hoping to gather new material on the early eighteenth century. While there he went to visit the historian Soloviev, of whose approach to history he was so critical. Earlier in the decade while working on Peter he had received some help from him, and now he wanted some more advice. Unfortunately, Soloviev was not at home. By the end of that year, Tolstoy had lost any enthusiasm for working on a historical novel.

Turgenev arrived at Yasnaya Polyana on May 2nd, 1880 and stayed for two days. He hoped while there to persuade Tolstoy to take part in upcoming festivities surrounding the unveiling of a Pushkin monument in Moscow. Never one for such bustle and now more doubtful than ever of the value of elite literary activities, Tolstoy refused. Although he believed that Turgenev disapproved of his current immersion in religious questions and his neglect of art, the two men got along fairly well. Tolstoy thought that their conversations about literature and other subjects were interesting and found it "both painful and comforting" to be with Turgenev.[10]

Yasnaya Polyana was lovely at this time. Spring was in the air. The trees were coming alive, the birds were chirping. The two old friends went out to shoot snipe, Turgenev in a brown coat and wide-brimmed hat. Sonia and some of the older Tolstoy children accompanied them. While they waited in their positions for the snipe to fly over, Sonia asked her guest why he did not write any more. He told her that his writing had always in the past been provided by a "fever of love,"[11] but that now he was too old and could neither love nor write.

His statement, however, was not quite true, for a few days later he was at his Spasskoe estate writing anxiously to hear from Maria Savina about meeting her train.

The longed-for meeting finally occurred in the middle of the month. He boarded her train at the Mtsensk station, only about seven miles from his estate, and rode with her for about an hour until they reached Orel. For this brief time the sixty-one-year-old Turgenev felt almost like a young man again. He later said if he lived for a hundred years he would not forget their kisses on the train that night. When he got out at Orel, he stood outside the open window of her cozy compartment and said good-bye. However, he was disappointed that she could not come to his estate with him for a day or two. He later confessed to her that for a brief moment he thought of pulling her from the window and carrying her off with him. The decision, he said, hung by a thread. But surely he exaggerated. One can hardly imagine the irresolute Turgenev performing such a bold action.

After spending the night in Orel, he returned to his estate and for the next few days could not get the young Maria out of his mind. The weather was beautiful, sunny and warm, but whether walking among the tree-lined alleys of his park or sitting on his terrace, images of her continued to haunt him. "What a night … [they] could have spent" if she had come to his estate!"[12] What happiness she would have given him! Such were his thoughts.

32

"PROPHET, PROPHET": DOSTOEVSKY'S PUSHKIN SPEECH

On July 1st, 1879, Vladimir Soloviev wrote to a friend: "I am living through a very sad time."[1] He went on to explain that his father was suffering from an incurable heart disease. The son was then with his sick father at the Neskuchny Garden. On a summer night, amidst the trees, ponds and ravines of this large park, one could sometimes hear from down below on the Moscow River voices singing "Down along the Mother Volga." The Solovievs stayed that summer in the best part of Neskuchny, at one of the pavilions near the royal-owned Alexander Palace.

Just a few days before, they had celebrated the father's name day. Family and friends were there, and Tsar Alexander's tall sons Sergei and Paul, whom the professor had tutored, stopped by. He sat on the flagstone terrace with a blanket wrapped around his swollen legs. His receding hair and full beard were white and his eyes seemed calm and benign, but he knew that although he was only fifty-nine, he probably had not much longer to live. Nevertheless, as he had done now for almost three decades, he continued writing his *History of Russia from Ancient Times*. That summer he worked over volume twenty-nine, dealing with an early portion of Catherine the Great's reign.

Early in October, after the family had moved back to its spacious apartment about a mile west of the Kremlin, the professor died. Shortly before his death, he asked his wife to be brave and told her of the financial provisions he had made for the family after his death. The legacy he left her and the eight children, five daughters and three sons, was quite substantial – professors were part of the state bureaucracy, and in his distinguished career he had reached a rank equivalent to that of a lieutenant general. Upon his father's death, Vladimir sobbed heavily and remained up almost all night reading prayers over the body.

By the middle of October, Vladimir was back in the capital and arrived at Dostoevsky's apartment one morning carrying a large cardboard package. Dostoevsky had returned late that summer from Bad Ems, and the Dostoevskys were now living on the second floor of a four-storey building near the Church of Our Lady of Vladimir, about a half a mile west of the Nicholas train station. They had six rooms in addition to a kitchen, hall and large store-room.

When Soloviev arrived, Dostoevsky was still asleep. Fortified by cigarettes and strong tea, he generally worked at his study desk until the early morning hours. He was still writing *The Brothers Karamazov*. About half of it had already been written and published in instalments in *The Russian Messenger*.

Inside Soloviev's package was a large photographic reproduction of Dostoevsky's favorite painting, Raphael's *Sistine Madonna*, which the novelist had admired many times in the Dresden Art Gallery. A mutual female friend of Dostoevsky and the young philosopher had heard of Dostoevsky's fondness for the picture and arranged to have it sent to her by friends in Dresden. Dostoevsky's wife, Anna, decided to have it framed and to surprise her husband on his fifty-eighth birthday, which was coming up on the thirtieth of the month.

When he found out who was ultimately responsible for the gift, he went over on his birthday to thank her. The lady was Countess Sophia Tolstaya, now in her fifties, and the widow of the poet Alexei Tolstoy. The poet had been a distant cousin of Leo Tolstoy and like him had been more distantly related to Alexander II's Minister of Education, Dmitry Tolstoy. He also had been a first cousin to Lev Perovsky, the father of the young radical Sophia Perovskaya. Alexei Tolstoy had been a childhood friend of Alexander II's and early in his reign an aide-de-camp to him and a good friend of the Empress. In addition to his poetry, some of which Tchaikovsky and Mussorgsky had recently put to music, he had also written historical novels and dramas.

Sophia Tolstaya, who had been a widow now for four years, was a strong-willed woman of great culture: she spoke numerous languages, had a beautiful singing voice, loved music, poetry, art and philosophy and was her husband's best critic. Soon after Dostoevsky's birthday visit to her, the conservative poet Fet would write to her, "I was highly amazed by your intellectual capacities … There are very few women who read poets and philosophers in the original; but I know of no other woman but you who reads and really understands [them]."[2] Some thought that Fet's friend Leo Tolstoy had used her as one of his prototypes for *Anna Karenina*.[3]

In the late seventies, this cultured widow hosted one of the most fashionable salons in the capital. There, dressed in black, amidst dimly-lit rooms decorated with Hindu statues and smelling of hyacinths, the countess welcomed numerous writers and thinkers. Among them were Dostoevsky, Soloviev and occasionally, when he was in town, Turgenev. Writers mixed there with society women possessing literary interests, such as Countess Volkonskaya, the daughter-in-law of the old Decembrist, and Julia Abaza, the wife of the man who in earlier days had lost huge sums of money playing cards with Nekrasov and who in 1880 would be named Alexander's Minister of Finance. At times Countess

Tolstaya prevailed upon one of the writers to read from his works, and Dostoevsky read there some selections from *The Brothers Karamazov*. He also often stopped in to see the countess and have tea with her when he went out on his afternoon walks.

Staying with the countess in those years was her niece Sophia Khitrovo, who had three young children. Dostoevsky also became friendly with her and enjoyed bringing her children and his together to play. While Sophia Khitrovo was a friend to Dostoevsky, she was much more to the young Soloviev. He was deeply in love with this married woman who was several years older than he. Her husband, from whom she was estranged, was a career diplomat who served under General Ignatiev in Constantinople and in 1880 became the Russian general counsel in Bulgaria.

Soloviev had become friendly with the two women partly as a result of his friendship with the man who had joined him in Cairo, Prince Dmitry Tsertelev. He was a nephew of Alexei Tolstoy. In addition, Soloviev greatly valued Tolstoy's poetry, especially that which dealt with human and divine love and their interconnection. Soloviev also liked much of the humorous poetry that Tolstoy had written and was so good at, and Soloviev himself had tried his hand at the writing of such verse. His friendship with the wife of this man, who shared her husband's spiritual interests, and his attraction to her niece were thus not surprising. The two women attended Soloviev's Lectures on Godmanhood, and he often visited them at the lovely Tolstoy estates, Pustynka, not far from the capital, and Krasny Rog, which was near the city of Bryansk, about two hundred and fifty miles southeast of Moscow. The latter estate consisted of more than sixty thousand acres. Contemporary visitors to those estates, such as the poet Fet, found them among the most beautiful in Russia.

But whether walking along the shores of the Tosno River or among the large old pines, both at Pustynka, or down the lime alleys or among the rare and beautiful flowers and plants of Krasny Rog, Soloviev was often melancholy. For his love of Sophia Khitrovo was not fully reciprocated. She was a refined, graceful, cultured and well-traveled woman. Her small, round, youthful face with its slanted hazel eyes had an Asiatic look about it. She had a regal walk and beautiful hands. But she seemed at times to toy with Soloviev's affections. There was an element of sado-masochism in their relationship, with Soloviev on the receiving end. He seemed to be attracted to such strong, complex women, to whom he could subordinate himself. Some of his poems of this period captured his fluctuating, agonizing feelings towards her.

> You are more slender and beautiful than a wild gazelle
> And your speech is infinitely profound –
> Touranian Eve, Madonna of the steppes
> from "*Gazeli pustyn …* " 1878[4]

You are leaving and my heart in this hour of parting
No longer resounds with longing and supplication;
It is weary from years of long torment,
From unnecessary lies, despair, and tedium,
It has surrendered and resigned to its fate.

from "*Ukhodish ty*," 1880[5]

Oh, how in you the pure azure
Is mixed with many dark, dark clouds!
How clearly above you shines the reflection of God,
But how oppressive and burning in you is the evil fire.

from "*O kak …* " 1880[6]

Besides his friendship with Vladimir Soloviev, Sophia Tolstaya and Sophia Khitrovo, Dostoevsky continued his good relations with Constantine Pobedonostsev, the chief adviser of the Tsar's oldest son, the Tsarevich Alexander. Although the ascetic-looking adviser possessed a much more skeptical disposition than did Dostoevsky, the novelist admired his wide-ranging intellect and shared his interest in religion and politics. Because Dostoevsky's writings seemed to support the Autocracy, Orthodoxy and conservative nationalism so dear to Pobedonostsev, the adviser recommended these works to various members of the royal family. He also played a part in arranging from time to time for Dostoevsky to meet and talk with the Tsar's two youngest sons, Sergei and Paul, the same two who had visited Professor Soloviev.

Early in April 1880, Dostoevsky and Anna attended Vladimir Soloviev's defense of his doctoral dissertation at St Petersburg University. He entitled it "A Critique of Abstract Principles," and in it he tried to demonstrate that the rationalism, empiricism and positivism of the West were an insufficient basis for personal, social and political life, and that faith and religion were also necessary. Although his dissertation reflected his considerable knowledge of Western philosophy, and was especially influenced by the thinking of German philosophers such as Boehme, Kant, Schelling and Schopenhauer, young Soloviev's mystical longing for the unity of the human and divine, for the Sophia of the Egyptian desert, was never far below the surface. The Dostoevskys thought that Soloviev performed brilliantly at the defense, and after the crowd on hand dispersed, the novelist congratulated his friend on his successful performance.

About a month and a half later, Dostoevsky left Anna and the two children at their summer home in Staraya Russa and took a train to Moscow. He had thought of taking his family with him, but he and Anna finally concluded that they could not afford the expense. Although they might have been able to finance it if just Anna accompanied him, he had become too anxious about the health and safety of their children to leave them with anyone besides Anna.

The primary reason for the trip was to give a speech as part of the celebrations surrounding the unveiling of a monument to his favorite writer, Alexander Pushkin. Before reaching Moscow, however, while stopped at the Tver station, he discovered that the Pushkin festivities had been postponed by government order.

After arriving in Moscow and checking in at the Loskutnaya Hotel, across from the historical museum being constructed at the end of Red Square, he wrote to Anna that he was thinking of leaving Moscow in four or five days. In fact, however, once he discovered that the Pushkin celebration had been rescheduled for early June, he remained for two and a half weeks.

Nevertheless, in letters to Anna he agonized over the decision of whether to stay or return to Staraya Russa. He was still writing *The Brothers Karamazov* and, as always, he had deadlines to meet. He disliked taking too long away from his desk at Staraya Russa, and he hated being separated from Anna and the children. He complained of sleeping poorly and of having nightmares, including dreams of Anna being unfaithful to him. On the other hand, his participation in the events surrounding Pushkin was too important to him and to others for him to return without participating. If his speech was a success, he thought he would be more famous as a writer, more on a level perhaps with Tolstoy and Turgenev. Then there were the political considerations. Dostoevsky knew that in his speech he intended to praise Russia and to criticize those who would deny Russia's real and potential greatness. He feared that in their speeches liberal Westernizers such as his rival Turgenev, who had returned to Moscow from his estate, would attempt just such a denial. Dostoevsky seemed to think of the speaker's platform as a field of battle on which Westernizers and Slavophiles would joust with each other, using their talks on Pushkin as their lances. And as he explained to Anna, he was the main hope of the Slavophile camp.

Dostoevsky's assessment was partly correct. Turgenev was part of the event's organizing committee operating in behalf of the Society of Lovers of Russian Literature. He and many others hoped that the celebration might mark an important turning point, signaling the increased participation of educated public opinion in the country's important affairs, whether cultural, social, or political. Turgenev's liberal aspirations, however, did not prevent him from attempting to block any official participation in the ceremonies by the conservative editor Katkov.

During the two weeks in which Dostoevsky waited impatiently for the festivities to begin, he visited with friends and relatives, went to the opera and visited the Armoury Museum. One evening the staff of the journal *Russian Thought* hosted a luxurious dinner at the Hermitage Restaurant for him. The already published installments of *The Brothers Karamazov* had increased his reputation, and he was happy with the attention lavished upon him. Included in those who honored him that night was Nicholas Rubenstein, one of the famous brothers who had done so much to further Russian music. Among the gossip that Dostoevsky heard in Moscow was the news that Turgenev had just visited Tolstoy and that the latter was deranged.

During all this time, Anna worried about her husband's health. His doctor had told Anna that due to his emphysema and the weak blood vessels in his lungs, he should be kept from too much excitement. She was also afraid that he might have one of his epileptic seizures, which he had not had since March, and be taken for a madman.

Meanwhile, enthusiasm among educated society increased dramatically as the celebration neared. A temporary relaxation of newspaper censorship and speculation about the upcoming events' significance helped fuel the growing excitement. Even commercial vendors attempted to cash in on it, as candy, cigarettes and vodka packaged with Pushkin's image or words suddenly appeared.

Finally on June 6th, after a two-hour religious service at the monastery across the street, bells pealed, a chorus sang the Russian anthem, and the new statue of Pushkin was unveiled on Strastnaya Square. The square was packed with men in frock coats and top hats and ladies in long dresses and bonnets. Some carried banners and wreaths. To the accompaniment of music, those carrying the wreaths came forward and placed them at the base of the monument. Beyond the square itself, crowds stretched in various directions, with overall estimates of those on hand ranging from a hundred thousand to over half a million.

That afternoon there were more ceremonies at Moscow University, where Turgenev was elected an honorary faculty member, followed by a dinner at the Noblemen's Club and musical and literary activities based on Pushkin's works. Nicholas Rubenstein conducted an orchestra accompanied by a chorus and several opera singers. One of the works performed that night was a scene from *Eugene Onegin*, the recently composed Tchaikovsky opera based on Pushkin's great work. Among those who read from Pushkin's works were Dostoevsky and Turgenev. But Turgenev, to the former's chagrin, received more applause than he. Dostoevsky told Anna that a good deal of the applause for Turgenev had come from students of a "westernizing" professor who had packed the room with them. In general, however, Dostoevsky was pleased with the reception that he and his reading received.

The next day there were more speeches and another literary dinner. Turgenev gave his speech on Pushkin that day, but neither its delivery nor content made much of an impression. Dostoevsky thought that the speech underrated Pushkin. However, compared to the one Dostoevsky was planning to deliver the next day, almost any speech would not have been enthusiastic enough.

Dostoevsky's turn was to come at the Noblemen's Club on the following day, June 8th. On the night before his speech he wrote to Anna telling her that he was afraid he might have an epileptic seizure.

When on the next day he walked up to the podium and looked out on the packed crowd, he was greeted with thunderous applause. As compared to the majestic white-haired and bearded Turgenev, who sat not far away with some of the other writers, Dostoevsky seemed unimposing. His hair and long beard were still mostly reddish-brown, with some traces of gray. He stood there a little stoop-shouldered in a loose fitting frock coat, wrinkled shirt and white tie. In response to the applause, he bowed and tried to quiet the crowd. Finally, he began to read his speech. And as he did, he seemed transformed. His usual low voice became strong and firm as he spoke with emotion and deep conviction. He seemed to stand straighter and his usually tired-looking eyes came alive. Time and again his speech was interrupted by applause.

In it he told his listeners that Pushkin had well understood that a Russian could not find meaning and happiness if he cut himself off from the Russian people and their traditions. Dostoevsky depicted Pushkin's Eugene Onegin as such a rootless man, but the heroine Tatyana as one who remained true to her Russian roots. Listeners might have been reminded of the parallel with Raskolnikov and Sonia in *Crime and Punishment*. Dostoevsky also spoke of Pushkin's unique ability among world writers to depict the spirit of foreign peoples, to empathize with them. In manifesting this aptitude, Dostoevsky believed that Pushkin was a prophet or forerunner of other Russians who would follow after him. For it was Russia's role to understand and reconcile other nations or, as Dostoevsky stated it, "to include within our soul by brotherly love all our brethren, and at last, it may be, to pronounce the final Word of the great general harmony, of the final brotherly communion of all nations in accordance with the law of the gospel of Christ."[7]

By the time he finished his speech, the people in the audience were ready to unleash a barrage of Russian emotion. They rushed up to embrace him, to kiss him, to present him with a wreath of flowers. There were tears, endless cheers and even a fainting. The other writers on the platform with him also kissed and embraced him. Even a teary-eyed Turgenev, who earlier in the festivities had refused to respond to Katkov's efforts at reconciliation, now hugged Dostoevsky. The Pushkin speech was perhaps the crowning moment of his difficult life. He had always felt slighted when he compared the accolades received by others, especially by his rival Turgenev. As he wrote to Anna that night: "This is a great victory for our ideas over twenty-five years of mistakes!"[8]

The tremendous impact of the speech was due in part to an appeal to Russian pride, which had been heightened by all of the events calling to mind the country's greatest poet. But despite its appeal to Russian nationalism and messianism, the speech seemed at first less anti-Western and more conciliatory than some of Dostoevsky's writings. He stated that "all our Slavophilism and Westernism is only a great misunderstanding." To a true Russian, he said, the fate of Europe was "as dear as Russia herself" because Russia's "destiny is universality, won not by the sword, but by the strength of brotherhood and our fraternal aspiration to reunite mankind."9

Words such as these, plus a brief, but most favorable passing comment by him about one of Turgenev's heroines, helped in the atmosphere of the day to foster a spirit of reconciliation. That night Dostoevsky wrote to Anna that Ivan Aksakov came to the platform after his speech and said that it was not just a speech but a political event and that his words, like the sun, had shed new light, and from that moment on there would be true brotherhood and no more misunderstanding. Dostoevsky also told her of two old men who came up to him and said they had been enemies for twenty years, but that his speech had reconciled them. They called him a saint and a prophet and others took up the cry, "prophet, prophet." That same evening he read at a final literary-musical event. By coincidence it had earlier been arranged for him to recite Pushkin's poem "The Prophet," which he did by heart. To many in attendance that night it seemed strangely fitting.

For a brief period before and during the Pushkin celebration, culminating on the day of Dostoevsky's triumph, optimism was the dominant note expressed by newspapers and public opinion in general. The spirit of these days calls to mind that of 1856 when Kavelin and Chicherin had hoped to unite public opinion around a banner of liberalism. The educated public, specifically Russia's intellectuals, had played the leading part in organizing the Pushkin events, and this fact gave rise to increased expectations for a greater role for educated society in determining Russia's future. To fulfil such a role, however, required not only a continuing reduction of government controls, but a more unified sense of purpose on the part of intellectuals than they had displayed in the past. Dostoevsky's speech temporarily offered hope that some of the divisions separating intellectuals could be overcome. Yet moments of reconciliation, like warm days in winter, never lasted long in the Russia of Alexander II.

Two days after his triumphant speech he left Moscow and returned, exhausted, but very happy, to Anna and the children at Staraya Russa. Vladimir Soloviev, Countess Tolstaya, and Julia Abaza, meanwhile had sent a telegram of congratulations to Staraya Russa. Dostoevsky's call for Russia to peacefully help bring about the "brotherly communion of all nations in accordance with the law of the gospel of Christ" was very much in keeping with the young Soloviev's most ardent hopes for world unity.

Back in the study of the family's two-storey summer home across the road from the Pererytitsa River, Dostoevsky continued working on *The Brothers*

Karamazov. But he also noted to his dismay that after Katkov printed the Pushkin speech in his conservative newspaper, many of the liberal papers in Moscow and St Petersburg came out with critical articles about it – throughout Russia in the six months following his speech it was reviewed in over forty journals and newspapers. As Anna put it, it was as if they had "awoken from their trance, and began to excoriate the speech and demean its author."[10] Although Turgenev did not publicly join the criticism, he also "awoke" and was privately critical, saying that despite the brilliance of it, it was based on deceit. Dostoevsky answered another liberal critic in a polemical article which he published along with his Pushkin speech in a special edition of *The Diary of a Writer*, which he had not published for several years.

Dostoevsky's critics insisted that his speech had little practical usefulness, that it offered no help in confronting Russia's real problems. The main difference between his liberal critics and him, however, continued to revolve around two topics: Russia and the West; and the respective roles of intellectuals and common people. Although always valuing education, Dostoevsky continued to insist that the common people's Orthodoxy was more valuable than any Western-based ideas that intellectuals might wish to instil in them.

By early autumn, Dostoevsky had completed *The Brothers Karamazov* and the family had returned to St Petersburg. That autumn and early winter he began planning to regularly publish once again his *The Diary of a Writer*, and he wrote several articles for the January issue. One dealt with the sad state of Russian finances and with spreading poverty – exacerbated, of course, by the Russo-Turkish War, which Dostoevsky had so ardently supported. He, however, also blamed others such as Jews and railway financiers. And even though earlier he had advocated railway expansion, he now wrote that "the railroads were built at the expense of the destruction of agriculture."[11] But more fundamentally, he blamed Western influence and the intellectuals' failure to learn Orthodox values from the Russian people – who, he noted in passing, looked to the Tsar for "their whole ideology, their hopes and beliefs."[12] He told his readers to worry less about budget deficits, foreign debts and the value of the ruble, and to disregard talk of military cuts. Let educated society turn to the people, join with them spiritually, and economic improvements would naturally follow.

Another article dealt with Russia and Asia. Dostoevsky was heartened by the most recent victories of General Skobelev, whose activities on several fronts during the Russo-Turkish War had won him wide acclaim as a daring young general. Now in Central Asia, he conquered Geok-Tepe, which lengthened Russia's border with Persia. Dostoevsky applauded such Russian advances in Asia. Since Europe despised Russia, perhaps Russia would be better off for awhile abstaining from involvement in Europe and concentrating on playing a civilizing role in Asia. European nations being what they were would fight among themselves anyway, providing Russia with later opportunities. Dostoevsky was not very specific about goals and means, but he was hopeful that the "conviction of the invincibility of the White Czar and of his sword grow and spread ... to the very borders of India and in India herself."[13] Although Dostoevsky still hoped that sometime in a future hour of crisis Europe would turn to a reinvigorated Christian Russia for spiritual enlightenment, this article spoke less of the "brotherhood" of Russia and Western Europe and more of the hostility between them.

This piece, however, was not to appear during his lifetime. Nor was a sequel he planned of *The Brothers Karamazov*. In it, he told the editor A. Suvorin, Alyosha would leave his monastery, become a revolutionary and be executed.

During the last week of January, Dostoevsky began spitting up blood. The exact cause is not known. But his lungs had been weak for years, and his emphysema had progressively worsened. According to Anna, the hemorrhaging began following the exertion of moving a bookcase to obtain a dropped penholder – also used for rolling cigarettes – and an argument with a visitor over one of the forthcoming articles in *The Diary of a Writer*. According to their daughter, it was a visit of Dostoevsky's sister Vera and an argument over an inheritance that set off the flow of blood. In either case, the hemorrhaging continued for a few days. Dostoevsky lay on his couch underneath his picture of the Sistine Madonna. Doctors came and went. A priest from nearby St Vladimir's came and administered the sacraments. Dostoevsky told Anna he was going to die. He asked for the copy of the Gospels given to him by some of the Decembrist wives, decades ago when he was on his way to a Siberian prison. He said good-bye to Anna and the two children. On Wednesday, the 28th, at a little past 8:30 p.m., he died.

On that following Sunday he was buried at the Alexander Nevsky Monastery. The previous day his body had been escorted to the monastery by a crowd even larger than that which had accompanied Nekrasov's body to the Novodevichy Convent. Now on Sunday, just as at Nekrasov's funeral, the graveyard was packed with people. After the coffin was lowered into the ground, various speakers paid tribute to the novelist. One was Vladimir Soloviev. He spoke with great feeling about Dostoevsky's belief that evil could be overcome by Christian love and forgiveness and of the writer's life-long desire for the coming of a "kingdom of truth" on earth.[14] By the time the crowd left the cemetery, the street lights had already been lit.

33

A DEATH AND A MARRIAGE

On that May day in 1880 that Dostoevsky left Staraya Russa for the Pushkin celebration in Moscow, the Empress Maria died, finally succumbing to tuberculosis. Her death had been the reason for the delay in beginning the Pushkin festivities. The nation had been in official mourning.

When his wife died, alone in her oxygen-supplied bedroom in the Winter Palace, Alexander was with Katia and their children at Tsarskoe Selo. Since September 1878, when she was born, there had been a new member of the family, the couple's infant daughter, named Katia after her mother. On hearing the news of Maria's death, the Tsar immediately took the short train ride into the city. Days of mourning and requiem services followed.

After the Empress's body had lain in the Winter Palace for a few days, it was transferred to the cathedral of the Peter and Paul Fortress. It was a gloomy Monday, rainy, windy, almost stormy in the morning when the procession wound its way over the Neva to the fortress. On horseback and in military uniform, Alexander rode behind the body of his wife. Foreign dignitaries, family and others followed behind. After a few days of lying in state, the body of the Empress was finally buried in the fortress cathedral.

One of the foreign princes at the funeral was the Empress's nephew, Alexander of Battenburg. The previous year, the Russians had helped to put him on the Bulgarian throne, but only as a limited constitutional monarch. Although a Russian protectorate after the Russo-Turkish war, the new Bulgarian state was allowed to establish a constitution that allowed full civil liberties and the creation of a strong national assembly based on universal manhood suffrage.

Alexander II's role in helping to create such a government in Bulgaria had helped once again to stimulate hopes for movement in such a direction within Russia itself. In Tver, where two of Bakunin's brothers and others had spoken out and been briefly imprisoned for it in 1862, the provincial *zemstvo* assembly passed the following resolution:

> The Emperor, in his care for the Bulgars, liberated from the Turkish yoke, has
> found it necessary to grant them true self-government, inviolability of personal

rights, independence of the judiciary, and freedom of press. The *zemstvo* of the province of Tver ventures to hope that the Russian people who have borne all the burdens of the war with such readiness, with such unreserved love for their Tsar-Liberator, will be granted the same benefits, which alone will enable them to enter, in the words of the Tsar, on the way of gradual, peaceful and legitimate development.[1]

As with the war against Napoleon and the Crimean War, the war against the Ottoman Empire and the treaties which followed contributed to increasing agitation in Russia. *Zemstvo* spokesmen, peasants, workers, university faculty and students, revolutionaries, conservatives like Ivan Aksakov who were bitter over the Berlin peace treaty and moderates such as Professor Soloviev, none of them seemed very satisfied with the condition of the country. Many educated people, like Professor Soloviev, privately blamed Alexander himself for many of the problems. At court, Alexander's continuing preference for his beloved Katia continued to undermine respect for him. Dostoevsky's conservative friend Pobedonostsev thought at the end of the seventies that Alexander was a "pitiful and unfortunate man" whose will was exhausted and who wanted "only the pleasures of the belly."[2]

Following the acquittal of Vera Zasulich in 1878 and then again after the assassination that summer of the chief of the gendarmes, Alexander approved a number of new reactionary measures to stem the growth of resistance. To prevent juries from acting as they had in the Zasulich case, such cases and other types of political subversion were to be dealt with by military courts under wartime procedures. The government also beefed up police forces in the countryside and in the cities.

Following the assassination of the governor-general of Kharkov in February 1879, Alexander himself just missed being assassinated in April. He was returning to the Winter Palace from a morning walk when a revolutionary, but not a very good marksman, took four or five shots at him from close range. Alexander escaped without injury, but the young would-be assassin was hanged the following month before a crowd of thousands.

The Tsar and his ministers now stepped up the pace of repression. Alexander set up new military governors in the areas of St Petersburg, Kharkov and Odessa. In these areas and in those of Moscow, Kiev and Warsaw, where governor-generals already existed, he instituted martial law provisions. By the summer of that year, the government had curtailed not only some judicial rights, but also some of those of the *zemstvos*, of educational institutions and of the press.

In November and then again in February, the revolutionary organization the People's Will organized two more near-successful attempts on the Tsar's life. The first aimed at blowing up his train as it was coming into Moscow one night on the Kursk-Moscow line. Fortunately for Alexander, however, a last-minute change had put his baggage train in the position in which his personal train should have been. Instead of the flowing of the Tsar's blood, all that flowed was jam from containers being transported from the Tsar's Crimean estates. In the February attempt, blood did flow, but not Alexander's. A young revolutionary workman had obtained a job within the Winter Palace and managed to set off dynamite two floors beneath the Tsar's dining room. Usually Alexander was there by 6 p.m., but on this dreary evening he was delayed by a meeting with Alexander, the new Bulgarian monarch. Moreover, it is doubtful whether the explosion would have been powerful enough to kill the Tsar two floors above. But it did kill eleven and wound fifty-six others, mainly soldiers who were closer to the blast.

In both of these two attempts the main culprits escaped immediate apprehension, and the government was left looking inept and foolish. After the explosion in the Winter Palace, wild rumors spread around the city, and some who could afford to do so left the capital. The Tsar's brother, referring to the terrorists, lamented in his diary, "we do not see, do not know, do not have the slightest idea of their numbers ... Universal panic."[3] These words, like those earlier of the Tver assembly, reflected the general crisis of this period. It was a time of exaggerated hopes and fears. For better or worse, changes of some sort seemed inevitable.

Four days after the explosion in the Winter Palace, Alexander decided to establish a Supreme Administrative Commission with General Loris-Melikov as its head. This commission and particularly its chairman would soon prove to be much more powerful than the type of investigating commission headed by Muraviev "the Hangman" after the Karakozov attempt in 1866.

Loris-Melikov was a dark-haired and whiskered Armenian in his mid-fifties. As a young cadet in the early 1840s he had briefly shared an apartment with Nekrasov and maintained a life-long love of his poetry. He had also been a war hero in the Russo-Turkish war and had most recently proved himself an able administrator as governor-general of the Kharkov Province. He was an energetic, intelligent and flexible man whose appointment was welcomed by both the conservative and liberal press. His job and that of his commission was to deal with the revolutionaries. But he attempted to do this not only by strengthening direct government and police efforts against them, but also by gaining public support for the government.

By the time of the Empress's funeral, Loris-Melikov had made some important gains. His powers had gradually broadened, and he had become almost an assistant Tsar for internal affairs. Terrorism abated and the public became more favorable to governmental efforts. Loris-Melikov ended some of the abuses against personal rights brought about by the reaction of the last few years, and he was sympathetic with increasing the rights of the *zemstvos* and the press. The relatively free atmosphere surrounding the Pushkin celebrations and the hopes expressed for a greater role for public opinion owed not a little to the efforts of Loris-Melikov. His most popular move was obtaining the dismissal of the Minister of Education and Procurator of the Holy Synod, Dmitry Tolstoy. The general's contempt for this man matched that of Professor Soloviev, who had thought him such a "vile figure." Loris-Melikov blamed this Tolstoy more than any other person for inadvertently fostering the growth of the revolutionary movement. Despite Tolstoy's inadvertent help, however, the underground paper of the People's Will praised Loris-Melikov for his role in getting rid of this "Minister of Obscurantism."[4]

Forty days after his wife's death, the Tsar attended the traditional mourning service in her honor at the cathedral of the Peter and Paul Fortress. Shortly before this sad occasion, he told one of his closest friends and aides, Count Adlerberg, that he intended to marry Katia. In his memoirs, War Minister Milyutin, who thought that the Tsar "was completely in the hands" of Katia, recounted what happened next. Adlerberg tried to persuade the Tsar that such an early marriage would be a mistake, but Alexander insisted that his conscience dictated such a step.

Several days later, after the mourning service, the Tsar and Adlerberg again discussed the matter in the Tsar's study, and the count tried to persuade him to wait at least the year usually mandated by the Orthodox Church before remarrying. While Adlerberg spoke, Alexander sat silently listening to him with a pale face and trembling hands. He believed that he had to marry Katia because he owed it to her and their three children. For fourteen years Katia had sacrificed everything for him, including her youthful years; and considering the dangers to his life, he could no longer afford to put off his moral debt. When Adlerberg finished speaking, the Tsar silently left the room and Katia came in to berate the count for trying to dissuade the Tsar from fulfilling his "debt of honor." The two of them argued for some time. According to Adlerberg, when Alexander returned and stuck his head in the doorway to meekly ask if it were time for him to enter, Katia answered, "No, leave us to finish the conversation."[5]

Not surprisingly, Adlerberg did not much care for Katia. Like many at court he thought her uncultured and arrogant. It was not clear, however, exactly how many others Alexander told of his plans, but the number was certainly few. The Tsarevich and other members of the Tsar's family quite naturally resented Katia and had for some time. There were rumors that two years earlier Alexander had given Katia and their children rooms in the Winter Palace and that in her final time on earth the Empress could hear the rival family above her. There were other derogatory comments about Katia's supposed influence on the Tsar and about how the attempts on the Tsar's life were God's punishment for his "sinful" ways. Although the Tsar's attachment to Katia and his treatment of the

Empress were enough by themselves to create tension within the royal family, any plans to marry Katia could only increase the bitterness. To marry so soon after the death of his wife would seem disrespectful to her memory. There was also the question of the inheritance. Even though Alexander planned a morganatic marriage, the Tsarevich, his wife and other members of the Tsar's family could not be absolutely sure what rights Katia and her children might be able to gain in the future.

Several days after Adlerberg's argument with Katia, the Tsar married her in a secret ceremony at Tsarskoe Selo. It was a sunny, warm Sunday in early July, and the old Tsar and his much younger wife seemed as much in love as ever. The Tsarevich and his family were then vacationing at the seaside resort of Gapsal, where his mother and his father in 1856 had happily surprised him and his three brothers with a visit. A little over a month after their marriage, Alexander, Katia and their children left for the Tsar's Crimean estate. Security precautions were extensive. While at the Livadia estate, Alexander appeared officially for the first time with Katia and the children. Although most of the court remained cold to Katia, Loris-Melikov seems to have accepted and gotten along well with her.

By this time Alexander had abolished the Supreme Commission, which Loris-Melikov had headed, but instead made him the Minister of the Interior, in which position he remained the second most powerful man in Russia. In addition, he also continued his two-pronged attack of trying to use more effective means against the revolutionaries and pushing for modest reforms – he persuaded the Tsar, for example, to abolish the salt tax. He also managed to have the Tsar replace certain officials with ones more to his liking. In the fall Alexander appointed as Minister of Finance the liberal A.A. Abaza, the same Abaza who earlier had constantly been in debt to Nekrasov as a result of gambling losses – appropriate experience perhaps for a man who would manage the finances of a government now spending over twenty per cent of its total expenditures just to service its growing debt.

The new Finance Minister and the liberal War Minister, Dmitry Milyutin, were by the end of the year Loris-Melikov's closest political allies. However, the Tsarevich, who had at first supported him, gradually became more critical. This was probably due to the Tsarevich's perception that the Armenian general was becoming too friendly with Katia. The influence of the heir's liberal-hating adviser, Pobedonostsev, undoubtedly also played a part in increasing the Tsarevich's distrust of Loris-Melikov.

In November, Alexander and Katia left the mountains, sea and warmth of Livadia and came back to the cold capital. Before leaving, however, Alexander made up a will for his new family, for whom he had already deposited more than three million gold rubles in the state bank.

34

TWO CONSPIRATORS

Shortly after the Tsar's return from the Crimea, Sophia Perovskaya was on the streets watching his movement about the capital. She was one of the leaders of the People's Will, and she and her friends were again plotting to kill him. Her job and that of a small group aiding her was to detect any pattern in the Tsar's activities as his carriage sped around the city.

For a long time she had been against assassinations. After being released from prison in 1874 and spending some time with her mother in the Crimea, she had worked as a doctor's apprentice in the Simbirsk Province and then attended a course for doctors' assistants in Simferopol, where her father had once been vice-governor. After graduating, she was put in charge of arranging a couple of barracks for wounded soldiers who would be brought to Simferopol as a result of the hostilities just begun against the Ottoman Empire. But before any arrived, she was ordered to the capital to take part in the Trial of the 193, most of whose defendants had been arrested three years earlier for engaging in revolutionary propaganda. At the time of Zasulich's shooting of General Trepov, which occurred the day after Sophia's own acquittal, she still believed that the weapons of the revolutionaries should be words and not guns. Yet tales which she heard of mistreatment of prisoners angered her, and her opposition to actions such as those of Zasulich began to soften.

Following the Zasulich shooting and trial, more and more of her fellow revolutionaries began turning to the use of terroristic methods. The circumstances Sophia and others often found themselves in encouraged this: she worked in St Petersburg and then in Kharkov aiding imprisoned friends and trying to help some of them escape. By late 1878, she had joined the revolutionary group Land and Liberty, formed by her friend Mark Natanson, who had also begun the earlier Chaikovsky circle. After witnessing the mass arrests following the "going-to-the-people" movement of 1874, Natanson and others decided that the revolutionary movement needed a new organization. For it they adopted the same name used by the short-lived revolutionary group aided in the early sixties by Herzen, Ogarev and Bakunin. And the ideas of all three men, especially those of Bakunin, continued to live on in the new Land and Liberty.

By the time Sophia joined it, Natanson had been arrested, but about two hundred other members, scattered around the country, carried on the work. A small number of revolutionaries in the capital attempted to provide overall direction. The activities of Land and Liberty included propaganda among workers and peasants, the writing and clandestine printing of the group's publications, the forging of internal passports, fund raising and the gathering of intelligence about police and government movements. A number of activities fell under the classification "disorganization." These included liberating prisoners, killing informers and assassinating government officials.

As the number of assassinations increased in 1878 and 1879, it finally led to the break up of Land and Liberty into two opposing groups. Those who advocated using terror, hoping thereby to bring down the government, called themselves the People's Will. Those who opposed this emphasis, which they thought came at the expense of work among the people, became known as the Black Repartition. For a short time Sophia wavered between the two groups, but finally decided to join the People's Will. In November 1879, she was one of the small group that blew up the Tsar's baggage train.

At this time the ultimate stated goal of the People's Will was the creation of a society which would have the following characteristics: land would be owned by the peasants; the peasant commune would be the basic economic and administrative unit of the country; factories would be owned by the workers; a considerable degree of political power would be on the local level; freedom of speech, etc. would exist; and the army would be transformed into a militia. Most members of the People's Will concluded that the best way to create such a society was to quickly overthrow the present government and allow the will of the people to be heard in a freely elected constituent assembly.

The party's emphasis on haste was stimulated by its alarm at the quickening pace of capitalistic development, sponsored by "the greatest capitalist force in the country" – the government.[1] The underground journal of the party wrote of the evils of this Tsarist policy and especially pointed to the suffering caused by the government's support of railway tycoons and shareholders: "The building of railways in Russia provides a spectacle that is unique anywhere in the world; they are all built with the cash of peasants and the State which, for no apparent reason, hands out hundreds of millions to the various businessmen."[2] Fearing increasing exploitation as the capitalist class, aided by the state, grew stronger, the People's Will hoped to undercut its development by destroying its chief source of support. Terrorist methods were to be used in order to weaken, demoralize and panic the Tsar's government and to awaken the common people to the realization that the government could be overthrown. When the time was ripe for such a takeover, the People's Will hoped to play a central role.

Although Sophia had overcome her scruples about assassinations, she remained more skeptical than some of her fellow revolutionaries about the wisdom of attempting to establish a constituent assembly. She was afraid it would be dominated by manipulative politicians and financiers and never lead to the socialist type society she and other revolutionaries desired. More in the spirit of Bakunin, she hoped for a national peasant uprising, followed by the direct establishment of federated peasant communes. In the spring of 1880, following the failed attempt inside the Winter Palace, Sophia went to Odessa to direct still another effort on the Tsar's life. But Alexander II did not pass through the city as expected, and Sophia returned to St Petersburg.

By the time that Alexander II went to the Crimea that summer, the People's Will had organized at least six separate assassination efforts against him. Only two, the Moscow train attempt and the one in the Winter Palace, had gotten to the point of actually being carried out.

From Sophia's return to St Petersburg in the spring until the Tsar's return in the late fall of that year, she was busy propagandizing among the St Petersburg workers and helping her party to expand its influence and contacts. As a member of its executive committee of twenty to thirty members, she played a central role.

By the following winter, some five or six hundred people, primarily industrial workers in St Petersburg, Moscow, Odessa, Kharkov and Rostov-on-the Don, were associated with the People's Will. There were also several thousand sympathizers who offered sporadic assistance. One such individual was Nicholas Mikhailovsky, a leading journalist and editor of Nekrasov's former journal, *Notes of the Fatherland*. He hoped to help bring about a united opposition of the revolutionaries with less radical opponents of the Tsarist regime. On occasion he wrote under a pseudonym for the journal of the People's Will. Through this clandestine publication, which reached thousands, and by the organization's audacious attempts on the Tsar's life, it seemed a larger and more powerful group than it really was.

While the Tsar was in the Crimea, Sophia's party did not attempt to assassinate him. It would have been difficult to accomplish there, and there were also other considerations. Several of the members of the executive committee were in jail awaiting proceedings against them, and it is likely that their friends and fellow conspirators did not wish to jeopardize their fate. But when two of them, A. Kvyatkovsky and A. Presnyakov, the former a cousin of Bakunin's wife, were condemned and put to death in early November, Sophia and a majority of the committee decided to renew their attempts against Alexander II. Thus it was that upon his return the executive committee placed Sophia in charge of scouting his movements.

Early in December, Sophia made her report to the committee and soon afterwards it decided to rent a shop on Malaya Sadovaya Street, just off the Nevsky Prospect. From the cheese shop they would open there, the revolutionaries hoped to dig a tunnel out to the street, set dynamite under it, and blow up the Tsar's carriage as it passed over Malaya Sadovaya on its way to the riding stables, where the Tsar usually went on Sundays.

By the end of 1880, Sophia and most of her friends were wanted by the police. One of the conspirators of the Moscow attempt had been arrested and implicated them. His confession greatly aided the police; arrests increased, and the leaders who remained free felt the increasing danger that faced them. Life at this time offered few moments of relaxation.

But on New Year's Eve they tried to forget for an evening their revolutionary work and anxieties. About twenty of them met that evening in a flat on Zabalkansky Prospect, in the southern part of the city. Outside a blizzard whirled the snow around. Inside they ate, drank wine and sang folk songs. A large man with a dark beard insisted that no one talk of their work and that everyone should have fun. He danced with all the women.

The man's name was Andrei Zhelyabov, and Sophia had fallen in love with him and was now sharing his bed. What a contrast the two presented! He was tall and powerfully built; she was small and slender. He had dark hair and a long face ending in a long dark beard; her hair was lighter, and although she possessed a large forehead, her face ended in a small chin. He was born in the Crimea, the son of a serf; she in the capital, and her father had once been civilian governor of the St Petersburg Province. Despite being several years older than Sophia, he was the more impetuous, outgoing and magnetic of the two; she was quieter and more restrained. But they also shared a number of qualities: they were both strong-willed, intelligent, courageous and hated the Tsarist regime and the injustices that they thought it perpetrated. The two radicals shared a poorly furnished flat consisting of two rooms and a kitchen, not far from where the New Year's Eve party was being held. In addition to her revolutionary work, Sophia did the housework and shopping.

Late in November, Zhelyabov had suggested postponing the assassination of the Tsar while he and some others went to the Volga provinces. As a result of a crop failure that year, the peasants' misery and hunger were increasing. With his own peasant background, he was especially sympathetic to the plight of the peasants. He offered to lead a peasant revolt, which, if nothing else, would force the government to aid the hunger-stricken. But the executive committee did not support his suggestion. Therefore, he once again devoted his enormous energy to the plot against Alexander II. In January he and others began digging the tunnel from their newly opened cheese shop out to the street.

While the People's Will was preparing this assassination attempt, Alexander was not only trying to rule the Empire, but also to win some degree of acceptance for his new wife. In January he held a sumptuous state ball at the Winter Palace. There, amidst palm trees, orchids and gigantic chandeliers, his guests danced waltzes, quadrilles and mazurkas. The uniforms and decorations of Russian officials, officers and foreign ambassadors were matched by the diamond diadems and assorted pearl, emerald, sapphire and ruby rings, bracelets, necklaces and brooches of the noble women in their long dresses. As others sat down at midnight to eat the various delicacies prepared by the royal chefs, Alexander escorted Katia around from one table to the next to pay his hospitality calls. Katia looked nervous. Alexander tried to be pleasant. But it was probably not difficult for the couple to discern the hostility many still felt for the Princess Yurevskaya, the official name Alexander had bestowed upon Katia. Rumors circulated that she wanted to have herself crowned Empress and that Loris-Melikov encouraged the idea. Immediately after the meal, the royal couple, contrary to etiquette, departed. Despite all the powers of a Russian autocrat, he could not force society to feel kindly toward his new wife.

That same month, the People's Will received a letter from a man about whom many of them still had ambivalent feelings, the infamous Sergei Nechaev. Since being extradited to Russia almost a decade before, he had been imprisoned. Now in the dreaded Peter and Paul Fortress, he had managed to win over some guards and to smuggle out a request to help him escape. The committee agreed to do so, but the attempt was to occur only after they had completed the assassination of Alexander II. Meanwhile, Nechaev continued to bombard the committee with ciphered letters of advice. Zhelyabov was in charge of responding to him.

Zhelyabov also played the leading role in the preparations for the assassination attempt. He persuaded the executive committee, which continued to dwindle due to arrests, to agree to some back-up plans should the mine under the street fail to blow up Alexander. His fellow revolutionaries agreed that he could organize a bomb squad prepared to hurl five-pound bombs at the Tsar if the mine plot failed to come off. And if that also failed, Zhelyabov would attack the Tsar with a dagger.

By late February, Zhelyabov was showing signs of strain. Despite the comfort Sophia's love gave him, he had trouble sleeping and often paced the bedroom trying to sort out the schemes that percolated in his head. He was not eating enough and had fainted once or twice. Meanwhile, he tried to hurry on the preparations for the assassination. He, Sophia, and the others decided that Sunday, March 1, was to be the day. He continued helping to prepare the mine under the street, seeming to seek out physical work as a release for tension; and he recruited and prepared his youthful squad of four bomb throwers.

The Friday before the scheduled attempt, he and Sophia left their apartment in the dusky late afternoon and took a horse cab to the Imperial Library, where they separated. After parting, they both realized that they were being followed, but each of them seemed to successfully elude their police agents. Zhelyabov went later that evening to see one of his fellow revolutionaries, but the police had his friend's apartment under observation. They managed to seize both men. Before the night was out, Zhelyabov and his friend were in jail.

35
BOMBS AND BLOOD

The morning after Zhelyabov's arrest, the Tsar, Katia and their eight-year-old son, Gogo, attended a two-hour Lenten service in the chapel of the Winter Palace. The Tsarevich and other members of the royal family were also present. Later, sometime after breakfasting with Katia, the Tsar heard the welcome news that the terrorist leader Zhelyabov had been arrested. Alexander seemed in good spirits that day, the danger of assassination seemed to be receding.

On that same Saturday, after Zhelyabov had failed to come back to their apartment the previous night, Sophia Perovskaya also discovered that her companion was now imprisoned. In addition, she learned that on that very morning the police had checked out the cheese shop, but had not discovered the tunnel. She and the other remaining free members of the executive committee decided to go ahead with plans to assassinate the Tsar on the following day.

In a flat on the corner of the Voznesensky Prospect and the Catherine Canal, where they met that afternoon, the other revolutionaries accepted Sophia's request that she be allowed to take Zhelyabov's place directing the bomb throwers. They were, however, only to spring into action if plans to set off the mine under the street failed. Following the meeting, she and one of the other revolutionaries returned to Sophia's apartment to retrieve anything of importance left behind. Now that Zhelyabov had been arrested, it was no longer safe for her to remain there.

Later that evening, after several other trips, she returned to the flat on the Catherine Canal. A bathhouse was located in the same building, and the revolutionaries hoped, therefore, that their comings and goings would not attract special attention. Inside the apartment three of her friends were preparing bombs. A fourth, the "lady of the house" and a fellow revolutionary, Vera Figner, persuaded her to lie down and save her strength for the next day. Meanwhile, Figner and the three men continued making the bombs. When Figner went to bed at 2:00 a.m., the other three continued their work. At 7:00, when she and Sophia got up, they were still at it.

That same morning the Tsar attended a church service and then ate breakfast with Katia. Loris-Melikov came over to the palace to show him the final draft of a project that he had been working on for over a month. Alexander met with him in his study, a room filled with photographs and paintings, where he usually received his ministers.

The final draft now before him reflected some changes suggested by a Tsarist committee and was less liberal than the original plan. But it still called for the creation of several commissions – preparatory ones and a general commission – which would make legislative recommendations in the areas of finance and administration to the Tsar's advisory State Council. It also stipulated that some of the delegates to the general commission would be elected, as would fifteen others who would sit with the State Council to consider the recommendations. All of this, of course, was merely advisory to the Tsar, and the work of the commissions was to be strictly circumscribed. Yet, after giving the document his approval and upon Loris-Melikov's departure, Alexander turned to one of his sons, the Grand Duke Vladimir, and said that he agreed to approve the proposal, knowing that he was "going along the road toward a constitution."[1] This, however, was probably a statement of apprehension, and not one of commitment to continue walking down such a path. He still apparently believed that any constitution limiting his powers would harm his country, but he seemed less able than ever to steer Russia in the direction he wished, one in which a loyal and loving people would willingly follow their benevolent Tsar.

Alexander told one of his other ministers to schedule a meeting of his Council of Ministers for the following Wednesday. He wished his ministers to have a final look at the document before it was promulgated.

As he often did on Sunday afternoons, Alexander planned to ride to the nearby Manège to observe some of his troops on parade. At least there, where he knew the names of many of his elite guards officers and felt at home with them, he could still feel like a proper benevolent, fatherly and beloved Tsar. Reviewing his troops, listening to "God Save the Tsar," witnessing the outstanding horsemanship of Cossack riders and chatting with his officers probably helped dispel, at least momentarily, doubts about the reality of any mutual affection between him and his subjects. But before Alexander left the Winter Palace that day, according to Katia's later testimony, his passions got the best of him, and on a couch in one of the rooms set up for his young family near his study, he and Katia made love.

A little before 1:00 p.m. he set off for the Manège. As usual, he was in military uniform, topped of by a dark blue cloak and a white plumed helmet. It was a cold, dreary, sunless day. As his closed carriage moved along the roads, escorted by six mounted Cossacks, he could see dirty snow piled upon the sides of the streets. His carriage was a present from Napoleon III and was supposed to be bomb-proof. As an additional precautionary measure, he had agreed to avoid going down the crowded Nevsky Prospect and past the suspicious cheese shop.

Meanwhile, Sophia Perovskaya and her friends had continued their preparations. By the time Alexander left the palace, some were in the cheese shop waiting for him, and Sophia and her bomb throwers were dispersed near the end of the expected route to the Manège. When Sophia realized that Alexander had not come along the usual route, she moved closer to the Manège and waited for the review to end. When she saw him leave, she realized that his return route again would not lead him past the cheese shop nor her bomb squad. By a prearranged sign (blowing her nose), she signaled the bomb throwers to take up their secondary positions along the Catherine Canal, the other most likely way for him to return.

Alexander decided to stop on the way and visit a cousin, Grand Duchess Catherine, who resided nearby at the Mikhailovsky Palace. This gave Sophia and her men more time to take up their places. When he came out of this palace a short time later, three of the bomb throwers were waiting along the canal, each with a five-pound package. The fourth man had changed his mind and left the scene. On the other side of the canal Sophia watched as the Tsar's carriage, accompanied by mounted Cossacks, approached the Catherine Quay. As it did, she again gave a signal.

Alexander's carriage, also followed by several police sleighs, had gone only about a hundred to a hundred and fifty yards down the quay, when a heavyset youth in a fur cap stepped forward and threw his bomb. A loud explosion followed. Amidst bluish smoke it was possible to see that the Tsar's carriage had been hit, as well as a Cossack guard and a small boy, both of whom were lying on the ground and would soon die. But Alexander was able to get out of his carriage and appeared not to be seriously hurt. Against the advice of his security guard, he took time to assess the situation, rather than leaving immediately for the Winter Palace. He could be stubbornly courageous at times. He went up to question the heavyset youth now being held along the quay railing by the police and soldiers.

While Alexander was still assessing the confusing scene, a second young man approached him with a package in his hand. When the youth was within a few paces of the Tsar, he hurled it at his feet. Again a loud explosion and smoke, but this time amidst the snow and blood Alexander lay wounded with his legs ripped apart and bleeding profusely. (A church, that of the Resurrection of the Savior on the Blood, was subsequently built on this spot.) He feebly called for help and was placed in one of the gendarme sleighs. As it rushed to the Winter Palace, it left a trail of blood in the snow.

Upon reaching the palace, the Tsar was taken to his study and his bloody but still breathing body was placed on a cot. The room was soon crowded with his two families and several doctors, including Dr Botkin. Outside in the Palace Square a large crowd gathered, some on their knees in the snow in prayer. Inside there was little anyone could do but try to comfort Alexander and ease his pain. A sobbing Katia and the giant Tsarevich held the head of the Tsar. The Tsarevich ordered a priest to be brought in. One soon appeared and gave Alexander communion. Everyone else knelt down. A few minutes later, at about 3:30 p.m. on this first day of March, Alexander died.

After observing the explosions from the other side of the canal, Sophia Perovskaya walked away to keep a rendezvous with a couple of her fellow revolutionaries in a cafe. The third bomb carrier was also able to walk away undetected. The second, who was of Polish background, was fatally wounded in his successful attempt against the Tsar and died that same evening. The first, a nineteen-year-old youth by the name of Rysakov, soon confessed and implicated others.

The day of the assassination, however, was a happy one for some of the revolutionaries. Vera Figner believed that it was a day of recompense for all the suffering and death inflicted upon the revolutionary movement. She thought that "the dawn of the New Russia was at hand."[2] Another member of the executive committee began working on a letter to send to the new Tsar, Alexander III. It would tell him that there were two choices: either he could call a constituent assembly and grant amnesties for political crimes or the revolutionaries would continue their activities.

Although Sophia also hoped for better days, her main preoccupation now shifted to trying to free Zhelyabov. She was afraid he would be implicated in the assassination. Her fears were soon realized when within a few days she learned that he had willingly confessed his own guilt. She continued trying to persuade others to help her organize an escape attempt for him, but they realized it was nearly impossible.

Her friends became concerned for her. Almost always in the past, she had been self-controlled and a tower of strength. Now she seemed distraught, pale and exhausted. They tried to talk her into leaving the city, perhaps into escaping abroad, but she refused.

Meanwhile, the police net spread and arrests escalated. Rumors and fears gripped the city, now draped in mournful black. Police and mounted Cossacks could be seen everywhere. Sophia's picture was available to the police, and they knew that she was the woman who lived with Zhelyabov. A woman from a dairy store where Sophia had regularly bought milk was asked to accompany a detective, and they searched for her. On March 10th, they happened to see her in a horse cab on the Nevsky Prospect. They chased after it and caught her. After being interrogated, she was locked up in a room in the same gendarme prison, behind the Summer Garden, where she had been incarcerated seven years before.

36
THE TRIAL

On the next evening after her arrest, Sophia Perovskaya was led out of the three-storey gendarme building and taken to the Peter and Paul Fortress. Four days earlier, after still another long procession across the wind-blown Neva, her victim, Alexander II, had been buried in the fortress's cathedral. A gendarme led Sophia into a vaulted, half-dark room, where a gendarme colonel sat behind a large table covered with a green cloth. There waiting to identify her was the heavyset bomb-thrower Rysakov, now clad in prison garb.

At the time of her daughter's arrest, Sophia's mother was in the Crimea at the little house where Sophia had recovered after her first prison term. Four days after Sophia's arrest, a gendarme captain arrived and took away her brother Vasily, and told her mother and brothers that Sophia had been arrested. That same evening Sophia's mother and oldest brother, Nicholas, left for St Petersburg.

Not long after arriving in the capital, Mrs Perovskaya went to the office of the Minister of Internal Affairs, Loris-Melikov. His preoccupation these days was with security, that of the new Tsar in particular. He and others were still fearful that the People's Will might try to strike again. The reform proposal which Alexander II had approved the day of his death was for the present in abeyance.

Loris-Melikov agreed to see Sophia's mother. There was something he wished to tell her. After inviting her into his office and offering her a chair, he told her that it was the new Tsar's desire that she persuade her daughter to disclose the names of all her fellow conspirators. Mrs Perovskaya informed him, however, that Sophia had a strong, independent mind and that she would do only what her own convictions dictated. No one could persuade her to do otherwise.

Despite this rebuff, Loris-Melikov allowed Sophia's mother to see her. Several days after her interview with the minister, Sophia's mother was led into a room in the gendarme building. Her daughter had been returned here after her brief visit to the Peter and Paul Fortress. When Sophia entered the room and saw her mother, she rushed to her and began kissing her. They sat down on a couple of chairs in the middle of a room. A gendarme officer and an investigator also sat there listening to their conversation. Sophia asked her mother's forgiveness, but told her she could not have done otherwise and that she would meet death with happiness. She only feared that she might be treated differently than her co-conspirators.

On March 20th, a man by the name of Nicholas Kibalchich was put in the prison room beside Sophia. He was the technical expert responsible for making the bombs which Sophia's bomb throwers had used. While incarcerated, he worked on some ideas he had about jet propulsion. Kibalchich's arrest completed for the time being the authorities' apprehension of those involved in the assassination of Alexander II. The government now decided to put six of them on trial before the end of the month. In addition to Kibalchich, Sophia and Zhelyabov, who was being held at the Peter and Paul Fortress, the other three defendants were to be Rysakov, Mikhailov (the would-be bomb thrower who had changed his mind) and Gesya Helfman, a Jewish woman in her mid-twenties who had maintained one of the apartments for the bomb throwers. As Sophia sat in her prison room, with its walls of yellow ocher and with a sentry always present, she had much time to think. Some of her thoughts of that time are expressed in a letter she wrote to her mother two days after Kibalchich was brought into the room next to her. Here is the letter:

> My dear, adored Mama, – The thought of you oppresses and torments me always. My darling, I implore you to be calm, and not to grieve for me; for my fate does not afflict me in the least, and I shall meet it with complete tranquillity, for I have long expected it, and known that sooner or later it must come. And I assure you, dear mama, that my fate is not such a very mournful one. I have lived as my convictions dictated, and it would have been impossible for me to have acted otherwise. I await my fate, therefore, with a tranquil conscience, whatever it may be. The only thing which oppresses me is the thought of your grief, oh, my adored mother! It is that which rends my heart; and what would I not give to be able to alleviate it? My dear, dear mother, remember that you still have a large family, so many grown-up, and so many little ones, all of whom have need of you, have need of your great moral strength. The thought that I have been unable to raise myself to your moral height has always grieved me to the heart. Whenever, however, I felt myself wavering, it was always the thought of you which sustained me. I will not speak to you of my devotion to you; you know that from my infancy you were always the object of my deepest and fondest love. Anxiety for you was the greatest of my sufferings. I hope that you will be calm, that you will pardon me the grief I have caused you, and not blame me too much; your reproof is the only one that would grieve my heart.
>
> In fancy I kiss your hands again and again, and on my knees I implore you not to be angry with me.
>
> Remember me most affectionately to all my relatives.

And I have a little commission for you, my dear mama. Buy me some cuffs and collars; the collars rather narrow, and the cuffs with buttons, for studs are not allowed to be worn here. Before appearing at the trial, I must mend my dress a little, for it has become much worn here. Good-bye till we meet again, my dear mother. Once more, I implore you not to grieve, and not to afflict yourself for me. My fate is not such a sad one after all, and you must not grieve about it.[1]

Two days after writing the letter, Sophia, Kibalchich and Rysakov, who had also been moved to the gendarme prison, were transferred to the House of Preventive Detention. This recently built prison was attached by long corridors to the court where they would be tried. It was to be the same court building on the Liteiny Prospect, near the Neva river, where Vera Zasulich had been tried and acquitted. Although the new prison was clean and considered by the government as something of a showpiece, in both the men's and women's sections the cells were small (ten feet by five) and the ventilation exceedingly poor. Here Sophia was allowed one more brief visit from her mother; her father did not wish to see her.

The trial opened on Thursday, March 26th, at 11:00 a.m. Police and gendarmes surrounded the court building, allowing only those with tickets to enter. The proceedings were held in a square, white-walled room. Spread out over the front of it was a panel of government-appointed officials who would act as both judges and jury. All but a few of them were from the Russian Senate, a weak bureaucratic institution that also acted as a court of final appeal. These judges sat behind a long red-clothed table and in high-backed chairs. On their left, as the judges looked out on the courtroom, the six accused sat, the four men in black suits, the two women in black dresses. Sophia was placed next to Zhelyabov, who sat last in the line, furthest from the judges. In front of the six sat their court appointed lawyers, except for Zhelyabov, who chose to defend himself. In the corner of the room between the defendants and their judges hung, draped in black, a life-sized picture of Alexander II. He seemed to be looking out at his accused murderers. In front of the judges was a table containing exhibits for the prosecution, including boxes of dynamite. Behind the table, facing the judges, were the distinguished guests, mainly government officials but also some ladies of society. Representatives of the foreign and Russian press were also on hand. But the accounts of the trial, especially to the Russian public, were subject to strict censorship.

To the right of the judges sat the man who would prosecute the government case. He seemed rather young for such an important task. He was only the same age as Zhelyabov. But his superiors thought him a talented man and he had risen quickly within the government's judicial system. He was especially known for his oratorical skills. The fact that he was always most eager to please his superiors and that he was one of the famous Muraviev clan also undoubtedly helped his career. He was the nephew of the famous Muraviev-Amursky and the son of a former governor of Pskov. He was Nicholas Muraviev, the same Kolya with whom Sophia and her brothers and sisters used to play when their father was vice-governor of Pskov, the same Kolya whom they had once pulled out of the water onto a raft. Muravievs and Perovskys had once served one another and helped each other's careers. Now a Muraviev was going to prosecute one of the Perovsky clan for murder. Like Nekrasov's nemesis, Michael Muraviev, "the Hangman," and unlike some of the Decembrist Muravievs, Nicholas Muraviev intended to be one of those Muravievs who did the hanging, not one who got hanged.

On the first day of the trial each of the defendants was asked some basic questions about himself or herself. Sophia answered briefly and stated that her occupation was revolutionary affairs. The tall, bearded, angry-looking Zhelyabov answered at greater length. When asked his religion, he stated that although he no longer considered himself a member of the Orthodox Church, he based his moral convictions on the teachings of Christ and believed it the duty of Christians to fight and, if need be, suffer for the weak and oppressed.

Later on, after the charges were read, each of the accused was allowed to plead and make a statement. Rysakov tried to mitigate his own guilt. The young Mikhailov, a worker of peasant background, rejected some of Rysakov's allegations upon which a good part of the government's case was built. He admitted only to being a member of a party which tried to help the workers. Helfman, who had fled her Orthodox Jewish home as a teenager in order to avoid an arranged marriage, admitted belonging to the People's Will, but not to taking part in the assassination. Kibalchich, while not denying his guilt, vigorously explained that as the maker of the bombs his role was limited to the technical sphere. Sophia then stood up and admitted taking part in both the Moscow attempt and the successful assassination of March 1st. She spoke of her faith in the eventual triumph of the views of the People's Will. As Helfman had done, she stated that Mikhailov was not involved in the plot against the Tsar. Sophia also said that Helfman had not taken any part in the terroristic activities of their party.

A number of Tsarist officials present that day noted that Sophia looked like a young girl and that there seemed to be a discrepancy between her terroristic acts and her rather modest demeanor. Zhelyabov, who spoke after Sophia and admitted his involvement, also created a strong impression on observers of the trial. He was the most forceful speaker of the six, often objected to rulings of the judges, and was frequently interrupted by the chief judge when he attempted to introduce material that the court considered irrelevant.

As the trial continued and the witnesses for the prosecution testified, Zhelyabov objected to various points of their testimony. One of his concerns was to prevent the state from proving the guilt of Helfman and Mikhailov. Kibalchich objected whenever he thought the government witnesses misspoke about his explosives or their intended effects. As in the nearby cells, the ventilation in the courtroom was poor. The court met each day in the late morning and early afternoon and then again in the evening. As the hour got late and the room more stuffy, the number of observers dwindled.

On Saturday, the third day of the trial, Muraviev summed up the government's case. It took him five hours to do so. The sober, intelligent War Minister, Milyutin, although not able to remain for all of the speech, considered it magnificent, and Muraviev a "talented young man, an orator in the full sense of the word."[2]

With all of the gestures and modulations of voice and emotion of an accomplished orator, Muraviev pictured a saintly, heroic Tsar, struck down by beastly assassins. At one point he said: "Thus he fell, a warrior at his imperial post of danger, fell in the battle for God, for Russia … in mortal combat with the enemies of justice, of order, of morality, of family life."[3]

In the course of his speech, Muraviev mentioned Sophia's family background and connections and noted that, despite all of her advantages, she had gone wrong. In a way that surely must have offended her feminist sensibilities, he indicated that the People's Will could not have been a very strong organization if after Zhelyabov's arrest it had to turn over to a weak woman the tasks of organizing the assassination. Could it not find, he asked, "a stronger hand, a stronger mind, a more experienced revolutionary than Sophia Perovskaya?"[4] Muraviev also pointed out that it was especially horrible for a woman to be acting in such a beastly role.

After the completion of Muraviev's long speech, the counsels for the first five defendants spoke. Sophia's counsel, while admitting she had gone astray, spoke of her noble character and asked the court to show mercy towards her. Zhelyabov, speaking in his own behalf, was constantly interrupted by the chief judge for exceeding the limits set down by the court. The court did not intend to allow Zhelyabov the use of the courtroom as a forum to proclaim his many grievances against the Russian government.

After the five lawyers and Zhelyabov spoke, each of the six accused was allowed a few words before the court decided its verdict. Kibalchich used the occasion to announce that he had drawn up designs for a "flying machine" and that he was bequeathing them to his counsel. Sophia objected to Muraviev's charges that the six were immoral and brutal, and she added that anyone who really knew their lives and circumstances would not accuse them of either failing.

Sophia, of course, was speaking to judges beyond those in the courtroom: she was appealing to the world outside, and to posterity. While Muraviev depicted the Tsar as saintly and heroic, many on the Left thought that those like Perovskaya were the true heroes, the true saints.

At midnight the judges left to consider their verdicts. The accused were also led out. Several hours later the court reconvened and the chief judge read out the verdicts regarding each of the six. All were found guilty. Muraviev demanded the death penalty for them. The judges again retired to consider the sentence.

The darkness outside was already beginning to pale when the court once again reconvened and the exhausted prisoners and audience heard the sentences. On this early Sunday morning, all six were sentenced to be hanged. They had until 5:00 p.m. on Tuesday to appeal. Since Sophia was of the noble class, the court noted that her sentence would be carried out only after being approved by the Tsar.

37

TWO APPEALS

On the same Sunday when many in the capital discovered the court's verdict and sentence, they also heard rumors about a provocative speech given the night before which dared to recommend mercy for the assassins. The speaker was Vladimir Soloviev. In a large hall of the capital's Credit Society, before some eight hundred people, he had given a lecture entitled "A Critique of Contemporary Education and the Crisis in the World Process." Among the audience were many students and sitting in the front were Sophia Tolstaya and her niece, Sophia Khitrovo, with whom Soloviev was still in love.

Since the previous fall, Soloviev had been lecturing as a private docent at both St Petersburg University and the Higher Courses for Women, established in the capital in 1878 – women were not permitted to enroll in the universities. His reputation among the students seemed to increase with each lecture. He welcomed their questions and objections, and especially enjoyed answering the students who were sympathetic with the revolutionary left. In a lecture at the Higher Courses for Women following the arrest of Sophia Perovskaya, Soloviev had publicly stated that the path of revolutionary violence was the wrong way, that it was impossible to bring about truth and justice by force, that it would only lead to despotism.

On the Thursday when the trial of the assassins began, he gave the first of two speeches at the Credit Society lecture hall. But compared to the one he gave two nights later, the first one did not cause much controversy. Both of these speeches, however, were influenced by an address which the Slavophile Ivan Aksakov had given the previous Sunday to a meeting of the St Petersburg Slavonic Benevolent Committee. In it, Aksakov stated that the assassins were just the logical, extreme manifestation of the liberal, westernizing spirit in Russia. Thus, not only would he be willing to blame radicals such as Herzen, Bakunin and Nechaev for giving birth to those such as Zhelyabov and Perovskaya; but he also would gladly point the finger of blame at liberals such as Turgenev. Dostoevsky, Katkov and Pobedonostsev had earlier expressed similar viewpoints. Aksakov stated that it was not the renegade intellectuals who captured the true spirit of Russia but the peasants and their highest representative, the Tsar.

Although Soloviev had never been as ardent a glorifier of the Russian peasants as were his friends Dostoevsky and Aksakov, in his speeches at the Credit Society building he seemed to attribute to the Russian people his own beliefs: faith in the truth of Jesus Christ and belief in the essential oneness of the universe (his Holy Sophia) and in the possibility of realizing Christ's truth on this earth. In his second speech on Saturday night he agreed with Aksakov that the Tsar was the highest representative of the people. But here his speech took an unexpected turn. He dared to advise the new Tsar on his treatment of his father's assassins.

In a clear distinct voice, the bearded Soloviev stood in front of his audience and stated that the use of capital punishment was wrong and unchristian. He did not rule out the use of violence in self-defense, but the regicides on trial were now unarmed and could be separated from society without executing them. Therefore, if the Tsar was to be the true representative and embodiment of the Christian spirit of the Russian people, he must not sanction the killing of his father's assassins. While admitting that it was not up to himself or his audience to decide the matter or to pass judgment on the Tsar, he nevertheless insisted that the Christian path and that of the Russian people was to follow that of the "God of Love," and not the pagan way of retaliation or vengeance.

Eye-witness accounts disagree on exactly what happened at the end of Soloviev's speech. But the consensus indicates that it awakened strong and opposing emotions among the audience. Words such as "traitor," "scoundrel" and "terrorist" were apparently hurled at Soloviev, but so were shouts of approval, especially from many of the young, both male and female. Dostoevsky's widow, Anna, was apparently among those present who were critical of the speech, despite the fact that after the execution of Kvyatkovsky and Presnyakov in November 1880, Dostoevsky in his notebook had suggested an approach to capital punishment similar to that now taken by Soloviev.

Important government officials were less divided than the audience over the merits of Soloviev's speech. Even the liberal Milyutin thought that Soloviev's advice to the Tsar was an act of folly. The day after the speech, Soloviev was sent for by the governor of the city, Major-General Baranov, who had recently been appointed thanks to the influence of Dostoevsky's old friend Pobedonostsev. Baranov at this time was a frantic man who was discovering plots and revolutionary activities where they did not exist.

Soloviev was allowed to explain in writing his version of the previous evening's lecture. In this explanation, he indicated that in suggesting the pardoning of the assassins he was only following up on one of the Tsar's own statements that he stood on the Christian principle of mercy. Not knowing exactly what reports had reached Baranov, Soloviev indicated that it was possible that some people had misinterpreted his remarks. Yet he admitted to saying that "Capital punishment in general ... is an unforgivable act and in a Christian state must be abolished."[1]

That same day Soloviev decided to write directly to the new Tsar, whom his father had once tutored. He confessed to having expressed his belief that only Christ's truth could triumph over the forces of evil and that the present moment presented an unprecedented opportunity for the Tsar to perform a great moral deed by pardoning the assassins. Such an act, the philosopher stated, could only strengthen the foundations of the Tsar's power and bring him closer to the Russian people – both of which would have pleased Soloviev, providing that the Tsar acted in a fashion in keeping with true Christian principles.

General Baranov made a report about Soloviev's speech to Loris-Melikov, who in turn reported to the Tsar. Another minister who heard about the lecture was the dour, ascetic, constantly black-suited Pobedonostsev, who as Procurator of the Holy Synod was in charge of the Orthodox Church in Russia.

Since his former pupil had become Tsar, Pobedonostsev's power and influence had increased significantly. In addition to Baranov's appointment, he also managed to influence the Tsar to name Ignatiev, the former ambassador to Constantinople, to a government post. Pobedonostsev had hoped that Ignatiev might replace Loris-Melikov as Minister of Interior. The new Tsar, however, had not yet completely made up his mind about the Armenian general and the reform project which Alexander II had approved the morning before his death. Therefore, for the present, Ignatiev had to settle for the position of Minister of State Properties. Nevertheless, Loris-Melikov and his liberal supporters, such as Milyutin and Finance Minister Abaza, were now definitely losing influence at court to Pobedonostsev's faction.

To Milyutin the thought of Pobedonostsev gaining more influence was abhorrent. At a meeting in early March, Pobedonostsev severely criticized Loris-Melikov's projected reform plan. In that speech according to Milyutin, Pobedonostsev "dared to call the Great Reforms of Emperor Alexander II a criminal mistake."[2] Milyutin noted further in his diary that he and some others were not able to conceal their annoyance at some of the phrases of this "fanatic-reactionary."[3]

Shortly before hearing about Soloviev's lecture, Pobedonostsev had been asked to transmit the letter of still another individual who wished the Tsar to pardon the assassins. It was written by Leo Tolstoy.

That March, Tolstoy was in the midst of translating and unifying the four Gospels into one chronological account. He had by now concluded that one of the most important messages of the Gospels was: "Resist not him that is evil." The previous month Soloviev and their mutual friend Strakhov had come to

visit him. The three of them had discussed much, and Tolstoy and Soloviev differed on a number of points. Soloviev defended, for example, the doctrine of
the Trinity. One of the other guests at Yasnaya Polyana thought that the young
philosopher bested Tolstoy in their debates, but did it in a humble manner.
Nevertheless, Tolstoy treated him kindly, and believed that in general they con-
curred upon moral questions. One of the matters that they apparently agreed
on was the evil of capital punishment.

Judging from the rough draft of Tolstoy's letter to Alexander III – and that is
all that is available – he started out by explaining why an "insignificant" man
like himself would dare to advise the Tsar. As the rest of the letter made clear, he
did it as a matter of conscience and because he believed that Russia stood at a
crucial juncture in its history. One of three roads stood before it. Two had already been tried, that of repression and that of liberal concessions. Neither, according to Tolstoy, had worked or would in the future. So why not try "another
remedy," an untried but at least not a failed one. Tolstoy quoted his remedy
from the Gospels: "Love your enemies … Resist not evil." He boldly stated:
"This and only this needs to be done; this is the will of God."[4]

Like Soloviev in his letter to the Tsar, Tolstoy tried to convince Alexander III
that by pardoning his father's assassins he could only strengthen his authority.
He wrote "Your majesty, if you should do this … give them [the assassins]
money and send them away somewhere to America, and write a manifesto
starting with the words: 'but I say to you, love your enemies,' … from these
words, like a flood, goodness and love would pour forth over Russia."[5]

Anticipating objections that his "remedy" would only make matters worse,
Tolstoy stated that there was no proof that it would not work. He believed that
the revolutionary ferment resulted from the revolutionaries' dissatisfaction
with the existing order and their desire to replace it with one based more on the
general welfare and on equality and freedom. Repression could not stamp out
the radical's activities. In his rough draft, he closed his letter by writing:

> There is only one ideal that can be opposed to them. And that is the one which
> they began with, not understanding it and blaspheming against it – the one which
> includes their ideal, the ideal of love, forgiveness and the repayment of good for
> evil. Only a single word of forgiveness and Christian love, spoken and carried out
> from the height of the throne, and the path of a Christian reign, which stands
> before you to embark upon, can destroy the evil which is eating away Russia.
> Like wax before the face of fire, every revolutionary struggle will melt away before
> the Tsar-man who carries out the law of Christ."[6]

Tolstoy sent his letter to his friend Strakhov and asked him to transmit it to
Pobedonostsev, who could then see that it, or at least its thoughts, reached the
new Tsar. Tolstoy's wife, Sonia, was upset with him for writing such a letter; his
religious transformation was introducing new strains in their relationship. She

attributed the letter partly to the influence of the children's tutor and former radical Alekseev. In a postscript to her husband's letter to Strakhov, she asked him to consult with Pobedonostsev and not to send the letter on if they thought it would anger Alexander III. This, of course, was contrary to Tolstoy's intentions. He was willing to face any consequences.

It was apparently just a day or so before hearing about Soloviev's lecture that Pobedonostsev met with Strakhov. The Procurator of the Holy Synod stated that he had a different view of the meaning of Christianity than did Tolstoy, and in good conscience he could not transmit the letter to the new Tsar.

After Soloviev's lecture, Pobedonostsev realized that Alexander III would probably hear of one or both of the appeals made to him. Indeed, Tolstoy did find another way to transmit his letter to the Tsar. Therefore, two days after Soloviev's lecture and the day after the court's sentencing, Pobedonostsev wrote a letter of his own to his former pupil. In it he wrote of "perverted ideas" being enunciated by some possessing "weak minds and hearts" who wished the Tsar to pardon the assassins. To such appeals he told the Tsar that his own response was: "No, no, a thousand times no."[7] The revolutionaries' bloody deed called for vengeance, and the opinion of the Russian people was the same. If any of the assassins escaped death, Pobedonostsev wrote that they would just invent new plots against the government.

It was not until a few months later that Tolstoy himself received an explanation from Pobedonostsev, who then wrote to him: "Your faith is one thing, and mine and the church's another … Our Christ is not your Christ. Ours I know as a man of strength and truth … but yours appears to me to possess traits of weakness."[8] This letter reminds one of the words of Dostoevsky's Grand Inquisitor to Christ in *The Brothers Karamazov*, and the Grand Inquisitor does indeed bear some resemblance to Dostoevsky's reactionary friend.

By the time Pobedonostsev wrote his letter, Alexander III had retreated to the palace at Gatchina, almost thirty miles from the capital. Still fearful of plots by the People's Will, whose remaining strength was not known, he was surrounded there by sentries and guards on horses, as well as by plain-clothed police. The powerful six-foot three-inch Alexander was not a coward, but some of his advisers and prudence suggested such elaborate measures.

Was there really any reason for Pobedonostsev to fear an Imperial pardon? Perhaps he thought one or both of the women might be spared, for females had not previously been executed in Russia for political crimes. Otherwise, everything we know of Alexander III's personality would seem to indicate that Pobedonostsev's fear reflected more his own horror at such a pardon than it did any substantial doubts about Alexander III's potential behavior. Alexander III was an obstinate, straightforward, conservative man, not given to self-doubting. Some of his defenders would claim he was a man of common sense, but no one thought of him as especially intelligent or cultured. Growing up in Russia's Golden Age of Literature he had never even heard of Bazarov, Turgenev's famous hero of *Fathers and Sons*, and he did not like Tolstoy's works. In general, he seems to have read little. As compared to his father, he was more wilful, nationalistic and distrustful of the West and less cosmopolitan or comfortable among foreigners. These traits were clearly apparent during his years as Tsarevich. His view of Christianity was basically that of Pobedonostsev, more inclined to stress duty and obedience than love, the only discernible difference being that the Tsar's beliefs were ingested almost unconsciously, with little mental effort.

Upon receiving Pobedonostsev's note, Alexander wrote on it: "Don't worry, no one will dare come to me with such proposals, and all six will be hanged, that I guarantee."9

38
A SPECTACLE ON SEMENOVSKY SQUARE

Despite the intentions of Alexander III, his "guarantee" to Pobedonostsev was not fully carried out. Even the "Autocrat of all the Russias" could not completely control unforeseen circumstances. One such circumstance was the discovery that one of the two females sentenced to death was pregnant. As a result, Gesya Helfman's sentence was changed to life imprisonment. "All six" would therefore not be hanged. And how about the other five? Mikhailov and Rysakov petitioned the Tsar for a reprieve; the other three did not. The Tsar turned down the two petitioning prisoners. But even then no one could be absolutely sure what would occur. Had not the famous Dostoevsky thought that he was going to be executed until almost at the very last moment, with the firing squad already in place, a reprieve was announced?

The executions were scheduled for Friday, April 3rd. On Thursday, Rysakov wrote still one more letter in an attempt to save his life. He offered to help the police catch some of the revolutionaries still not apprehended. Once again, he was turned down. That same evening, Rysakov and Mikhailov each confessed their sins to a priest. Kibalchich went as far as talking to one; but Sophia and Zhelyabov each refused the opportunity. The prisoners were allowed no other visitors. Sophia lay down that Thursday night at 11:00 in her cell in the House of Preventive Detention, but she was not alone. Night and day, a gendarme officer and a gendarme soldier were present. Ironically enough, the government did not want her taking her own life. The same precaution was taken with the others.

The next morning the five were given tea shortly after 6:00 a.m. After putting on the black clothes presented to them, they came out into the prison court-yard. Sophia was pale and seemed to stagger. The big, friendly Mikhailov encouraged her to pull herself together, and she seemed to do so. The five prisoners were then placed on platforms high atop two carts. Sophia sat on the second, between Mikhailov and the bearded Kibalchich. All five were in shackles and wore large placards around their necks with the word "Tsaricide" on each.

Just before 8:00 a.m. the prison gate opened. First came a cart carrying soldiers and police, then the two holding the prisoners. Five priests in carriages, a cart of coffins, and additional soldiers followed behind. Military drummers accompanied this slow-moving procession, furnishing a muffled and somber tapping, designed to prevent any of the prisoners from addressing the large crowds lining the streets. Sophia and the others were shackled with their backs to the horses that pulled their springless carts slowly over the cobblestoned and potholed streets: Shpalernaya, Liteiny, Kirovhnaya, Nadezhdinskaya, and then across the Nevsky Prospect and down the long Nikolaevsky to Semenovsky Square. There a crowd of close to a hundred thousand people awaited them, as did a gallows. More than three decades before it had been a firing squad that awaited Dostoevsky on this same large unpaved square.

On a low platform in front of the gallows were gathered various dignitaries, including Procurator Muraviev, foreign diplomats and representatives of the press. Some privileged people had managed to obtain tickets which permitted them to come up on the scaffold once the bodies had been removed. This would enable them, if they wished, to take away pieces of the hanging ropes – considered good luck souvenirs.

Most of the large crowd stood behind thousands of foot soldiers and mounted Cossacks lined up to maintain order. Some people watched from nearby roofs. For a St Petersburg morning in early spring, the weather was good: not too cold and some sunshine, which before the day was over would melt some more of the snow on the square.

After the prisoners ascended the black-painted scaffold, they were chained to posts or to a railing on the platform while their sentences were read out. Zhelyabov was able to say a few words to Sophia. Both of them looked composed, as did Mikhailov and Kibalchich. Only Rysakov seemed agitated. A London *Times* reporter noted that Perovskaya seemed the calmest of all, and he even noticed a slight pinkish glow on her cheeks.

Five priests then climbed up the stairs of the scaffold and held out crosses for the condemned to kiss. Each of them did so. Even Zhelyabov had stated at his trial that he considered himself a follower of the true teachings of Christ. The priests blessed the prisoners and walked off the platform. Before being placed under their nooses, Zhelyabov kissed Sophia, as did Kibalchich and Mikhailov; but she, uncompromising to the end, turned away when the informer Rysakov approached her.

The hangman, dressed in a red shirt, and his assistants then placed white hoods over the prisoners' heads. The drums continued to beat. Kibalchich was helped up on to a little stand, the rope affixed to his neck, and the stand removed. Next it was Mikhailov's turn. The same procedure was followed, but after hanging for almost a minute, Mikhailov's big body hit the scaffold floor.

The crowd screamed. The noose had come undone. He was helped back up, but after hanging another minute and a half, the same thing happened again. On the third try, after a further last-minute adjustment prevented still another failed attempt, he was finally successfully hanged. A similar bungled hanging had taken place more than fifty years earlier with several of the Decembrists, but at least that hanging was not before a mass audience.

While poor Mikhailov was being hanged three times, Sophia stood next in line, dwarfed between him and Zhelyabov. One can only imagine what she was thinking. Several minutes later, however, her petite body hung limp from a noose. Her body had quivered only briefly. By 10:00 a.m. all five bodies were in their coffins, and most of the crowd had begun to leave the square.

EPILOGUE

The bloody struggle between revolutionaries and the government did not end with the deaths of Sophia Perovskaya and her four companions. During Alexander III's reign (1881–94), however, the Tsar seemed to have the upper hand. His increasingly reactionary policies temporarily stifled the radicals, and the spirit of Pobedonostsev seemed triumphant. He continued to be an important minister for the next quarter century. By the time he was replaced as Procurator of the Holy Synod in 1905, Nicholas II was Tsar. As a twelve-year-old boy, he had witnessed the painful death of Alexander II, his grandfather. The scene left a lasting impression on him, and he became as reactionary as his father, although not as strong-willed.

Crippled but not crushed, the radical spirit survived. In 1887, Alexander Ulyanov was executed for plotting against the Tsar, but his younger brother, subsequently best known by his revolutionary name of Lenin, came to power thirty years later and inaugurated seven decades of communist rule. Of course, the future of the Russian Empire was determined not just by its rulers, thinkers and revolutionaries, but by thousands of other causes as well, from the realities of geography to those of international relations.

In 1883, Ivan Turgenev died a painful death from cancer. At his funeral a now moribund People's Will distributed one of his poems mistakenly thought to have been a tribute to Sophia Perovskaya. A voice in the poem referred to its heroine as "Saint."[1] At the trial of the assassins, her companion Zhelyabov had declared his commitment to the true teachings of Christ, but prosecutor Muraviev countered that it was the heroic Alexander II who was the true "warrior" for God.

Yet, despite all of the talk of saintly and Christ-like behavior – and all of the variations on this theme from the pens of Dostoevsky, Vladimir Soloviev, Tolstoy and Pobedonostsev – Alexander II and other leading personalities of his time displayed their share of common human frailties. This was true in both their actions and socio-political thinking.

Although Alexander II's reforms of the early 1860s were a considerable achievement, after instituting them he failed to display the vision, energy, or leadership which Russia needed to propel it successfully towards the twentieth century. At his death Russian autocracy was still in place, and the economic condition of the great mass of the Russian people, the peasants, was perhaps no better than it had been a few decades earlier. In fact, the rapid growth of the rural population, coupled with low agricultural yields and high taxes and redemption payments, put increasing pressure on the meager resources of most peasants.

Turning to intellectuals such as Dostoevsky, Herzen and Tolstoy, it cannot be denied that they sometimes expressed important truths about the human condition. Nor were they necessarily wrong to argue that Western societies had many failings or that Russia needed to develop along its own unique path. But the intellectuals suffered from serious failings of their own. Two such deficiencies were especially damaging: a dogmatic intolerance of opposing viewpoints and a lack of pragmatism regarding social and political alternatives to the autocratic, patriarchal nature of Russian society.

Of course, these failings were more pronounced in some intellectuals than others. Vladimir Soloviev, for example, was more tolerant than most. Although his friend Dostoevsky sometimes expressed extreme antisemitic views, Soloviev became extremely critical of antisemitism during the 1880s.[2] In the early 1890s, he defended the concept of religious tolerance against those who, like Pobedonostsev, equated it with indifference. He argued that it must be allowed since no infallible, universally recognized judge existed who could decide what was true and what was not. Although many other intellectuals might support such a statement when arguing against religious discrimination or government censorship, in their own writings they frequently reflected a dogmatism which helped pollute the air inhaled by extremists such as Nechaev.

Although Soloviev appreciated the importance of tolerance and some of his philosophical thinking helped provide a basis for the further development of liberal ideas, his other-worldly personality reflected the lack of practicality that afflicted so many of the prominent Russian thinkers. After his death in 1900, a friend of his recalled that he had very confused ideas about economics and about the operations of the local government organs (the *zemstvos*) established by Alexander II.[3] Others like Bakunin or Tolstoy – who became more outspokenly utopian from 1881 until his death in 1910 – had little comprehension of how real human beings, with all their human failings, might harmoniously live together in society. Toward the end of his life, Herzen warned Bakunin that if the old order were ended by violence, the new order would have to maintained by it. But this practical bit of wisdom had no influence on Bakunin or on those like Perovskaya who believed that a new and better world could be created on soil scattered by the bombs of assassins.

In 1909, seven Russian thinkers published a book called *Signposts* (*Vekhi*), which was collection of articles criticizing the revolutionary intelligentsia. Their critique maintained that the intelligentsia had been too dogmatic, rationalistic, intolerant and impractical, placed too much faith in political revolution and ignored the importance of the inner spiritual transformation of each individual. Several of the contributors were strongly influenced by Vladimir Soloviev's ideas and wished Russia to evolve toward a more just Christian society. The collection also touched on a point brought up by Dostoevsky in his Pushkin speech: the relationship of the intelligentsia to the people and who should learn from whom.[4]

In the mid- and late 1980s, after seven decades of communist rule, Mikhail Gorbachev began a process of change that awakened great hopes, only to be followed by considerable disillusionment. Parallels with Russia under Alexander II were not difficult to identify, and Russia's pre-communist past was once again examined for possible guidance as Russia struggled to create a new political order.

In works of the 1980s and 1990s, the Russian scholar Yuri Lotman maintained that Russian culture predisposed individuals and groups to take absolute positions, favor radical rather than evolutionary approaches and shun compromise. Not only were these characteristics evident in earlier eras such as that of Alexander II, but Lotman and others continued to believe they were still present in abundance in post-Soviet Russia.[5]

Not only has the tone of post-Soviet debates sometimes been reminiscent of those of Alexander II's time, but often so too has the content – for example, the question of Russia's relationship to the West. The differences of Herzen, Dostoevsky and Turgenev about this question seemed almost as relevant in the 1990s as they did when they first surfaced. Related to this question are others debated in both periods: liberalism versus socialism; the role of religion in politics; the relationship of government to society. As Russia continued to search for principles upon which to construct a new political order, the socio-religious ideas of Dostoevsky, Tolstoy and Vladimir Soloviev, as utopian as they often were, again attracted attention.[6] In 1862, Chernyshevsky wrote *What Is To Be Done?* In 1886, Tolstoy completed *What Then Must We Do?* In 1902, Lenin's *What Is To Be Done?* was published. At the beginning of the twenty-first century, with Russia still in the midst of great difficulties, the question was still being asked.

WHO'S WHO?

PRINCIPAL FIGURES AND FAMILIES*

Alexander II (1818–81), Emperor and Tsar of Russia, 1855–81.
  Empress Maria (1824–80), wife of Alexander II.
  Alexander III (1845–94), son of Alexander II and Maria.
  Maria (1853–1920), daughter of Alexander II and Maria, became Duchess of Edinburgh in 1874.
  Catherine Dolgorukova (Katia) (1847–1922), longtime mistress and second wife of Alexander II.

Bakunin, Michael A. (1814–76), leading radical figure.
  Antonia, his wife.
  Antonia had a few children while married to Bakunin, but he was not their father.
  Several of Bakunin's brothers were involved in liberal political activities in the Tver province.

Dostoevsky, Fedor M. (1821–81), writer.
  Maria Isaeva (1826?-64), first wife of Dostoevsky.
  Anna Snitkina (1846–1918), second wife of Dostoevsky, with whom he had four children, but two died as infants, Sonia in 1868 and Alyosha in 1878.

The Herzens:

Alexander (1812–70), radical journalist; editor of *The Bell*.
  Natalia (1817–52), his wife.
  Alexander (Sasha) (1839–1906), their son.
  Natalia (Tata) (1844–1936), their daughter.
  Olga (1850–1953), their second daughter.
  In addition, the Herzens had two other sons, the first died when still a young boy in 1851, the second shortly after his birth in 1852.

The Ogarevs:

Nicholas P. (1813–77), poet, radical journalist, friend and co-editor with Herzen of *The Bell*.

---

* A note on Russian names: female last names often vary slightly from their male counterparts and most frequently end in "a"; thus Natalia Ogareva instead of Ogarev.

Maria (d. 1853), his first wife.
Natalia (1829–1923), second wife and Herzen's mistress from 1857.

Children of Alexander Herzen and Natalia Ogareva:
Liza (1858–75)
Elena (1861–4)
Alexei (1861–4)

The Muraviev clan:

Michael N. (1796–1866), Governor-general of Lithuania, 1863–65, the "hangman."

Nicholas N. Muraviev-Amursky (1809–81), Governor-general of Eastern Siberia, 1847–61, a distant relative of Michael N.

Nicholas V. (1850–1908), nephew of Muraviev-Amursky, public prosecutor in St Petersburg at the time of Alexander II's death.

Bakunin's mother, several Decembrists, and many distinguished officials and high-ranking officers were also Muravievs.

Nekrasov, Nicholas A. (1821–1877), radical poet and editor of *The Contemporary.*

The Perovskys:

Lev N. (1816–90), civilian governor of St Petersburg province in the mid 1860s.
Barbara, wife of Lev.
Peter N. (1818–65), Russian negotiator in Peking, 1858–9, brother of Lev.
Sophia L. (1853–81), one of four children of Lev and Barbara, a leading member of People's Will.
The uncles of Lev and Peter, Vasily A. and Lev A., both held important government posts under Nicholas I. The mother of the poet Alexei Tolstoy was a sister of these uncles.

The Solovievs:

Sergei M.(1820–79), distinguished historian, professor, and administrator at Moscow University.

Poliksena Romanova, wife of Sergei and daughter of Vladimir Romanov (1796–1864), a naval hero at Sevastopol.

Vladimir S. (1853–1900), son of Sergei and Poliksena; philosopher, poet, mystic.

Of the other seven Soloviev children who lived to adulthood, several had distinguished careers; Vladimir's older brother, Vsevolod, was a popular historical novelist and his youngest sister, Poliksena, became a fine poet.

The Tolstoys:

Leo N. (1828–1910), writer.
Maria (1830–1912), sister of Leo, briefly infatuated with Turgenev.
Sonia Bers (1844–1919), Leo's wife.
Leo and Sonia had thirteen children, ten of them born during the reign of Alexander II. Of these ten, three died by the age of two. The Tolstoys were a distinguished family related to a number of other famous Russian families, including different branches of Tolstoys, and the Volkonskys, Trubetskoys, and Gorchakovs.

Turgenev, Ivan S. (1818–83), writer.

Paulinette (1842–1919), illegitimate daughter of Turgenev.

OTHER INDIVIDUALS

Abaza, Alexander A. (1821–95), Minister of Finance, 1880–81.

Aksakov, Constantine S. (1817–60), historian, Slavophile.

Aksakov, Ivan S. (1823–86), journalist, Slavophile.

Baryatinsky, Prince Alexander I. (1814–79), Viceroy of the Caucasus, 1856–62.

Belinsky, Vissarion G. (1811–48), famous literary critic.

Bismarck, Prince Otto Von (1815–98), Minister-president of Prussia, Chancellor of Germany.

Chaikovsky, Nicholas V. (1850–1926), populist leader of radical Chaikovsky circle.

Chernyshevsky, Nicholas G. (1828–89), radical journalist.

Chicherin, Boris N. (1828–1904), historian, legal scholar, publicist.

Disraeli, Benjamin (1804–81), novelist and British Prime Minister, 1868 and again 1874–80.

Dobrolyubov, Nicholas A. (1836–61), radical literary critic.

Dolgorukaya, Alexandra S. (1836–1913?), lady-in-waiting to the Empress; rumors linked her romantically with Alexander II prior to his affair with Catherine Dolgorukova. Also the rumored prototype for Irena in Turgenev's *Smoke*.

Fadeev, General Rostislav A. (1824–83), leading panslavist.

Fet-Shenshin, Afanasy A. (1820–92), poet, friend of Tolstoy and Turgenev.

Filaret (1782–1867), Metropolitan of Moscow.

Garibaldi, Giuseppe (1807–82), fighter for Italian unity.

Gorchakov, Prince Alexander M. (1798–1883), Minister of Foreign Affairs, 1856–82.

Ignatiev, Count Nicholas P. (1832–1908), diplomat and statesman.

Karakozov, Dmitry V. (1840–66), terrorist who attempted to assassinate Alexander II.

Katkov, Michael N. (1818–87), influential journalist and editor.

Kavelin, Constantine D. (1818–85), historian, legal scholar, publicist.

Kramskoi, Ivan (1837–87), painter

Kropotkin, Prince Peter A. (1842–1921), radical populist, later a leading theorist of anarchism.

Lavrov, Peter L. (1823–1900), theorist of revolutionary populism.

Loris-Melikov, General Michael T. (1825–88), Minister of Internal Affairs, 1880–81.

Milyutin, Count Dmitry A. (1816–1912), Minister of War, 1861–81.

Mussorgsky, Modest P. (1839–81), composer.

Napoleon III (1808–73), Emperor of France, 1852–70.

Nechaev, Sergei G. (1847–82), nihilist who murdered student Ivanov.

Nikitenko, Alexander V. (1804–77), moderate government official, professor of literature, diarist.

Panaev, Ivan I. (1812–62), friend and co-editor of Nekrasov.

Panaeva, Avdotya Y. (1819–93), wife of above and longtime lover of Nekrasov.

Petrashevsky, Mikhail V. (1821–66), minor government official, coordinator of Petrashevsky circle.

Pisarev, Dmitry I. (1840–68), journalist, literary critic, major theoretician of nihilism.

Pobedonostsev, Constantine P. (1827–1907), conservative tutor and adviser to Alexander III.

Poggio, Alessandro (1798–1873), Decembrist.

Pogodin, Michael P. (1800–75), nationalist historian, panslavist.

Pushkin, Alexander, S. (1799–1837), Russia's most acclaimed poet.

Repin, Ilya E. (1844–1930), painter.

Reutern, Count Michael K. (1820–90), Minister of Finance, 1862–78.

Rubinstein, Nicholas G. (1835–81), pianist, conductor.

Ryleev, Kondraty F. (1795–1826), poet, Decembrist.

Savina, Maria G. (1854–1915), actress, friend of Turgenev.

Schopenhauer, Arthur (1788–1860), German philosopher.

Shamil (1797–1871), Caucasian Muslim leader in the struggle for independence.

Shuvalov, Count Peter A. (1827–89), head of the Third Division, 1866–74.

Strakhov, Nicholas N. (1828–96), literary critic.

Suslova, Appolinaria P. (1839–1917?), aspiring writer with whom Dostoevsky had an affair.

Tchaikovsky, Peter I. (1840–93), composer.

Tolstaya, Countess Sophia A. (1844–92), friend and patroness of writers, widow of poet Alexei Tolstoy (1817–75).

Tolstoy, Count Dmitry A. (1823–89), Minister of Education, 1866–80.

Totleben, Count Edward I. (1818–84), general, military engineer.

Trepov, Fedor F. (1812–89), police chief in St Petersburg, 1866–78.

Tyutcheva, Anna F. (1829–89), lady-in-waiting to Empress Maria, married Ivan Aksakov in 1866.

Valuev, Count Peter A. (1814–90), Minister of Internal Affairs, 1861–8.

Viardot, Pauline (1821–1910), opera singer and beloved friend of Turgenev.

Victoria, (1819–1901), Queen of England, 1837–1901.

Volkonskaya, Princess Maria N. (1805–63), wife of Decembrist.

Volkonsky, Prince Sergei G. (1788–1865), Decembrist.

William I (1797–1888), King of Prussia, 1861–88, Emperor of Germany, 1871–88.

Zasulich, Vera I. (1851–1919), revolutionary.

Zhelyabov, Andrei I. (1850–81), revolutionary; one of the leaders of the People's Will.

CHRONOLOGY

1855	Beginning of Alexander II's reign.
1856	Peace of Paris ends Crimean War.
	Coronation of the Tsar.
1857	Bakunin released from prison and exiled to Siberia.
	Tolstoy's first trip to Western Europe.
	Herzen and Ogarev begin publishing *The Bell*.
1858	Russia and China sign treaties of Aigun and Tientsin.
	Peter Perovsky arrives in Peking.
	Chicherin visits Herzen in London.
1859	Katkov and Chernyshevsky visit Herzen.
	Dostoevsky returns from Siberian exile.
1860	Treaty of Peking signed.
1861	Emancipation of the serfs.
	Tolstoy and Bakunin visit Herzen.
	Dmitry Milyutin becomes Minister of War.
	Tolstoy and Turgenev break off relations.
1862	*Fathers and Sons* published.
	Arrest of Chernyshevsky.
	Turgenev and Dostoevsky visit Herzen.
1863–4	Polish rebellion.
1864	Zemstvo and legal reforms.
1865	Herzen moves to Geneva.
1866	Karakozov attempts to assassinate Alexander II.
	Alexander begins affair with Catherine Dolgorukova.
	Dostoevsky completes *The Gambler* and *Crime and Punishment*.
1867	Assassination attempt on Alexander II in Paris.
	Dostoevsky and Turgenev meet in Baden-Baden.
1868	Dostoevsky's daughter, Sophia, dies in Geneva.
1869	Nechaev arrives in Geneva and meets Bakunin and Ogarev.
	Tolstoy completes *War and Peace*.
1870	Death of Herzen.
1870–71	Franco-Prussian War.

1874	Alexander II visits London.
	Thousands of young radicals "go to the people."
	Dostoevsky's first stay at Bad Ems.
	Sophia Perovskaya imprisoned for about five months.
1875	Vladimir Soloviev in Egypt.
1875–7	Tolstoy's *Anna Karenina* published.
1876	Death of Bakunin.
1877	Turgenev's *Virgin Soil* published.
	Death of Nekrasov.
1877–8	Russo-Turkish War.
1878	Dostoevsky and Vladimir Soloviev visit Optina Monastery.
	Tolstoy and Turgenev renew friendly relations.
1879	Death of Sergei Soloviev.
	The People's Will formed.
1880	Loris-Melikov named head of Supreme Administrative Commission.
	Death of Empress Maria and remarriage of Alexander II.
	Dostoevsky and Turgenev give speeches at Pushkin festivities.
1881	Death of Dostoevsky.
	Assassination of Alexander II.

ENDNOTES

(See Bibliography for full references)

PART ONE

Chapter 1

1. Lincoln (2), p. 351, quoting C. Kavelin.

Chapter 2

1. Tolstoy (2), XLVII, 37.
2. Ibid., XLVI, 31.
3. Ibid., IV, 59.
4. Alston, p. 70.
5. For example, Chicherin, II, 242–3, states that Anna Tyutcheva spoke Russian badly because she had spent her life at court.

Chapter 3

1. Lampert, p. 68.
2. Quoted in Alston, pp. 47–8. For several articles which challenge some aspects of the traditional view of the Orthodox church as a "handmaiden" of the state and indicate that not all clergymen were as conservative as Filaret, see Freeze (2) and (3).

Chapter 4

1. In his younger days, Vladimir Romanov had sailed to the Russian territories in America and become acquainted with the Russian-American company's office manager, a young poet named Ryleev, who also turned out to be one of the leaders of the Decembrist conspiracy of 1825. As a result of this takeover plot, Ryleev was hanged along with four others. Over a hundred more were sent to Siberia, and still others received lesser punishments. Romanov himself was imprisoned for months in the Sts Peter and Paul Fortress before he was released and allowed to continue his naval career. See *Russkii …* , XVII, 26–8.
2. Fadner, pp. 388–9, n. 107.
3. Ibid., p. 210.
4. Sergei Soloviev (3), p. 105.

5. Kornilov (2), p. 29, quoting the government official V.A. Mukhavov. The term *glasnost*, which Mikhail Gorbachev made one of his chief watchwords, was a term that was also frequently used in the first few years of Alexander II's reign. Only then it was put forth as a central aim not by the political leader, but by intellectuals and a few reform-minded government officials. In October 1855, Alexander Nikitenko wrote: "Many are now beginning to talk about lawfulness and openness (*glasnost*)." A few months later he mentioned an order of Grand Duke Constantine, head of the navy, which was critical of administrators who tried to cover up defects. Nikitenko thought the order was wonderful, but added that many were displeased with such indications of *glasnost*. Nikitenko, I, 422, 426. See also below, Ch. 5, where Chicherin writes of *glasnost*; Lincoln (3), p. 42; and Venturi, p. 103, on Herzen and "publicity," which is another English word for *glasnost*.
6. N. Barsukov, XIV, 494.
7. Quoted in Riasanovsky, p. 265.

Chapter 5

1. Tolstoy (2), XVII, 8.
2. Fet, I, 107.
3. Tolstoy (3), I, 59–60; Russian original in Tolstoy (2), LX, 74.
4. *Golosa* ... , II, 111.
5. Barsukov, XIV, 203.
6. Tolstoy (2), XLVII, 69.
7. Ibid., p. 71.

Chapter 6

1. *1857–1861*, p. 17.
2. Ibid., p. 208. A picture of Alexandra Dolgorukaya is on p. 207.
3. Tyutcheva, II, 123.

Chapter 7

1. See Frank (1), pp. 85–9, on the death of Dr. Dostoevsky, the guilt of Fedor, and the possibility that, contrary to long-held beliefs, the father was not killed by his serfs.
2. Quoted in Grossman (1), pp. 159–60.
3. Dostoevsky (8), II, 405, 408, 409.
4. Pereira, p. 25, quoting from Tatishchev.
5. Rieber (2), p. 47, quoting from a letter written by Alexander II in French and reproduced in full on pp. 116–18.
6. Dostoevsky (7), I, 190.
7. Ibid., p. 246.
8. Ibid., p. 398.
9. Ibid., p. 267.

Chapter 8

1. Quoted in Mendel, p. 22.

2. See the excellent article by Marshall S. Shatz, "Michael Bakunin and His Biographers: The Question of Bakunin's Sexual Impotence," in Mendelsohn and Shatz, pp. 219–40, for a view which faults historians for accepting Bakunin's impotence as a fact. Mendel, p. 28–31, using a psycho-historical approach, argues that Bakunin was impotent and avoided sexual contact because in his subconscious sex was associated with incest.
3. Quoted in Mendel, pp. 261–4.

Chapter 9

1. Cited in Seton-Watson, p. 336.
2. Kropotkin, p. 184.
3. For the Kropotkin quote, see ibid., p. 155.; see also Bassin, Chapter 5, for "Dreams of A Siberian Mississippi," where the author details both Russian and American hopes that Russian activity in the Amur area would lead to closer ties, and Chapter 6 on "Civilizing a Savage Realm."
4. Nikolai Barsukov, XVII, 73–4.

Chapter 10

1. Nekrasov, X, 336.
2. Tolstoy (2), XLVII, 118.
3. Tolstoy (3), I, 97; Tolstoy (2), LX, 167.
4. Tolstoy (3), I, 97; Tolstoy (2), LX, 170.
5. Tolstoy (3), I, 115–16; Tolstoy (2), LX, 247–8.
6. Tolstoy (2), XLVIII, 15.
7. Turgenev (3), III, 170.
8. Turgenev (5), VI, 80–81.
9. Ibid., IV, 213.
10. *Turgenevskii sbornik*, II, 250; Pushkin, I, 92–3.
11. Turgenev (3), III, 418.
12. Ibid., p. 292.
13. Ibid., p. 325.

Chapter 11

1. Herzen (3), XII, 273.
2. See Zakharova (2), pp. 66, 107–09, 123–4, on Herzen's influence at this time.
3. *Kolokol*, I, 67. This is from the edition of February 15, 1858.
4. Chicherin, II, 50.
5. Ibid., p. 52–3.

Chapter 12

1. See Wilson, pp. 131–5, 154–8 on the death of Nicholas and the earlier death of another brother, Dmitry, and on the influence of both of these deaths on Tolstoy and his writings.
2. Tolstoy (2), XVII, 470.

3. Ibid., LXII, 199.
4. Berlin (2), 212.
5. Burke, p. 85.
6. Tolstoy (2), LX, 377.
7. Florinsky, II, 922.
8. Valuev would later become one of the prototypes for the unlikeable Alexis Karenin in Tolstoy's *Anna Karenina*; see Tolstoy (2), XX, 640.
9. Herzen (3), XV, 176.
10. For an account of Bakunin in the United States, see Avrich, pp. 79–106.
11. Tuchkova-Ogareva, p. 185.
12. Quoted in Carr (2), p. 220.

Chapter 13

1. Yarmolinsky (1), p. 125.
2. Dostoevsky (8), XVIII, 37.
3. Ibid., p. 68.
4. Turgenev (5), XI, 87.
5. Frank (3), p. 151.
6. Quoted in Grossman (1), p. 252.
7. Tolstoy (2), 5, 24.
8. Berdyaev, p. 99.
9. Dostoevsky (1), p. 6.
10. Emmons, p. 344.
11. Herzen (1), III, 1366.
12. Dmytryshyn, p. 318.
13. On Turgenev's pessimism, see Moss (3), 242–7, and "The Nihilism of Ivan Turgenev" in Kelly (2), pp. 91–118.

Part Two

Chapter 14

1. Bourne and Watt, p. 81.
2. Quoted in Geyer, p. 40.
3. Emmons, p. 408.
4. Ibid., p. 411.
5. Pereira, p. 87.
6. See Wortman, II, 92–109, for much more on Tsarevich Nicholas and his significance.
7. Tarsaidzé, p. 108. Many of the Tsar's letters to Katia and some of hers to him appear in this work.

Chapter 15

1. N. Barsukov, XX, 186.
2. Bourne and Watt, p. 83.
3. Quoted in Chukovsky, pp. 40–41.

4. Ibid., p. 49.
5. Ibid., p. 9.
6. Ibid., p. 16.

Chapter 16

1. Herzen (3), XX (2), 606.
2. Quoted in Carr (2), p. 257.
3. *Kolokol*, IX, 1789. This is from the edition of May 1, 1866.
4. Quoted in Carr (2), p. 265.
5. Ibid.

Chapter 17

1. Dostoevsky (3), p. 215.
2. Dostoevsky (7), I, 438.
3. Dostoevsky (8), VIII, 188.
4. *Literaturnoe nasledstvo*, Vol. 86, p. 234; see also Dostoevskaya (3), p. 30.
5. Dostoevskaya (3), p. 46.

Chapter 18

1. Kavelin, I, 584.
2. V. Soloviev (4), p. 171.
3. V. Soloviev (2), IV, 60.

Chapter 19

1. Tolstaya (2), pp. 87–8.
2. Ibid., p. 90.
3. Tolstoy (2), XLVIII, 15, 25.
4. Tolstaya (2), p. 92.
5. Ibid., p. 147.
6. Tolstoy (4), 1283; Russian original in Tolstoy (2), XII, 267–8.
7. Turgenev (3), VIII, 200.
8. Tolstoy (3), I, 199; Tolstoy (2), LXI, 115.
9. Quoted in Berlin (1), p. 13.
10. Tolstoy (2), VIII, 334.
11. Ibid., XLVIII, 124.

Chapter 20

1. Tarsaidzé, p. 101.
2. Ibid., p. 106.
3. Ibid., p. 115.
4. *The Times*, June 8, 1867.
5. Goncourt and Goncourt, p. 233.
6. Herzen (1), III, 1429.
7. Ibid., p. 1428.

Chapter 21

1. Quoted in Schapiro (3), pp. 201–2.
2. Turgenev (3), V, 279.
3. Ibid., VI, 109.
4. Dostoevsky (7), II, 30.

Chapter 22

1. Bakunin, pp. 93–4.
2. Dostoevsky (7), II, 71.
3. Ibid., pp. 101–2.
4. Ibid., II, 101.
5. Confino, p. 75.

Chapter 23

1. *Literaturnoe nasledstvo*, Vols. 39–40, p. 542.
2. Ogarev, pp. 342–3, 833; see also Pomper (2), p. 96.
3. From a Bakunin letter to Nechaev in Confino, pp. 273–5.
4. Quoted in Pomper (2), p. 82.
5. Carr (1), p. 393.
6. Confino, p. 151.
7. Herzen (3), XXX (1), 299.
8. Ibid., p. 301.
9. Confino, p. 152.
10. Herzen (3), IV, 264.

PART THREE

Chapter 24

1. Tarsaidzé, pp. 161–6.
2. Queen Victoria (2), II, 189, 191.
3. Queen Victoria (3), II, 337.
4. Disraeli, I, 106.

Chapter 25

1. Dostoevsky (8), XVI, 5, 7, 16.
2. Ibid., p. 38.
3. Bater, pp. 205–6; Ransel, pp. 94–6, 306.
4. Dostoevsky (7), III, 115.

Chapter 26

1. Kropotkin, p. 306.
2. Quoted in Venturi, p. 488.

Chapter 27

1. V. Soloviev (2), III, 85.
2. Ibid., p. 291.
3. V. Soloviev (4), p. 174.
4. Anderson, pp. 208–9.
5. V. Soloviev (4), p. 177.
6. Ibid.
7. Ibid., p. 63.

Chapter 28

1. Forbes, pp. 190, 194.
2. Hozier, p. 472.
3. Tolstoy (1), 698; Russian original in Tolstoy (2), XIX, 352–3.
4. Milyutin, II, 187.
5. Tarsaidzi, p. 185.
6. Dostoevsky (1), II, 636.
7. Tatishchev, II, 394.
8. Tarsaidzi, p. 175.
9. Ibid., p. 173.
10. Forbes, p. 199.
11. Tarsaidzi, p. 192.
12. Ibid., p. 193.
13. Ibid., p. 191.
14. MacKenzie, p. 327.

Chapter 29

1. Vasily Botkin, like his good friend Turgenev, had broken with Nekrasov once Chernyshevsky and Dobrolyubov became influential on *The Contemporary*. Botkin had been too much of an aesthete to tolerate such radicals. On his deathbed in 1869 he arranged for musicians to be brought in, and he died as they played a Beethoven string quartet. The brothers also had a sister who was married to another aesthete and hater of radicals, the poet Fet.
2. Nekrasov, II, 369.
3. Ibid., p. 407.
4. Turgenev (3), VIII, 312.
5. Quoted in Schapiro (3), p. 235.
6. See above, Chapter 23, note 9.
7. Turgenev (3), XII (1), 135.
8. Turgenev (5), X, 147.
9. Quoted in Ashukin, p. 512.
10. Dostoevsky (1), II, 584.
11. Ibid., p. 936.
12. Ibid., p. 937.

Chapter 30

1. V. Soloviev (1), p. 159.
2. See above, chapter 27, note 1.
3. Tolstoy (3), I, 322; Tolstoy (2), LXII, 413.
4. Dostoevsky (7), IV, 17.
5. Dostoevsky (9), II, 64. See also "Dostoevsky and the Divided Conscience," in Kelly (2), pp. 55–79, and Bakhtin, 6, 18, on the "polyphonic" nature of his fiction that allows his characters to express different ideologies and speak with many different, often mutually exclusive, but yet convincing, voices. For an approach to Dostoevsky's *Diary of A Writer* that also detects considerable ambivalence in this work, see Morson.
6. Turgenev (3), X, 305.
7. For a more balanced assessment of the 1863 change in the liquor laws, see David Christian's "A Neglected Great Reform: The Abolition of Tax Farming in Russia," in Eklof, Bushnell, and Zakharova (2), pp. 102–114.
8. Chicherin, III, 192.
9. Dostoevsky (7), IV, 170.
10. Fictional characters, however, often reflect multiple creative sources. See Perlina, for example, where she emphasizes the similarity of many of Ivan's ideas to those of Herzen.

Chapter 31

1. Tolstoy (2), LXII, 406–7.
2. Tolstoy (3), I, 288; Tolstoy (2), LXII, 226.
3. Tolstoy (2), XXIII, 26.
4. Tolstoy (3), I, 314; Tolstoy (2), LXII, 381.
5. Tolstoy (3), I, 320; Tolstoy (2), LXII, 409.
6. Tolstoy (3), I, 321; Tolstoy (2), LXII, 411.
7. See Loshchinin, pp. 67–9, where he revises the traditional view that Turgenev did not like *Anna Karenina* by pointing out that Turgenev's critical comments about it were directed mainly at the first quarter of the novel and that Turgenev's attitude toward the work as a whole was much more favorable.
8. Tolstaya (2), p. 78.
9. Quoted in Schapiro (3), p. 275.
10. Tolstoy (3), II, 338; Tolstoy (2), LXIII, 116.
11. S. Tolstoy, p. 169.
12. Turgenev (3), XII (2), 260. See Turgenev (1) for translations of his letters to Savina and for more on their romance.

Chapter 32

1. V. Soloviev (2), II, 248.
2. Quoted in Dalton, p. 23.
3. Troyat (2), p. 422.
4. V. Soloviev (4), p. 228.

5. Ibid., p. 71.
6. Ibid., p. 74.
7. Dostoevsky (2), p. 58.
8. Dostoevksy (7), IV, 171.
9. Dostoevsky (2), pp. 57, 58.
10. Dostoevskaya (3), p. 336.
11. Dostoevsky (1), p. 1019. For a brief overview of the anti-Semitism of Dostoevsky, Pobedonostsev, and others see Klier, 412–16; for a fuller treatment of Dostoevsky's views on the Jews, see Goldstein.
12. Ibid., p. 1032.
13. Dostoevsky (1), II, 1044; and see above Ch. 24, where Gorchakov in 1864 had defended earlier Russian advances as part of a civilizing mission. See also Bassin, pp. 262–5, on Dostoevsky's views on Central Asia and how they relate to earlier Russian expansionist hopes including those in the Amur region.
14. V. Soloviev (3), III, 170.

Chapter 33

1. Cited in Kornilov (1), II, 237.
2. Quoted from Byrnes, pp. 143–4.
3. Cited in Zaionchkovsky (1), p. 92.
4. Ibid., p. 135.
5. Milyutin, IV, 79.

Chapter 34

1. Venturi, p. 667, quoting from the first issue of *The People's Will*, the underground journal of the party.
2. Ibid., p. 668, quoting from the second issue of the same journal. See also Stepniak (1), pp. 11–24, for a more detailed radical view regarding the connection of railway financing and peasant impoverishment.

Chapter 35

1. Milyutin, IV, 62.
2. Cited in Footman, p. 266.

Chapter 36

1. Stepniak (2), pp. 131–3.
2. Milyutin, IV, 49.
3. Cited in Footman, p. 298.
4. Quoted in Segal, p. 368.

Chapter 37

1. Cited in Mochulsky (2), p. 127.
2. Milyutin, IV, 35.
3. Ibid.

4. Tolstoy (2), LXIII, 46–7.
5. Ibid., p. 50.
6. Ibid., p. 52.
7. Ibid., p. 58.
8. Ibid., pp. 58–9.
9. Ibid., p. 58.

Epilogue

1. Turgenev (5), X, 147–8. See also Schapiro (3), p. 287.
2. See, Chapter 32, n. 11; Moss (2).
3. Trubetskoi, I, 7.
4. See Shatz and Zimmerman, and "Which Signposts?" in Kelly (2), pp. 155–200.
5. See, for example, McDaniel, pp. 17–18, 28, 184, 186, where he discusses such characteristics and acknowledges Lotman's influence.
6. See Ragsdale, pp. 274–5, where he suggests that some type of Christian socialism might be most appropriate for Russia. The most fully developed Christian socialist ideas of the late tsarist period came from Sergei Bulgakov (See Evtuhov, 101–14). Bulgakov was one of the contributors to *Signposts* who was strongly influenced by the ideas of Vladimir Soloviev.

A NOTE ON PRINCIPAL SOURCES

(See Bibliography for full references)

The most valuable primary source for Alexander II in chapters 1, 3 and 6 was the diary of A. Tyutcheva, one of the Empress's ladies-in-waiting. The correspondence between the Tsar and his brother Constantine and the latter's diary are valuable for the years 1857–61 (see *1857–1861...*). For Alexander's relations with Catherine (Katia) Dolgorukova, Tarsaidzé was most helpful. Many of the Tsar's letters to her and a few of hers to him are reproduced there. Alexander's trips to Paris (Chapter 20) and to London (Chapter 24) were reported on in detail in *The Times* (London), and Van der Kiste also describes the trip to London, as well as British-Russian royal relations in general. The diaries of two of the Tsar's ministers, Valuev and D. Milyutin, proved useful, the first for the period 1861–76, the second for the years 1873–81. The principal biographies of Alexander which I used were those of Almendingen, Lyashenko, Mosse (1), Pereria and Tatishchev. Zakharova (1) and (2) were also helpful. Zaionchkovsky (2) and (3) were excellent sources for the last several years of Alexander II's reign and the first month of Alexander III's, and the Eklof, Bushnell, and Zakharova collection, Lincoln (2), Rieber (1) and (2), and Wortman's second volume of *Scenarios of Power* offer useful interpretations of Alexander II's policies.

The daily activities of Tolstoy are chronicled in Gusev (1) and fleshed out in more detail in Gusev (2). Chronological listings of events in the lives of Dostoevsky, Herzen, Nekrasov and Turgenev are in Grossman (2), Egorov, Ashukin and Kleman respectively. The letters and other writings of all five writers provided valuable material. Since numerous translations of some of those works exist, I have listed in the bibliography only those of which I have made direct use. Tolstoy's diaries in Tolstoy (2) and those of his wife are also useful. Birukoff's work on Tolstoy contains much material (and some good photos) on Tolstoy up until the early 1860s. For the chapters dealing with the Dostoevskys between 1866 and 1868, I relied heavily on the diaries and reminiscences of Dostoevsky's second wife, Anna. In addition to the English translations of her works listed in the bibliography, her untranslated Geneva diary, reproduced in *Literaturnoe nasledstvo*, Vol. 86, also contains important remembrances, including some of the months she worked with Dostoevsky before their marriage. The reminiscences of Dostoevsky's friend Wrangel are helpful for some of the novelist's Semipalatinsk years. Secondary works in English on Dostoevsky, Tolstoy and Turgenev are plentiful, and I have listed in the bibliography only those that were most useful. Of those listed, Frank's multi-volume biography of Dostoevsky was especially helpful. *N.A. Nekrasov ...*

contains valuable first hand accounts of the editor and poet, and the works by Chukovsky, Peppard, and Zhdanov are all useful secondary sources on him. The remembrances of Fet and Panaeva provided additional material, especially on the interrelationships of Nekrasov, Tolstoy, and Turgenev. Levitt's book on the Pushkin Celebration is a thorough study of its political significance and the role of Dostoevsky and Turgenev in the celebration.

For Sergei Soloviev, his memoirs (*Zapiski*), Illeritsky and several articles on him by Klyuchevsky were most helpful. Nikolai Tsimbaev's biography is also a solid work, but I consulted it only after completing the chapters on Soloviev. Information on his father-in-law, Vladimir Romanov, was found in *Russkii biographicheskii slovar*, Vol. 17. For Vladimir Soloviev and his family and life up to the mid 1870s, Lukyanov (1) and (2) were invaluable. The recollections of Bezobrazova and Eltsova, as well as the philosopher's own letters and works, provided additional information. I also benefited from the biographical studies of Mochulsky, Soloviev's nephew (S.M. Soloviev), and Stremoukhoff. Kostalevsky's work on Dostoevsky and Vladimir Soloviev is a good recent examination of the ideas and relationship of the two men.

For Bakunin I relied on Bakunin (1) and (2), Carr (1), Dolzhikov, Kelly (1) and Mendel; for Muraviev-Amursky on Ivan Barsukov and Sullivan; for Herzen on Acton (1), Carr (2) and Herzen (1), (2) and (3), the last of which contain his letters, as well as other writings. Some valuable information on Herzen and Ogarev can also be found in *Literaturnoe nasledstvo,* Vols. 39–40, 41–2 and 61 and in Confino, which contains translations of many valuable letters of the Herzens, Bakunin, Ogarev, and Nechaev. Zimmerman provides good background material on Herzen for the years 1847–52. An interesting, but at times misleading, memoir is that of Ogarev's second wife, Natalia Tuchkova-Ogareva.

On Peter Perovsky and Igantiev in Peking, Quested was most valuable. On Lev Perovsky and his revolutionary daughter, Sophia, I used primarily the memoirs of Sophia's brother Vasily, the biography of Segal, and remembrances of her by her fellow revolutionaries in "*Narodnaya volya …* ," Kropotkin and Stepniak (2).

On public opinion in Russia, Kornilov (2) and Nikitenko were most useful. I discovered Bassin's valuable book *Imperial Visions* (1999) only after completing earlier versions of my work, but made some minor revisions as a result. Kelly (2) offers valuable insights on various important figures including Chicherin, Dostoevsky, Herzen, Tolstoy and Turgenev. On the revolutionary movement in Russia, Footman, Gleason, Hardy, Pomper (1), Ulam, Venturi and Yarmolinsky (1) were all helpful. For Chrenyshevsky, Woehrlin was most valuable and for Nechaev, Pomper (2).

For descriptions of the various cities and other locales mentioned in the book, I used a wide variety of nineteenth-century and modern-day sources, including old Baedeker and Murray guidebooks. I have listed only a few of these in the bibliography. Among them, Bater's book on St Petersburg deserves special mention because of its thoroughness. Visits to most of these places, including estates such as those of Tolstoy and Nekrasov and resort towns such as Baden-Baden and Bad Ems, have also, I hope, enabled me to describe them more accurately.

BIBLIOGRAPHY OF PRINT MATERIALS*

Acton, Edward. (1) *Alexander Herzen and the Role of the Intellectual Revolutionary.* Cambridge, Eng., 1979.

—— (2) "The Russian Revolutionary Intelligentsia and Industrialization", in *Russian Thought and Society, 1800–1917: Essays in Honour of Eugene Lampert.* Edited by Roger Bartlett. University of Keele, 1984.

Akademiya nauk ssr. Institut istorii. *Istoriya Moskvy.* Vols. III and IV. 1954.

Allen, Paul M. *Vladimir Soloviev: Russian Mystic.* Blauvelt, N.Y., 1978.

Almendingen, E.M. *The Emperor Alexander II: A Study.* London, 1962.

Alston, Patrick L. *Education and the State in Tsarist Russia.* Stanford, 1969.

Anderson, M.S. *The Eastern Question, 1774–1923: A Study in International Relations.* London, 1966.

Ashukin, N.S. *Letopis zhizni i tvorchestva N.A. Nekrasova.* Moscow-Leningrad, 1935.

Avrich, Paul. *Anarchist Portraits.* Princeton, 1988.

Bakhtin, M.M. *Problems of Dostoevsky's Poetics.* Edited and translated by Caryl Emerson. Minneapolis, 1984.

Bakunin, Mikhail. (1) *Bakunin on Anarchism.* Edited, translated and with an introduction by Sam Dolgoff. Montreal, 1980.

—— (2) *Sobranie sochinenii i pisem, 1828–76.* Edited by Yu. M. Steklov. 4 vols. Moscow, 1934–5.

Banno, Mastaka. *China and the West, 1858–1861: The Origins of the Tsungli Yamen.* Cambridge, Eng., 1964.

Baron, Samuel H. *Plekhanov: The Father of Russian Marxism.* Stanford, 1963.

Barsukov, Ivan. *Graf Nikolai Nikolaevich Muraviev-Amursky po ego pisman, offitsialnym dokumentam, razskazasill sovremennikov i pechatnym istochnikam: Materialy dlya biografii.* 2 vols. Moscow, 1891.

Barsukov, Nikolai. *Zhizn i trudy M.P. Pogodina.* 22 vols. St. Petersburg, 1888–1910.

Bassin, Mark. *Imperial Visions: Nationalist Imagination and Geographical Expansion in the Russian Far East, 1840–1865.* Cambridge, Eng., 1999.

Bater, James H. *St Petersburg: Industrialization and Change.* Montreal, 1976.

Berdyaev, Nicholas. *The Russian Idea.* Translated by R.M. French. Boston, 1962.

Bergman, Jay. *Vera Zasulich: A Biography.* Stanford, 1983.

* For online links to visual and other textual materials see http://www.emich.edu/public/history/moss.

Berlin, Isaiah. (1) *The Hedgehog and the Fox: An Essay on Tolstoy's View of History*. New York, 1966.

—— (2) *Russian Thinkers*. New York, 1979.

Bezobrazova, S.M. "Vospominaniya o brate V. Solovieve," *Minouvshie gody*, V–VI (May–June, 1908), 128–66.

Billington, James H. (1) *The Icon and the Axe: An Interpretative History of Russian Culture*. New York, 1966.

—— (2) *Mikhailosky and Russian Populism*. New York, 1958.

Birkenmayer, Sigmund S. *Nikolaj Nekrasov: His Life and Poetic Art*. The Hague-Paris, 1968.

Birukoff [Biriukov], Paul. *Leo Tolstoy, His Life and Work; Autobiographical Memoirs, Letters, and Biographical Material*. New York, 1906.

Bourne, Kenneth, and Watt, D. Cameron. *British Documents on Foreign Affairs: Reports and Papers from the Confidential Print*. Part I: *From the Mid-Nineteenth Century to the First World War*. Series A: *Russia, 1859–1914*. Edited by Dominic Lieven.[Frederick, Maryland], 1983.

Brower, Daniel R.(1) *The Russian City between Tradition and Modernity, 1850–1900*. Berkeley, 1990.

—— (2) *Training the Nihilists: Education and Radicalism in Tsarist Russia*. Ithaca, N.Y., 1975.

Buel, J.W. *Russian Nihilism and Exile Life in Siberia*. St. Louis and Philadelphia, 1884.

Burke, Edmund. *Speech of Edmund Burke Esq. on Moving His Resolutions for Conciliation with the Colonies, March 22, 1775*. Reprint of 2nd ed. Taylors, S.C., 1975.

Byrnes, Robert F. *Pobedonostsev: His Life and Thought*. Bloomington, 1968.

Carr, E.H. (1) *Michael Bakunin*. New York, 1961.

—— (2) *The Romantic Exiles: A Nineteenth-Century Portrait Gallery*. Boston, 1961.

Chernyshevsky, N.G. *What is to Be Done? Tales about New People*. The Benjamin E. Tucker translation, revised and abridged by Ludmilla Turkevich. New York, 1961.

Chicherin, B.N. *Vospominaniya Borisa Nikolaevicha Chicherina*. 4 vols. Moscow, 1929–34.

Christoff, Peter K. *K.S. Aksakov: A Study in Ideas*. Princeton, 1982.

Chukovsky, Koreni. *The Poet and the Hangman*. Translated by R.W. Rotsel. Ann Arbor, 1977.

Collins, Perry McDonough. *A Voyage Down the Amoor*. New York, 1860.

Confino, Michael, ed. *Daughter of a Revolutionary: Natalie Herzen and the Bakunin-Nechayev Circle*. Translated by Hilary Sternberg and Lydia Bott. LaSalle, Ill., 1974.

Curtiss, John Shelton. *Russia's Crimean War*. Durham, N.C., 1979.

Dalton, Margaret. *A.K. Tolstoy*. New York, 1972.

David, Zdenek V. "The Formation of the Religious and Social System of Vladimir Soloviev." Unpublished Ph.D. dissertation. Harvard University, 1960.

De Jonge, Alex. *Dostoevsky and the Age of Intensity*. New York, 1975.

De Vogüé, E.M. *Journal: Paris-Saint Petersburg, 1877–1883*. Paris, [1932].

Dilthey, Wilhelm. *Pattern & Meaning in History: Thoughts on History & Society*. Edited and introduced by H.P. Rickman. New York, 1962.

Disraeli, Benjamin. *The Letters of Disraeli to Lady Chesterfield and Lady Bradford*. Edited by the Marquis of Zetland. 2 vols. London, 1929.

Dmytryshyn, Basil. *Imperial Russia: A Source Book 1700–1917*. 3rd ed. New York, 1990.

Dolzhikov, V.A. *M.A. Bakunin i Sibir (1857–61 gg.)*. Novosibirsk, 1993.

Dostoevskaya, Anna. (1) *The Diary of Dostoevsky's Wife*. Translated from the German by Madge Pemberton. New York, 1928.

—— (2) *Dostoevsky Portrayed by His Wife: The Diary and Reminiscences of Mme Dostoevsky*. Translated and edited by S.S. Koteliansky. London, 1926.

—— (3) *Dostoevsky: Reminiscences*. Translated and edited by Beatrice Stillman. New York, 1975.

Dostoevsky, Aimee. *Fyodor Dostoevsky: A Study*. London, 1921.

Dostoevsky, F.M. (1) *The Diary of a Writer*. Translated and annotated by Boris Brasol. New York, 1954.

—— (2) *The Dream of a Queer Fellow and the Pushkin Speech*. Translated by S. Koteliansky and J. Middleton Murray. London, 1960.

—— (3) *The Gambler, with Polina Suslova's Diary*. Edited by Edward Wasiolek, translated by Victor Terras. Chicago, 1972.

—— (4) *The Letters of Dostoevsky to His Wife*. Translated by Elizabeth Hill and Doris Mudie. London, 1930.

—— (5) *Letters of Fyodor Dostoevsky to His Family and Friends*. Translated by Ethel Colburn Mayne. New York, 1964.

—— (6) *The Notebooks for a Raw Youth*. Edited by Edward Wasiolek, translated by Victor Terras. Chicago, 1969.

—— (7) *Pisma*. Edited by A.S. Dolinin. 4 vols. Moscow, 1928–59.

—— (8) *Polnoe sobranie sochinenii v tridsati tomakh*. 30 vols. Leningrad, 1972–90.

—— (9) *The Unpublished Dostoevsky: Diaries and Notebooks, 1860–1881*. Edited by Carl Proffer. 3 vols. Ann Arbor, 1973–5.

—— (10) *Winter Notes on Summer Impressions*. Translated by Richard Lee Renfield. New York, 1965.

Dryzhakova, E.I. (1) "Dostoevsky i Gertsen: Londonskoe svidanie, 1862 goda," *Canadian-American Slavic Studies* 17 (Fall 1983), 325–48.

—— (2) "Dostoevsky i Gertsen: U istokov romana 'Besy,'" *Dostoevsky: Materialy i issledovaniya*. Vol. 1. Leningrad, 1974.

Durman, Karel. *The Time of the Thunderer: Mikhail Katkov, Russian Nationalist Extremism and the Failure of the Bismarckian System, 1871–1887*. New York, 1988. *1857–1861: Perepiska Imperatora Aleksandra II s Velikim Kniazem Konstantinom Nikolaevichem: Dnevnik Velikogo Kniazia Konstantina Nikolaevicha*. Moscow, 1994.

Eikhenbaum, Boris. (1) *Tolstoi in the Seventies*. Translated by Albert Kaspin. Ann Arbor, 1982.

—— (2) *Tolstoi in the Sixties*. Translated by Duffield White. Ann Arbor, 1982.

Egorov, B.F. et al., eds. *Letopis' zhizni i tvorchestva A.I. Gertsena*. Vols. II-IV. Moscow, 1976–87.

Eklof, Ben. *Russian Peasant Schools: Officialdom, Village Culture, and Popular Pedagogy, 1861–1914*. Berkeley, 1986.

Eklof, Ben, Bushnell, John, and Zakharova, Larissa, eds. *Russia's Great Reforms, 1855–1881.* Bloomington, 1994.

Eltsova, K., "Sny nezdeshnie," *Sovrmenniya Zapiski* 28 (1926), 225–75.

Emmons, Terence. *The Russian Landed Gentry and the Peasant Emancipation of 1861.* Cambridge, Eng., 1968.

Engel, Barbara. *Mothers and Daughters: Women of the Intelligentsia in Nineteenth-Century Russia.* Cambridge, Eng., 1983.

Engel, Barbara Alpern, and Rosenthal, Clifford N., eds. and translators. *Five Sisters: Women Against the Tsar.* New York, 1975.

Engelgardt, A.N. *Aleksandr Nikolaevich Engelgardt's Letters from the Country, 1872–1887.* Translated and edited by Cathy A. Frierson. New York, 1993.

Evgeniev-Maksimov, V. (1) *N.A. Nekrasov i ego sovremenniki: Ocherki.* Moscow, 1930.

—— (2) *Zhizni deyatelnost N. A. Nekrasova.* 3 vols. Moscow, 1947–52.

Evtuhov, Catherine. *The Cross & the Sickle: Sergei Bulgakov and the Fate of Russian Religious Philosophy.* Ithaca, N.Y., 1997.

Fadner, Frank. *Seventy Years of Pan-Slavism in Russia: Karamzin to Danilevskii, 1800–1870.* Washington, D.C., 1962.

Feoktistov, E.M. *Vospominaniya za kulisami politiki i literatury, 1848–1896.* Leningrad, 1929.

Fet, A.A. *Moi vospominaniya.* 2 vols. Moscow, 1890.

Feuer, Kathryn B. *Tolstoy and the Genesis of "War and Peace."* Ithaca, N.Y., 1996.

Field, Daniel. *The End of Serfdom: Nobility and Bureaucracy in Russia, 1855–1861.* Cambridge, Mass., 1976.

—— "Kavelin and Russian Liberalism," *Slavic Review* 32 (March 1973), 59–78.

Florinsky, Michael T. *Russia: A History and Interpretation.* 2 vols. New York, 1953.

Footman, David. *The Alexander Conspiracy: A Life of A.I. Zhelyabov.* LaSalle, Ill., 1974.

Forbes, Archibald. *Barracks, Bivouacs, and Battles.* London, 1910.

Frank, Joseph. (1) *Dostoevsky: The Miraculous Years, 1865–1871.* Princeton, 1995.

—— (2) *Dostoevsky: The Seeds of Revolt, 1821–1849.* Princeton, 1976.

—— (3) *Dostoevsky: The Stir of Liberation, 1860–65.* Princeton, 1986.

—— (4) *Dostoevsky: The Years of Ordeal, 1850–1859.* Princeton, 1983.

Freeze, Gregory L. (1) *From Supplication to Revolution: A Documentary Social History of Imperial Russia.* Pt. 2. New York, 1988.

—— (2) "Handmaiden of The State? The Church in Imperial Russia Reconsidered." *The Journal of Ecclesiastical History* 36 (Jan 1985), 82–102.

—— (3) *The Parish Clergy in Nineteenth-Century Russia: Crisis, Reform, Counter-Reform.* Princeton, 1983.

Frierson, Cathy A. *Peasant Icons: Representations of Rural People in Late Nineteenth-Century Russia.* New York, 1993.

Gammer, Moshe. *Muslim Resistance to the Tsar: Shamil and the Conquest of Chechnia and Daghestan.* London, 1994.

Gernet, Mikhail. *Istoriya tsarskoi tyurmy.* Vol. III: *1870–1900.* Moscow, 1961.

Gerschenkron, Alexander. "The Problem of Economic Development in Russian

Intellectual History of the Nineteenth Century," *Continuity and Change in Russian and Soviet Thought.* Edited by Ernest J. Simmons. Cambridge, Mass., 1955.

Geyer, Dietrich. *Russian Imperialism: The Interaction of Domestic and Foreign Policy, 1860–1914.* Translated from the German by Bruce Little. Leamington Spa, N.Y., 1987.

Gleason, Abbott. *Young Russia: The Genesis of Russian Radicalism in the 1860s.* New York, 1980.

Goldstein, David I. *Dostoevsky and the Jews.* Austin, 1981.

Golosa iz Rossii: Sbornik A.I. Gertsena i N.P. Ogareva. 9 books. London, 1856–60. Facsimile ed. in 3 parts, with commentaries and index in 4th part, Moscow, l974–5.

Goncourt, Edmond, and Goncourt, Jules. *The Goncourt Journals, 1851–1870.* Edited and translated by Lewis Galantiere. Garden City, N.Y., 1958.

Graham, Stephen. *Tsar of Freedom: The Life and Reign of Alexander II.* New Haven, 1935.

Greene, F.V. *Sketches of Army Life in Russia.* New York, 1880.

Grossman, Leonid. (1) *Dostoevsky: A Biography.* Translated by Mary Mackler. Indianapolis, 1975.

——— (2) *Zhizn i trudy F.M. Dostoevskogo: Biografiya v datakh i dokumentakh.* Moscow-Leningrad, 1935.

Gusev, N.N. (1) *Letopis zhizni i tvorchestva Leva Nikolaevicha Tolstogo.* 2 vols. Moscow, 1958–60.

——— (2) *Lev Nikolaevich Tolstoi: Materialy k biografii.* 4 vols. Moscow, 1954–70.

Gustafson, Richard F. *Leo Tolstoy, Resident and Stranger: A Study in Fiction and Theology.* Princeton, 1986.

Hamburg, Gary M. *Boris Chicherin and Early Russian Liberalism, 1828–1866.* Stanford, 1992.

Hardy, Deborah. *Land and Freedom: The Origins of Russian Terrorism.* New York, 1987.

Herzen, Alexander. (1) *My Past and Thoughts.* 4 vols. Translated by C. Garnett, revised by Humphrey Higgens. London, 1968.

——— (2) *Selected Philosophical Works.* Translated by L. Navrozov. Moscow, 1956.

——— (3) *Sobranie sochinenii.* 30 vols. Moscow, 1954–66.

Hozier, H.M., ed. *The Russo-Turkish War: Including an Account of the Rise and Decline of the Ottoman Power, and the History of the Eastern Question.* 2 vols. London, [1878].

Illeritsky, V.E. *Sergei Mikhailovich Soloviev.* Moscow, 1980.

"Iz rechei na sude A.I. Zhelyabova, N.I. Kibalchicha, i S.L. Perovskoi," *Byloe,* 1906, no. 3, 62–70.

Jelavich, Barbara. *St Petersburg and Moscow: Tsarist and Soviet Foreign Policy, 1814–1974.* Bloomington, 1974.

Kagan-Kans, Eva. *Hamlet and Don Quixote: Turgenev's Ambivalent Vision.* The Hague-Paris, 1975.

Katz, Martin. *Mikhail Katkov: A Political Biography, 1818–1887.* The Hague, 1966.

Kavelin, K.D. *Sobranie sochinenii.* 4 vols. St Petersburg, 1897–1900.

Kazemzadeh, Firuz. *Russia and Britain in Persia, 1864–1914: A Study in Imperialism.* New Haven, 1968.

Kelly, Aileen. *Mikhail Bakunin: A Study in the Psychology and Politics of Utopianism.* Oxford, 1982.

—— (2) *Toward Another Shore: Russian Thinkers Between Necessity and Chance*. New Haven, 1998.

—— (3) *Views from the Other Shore: Essays on Herzen, Chekhov and Bakhtin*. New Haven, 1999.

Kingston-Mann, Esther. *In Search of the True West: Culture, Economics, and Problems of Russian Development*. Princeton, 1999.

Kingston-Mann, Esther, and Mixter, Timothy, eds. *Peasant Economy, Culture and Politics of European Russia, 1800–1921*. Princeton, 1990.

Kipp, Jacob W., and Lincoln, W. Bruce. "Autocracy and Reform: Bureaucratic Absolutism and Political Modernization in Nineteenth-Century Russia," *Russian History* 6, no. 1 (1979), 1–21.

Kleman, M.K. *Letopis zhizni i tvorchestva I.S. Turgeneva*. Moscow-Leningrad, 1934.

Klier, John Doyle. *Imperial Russia's Jewish Question, 1855–1881*. Cambridge, Eng., 1995.

Klyuchevsky, V. *Sbornik statei*. Vol. II: *Ocherki i rechi*. Moscow, 1918.

Kohn, Hans. *Pan-Slavism: Its History and Ideology*. 2nd ed. rev. New York, 1960.

Kolokol: Gazeta A.I. Gertsena i N.P. Ogareva, 1857–1867. 10 vols. Moscow, 1962–4.

Kornilov, Alexander. (1) *Modern Russian History*. Translated and extended by Alexander S. Kaun. 2 vols. in 1. New York, 1924.

—— (2) *Obshchestvennoe dvizhenie pri Aleksandre II (1855–1881): Istoricheskie ocherki*. Moscow, 1909.

Kostalevsky, Marina. *Dostoevsky and Soloviev: The Art of Integral Vision*. New Haven, 1997.

Kropotkin, Peter. *Memoirs of a Revolutionist*. New York, 1971.

Kuzminskaya, Tatyana, A. *Tolstoy as I Knew Him: My Life at Home at Yasnaya Polyana*. Translated by Nora Sigerist et al. New York, 1948.

Lampert, E. *Sons against Fathers: Studies in Russian Radicalism and Revolution*. Oxford, 1965.

Leslie, R.F. *Reform and Insurrection in Russian Poland, 1856–1865*. London, 1963.

Levitt, Marcus C. *Russian Literary Politics and the Pushkin Celebration of 1880*. Ithaca, N.Y., 1989.

Lincoln W. Bruce. (1) *The Conquest of a Continent: Siberia and the Russians*. New York, 1994.

—— (2) *The Great Reforms: Autocracy, Bureaucracy, and the Politics of Change in Imperial Russia*. Dekalb, Ill., 1990.

—— (3) "The Ministers of Alexander II," *Cahiers du Monde russe et soviétique*, no. 4 (1976), 467–84.

—— (4) *Nicholas I, Emperor and Autocrat of All the Russians*. Bloomington, 1978.

Literaturnoe nasledstvo. Vol. 39–40 (1941): *A.I. Gertsen, I*. Vol. 41–42 (1941): *A.I. Gertsen, II*. Vol. 61 (1953): *Gertsen i Ogarev, I*. Vol. 67 (1959): *Revolyutsionnye demokraty: Novye materialy*. Vol. 83 (1971): *Neizdannyi Dostoevsky: Zapisnye khnizhki i tetradi, 1860–1881 gg*. Vol. 86 (1973): *F.M. Dosteovsky: Novye materialy i issledovaniya*.

L.N. Tolstoi v vospominaniyakh sovremennikov. 2 vols. Moscow, 1978.

Loshchinin, N.P. *L.N. Tolstoi i I.S. Turgenev: Tvorcheskie i lichnye otnosheniya*. Tula, 1982.

Lotman, Yu. M. *Kultura i vzryv*. Moscow, 1992.

Lukyanov, Sergei. (1) "O Vl. S. Solovieve v ego molodye gody," *Zhurnal Minsterstva Narodnago Prosveshcheniya*, LVI (March, 1915), 1–57; LVII (May 1915), 62–129; LVIII (July 1915), 27–52; LIX (Sept. 1915), 55–86; LX (Nov. 1915), 1–36; LXI (Jan., 1916), 24–69; LXII (March, 1916), 34–79; LXIII (May, 1916), 32–70; LXIV (July, 1916), 38–80; LXV (Sept. 1916), 25–71; LXVII (Jan. 1917), 1–42; LXVIII (March–April, 1917), 1–43; LXIX (June, 1917), 209–47; LXXI (Sept., 1917), 1–32; LXXII (Nov.–Dec., 1917), 27–60.

—— (2) *O Vl. S. Solovieve v ego molodye gody: Materialy k biografii*. Vol. III. Petrograd, 1921.

Lyashenko, L.M. *Tsar-Osvoboditel: Zhizn i deyaniya Aleksandra II*. Moscow, 1994.

MacKenzie, David. *The Serbs and Russian Pan-Slavism,1875–1878*. Ithaca, N.Y., 1967.

Malia, Martin. *Alexander Herzen and the Birth of Russian Socialism*. Cambridge, Mass., 1961.

Maud, Aylmer. *The Life of Tolstoy*. 2 vols. London, 1930.

Mazour, Anatole G. *The First Russian Revolution, 1825: The Decembrist Movement, Its Origins, Development, and Significance*. Stanford, 1961.

McCauley, Martin, and Waldron, Peter, eds. *The Emergence of the Modern Russian State, 1855–81*. Totowa, N.J., 1988.

McDaniel, Tim. *The Agony of the Russian Idea*. Princeton, 1996.

Mendel, Arthur P. *Michael Bakunin: Roots of Apocalypse*. New York, 1981.

Mendelsohn, Ezra, and Shatz, Marshall S., eds. *Imperial Russia, 1700–1917: State, Society, Opposition: Essays in Honor of Marc Raeff*. DeKalb, Ill., 1988.

Miller, Forestt A. *Dmitrii Miliutin and the Reform Era in Russia*. Nashville, 1968.

Milyutin D.A. *Dnevnik*. Edited by P.A. Zaionchkovsky. 4 vols. Moscow, 1947–50.

Mitchell, B.R. *European Historical Statistics 1750–1970*. New York, 1975.

Mochulsky, Konstantin. (1) *Dostoevsky: His Life and Work*. Translated by Michael Minihan. Princeton, 1967.

—— (2) *Vladimir Soloviev: Zhizn i uchenie*. 2nd ed. Paris, 1951.

Morson, Gary Saul. *The Boundaries of Genre: Dostoevsky's Diary of a Writer and the Traditions of Literary Utopia*. Austin, 1981.

Moss, Walter G. (1) *A History of Russia*. Vol. 1. New York, 1997.

—— (2) "Vladimir Soloviev and the Jews in Russia," *The Russian Review* 29 (April 1970), 181–91.

—— (3) "Why the Anxious Fear? Aging and Death in the Works of Turgenev," *Aging and the Elderly: Humanistic Perspectives in Gerontology*. Edited by Stuart Spicker et al., Atlantic Highlands, N.J., 1978.

Mosse, W.E. (1) *Alexander II and the Modernization of Russia*. Rev. ed. New York, 1962.

—— (2) *An Economic History of Russia, 1856–1914*. London, 1996.

—— (3) *The European Powers and the German Question, 1848–1871, with Special Reference to England and Russia*. Cambridge, Eng., 1958.

N.A. Nekrasov v vospominaniyakh sovremennikov. Moscow, 1971.

"Narodnaya volya" i "Chernyi predel": Vospominaniya uchastnikov revoliutsionnogo dvizheniya v Peterburge v 1879–1882 gg. Leningrad, 1989.

Naryshkin-Kurakin, Elizabeth. *Under Three Tsars: The Memoirs of the Lady-in-Waiting*. Translated from the German by Julia E. Loesser. New York, 1931.

Natova, N.A. *F.M. Dostoevsky v Bad Emse.* Frankfurt/Main, 1971.

Nekrasov, N.A. *Polnoe sobranie sochinenii i pisem.* Edited by V.E. Evgeniev-Maksimov, A.M. Egolin, and K.I. Chukovsky. 12 vols. Moscow, 1948–53.

Nikitenko, A.V. *Dnevnik.* 3 vols. Leningrad, 1955–6.

Nikolaev, Vsevolod. *Aleksandr Vtoroi – chelovek na prestole: Istoricheskaya biografiya.* Munich, 1986.

Nolan, E.H. *The Illustrated History of the War against Russia.* 2 vols. London, [1857].

Ogarev, N.P. *Stikhotvoreniya i poemy.* Leningrad, 1956.

Ollier, Edmund. *Cassell's Illustrated History of the Russo-Turkish War.* 2 vols. London, [1877–9].

Orlovsky, Daniel T. *The Limits of Reform: The Ministry of Internal Affairs in Imperial Russia, 1802–1881.* Cambridge, Mass., 1981.

Orwin, Donna Tussing. *Tolstoy's Art and Thought, 1847–1880.* Princeton, 1993.

Paine, S.C.M. *Imperial Rivals: China, Russia, and Their Disputed Frontier.* Armonk, N.Y., 1996.

Paléologue, Maurice. *Le roman tragique de l'empereur Alexandre Roman Imperatora.* Paris, [1923].

Panaeva, A.Ya. *Vospominaniya.* Moscow, 1956.

Paperno, Irina. *Chernyshevsky and the Age of Realism: A Study in the Semiotics of Behavior.* Stanford, 1988.

Peppard, M.B. *Nikolai Nekrasov.* New York, 1967.

Pereira, N.G.O. *Tsar-Liberator: Alexander II of Russia, 1818–1881.* Newtonville, Mass., 1983.

Perlina, Nina. "Herzen in *The Brothers Karamazov*," *Canadian-American Slavic Studies* 17 (Fall 1983), 222–56.

Perovsky, V.L. *Vospominaniya o sestre.* Moscow, 1927.

Pirumova, N. *Bakunin.* Moscow, 1970.

Pollard, Alan P. "Dostoevsky's Pushkin Speech and the Politics of the Right under the Dictatorship of the Heart," *Canadian-American Slavic Studies* 17 (Summer 1983), 222–56.

Pomper, Philip. (1) *The Russian Revolutionary Intelligentsia.* New York, 1970.

—— (2) *Sergei Nechaev.* New Brunswick, N.J., 1979.

Pushkin, A.S. *Izbrannye Proizvedeniya.* 2 vols. Moscow, 1965.

Quested, R.K.I. *The Expansion of Russia in East Asia, 1857–1860.* Kuala Lumpur, 1968.

Raeff, Marc, ed. *Russian Intellectual History: An Anthology.* New York, 1966.

Ragsdale, Hugh. *The Russian Tragedy: The Burden of History.* Armonk, N.Y., 1996.

Ransel, David L. *Mothers of Misery: Child Abandonment in Russia.* Princeton, 1988.

Riasanovsky, Nicholas V. *Nicholas I and Official Nationality in Russia, 1825–1855.* Berkeley, 1969.

Rieber, Alfred J. (1) "Alexander II: A Revisionist View," *Journal of Modern History* 43, no. 1 (March, 1971), 42–58.

——, ed. (2) *The Politics of Autocracy: Letters of Alexander II to Prince A.I. Bariatinskii, 1857–1864.* Paris, 1966.

Roosevelt, Priscilla. *Life on the Russian Country Estate: A Social and Cultural History.* New Haven, 1995.

Russell, William Howard. *Russell's Dispatches from the Crimea, 1854–1856.* Edited by Nicholas Bentley. London, 1966.

Russkii biograficheskii slovar. 25 vols. St. Petersburg, 1896–1918.

Sampson, R.V. *Tolstoy: The Discovery of Peace.* London, 1973.

Sanders, Thomas, ed. *Historiography of Imperial Russia: The Profession and Writing of History in a Multinational State.* Armonk, N.Y., 1999.

Saunders, David. *Russia in the Age of Reaction and Reform, 1801–1881.* London, 1992. Chs. 8–11.

Schapiro, Leonard. (1) *Rationalism and Nationalism in Russian Nineteenth-Century Political Thought.* New Haven, 1967.

—— (2) *Russian Studies.* Edited by Ellen Dahrendorf. London, 1986.

—— (3) *Turgenev: His Life and Times.* New York, 1978.

Segal, Elena. *Sophia Perovskaya.* Moscow, 1962.

Sekirin, Peter. *Dostoevsky Archive: Firsthand Accounts of the Novelist from Contemporaries' Memoirs and Rare Periodicals.* Jefferson, N.C., 1997.

Semyonov, Yuri. *Siberia: Its Conquest and Development.* Translated from the German by J.R. Foster. Baltimore, 1963.

Sergeenko, P. *Tolstoi i ego sovremenniki: Ocherki.* Moscow, 1911.

Seton-Watson, Hugh. *The Russian Empire, 1801–1917.* Oxford, 1967.

Shatz, Marshall, and Zimmerman, Judith, eds. *Signposts: A Collection of Articles on the Russian Intelligentsia.* Irvine, Calif., 1986.

Shchegolev, P. "Sobytie l-go marta i Vladimir Sergeevich Soloviev," *Byloe,* 1906, no. 3, pp. 48–55.

Shelgunov, N.V., Shelgunova, L.P., and Mikhailov, M.L. *Vospominaniya,* 2 vols. [Moscow], 1967.

Shirer, William L. *Love and Hatred: The Troubled Marriage of Leo and Sonya Tolstoy.* New York, 1994.

Shklovsky, Victor. *Lev Tolstoy.* Translated from the Russian by Olga Shartse. Moscow, 1978.

Simmons, Ernest J. *Leo Tolstoy.* 2 vols. New York, 1960.

Slonim, Marc. *Three Loves of Dostoevsky.* New York, 1955.

Slonimsky, L. "Pisma v redaktsiyu" *Byloe,* 1907, no. 3, 306–7.

Soloviev, Sergei M. (1) *Istoriya Rossii s drevneishikh vremen.* 29 vols in 15. Moscow, 1959–66.

—— (2) *Sochineniya.* St. Petersburg, 1882.

—— (3) *Zapiski: Moi zapiski dlya detei moikh, a esli mozhno, i dlya drugikh.* Petrograd, [1914].

Soloviev, S.M., *Zhizn i tvorcheskaya evolyutsiya Vladimira Solovieva.* Brussels, 1977.

Soloviev, Vladimir Sergeevich. (1) *Lectures on Godmanhood.* Introduction by Peter Zouboff. London, 1948.

—— (2) *Pisma.* Edited by E.L. Radlov. 4 vols. St. Petersburg, 1908–23.

—— (3) *Sobranie sochinenii.* Edited by Mikhail Soloviev and G.A. Rachinsky. 9 vols. St. Petersburg, 1901–7.

—— (4) *Stikhotvoreniya i shutochnye piesy.* Munich, 1968.

Stepniak [Kravchinsky, Sergei] (1) *The Russian Peasantry: Their Agrarian Condition, Social Life, and Religion.* New York, 1888.

—— (2) *Underground Russia: Revolutionary Profiles and Sketches From Life.* Westport, Conn, 1973.

Stites, Richard. *The Women's Liberation Movement in Russia: Feminism, Nihilism, and Bolshevism, 1860–1930.* Princeton, 1978.

Strémoukhoff, D. *Vladimir Soloviev and His Messianic Work.* Translated from the French by Elizabeth Meyendorff. Belmont, Mass., 1980.

Sullivan, Joseph Lewis. "Count N.N. Muraviev-Amurksy." Unpublished Ph.D. dissertation, Harvard University, 1955.

Sumner, B.H. *Russia and the Balkans, 1870–1880.* Oxford, 1962.

Sutherland, Christine. *The Princess of Siberia: The Story of Maria Volkonsky and the Decembrist Exiles.* New York, 1984.

Svetaeva, M.G. *Mariya Gavrilovna Savina.* Moscow, 1988.

Tarle, E.V. *Krymskaya voina.* 2nd ed., rev. and enl. 2 vols. Moscow, 1950.

Tarsaidzé, Alexandre. *Katia, Wife before God.* New York, 1970.

Tatishchev, S.S. *Imperator Aleksandr II, ego zhizn i tsarstvovanie.* 2 vols. St Petersburg, 1903.

Thaden, Edward C. *Conservative Nationalism in 19th Century Russia.* Seattle, 1964.

Timberlake, Charles E., ed. *Essays on Russian Liberalism.* Columbia, Mo. 1972.

The Times (London). June 1–12, September 11–13, 1867; May 12–16, 18–21, 1874; April 9, 11, 1881.

Tolstaya, Sophia. (1) *The Diaries of Sophia Tolstoy.* Edited by O.A. Golinenko et al. Translated by Cathy Porter. New York, 1985.

—— (2) *The Diary of Tolstoy's Wife, 1860–1891.* Translated by Alexander Werth. London, 1928.

Tolstoy, Leo. (1) *Anna Karenina.* Edited by George Gibian. Norton Critical Edition. New York, 1970.

—— (2) *Polnoe sobranie sochinenii.* 90 vols. Moscow, 1928–58.

—— (3) *Tolstoy's Letters.* Edited and translated by R.F. Christian. 2 vols. New York, 1978.

—— (4) *War and Peace.* Edited by George Gibian. Norton Critical Edition. New York, 1966.

Tolstoy, Nikolai. *The Tolstoys: Twenty-four Generations of Russian History, 1353–1983.* New York, 1983.

Tolstoy, Sergei. *Tolstoy Remembered by His Son.* Translated by Moura Budberg. London, 1961.

Troyat, Henri. (1) *Alexandre II: Le Tsar Libérateur.* [Paris], 1990.

—— (2) *Tolstoy.* Translated from the French by Nancy Amphoux. New York, 1967.

Trubetskoi, Evgenii. *Mirosozertsanie Vl. S. Soloveva.* 2 vols. Moscow, 1913.

Tsimbaev, Nikolai. *Sergei Soloviev.* Moscow, 1990.

Tuchkova-Ogareva, N. A. *Vospominaniya.* [Moscow], 1959.

Turgenev, Ivan. (1) *Letters to an Actress.* Translated and edited by Nora Gottlieb and Raymond Chapman. London, 1973.

—— (2) *Literary Reminiscences and Autobiographical Fragments*. Translated by David Magarshack. London, 1958.

—— (3) *Polnoe sobranie sochinenii i pisem v dvadtsati vosmi tomakh. Pisma v trinadtsati tomakh*. Moscow-Leningrad, 1961–8.

—— (4) *Polnoe sobranie sochinenii i pisem v dvadtsati vosmi tomakh. Sochineniya v pyat-nadtsati tomakh*. Moscow-Leningrad, 1960–68.

—— (5) *Polnoe sobranie sochinenii i pisem v tridtsati tomakh. Sochineniya*. Moscow, 1978–86.

Turgenevskii sbornik: Materiay k polnomu sobraniyu sochinenii i pisem I.S. Turgeneva. 5 vols. Moscow -Leningrad, 1964–9.

Tyutcheva, A. F. *Pri dvore dvukh imperatorov: Vospominaniya-Dnevnik*. 2 vols. Moscow, 1928.

Ulam, Adam B. *In the Name of the People: Prophets and Conspirators in Prerevolutionary Russia*. New York, 1977.

Valuev, P. A. *Dnevnik*. 2 vols. Moscow, 1961.

Van der Kiste, John. *The Romanovs 1818–1959: Alexander II of Russia and His Family*. Gloucestershire, Eng., 1998.

Venturi, Franco. *Roots of Revolution: A History of the Populist and Socialist Movements in Nineteenth Century Russia*. Translated from the Italian by Francis Haskell. New York, 1966.

Victoria, Queen of Great Britain. (1) *Darling Child: Private Correspondence of Queen Victoria and the Crown Princess of Prussia, 1871–1878*. Edited by Roger Fulford. London, 1976.

—— (2) *The Girlhood of Queen Victoria: A Selection From Her Majesty's Diaries between the Years 1832 and 1840*. Edited by Viscount Esher. 2 vols. London, 1912.

—— (3) *The Letters of Queen Victoria: A Selection of Her Majesty's Correspondence. Second Series, 1862–1885*. Edited by George Earle Buckle. 3 vols. New York and London, 1926–8.

Volgin, Igor. *Poslednii god Dostoevskogo: Istoricheskie zapiski*. Moscow, 1986.

Von Laue, Theodore H. *Sergei Witte and the Industrialization of Russia*. New York, 1969.

Walicki, Andrezej. *A History of Russian Thought, From the Enlightenment to Marxism*. Translated from the Polish by Hilda Andrews-Rusiecka. Stanford, 1979.

Weeks, Theodore R. *Nation and State in Late Imperial Russia: Nationalism and Russification on the Western Frontier, 1863–1914*. DeKalb, Ill., 1996.

Weidemaier, William Cannon. "Herzen and the Existential World View: A New Approach to an Old Debate," *SlavicReview* 40 (Winter 1981), 557–69.

Wieczynski, Joseph L., ed. *The Modern Encyclopedia of Russian and Soviet History*. 60 vols plus supplements. Gulf Breeze, Fla., 1976ff.

Williams, Roger L. *The World of Napoleon III, 1851–1870*. New York, 1962.

Wilson, A.N. *Tolstoy*. New York, 1988.

Woehrlin, William F. *Chernyshevskii: The Man and the Journalist*. Cambridge, Mass., 1971.

Worobec, Christine. *Peasant Russia: Family and Community in the Post-Emancipation Period*. Princeton, 1991.

Wortman, Richard S. *Scenarios of Power: Myth and Ceremony in Russian Monarchy*. 2 vols. Princeton, 1995, 2000.

Wrangel, A.E. *Vospominaniya o F.M. Dostoevskom v Siberii*. St Petersburg, 1912.

Yarmolinsky, Avrahm. (1) *Road to Revolution: A Century of Russian Radicalism*. New York, 1962.

—— (2) *Turgenev, The Man, His Art, and His Age*. New York, 1961.

Zaionchkovskii, Peter A. (1) *The Abolition of Serfdom in Russia*. Gulf Breeze, Fla., 1978.

—— (2) *The Russian Autocracy in Crisis, 1878–1882*. Edited and translated by Gary M. Hamburg. Gulf Breeze, Fla., 1979.

—— (3) *The Russian Autocracy under Alexander III*. Edited and translated by David R. Jones. Gulf Breeze, Fla., 1976.

Zakharova, L.G. (1) "Alexander II," *Russian Studies in History* 32 (Winter 1993–4), 57–88.

—— (2) "Autocracy and the Abolition of Serfdom in Russia, 1856–1861," *Soviet Studies in History* 26 (Fall, 1987). Whole issue is devoted to this work except for introduction by the editor/translator, Gary M. Hamburg.

Zernov, Nicolas. *Three Russian Prophets: Khomiakov, Dostoevsky, Soloviev*. 3rd ed., London, 1973.

Zhdanov, V. *Nekrasov*. Moscow, 1971.

Zhitova, V. *The Turgenev Family*. Translated by A.S. Mills. London, 1947.

Zimmerman, Judith E. *Midpassage: Alexander Herzen and European Revolution, 1847–1852*. Pittsburgh, 1989.

INDEX

This index covers the introduction and epilogue, as well as the main body of the text, but not the 'Who's Who', chronology, endnotes, principal sources or bibliography. Book titles are given in *italic*.